The Latin America Readers

A Series Edited by Robin Kirk and Orin Starn

THE

History, Culture, Politics

BRAZIL

READER

Edited by Robert M. Levine and John J. Crocitti

Duke University Press   Durham   1999

© 1999 Duke University Press

All rights reserved

Printed in the United States of America on acid-free paper ∞

Designed by C. H. Westmoreland

Typeset in Dante by Keystone Typesetting, Inc.

Library of Congress Cataloging-in-Publication Data

The Brazil reader : history, culture, politics / edited by
Robert M. Levine and John J. Crocitti.
p.   cm. — (Latin America readers)
Includes bibliographical references (p.   –   ) and index.
ISBN 0-8223-2258-7 (cloth : alk. paper). — ISBN 0-8223-2290-0
(pa. : alk. paper)
1. Brazil—History.   2. Brazil—Social conditions.   3. Brazil—
Economic conditions.   I. Levine, Robert M.   II. Crocitti,
John J.   III. Series.
F2521.B768   1999
981—dc21   98-45699

This book is dedicated to all present and past

students in the University of Miami's graduate

program in Latin American history.

John adds a dedication to his mother,

Helen M. Crocitti.

Contents

V Seeking Democracy and Equity

VI Women's Lives

VII Race and Ethnic Relations

VIII   *Realities*

IX   *Saudades*

Acknowledgments

Many people have assisted in making this book possible. Requests for permission to reprint material from printed sources and the Internet were almost invariably received kindly and often with enthusiasm. Special thanks go to Maria Lisbôa and Rosane Pereira, Fabiano Maissonave, Maria Leal, Norman Gall, Lyn MacCorkle, Alice Morales, Jens R. Hentschke, Marieta Ferreira Moraes, Edson Oliveira Balotta, and Hans Christian de Salas del Valle. We are especially indebted to the contributors who wrote or adapted essays for this anthology: Peter M. Beattie, Dain Borges, Gerald M. Greenfield, Cristina Mehrtens, Christopher Dunn, Elizabeth Ginway, Juliano Spyer, José Carlos Sebe Bom Meihy, Ted G. Goertzel, Carol Damian, Seth Garfield, Amelia Simpson, Jeffrey Lesser, Tobias Hecht, Bruce P. Chadwick, Roger M. Allen, James N. Green, Robin Nagle, Bryan McCann, Bill Hinchberger, Jessica Calloway, and Janet Lever. We also are indebted to Pedro Ribeiro for his stunning photographs of Brazilian men and women.

A Note on Style

Most of the translations in this anthology were done by Robert M. Levine and John J. Crocitti. We attempted to retain the original wording where necessary for clarity. Where explanations were needed, we preferred to use brackets rather than footnotes, which are usually more cumbersome. Portuguese names and terms are spelled according to modern usage, except when traditional spellings are still preferred. Thus, *mil-réis,* Gilberto Freyre, or Bahia, and not *milréis,* Freire, or Baía.

Map of Brazil

Introduction

Exotic images of Brazil's tropicality have dominated the West's perception of this vast subcontinent. Perhaps because Brazilians speak Portuguese, not Spanish, the country is less known, shrouded in mystery beyond the usual touristic clichés about coffee, Carnival, and soccer. Few appreciate that Brazil is urban, that more than a dozen cities have more than a million residents, that migration from the countryside to the sprawling industrial metropolitan areas has dominated demographic trends, or that Rio de Janeiro and São Paulo have two of the longest and cleanest subway systems in the world.

Dualism has long influenced ways of seeing the country and predicting its future. Its seemingly larger-than-life size, and many complexities, have led to explanations of Brazil's culture, economy, and promise that cluster at the extremes of the spectrum, not unlike similar analyses of the United States of America. If the Spanish pursued the Seven Cities of Gold and the Fountain of Youth in North America, explorers of Brazil followed tales of warlike Amazonian women who cut off one of their breasts to make shooting more efficient; others viewed the land as a storehouse of wealth as they searched relentlessly for gold and diamonds. In these cases, not all of the tales were myths. There were Amazonian tribes dominated by women who were fierce in battle; there were cannibals; and there were gigantic lodes of gold and diamonds, although they were not discovered until the closing years of the seventeenth century. In the nineteenth century, another dual set of interpretations emerged. One was based on praise for Brazil's stability under its monarchy; another warned of what was considered by many to be the harmful legacy of Brazil's continued reliance on slave labor. Still later, some praised Brazil as the "Land of the Future" and called it a "racial democracy"; others warned of potentially explosive pent-up rage and the hypocrisy in denying the existence of prejudice. Social scientists borrowed from the dual model in dubbing the country "Belindia," a place where a small minority live in First World archipelagoes with a standard of living like that of Belgium, whereas the rest of the population lives under Third World conditions not unlike those in India.

Not only was Brazil from the first settlement a land of continental size, but successful diplomatic efforts in the nineteenth century added even more territory, in the southwest and in the region of the Amazon. Brazil's current 3,286,426 square miles, occupying nearly half of South America, makes it the fifth largest nation in the world after Russia, Canada, China, and the United States. Bordering every country in South America except Chile and Ecuador, only a tiny portion, in the far south, lies in the temperate zone. Its shoreline stretches for 4,600 miles, and it is as near to Africa as it is to the United States. In the primeval past, until the early Cretaceous period, eastern Brazil and the African Gulf of Guinea joined in one "supercontinent," known by geologists as West Gondwana. Today, Brazil is four times the size of Mexico. While Brazil is not prone to either earthquakes or hurricanes, devastating droughts, their effects exacerbated by ill-conceived human-made strategies, have caused widespread misery over the centuries. Few rivers run east to west. The central plateau and its hinterland are cut off from the coastal region by a wall-like slope known as the Great Escarpment. Ocean-going ships cannot reach the interior, although by entering the Amazon River at Belém in the far north, they can journey almost 1,000 miles to the steamy jungle city of Manaus. These physical barriers have long made access to the interior especially difficult; only in recent decades has Brazil's frontier opened to settlement of any size.

To outsiders, Brazil seemed an earthly paradise ripe for the picking. Brazil's natural resources make it one of the potentially wealthiest countries in the world. Although there is only a small amount of coal, most of it low grade, mining has yielded immense quantities of iron ore, manganese, bauxite, nickel, tungsten, tin, uranium, gold, semiprecious stones, and industrial diamonds. Brazilian forests provide rubber, pulp for paper, hardwoods, waxes, firewood, and charcoal. Formerly energy dependent, by the 1990s, more than two-thirds of the country's electricity came from offshore petroleum and its enormous hydroelectric plants; indeed, the plant at Itaipú is the largest hydroelectric project in the world, jointly shared by Argentina, Brazil, and Paraguay. In the 1970s, scientists converted most of the nation's fleet of trucks and official vehicles to the use of alcohol produced from sugarcane stalks. But consumers resisted the alcohol-burning engines. Consequently, two decades later, Brazilian dependence on imported petroleum continued, since domestic oil only provided half of the nation's needs.

Brazil's huge size gave birth to significant regional variations, much like Russia's. The country's five major areas—the Amazonian North, the arid Northeast, the dynamic Southeast (or Center-South), the pastoral South, and the undeveloped Center-West—have been likened to islands in a huge archipelago, spread across a sea of geographic diversity. Although Portuguese is universally spoken, regional differences in pronunciation are almost as sharp as the difference between English spoken in Mississippi and New England.

The Amazon region contains more than 2.4 million square miles of rain forest, under assault for centuries by settlers (mostly landless claim jumpers), rubber tappers, and only in the last few years, contracted developers. More than 12 percent of the original rain forest has been cut down and nearly 10,000 square miles are destroyed each year. In the last decade, the Amazon region has been integrated into the international economy, for better or worse. New towns have sprung up out of the jungle; the construction and agro-industrial sectors are booming, and the impact on the formerly desultory way of life has yet to be understood.

The rainy coast from Maranhão to Espírito Santo was covered by nearly 700,000 square miles of lush trees—the *zona da mata,* literally "the forest zone"—but is now mostly stripped. Only 8 percent of the original forest remains, providing erosion control and other ecological benefits for the 70 percent of Brazil's population that lives along the coast. The northern states—Pará, Maranhão, Piauí, and Ceará—have long suffered from overpopulation, lack of industry, and fierce domination by the landed oligarchy, although Ceará, in recent years, has made great economic strides under a dynamic state government. The Northeast, from Rio Grande do Norte to Bahia, has been plagued by centuries of periodic drought, overpopulation, and lack of economic opportunity. Pernambuco during the early colonial period was one of the most profitable agricultural colonies in the world, but decline set in by the seventeenth century, exacerbated by its own entrenched elite whose efforts in the late nineteenth century to modernize sugar production failed, further lowering the quality of life for its wretched inhabitants.

The São Francisco River starts on the Atlantic coast and winds west and south through the dusty backlands of Pernambuco and Bahia, ending in the low mountains of Minas Gerais. For generations—until the arrival of the airplane—the river, filled with sandbars and treacherous for navigators, was the easiest way to the interior, and therefore, the route of immigrants, settlers, and migrants. The lands on either side of the river-bank are covered by thornwood and scrub brush, and where fresh water is available, the sites of cattle ranches. Clusters of small farms produce subsistence crops, maize, and manioc. The vast and ruggedly beautiful central plateau is still largely unpopulated, despite the creation of the new national capital of Brasília in the late 1950s. Northwest of the Paraná River is the Pantanal, home to a large but shrinking environment of pristine natural flora and fauna, and Indian reservations. It is the world's biggest wetland, filled with legions of rare and endangered species, including hyacinth macaws and jabiru storks. Developers are planning to utilize the wetland as one link in the *hidrovia,* a 2,150-mile navigation project to connect Brazil, Bolivia, Paraguay, Argentina, and Uruguay. This threatens, of course, to destroy the Pantanal.

Brasília rose out of the bare earth of the central plateau as a symbol of the country's confidence in its future, and also as an effort to shift the political center away from the primate cities of São Paulo and Rio de Janeiro. Brasília's architecture, considered futuristic when it was built, has become weathered and in places dilapidated, and the utopian goals of its visionary architect, Oscar Niemeyer, were never achieved. It did attract thousands of urban pioneers from all over the country, however, and by the 1990s, had realized at least some of the hoped-for stimulation of national integration.

The Center-South is so densely populated in comparison with the rest of Brazil that geographers use the term *hyperconcentrated* to describe it. Mountainous Minas Gerais balances agricultural productivity with mining and urban centers, and is linked commercially with Rio de Janeiro, the steadily declining former capital and tourist mecca to the east, and vigorous São Paulo to its south. Rio de Janeiro's beaches are polluted, and residents cope with an alarmingly high frequency of crime, centered in the drug-ridden hillside shantytowns that look down on the beautiful city. Once the nation's major port of entry, it has lost that distinction to Santos, in the state of São Paulo. Rio's 5.5-million inhabitants live in some of the wealthiest (and most heavily guarded) residential districts any-where, but there are also more than 500 *favelas,* the substandard hillside slums. On the city's outskirts lie industrial districts mired in poverty, such as the violent Baixada Fluminense, with the highest murder rate in the world. Atmospheric pollution in many of Brazil's industrial cities is so bad that, according to political scientist Ronald M. Schneider, it may pose a more serious environmental peril for Brazilians than the depredation of the tropical Amazonian rain forest.

The southeastern plateau between the cities of Rio de Janeiro and São Paulo is the site of the once-prosperous coffee plantations of the Paraíba Valley, recently abandoned for the more productive coffee lands further to the south. The Paraíba Valley has since blossomed as a region of heavy and light manufacturing, favored by multinational investors for its proximity to Brazil's two major cities, but overbrimming with population and traffic, and plagued by industrial and vehicular pollution. In the South are the states of Paraná, Santa Catarina, and Rio Grande do Sul. Temperate in climate—even to the point of receiving some light snowfall at higher elevations during the winter months of July and August—this agricultural and ranching region has received hundreds of thousands of immigrants since the mid-1800s; today, many communities in this region are populated by descendants of Japanese, Poles, Germans, Ukrainians, and Italians. Although dictator Getúlio Vargas banned foreign-language newspapers and instruction in 1938, the languages of the immigrants are still spoken in many small towns. *Gaúchos*—the term for the residents of Rio Grande do Sul, but also used loosely for southerners in general—have not only played a major role in national politics since the late–nineteenth century, but in recent decades, have contributed to an out-migration to other parts of Brazil in search of cheaper land. This *"gaúcho diaspora"* started within the region, in the 1930s and 1940s, when settlers moved further north and west into the forested parts of Santa Catarina and Paraná. It crossed regional boundaries in the 1950s and 1960s when southerners began to migrate to Mato Grosso, and in the 1970s, to the Amazon. Just as northeastern migration to the South was not always well received, *"gaúcho"* settlers in other parts of Brazil were criticized for their aggressiveness and the perception that they felt superior to the populations in whose midst they settled.

North of Rio and east of Minas Gerais is the large state of Bahia, the heart of Brazil's Afro-Brazilian culture, and home to community and cultural groups organized during the last decade to preserve and celebrate the African heritage. Southern Brazil is a region of agriculture and ranching, more prosperous than most of the country and marked by a fairly highly educated population, hilly terrain, and a relatively prosperous economy. To the far west are the underpopulated and undeveloped former territories of Acre, Rondônia, and Roraíma, elevated to statehood by cynical politics (new states send senators to the national legislature and create patronage jobs in their new state bureaucracies). The resource-rich state of Mato Grosso bordering Bolivia was divided in two for similar reasons during the 1980s, as was the state of Goiás in central Brazil. The new state carved out of Goiás—Tocantins—has virtually no cities nor any viable sources of income for most of its sparsely settled population.

In the year 1500, Brazil was accidentally discovered by a fleet of ships sailing from Portugal to India under the command of Pedro Álvares Cabral. He landed on the coast of what later would be known as the province of Bahia. Composer and essayist Caetano Veloso finds noteworthy the fact that Brazilians in the year 2000 will celebrate not only the millennium, but also the 500th anniversary of Cabral's landfall, since all other countries in the hemisphere commemorate Columbus's 1492 voyage. In so doing, he points out, Brazil sets itself apart from the rest of Latin America.[1] The Portuguese, who had already developed commercial ties to Asia, did little to develop Brazil. Portugal's resources were thin, and before long, the administration of active trading posts up and down the African coast, in India and in the Far East, began to overwhelm a country of only two million inhabitants. Until the seventeenth century, the Far East was the top priority of the Portuguese empire, with Africa second, and Brazil a distant third.

To discourage the designs of rival European powers on the nearly empty Brazil, the Portuguese Crown, lacking the resources to follow the Spanish New World model, granted titles to huge tracts of land to a handful of private citizens. The rigid centralization that so clearly defined early Spanish American history was not a feature of Portuguese settlement. Nor was the use of Indians for labor. In Brazil, Native Americans' resistance to working on the land led the Portuguese to import slaves from their trading posts in Africa.

Like North America, Brazil had been a land where indigenous tribes hunted and gathered food. This was not the case in most of Spanish America. There—except in the far south—the conquerors encountered Indian civilizations based on stable agriculture. Indigenous villages were left intact: to their inhabitants, it did not much matter whether they worked and paid tribute to Inca or Aztec rulers, or Spanish viceroys.

Throughout its entire colonial period, Brazil remained sparsely populated, its settlements cut off from one another by great distances and
difficult transportation. Its urban centers more closely resembled shabby
towns than cities. Brazil had few schools, whereas Spanish America had
universities as early as 1553 (in Mexico City) and 1572 (in Lima). It caught
up, however, in the twentieth century, when Brazilian culture flourished, and when a combination of impressive population growth and
government-directed industrialization made Brazil primary if not dominant among the Latin American nations. It is Brazil's singularity—and
its character, self-perceptions, and transitions—that provides the central
theme of *The Brazil Reader.*

The editors hope that readers will pick up this anthology, browse through
it, and find it engaging reading. There is no effort to be all-inclusive: this
would be impossible in a book of this length. This is not an anthology of
Brazilian history. A good one is E. Bradford Burns's compilation, *A Documentary History of Brazil* (New York: Borzoi Books, 1966); another is
Richard Graham's *A Century of Brazilian History since 1865* (New York:
Borzoi Books, 1969). Until recently, writing on Brazil has concentrated
on political economy, trade and neodependency, slavery, and latifundia.
These interests remain, but they have broadened. Scholars are probing
gender, the history of the family, collective memory, and patronage, corruption, and the uneven distribution of justice. Studies of the church, the
armed forces, and labor, traditionally examined institutionally, are now
focusing on the lives of recruits, working women, and parish priests.
Works are being published on interpersonal behavior and sexuality, on
violence in everyday life, on ideas and attitudes, and on the relationship,
as Mikhail Bakhtin put it, between learned culture and subaltern cultures.
The Brazil Reader incorporates both traditional viewpoints and the
newer approaches to understanding the past. Its entries were selected
because they probe beneath the surface of stereotype, looking, as often
as not, behind the scenes or explaining lived experience. This is neither
an anthology of official versions nor of highly specialized analyses. Although much scholarship on Brazil is limited geographically, this anthology attempts to offer selections from different regions—from the Amazon to the Northeast to the Central-South. It is as interested in political
culture as it is in politics. This reader includes "history from below" as
well as "history from above." It seeks historical consciousness, the desire
for experiences to be understood historically. It ranges widely and is

purposefully eclectic. More than anything else, it presents a variety of perspectives, from foreign visitors to native-born analysts to ordinary people. The result is deliberately kaleidoscopic. It has been designed so that its chapters stand alone, so that readers may open the book at any place and enjoy what they find.

In selecting material for this volume, we attempted to complement traditional sources with unorthodox ones. Many of the entries are based on oral testimonies and unpublished documents. More than a dozen were written specifically for *The Brazil Reader*. Some of the entries were taken, with permission, from the Internet. The beauty of surfing the Internet is that it permits contact with diverse groups that can make their case without either being sanctioned officially or having a large budget; it costs little to put up a web site and maintain it. In earlier times, people did this by handing out leaflets on street corners or publishing clandestine newspapers. Now, they can reach a worldwide audience linked simply through curiosity and on-line networks.

The volume's entries span the spectrum of ideology and point of view. They include the emotional voices of blacks angry at their treatment and students enraged by police brutality; they also include writing by militants on the far Left and far Right. The following pages contain letters, official reports, regulations, reminiscences, photographs, fiction, laws, lists, photographs, artwork, analyses of songs, and interviews with people whose lives were impacted, for better or worse, by social conditions and government. The anthology sets out to do more than sample the writing of Brazilian politicians and intellectuals. Indeed, we know of no other collection of writing about Brazil that presents so much analysis of Brazilian reality by ordinary citizens. Many are critical of the conditions under which the poor and marginalized live, but others exhibit great pride in being Brazilian, and show that even in a country with structural barriers to upward mobility and a weak record of effective reform, many have managed, by a combination of hard work and good fortune, to better their lives and see their children ascend to a higher standard of living.

The Brazil Reader, however, balances the voices of Brazilians with analyses written by non-Brazilians. They include scholars, visitors, and travelers from many places—including the United States, South Africa, Great Britain, and Portugal—captivated by Brazil's culture, history, and people. Just as the French visitor Alexis de Tocqueville saw things about the

United States in the nineteenth century that many citizens of that new country may not have seen for themselves, so too, do we believe that our non-Brazilian authors provide useful insights into Brazilian life.

As in the case of the first book in this series, *The Peru Reader*, this anthology does not seek to assert the superiority of nonscholarly writing or knowledge; nor does it suggest that academic analysis is more revealing than journalism, memoir literature, or testimonies from real life. We have not only excerpted works of traditional scholarship, but we also present work by journalists, eyewitnesses, web site operators, and ordinary people of all colors, sexual preferences, and social categories. Being ordinary, of course, does not make them less special than anyone else. It is in these accounts of travail, frustration, and hope that the core of what Brazilians call their "reality" resides. We have included selections, then, from many kinds of sources. Taken together, we hope that they will provoke thought about Brazil, and its fascinating past, and its present condition.

The anthology contains nine parts. The first five, looking at Brazil from before the conquest to the recent return to democratic practice, follow historical chronology, the exception being the chapter on slavery and its aftermath. The country's historical evolution profoundly influenced the way that Brazil is today and will continue to be into the next century. The historical sections are intended not only to be of interest by themselves, but to frame many of the themes introduced later in the volume. They are followed by four sections that are topical and thematic in nature. There is also some overlap in chronology here, but the sections stand by themselves and are mostly contemporary. They deal with issues that affect Brazil and Brazilians today.

The book closes with a section titled *"Saudades"*—a singular Luso-Brazilian term referring to longing and nostalgia. This section deals with Brazilian music and popular culture, ways of expressing feelings about the nation and its heritage. Brazil is a warm, welcoming, compassionate country, and these qualities are communicated in its rhythms and lyrics.

Note

1 Caetano Veloso, *Verdade Tropical* (São Paulo: Companhia das Letras, 1997), p. 13.

I

Origins, Conquest, and

Colonial Rule

Hundreds of native tribes inhabited Brazil at the time of the arrival of Europeans, the earliest going back at least 10,000 years in the highlands of Minas Gerais. They divided into four main language groups: the Tupí-Guaraní, the Gê, the Carib, and the Arawak. The Tupí-Guaraní predominated along the Atlantic coast; the Gê peoples lived on the open central plateau. Caribs and Arawaks, who were more advanced in technology, especially pottery making, lived in the Amazon basin. The most aggressive were the Caribs, who were warlike and sometimes practiced cannibalism, as did the Tupí living on the seacoast. Most Brazilian Indians dwelled in temporary villages. Lowland South America had no animals that could be domesticated—like the llamas and guinea pigs of the Andes—and therefore, the Brazilian tribes kept moving in search of wild game. The Amazon river system flooded regularly, making life on its edge precarious. Its soils were weak, discouraging planting. There were no written languages, so that recorded histories of the Indian peoples date only from the arrival of Europeans, untrained observers at best, who wrote down what they could understand from the tales of the indigenous storytellers.[1]

The Portuguese navigators who arrived at the New World on April 22, 1500, were long experienced in the business of seafaring and voyages of discovery, and as a result, were not as consumed by the dreams of gold and fabulous peoples that motivated less experienced explorers, including the Spanish. Portugal had taken the Moroccan seaport of Ceuta in 1415, the same year as Henry V's victory at Agincourt, although the campaign led to neither a North African empire nor further military victories against the Moors.[2] Later, they explored the islands of the Atlantic (Madeira, the Azores, and Cabo Verde), creating the patterns that were employed in further voyages of discovery and reconnaissance. Lacking national wealth and with its always-small population in the fifteenth century at a low ebb, the Portuguese Crown was ill-equipped to launch the kind of military-backed settlement ventures that would be carried out by the Spanish, English, and French.

In response to the need for ventures that were limited to commercial exploitation, the Portuguese established trading posts all along the African coast and, after Vasco da Gama's 1497 landing at Goa, in India, gained access to the riches of Asia. The Brazilian natives encountered by the Portuguese wore no gold or silver adornments, and their rustic settlements displayed neither artistic grandeur nor artifacts of material value. Pedro Álvares Cabral's fleet departed after only eight days, heading southeast on its original course for the Far East. The supply vessel, its cargo redistributed among the other twelve ships in the fleet, returned to Portugal to report to the king.[3]

In the context of Portugal's prior Atlantic experience, Harold B. Johnson observes, the nature of Brazil was ambiguous. Colonial administrators bypassed opportunities to import cattle or to send settlers; instead, they concentrated on establishing trade with the native population in local commodities (dyewood, monkeys, Indian slaves, and parrots) and leased out vast tracts of territory—stretching far into the unknown interior—to Lisbon merchants, the basis for what came to be known as the donatary or captaincy system.[4] This proprietary arrangement minimized the financial risk for the Crown, but it also made development of the colony dependent on the resources and motivation of the investors who received the donatary grants. Only one of the ventures succeeded, in Pernambuco, where sugarcane cultivation proved prosperous, and eventually all of the proprietary leases were canceled and the land reverted to the Crown.

After the Spanish discovered silver at Potosí, and in the wake of the decline of the Far East spice trade, the Portuguese Crown established a royal government for the first time in Brazil in the 1540s. The first governor was Tomé de Sousa, a relative of the overseer of the Treasury in

Lisbon. As soon as he arrived, he faced the need to defend Portuguese territory from incursions and attacks all along the frontier, from Indians and would-be French conquerors. The Crown also wanted to increase revenues from the colony, and Tomé de Sousa was given instructions to build a fort at the site of the royal captaincy, in Bahia. To pacify and Christianize the Indians, the king sent Jesuits, only nine years after its order was founded in 1540. The first group, including Father Manoel de Nóbrega, arrived with Tomé de Sousa. Only 128 Jesuits came to Brazil during the entire period up to 1598, but because the territory was so sparsely populated, larger numbers did not seem necessary. When the initial efforts of the Jesuits to convert the native population failed—the Indians soon reverted to their old practices—the Jesuits decided to remove the Indians from their native habitats to fortified villages, called *aldeias,* where they would be taught to cultivate and instructed in the catechism. A diocese for Brazil was created in 1551, but the first bishop proved too rigid (he opposed the Jesuit practice of permitting Christianity to be taught without forcing full acculturation), and as a result, the Jesuits moved further into the interior, away from the bishop's purview. When word reached Lisbon of the bishop's quarrelsome demeanor, he was recalled in 1556, but his ship was wrecked along the coast; he was captured and eaten, as we are reminded, "by the Caeté Indians he so heartily disdained."[5]

Brazil's development as time passed was characterized by agricultural expansion, but little else, until the discovery of gold at the end of the seventeenth century. In the time of Viceroy Lavradio (1769–1779), there were fewer than 1,500 colonial officials in the colony, or 1 per 1,036 registered inhabitants. Portuguese officials were legalistic and authoritarian, but they were not despotic. Most, as Dauril Alden explains, were less interested in making a record of achievement than in marking time and keeping their records sufficiently unblemished so that they could return to Portugal.[6] Alden makes another point worth pondering: there really were several "Brazils" during the colonial period, the result of the founding of quasi-feudal captaincies during the sixteenth and seventeenth centuries, which led to regional divisiveness and postindependence revolts. Portugal did not integrate its colony socially, culturally, economically, or administratively.[7] Inconsistency and frequent changes in policy hindered commerce, and raised awareness among merchants that they might be better off without Portuguese restrictions on free trade, especially with the British.[8] The eighteenth-century gold rush did, however, spur public works, church building, and urban development. Immediately before the arrival of the Portuguese royal family in flight from the Napoleonic invasion of the Iberian Peninsula, Bishop J. J. de Azeredo Coutinho wrote of the state of affairs in the colony:

> If Portugal . . . preserves an adequate navy and merchant marine; if, satisfied with her vast dominions in the four quarters of the globe, she renounces further conquests; if she promotes by every [possible] means the development of the riches which her possessions have the capacity to produce; if she maintains her vassals in peace and tranquility and assures their right to enjoy the fruits of their estates; if she establishes manufactures only of the most indispensable necessities, and abandons those of luxury to foreigners, in order to allow them an opportunity to purchase her superfluities . . . no enemy will molest her, or disturb her quiet . . .[9]

This, of course, was not to be. And for the inhabitants of Brazil—throughout the colonial period, more than two-thirds of them slaves—Brazilian plantations were, in the words of Father Andrés de Gouvea in 1627, "hell [with] masters [who were] damned."[10] Government and society, Stuart B. Schwartz reminds us, formed two interlocking systems, which worked together to ensure the continued flow of profits to Portugal and to hold society together. Little sense of nationality or citizenship developed in this world. Elites dreamed of being transferred elsewhere in Portugal's overseas empire or sent back to the mother country. Brazil remained firmly based on the institution of slavery. Signs of political unrest, so prevalent in Spanish America, were few and far between. Only the fateful (and fortuitous) transfer of the Portuguese royal family to Brazil in 1808 in flight from Napoleon brought sufficient change to the colonial equation to set Brazil, once and for all, on the road to independence.

Notes

1 John Hemming, "The Indians of Brazil in 1500," in *Cambridge History of Latin America,* edited by Leslie Bethell (Cambridge: Cambridge University Press, 1986), Vol. 1, pp. 119–22.
2 H. B. Johnson, "The Portuguese Settlement of Brazil," in *Cambridge History of Latin America,* edited by Leslie Bethell (Cambridge: Cambridge University Press, 1986), Vol. 1, p. 249.

3 Warren Dean, *With Broadax and Firebrand: The Destruction of the Brazilian Atlantic Forest* (Berkeley: University of California Press, 1995), p. 44.

4 Johnson, "The Portuguese Settlement of Brazil," p. 255.

5 Ibid., p. 272.

6 Dauril Alden, *Royal Government in Colonial Brazil* (Berkeley: University of California Press, 1968), pp. 491–92.

7 Ibid., p. 494.

8 A. J. R. Russell-Wood, "Colonial Brazil: The Gold Cycle," in *Cambridge History of Latin America,* edited by Leslie Bethell (Cambridge: Cambridge University Press, 1984), Vol. 2, p. 587.

9 Bishop J. J. de Azeredo Coutinho, *Obras económicas de J. J. da Cunha de Azeredo Coutinho (1794–1804),* quoted in Dauril Alden, "Late Colonial Brazil," in *Cambridge History of Latin America,* edited by Leslie Bethell (Cambridge: Cambridge University Press, 1984), Vol. 2, p. 659.

10 Father Andrés de Gouvea, Bahia, 1627, quoted in Stuart B. Schwartz, "Colonial Brazil, c. 1580–c. 1750: Plantations and Peripheries," in *Cambridge History of Latin America,* edited by Leslie Bethell (Cambridge: Cambridge University Press, 1984), Vol. 2, p. 423.

The Origin of Fire

Cayapo Legend

Deep within central Brazil dwell a number of Amerindian societies belonging to the Gê linguistic group. The Gê have interested anthropologists because their complex social and religious organizations seem incongruent with their hunting-gathering economy. Beginning with Curt Nimuendajú's pioneering work of 1914, Gê folk narratives have drawn special attention. Animals, natural phenomenon, creation myths, and the sun and moon appear regularly in Gê tales. Alfred Métraux continued Nimuendajú's work in 1954 when he recorded narratives from the Cayapo, a Gê society on the verge of extinction. The following Cayapo legend about the origin of fire is fairly standard among the various Gê societies.

Formerly men did not have fire. When they killed game, they carved the flesh into thin strips, which they laid on stones to dry in the sun. They also ate rotten wood.

A man walking in the forest saw two macaws fly away from a hole in a rock. Thinking that the nest of the birds must be there and that it would contain young macaws, he returned to the village and said to his wife: "I saw a hole in a rock where there must be some young macaws. Tomorrow I will go with your brother to get them out." So, the next day, he left with his brother-in-law. When they arrived at the foot of the rock, the husband cut down a tree, notched it, and placed it as a ladder against the rock so that the brother-in-law could reach the nest. But the latter found only some round stones there. The husband, who stayed at the foot of the cliff, asked what was in the nest. "Nothing at all." "That's not true," answered the other. "Yesterday I heard a noise in that crack in the rock." "No, there is nothing there." "There must be something there." The climber finally cried: "Yes, there are two eggs; here they are." He dropped the stones on his brother-in-law, and they fell on his hands and hurt him. The brother-in-law stepped aside, turned his head away, and took down the ladder and threw it far into the brush. Abandoning the man on the rock, he returned home. His wife asked where his companion was. "In the forest: he is late, but he will arrive soon," answered the husband. The woman repeatedly asked the question and each time the answer was the same: "He'll arrive soon." When night fell, the woman accused her husband of having killed her brother. He denied it, repeating that the other would return. All night she waited and cried. The next day, the husband said that he was going into the forest to look for his brother-in-law. When he returned in the evening, he said he had seen his brother-in-law's tracks near the house, but had not been able to find him.

During all this time, the brother-in-law was dying of hunger and thirst on the rock. He was reduced to eating his own excrement and drinking his own urine. He became very thin and was near death when a jaguar, carrying a peccary on his shoulders, went by. The jaguar saw the man's shadow on the ground and tried to catch it. The man pulled back, but when he leaned forward once more, the jaguar took a swipe at the shadow with his bared claw. The animal looked in all directions, and then he covered his mouth, raised his head, and noticed the man on the rock. He asked the man what he was doing, why he was perched up there, and who he was. The man answered: "My brother-in-law discovered a macaw's nest, made me climb up this rock, and then took away the ladder. I am eating my own excrement." The jaguar dropped the peccary, cut down a tree, notched it, and climbed up to the man. He told him to climb onto his back, but the man, having seen the jaguar's teeth, was afraid and twice refused. The jaguar insisted, and still the frightened man refused. The jaguar descended, put the peccary on his back, and suggested that the man straddle the animal. Reassured, the man agreed. They went to the jaguar's home. When they arrived, the jaguar's wife was spinning. Seeing her husband, she said: "You bring someone else's son." The jaguar explained: "I have no companion. This man will be my companion and will go hunting with me. But he is very thin; he must be given a lot of food to fatten him up."

So the man remained at the jaguar's home, where he was given food to eat. He had almost regained his weight when the jaguar, who was leaving to hunt, told him: "Stay with my wife. If you are hungry, take a piece of tapir, which is cooking on the hearth." When he became hungry, the man wanted to take a piece of tapir, but the jaguar's wife suggested a piece of deer instead. The man paid no attention to her and went over to the hearth, but the woman called to him: "Look at me," she said, showing her claws. The man was frightened and fled into the forest. He walked a long time and finally climbed a tree. The jaguar, who was on his way home, saw him and asked what he was doing there. The other told all that had happened and that the female jaguar had wanted to kill him. The jaguar brought him back home and scolded his wife: "Don't do that; he is our son." "I was only joking," said the wife. Once more, the man stayed home alone with her. Again, he wanted to take a piece of tapir, but the jaguar's wife again told him to content himself with deer meat. As he insisted on having some tapir meat, she threatened him: "Look at me," and she showed her claws. The man ran away, and meeting the jaguar, he told him that once again the female had sought to kill him. The jaguar took him back to his house and scolded his wife, but she said again, "I was only joking."

When the jaguar again went hunting, the man accompanied him, and in the forest the jaguar said to his friend: "I will make you a bow and arrows to kill my wife if she shows her claws again. Don't be afraid, and aim straight at her heart." He made the weapons and gave them to the man. The man stayed with the jaguar's wife and, as before, he approached the hearth to get some tapir meat. While he was pretending to remove the leaves in which the meat was wrapped, the female bared her claws. He turned around and let fly two arrows, which pierced her through and through, and she fell dead. The man filled one basket with cotton thread and another with meat. He also wanted to take the fire, but was not able, by himself, to carry the jatoba tree trunk. He cut off a piece with an ax.

The jaguar had shown him the road to his village. He walked through the forest, crossed some streams, and finally found a path that took him to the village. At the edge of the forest, he hid the fire and all that he had taken from the jaguar's house. Then he went on toward the village. He saw his sister and called to her. When she saw him, she began to cry [tears of welcome], then went to tell her mother. Learning of the arrival of her son, the mother wept, but he did not answer her and hid in the forest. He slept beside the fire, and the next day, he went to his mother's house with all the things he had taken from the jaguar's home. The mother wept and cried: "My son brings so many things: meat, thread, fire." They lit the fire and warmed themselves by it, cooked the meat, and found it good.

The men of the men's house gathered and sent a *me-okre* to fetch the one who had brought the fire. They asked him to take them to the place where he had found it. The man told his story, and everyone decided to go look for the fire and the possessions of the jaguar. To succeed in their venture, they changed themselves into animals, and each was given a task. A big strong man was to transform himself into a tapir and carry the jatoba trunk; a second was to transform himself into a *yao* bird and extinguish the coals; a third, who had changed into a deer, was chosen to carry the meat; and a fourth, having become a peccary, had to carry the cotton thread. The hero of the adventure put himself at the head of the expedition and took them to the jaguar's house. The tapir went forward quietly to reconnoiter, but he saw no one. The jaguar had left. The tapir took the jatoba trunk, the peccary took the cotton thread, and the deer took the meat. They returned home and the women eagerly gathered dry leaves to make the fire. They cut up the jatoba trunk and each took a piece of it to make fire.

Noble Savages

John Hemming

The first Portuguese sighting of Brazil was on April 22, 1500. A fleet of thirteen ships commanded by the young nobleman Pero [Pedro] Álvares Cabral was on its way to India around the recently discovered Cape of Good Hope, but was blown too far to the west, across the Atlantic toward Brazil. Its sailors realized that they were approaching land. They pressed on and sighted a high, round mountain, which their commander named Mount Pascoal ("Easter Mountain"). They sailed closer and anchored in nine fathoms, a mile from the mouth of a forested river.

The first meeting between the Portuguese and the Brazilian natives occurred immediately. "We caught sight of men walking on the beaches. . . . [a chronicler wrote] The Admiral sent Nicolau Coelho ashore in a longboat to examine the river. As soon as he approached it, men began to assemble on the shore in twos and threes: by the time the boat reached the mouth of the river eighteen or twenty men were already there. They were dark and entirely naked, with nothing to cover their private parts, and carried bows and arrows in their hands. Nicolau Coelho made a sign to them to lay down their bows, and they laid them down. He could not speak with them there . . . because of the breaking of the sea on the shore. He merely threw them a [four-cornered] red hat, and a linen [conical cap] he was wearing on his head, and a black hat. One of them gave him a headdress of long feathers with a small tuft of red and grey feathers like those of a parrot. Another gave him a large string of very small white beads which looked like seed pearls."

Cabral's expedition spent only nine days sailing along the coast of Brazil before moving off towards India. But it fortunately contained a chronicler, Pero Vaz de Caminha, who described the thrilling discovery in a long letter to King Manoel I that was sent back by ship directly from

Brazil. Caminha was a narrator equal to the magnitude of the event. He combined sharp observation with plenty of delightful detail and has earned a place as Brazil's first ethnological observer. Every word in the letter carries information, all of it accurate; and yet, Caminha managed to convey his excitement and wonder at the marvels of the new discovery. He also touched on many of the aspects of relations between European and Brazilian natives that were to become constants during the years ahead.

Even during its short visit, Cabral's expedition held the first Christian service in Brazil. Native Indians watched in fascination as the Portuguese celebrated mass on an empty beach. "And when the mass was finished and we sat down for the sermon, many of them stood up and blew a horn or trumpet and began to leap and dance for a while." Cabral later ordered two ship's carpenters to build a large cross. "Many of them came there to be with the carpenters. I believe that they did this more to see the iron tools with which these were making it than to see the cross itself." This was the intense thrill of Stone Age people at their first sight of the cutting power of metal. "For they have nothing made of iron. They cut their wood and boards with wedge-shaped stones fixed into pieces of wood and firmly tied between two sticks." Once the cross was made, Cabral had his men "kneel down and kiss the cross so that [the Indians] might see our veneration for it. We did so, and motioned to them to do the same: they at once all went to kiss it." When the cross was finally planted, the natives joined in the ceremony, kneeling for the prayers and imitating the Portuguese when they rose for the sermon. "And at the elevation of the Host, when we knelt, they placed themselves as we were with hands uplifted, and so quietly that I assure Your Highness that they gave us much edification."

During the first thirty years after the discovery of Brazil, European visits consisted of a steady trickle of small ships seeking brazilwood and a few other commodities. The trees at first were close to the sea and river estuaries, and the Indians were content to barter the cut logs for trade goods. The visiting merchants were on their best behaviour, dependent as they were on Indian help, and in some awe of the large warrior tribes that they found inhabiting the Brazilian coast.

The profitable brazilwood trade depended entirely on the Brazilian Indians. Their lands produced the trees, and the natives themselves felled the brazilwoods, cut their hardwood into logs, and transported these to the coast for loading onto European ships. "The ships are sometimes far from the place where the cutting is done, perhaps four or five leagues [eleven to fourteen miles]. The only profit that these poor people derive from so much effort might be some miserable shirt or the lining from some clothing of little value. . . . After they have carried the logs to the ships during several journeys, you see their shoulders all bruised and torn by the weight of the wood—which is well known to be heavy and massive. This is hardly surprising, since they are naked and carry these loads so far. And yet they consider themselves very fortunate . . . to do this service for the Christians, whom they love, cherish and honour . . . because they showed them the way to cut wood with iron, with which they supply them."

Metal axes and tools seemed miraculous to peoples who spent much of their year in the laborious business of clearing forests with stone axes. Indians had always made skilled artifacts, but as one chronicler explained, "they took a very long time to make anything. This is why they value metal so greatly—because of the ease they experience in making things with it. For this reason they delight in communication with the whites." It was a fatal fascination, the greatest weakness of Brazilian Indians. Throughout Brazilian history, knives and axes have always been the surest way of winning Indian friendship, and they are still the main instrument in the attraction and pacification of hostile tribes.

The French organised their trading slightly differently from the Portuguese. They sent interpreters to live in the midst of the Indians—blond Normans who settled in the native villages and organised the gathering of logs for the next ship from France. These men went native, living as naked sultans among the tribes that adopted them. "I must record, to my great regret," the French Protestant pastor Jean de Léry wrote in 1556, "that some interpreters from Normandy who have lived eight or nine years in that country accommodated themselves to the savages and led the lives of atheists. They not only polluted themselves with all sorts of lewdness and villainy among the women and girls . . . but surpassed the savages in inhumanity: I have heard them boasting of having killed and eaten prisoners!" The Portuguese were more restrained and business-like. They established small warehouses at half a dozen places along the coast. A few Portuguese lived in these, trading with the tribes and accumulating the precious wood.

The French were as active as the Portuguese in bringing Brazilians back to Europe during those early years. Paulmier de Gonneville, the captain from Honfleur who so impressed the Carijó with his ship full of trade goods, took the son of the Carijó chief to France in 1505. He promised the father that he would teach the boy "artillery, which they greatly desired to dominate their enemies, and also how to make mirrors, knives, axes and all that they saw and admired among the Christians. Promising them all this was like promising a Christian gold, silver and jewels, or to teach him about the philosopher's stone." Back in France, the boy was "well regarded in Honfleur and in all the places we passed: for there had never been in France a person from so distant a country." Gonneville christened the boy Binot, gave him a good education, married him to his daughter Suzanne, and bequeathed him some property and the name and arms of Gonneville. But Binot never returned to his people to teach them how to make the magical artillery, mirrors, and knives.

Four years later, Captain Thomas Aubert brought seven Indians back from Brazil in his ship *La Pensée*. They were paraded through Rouen wearing feathers and loincloths, and carrying bows and arrows and bark canoes. One Frenchman noted with disgust that they lacked the fundamentals of French culture: "They speak with their lips and have no religion. . . . And they know nothing about bread, wine or money."

By the middle of the century, Brazilians brought back by French sailors were a familiar sight in Normandy. When the city of Rouen wished to stage a lavish welcome for Henry II and Catherine de' Medici when they visited with their court in 1550, someone thought of importing more Indians and using them in a tableau. A meadow beside the Seine was decked out to resemble Brazil. New trees and bushes were planted. Existing trees were made more luxuriant with extra branches and festooned with imitation fruit. Parrots, monkeys, coatis, and other American animals clambered about in this jungle. Thatched cabins were built at either end of the meadow, each surrounded by a log palisade: these were intended to represent villages of the Tupinambá and Tabajara, two warring tribes from the northern coast of Brazil. "All along this site as many as three hundred men busied themselves here and there. They were completely naked, tanned and shaggy, without in any way covering the parts that nature commands, and were decorated and equipped in the manner of those savages of America from whom brazilwood is brought. Among their number there were a good fifty natural savages freshly brought from that country. . . . The remainder of the company were French sailors who had frequented that country: they spoke the language as well, and expressed themselves as naively in the gestures and mannerisms of the savages, as if they were natives of that same country."

The pageant opened with the real natives and the naked sailors going about their daily life, demonstrating archery, chasing game "like troglodytes after water-fowl," swinging in hammocks, or loading wood onto a French ship anchored in the river. This peaceful scene was suddenly broken by an attack on the Tupinambá village by their Tabajara enemies. Norman sailors and real Indians staged a mock battle, wielding clubs and bows and arrows; but the Tupinambá—traditional allies of the French—were victorious. The spectacle's climax was the burning of the Tabajara hut. The king and his court were enchanted by it all.

It was in such a world of fantasy that Europeans came to imagine the native peoples of Brazil. Pero Vaz de Caminha's letter to the king had been a sober description of the people he saw; but even he paused frequently to marvel at the Indians' simplicity, beauty, and natural innocence. Cabral sent back one Tupinikin who "was received with joy in Portugal by the King and kingdom. Great and small could never tire of seeing and hearing the gestures, talk or movements of that new individual of the human race. Some took him to be half-goat, others a faun or some kind of ancient monster." Later visitors to Brazil were less objective than Caminha. A letter from a pilot on one of the first voyages was widely diffused through Europe: it depicted the Brazilians as beautiful, naked people living innocently in a perfect climate surrounded by birds and animals.

A Description of the Tupinambá

Anonymous

Unlike the Aztecs and Incas encountered by Spaniards, Brazil's Amerindians produced few artifacts and no monuments or codices from which historians might piece together their pre-sixteenth-century way of life. Furthermore, by 1600, European diseases, warfare, trade, and culture had drastically altered life for the Tupí who dwelled along the coast. Therefore, sixteenth-century descriptions written by Europeans are invaluable tools for retrieving, at least partially, the indigenous past. An anonymous author left the following account in 1587 after seventeen years of Brazilian travels. Focusing on one Tupí tribe, the Tupinambá, this account belies the idyllic image that Europeans of this era often assigned to Brazilian Indians.

The Tupinambá live arranged in villages; in each one, everybody recognizes one person as their leader, or chief, so that in war he directs them; this is the only act in which they offer him any demonstration of obedience. They elect him by the proof he has given of having more power and valor than others; yet outside of instances of war, he does not receive better treatment, esteem, or respect than the rest, from whom he is not distinguished.

When this chief heathen settles his village, he always looks for some high, clear site, bathed by winds, that there might be good and nearby water, and that the land might be compatible for their crops. After the site is chosen and approved by the oldest men, the leader makes his home very long, covered with palms; and the rest, by the same method, also go about forming their houses, arranging them in squares that appear like plazas, in which they conduct their gatherings and dances. In each house there is an old Indian, who serves as head of the household and is related to the rest.

These houses last as long as the palms, which serve as a roof, keep from rotting, which is always past three or four years; as often as this happens, they move the site. In the houses, there is not any quality of a room other than the beams, which fall between the branches where each clan is sheltered. The old heathen chooses a place for their hut, where he settles with his woman, friends, children, and the old unmarried women who serve him. And soon, the rest go about settling. They do not move from these huts, except when a single male marries and wants to make a hut for himself because, in this instance, he does it with his woman.

On top of the beams of the houses, they insert some tightly joined poles, in which they store their utensils, vegetables, and everything else they have. When they eat, the whole hut gathers and, squatting over their legs (except the chief, who remains resting in the hammock), they eat what they have. In these same houses, they hold their carnal gatherings without safeguards or discretion for sex and age, with all the publicity of brutes.

If the villages adjoin those of their rivals, they make fences of wattle and daub, strong and tightly joined, with their doors and openings from twenty to thirty palms [spans of a hand] distant from the houses; and of a manner that there becomes formed a sufficient rampart, which hinders entrance to the enemy, and defends the villagers and facilitates them being able to shoot arrows from inside, if the enemies intend to assault them, as very often occurs . . .

The true woman of the Tupinambá is the first whom he knew. In their marriages, the ceremonies are nothing more than the father giving the daughter to the son-in-law, and as long as they know each other carnally, they remain married. In addition to this, each one has whomever else he wants; and the best nobility or dignity among them is judged by the greatest number of women had. However, all the women recognize the superiority of the first one and serve her, and she is not offended to have them as companions in the art of cohabiting with her husband. She is the one who has her hammock joined to that of the husband; the others are more distant, and between each a fire is always burning at night.

In that which regards cohabitation, however, there is neither subordination nor discretion among the women; the husband gets up from his hammock when it strikes him and lies down in the hammock of the one whom he craves, and in view of the rest, satisfies his desires, without the others being stimulated for being passed over. Still, he can be with the first woman as much time as it strikes him and with the rest only the time necessary for the conclusion of his lustful acts.

Despite this, secret jealousies gravely torment the women, especially the first woman; although they might not be able to complain about these communications, by custom, it does not avoid nor impede stimuli for rivalry because of the knowledge of there being women more to the liking of the common husband, those whom he more often seeks for cohabitation.

[For] the Indian who is not chief of the village, the more children he has, the more honorable his reputation among the rest. They seek daughters from him (especially single men seeking their first woman) and serve [him for] two or three years, primarily so that the father might facilitate the daughters' relationship with them. The daughters are awarded to those who better serve the father, and for that the lovers willingly care about doing good for him, in order to win their intended loves. This service consists of going to cultivate the field for him, to kill game and fish, to bring him firewood from the forest, and to perform every salutation to him with fine diligence.

As soon as the father awards the daughter to the pretender, he lies down with her in the hammock of the said father, from which they arise married, and the daughter, then leaving the father's hut, parting from siblings and relatives, goes with the husband to his hut. If she still is not a woman, she is not offered to the husband until she arrives at that age, which is known easily.

[This is] because the female, until she is a perfect woman, walks without any division; and as soon as she is [a perfect woman], she has the obligation to wear a string of cotton around the waist, and another around the wrists, by which is given the news that she is fit for marriage. However, if some man who is considered one of the most important of the village asks for a woman from some father whose daughter is still a girl, the father awards her to him, and the husband offers the infallible guarantee in which he specifies that he will not touch her too early. The father brings her immediately with him and sends her to grow in his hut; until the said time, the son-in-law does not offend [have sexual relations with] her.

If some Indian deflowers an Indian woman, although no one might know about it, she immediately breaks the cords that she has worn on her waist and wrists since she reached womanhood, so that all might know that she already was penetrated, and the Indian will not consider her a virgin, which she now is not. That is not a misdeed, whether known by the husband or by any other man; nor by this fact is the father offended, nor does the daughter lose the husband, since there is never lacking anyone who might want her for a woman if the man who deflowered her rejects her . . .

The Tupinambá only work in their fields from seven in the morning until noon, and those who are most concerned do not work past two in the afternoon, which they know quite well by the height of the sun. In this work, they are excellent practitioners, and the work completed, they gather at the house.

At the same time, the males prepare the forest for planting; they burn and clean the land. The females plant food crops and cultivate them. The former cut and bring wood to the house, where there always is a lit fire (since, as I already said, even at night they keep it between the hammocks, and without which they do not sleep). The women bring water, make food to eat, and care for the house; they tell the males when the hammocks are dirty so that they will wash them in the river, as it is the men to whom this work belongs.

The most famous projects, which the males perform, are [the making of] baskets of palm leaves and many other pots of the same type, very cleverly fabricated from the same leaf and some with a special blend of colors because they dye them various shades with water from wood. They make hampers from vines, and other concave utensils, in which they save their ornaments, with ingenious construction and workmanship. They make bows and sharp, very penetrating arrows; hoods and capes from bird feathers; and other manufactures from the same things, finely colored. With the same dyes from wood, they change and transform the natural colors of the feathers into that which they desire. Also, they make embroidered hammocks and other textiles from cotton, very finely done and with great workmanship.

When they want to collect many fish in the freshwater rivers or saltwater estuaries, they capture them with a fabric of sticks and beat the fish that remain on the surface, after throwing them an ample quantity of an herb, which they call *timbó,* that intoxicates them and, as they die, makes them come to the surface. They then collect as much as they want and of the type that they intended.

The females do not sew, nor spin cotton, and therefore they do not make looms, as they could if they had anyone who would teach them; but they make, from their own idea, a type of textile, from which they form the hammocks in which they sleep and some ribbons, as braids, with which they encircle the head, arms, legs, waist, and anything they desire. From the same fibers, they form cords of various thicknesses that are very strong and serve their uses.

Those women who are of middle age go to the fields and bring to the house, on their backs, the manioc from which they make meal to sustain the family. Those women who are older make the clay pots—as there are pots, bowls, pans, cups, and other vessels and pieces for their use, and some in which they keep wines—and they carry a pipe and make other things, all carved, painted, and finely made, according to their use. They shape these clay pots by hand, and later insert them into holes in the ground, cover them with wood, and bake them with fire; this makes them good and durable. Also, they are very inclined to raise dogs, with which the husbands go to the hunt, and the women carry them on their backs when they go to the field. They also raise chickens and other fowl and animals . . .

As soon as the Tupinambá halt their march [to the enemy village], they stop making daytime fires, so that they cannot be sensed by their enemies because of the smoke. They are predisposed to the method by which, suddenly at night, they fall on their enemies; they hope that the moon might be full in order to make the rest of the march at night. They reach the enemy's village all together, and with great silence, sometime in the early morning before dawn; and as soon as it is surrounded, they enter it giving thunderous howls with the beating of their drums and other instruments, and at the same time, everyone swings clubs with such fury and cruelty that not a single person remains alive from those who receive blows from the first rush, whether male or female, big or small. Each one swings a heavy club, shaped into nubs, with which they strike their enemy's head with such violence that only one blow suffices and is more than enough to take a life.

They are so barbarous that, not satisfied to deny quarter to whoever surrenders, they cut the parts natural to men and the female ducts to carry back to their women, who dry them with smoke, and make those of the same nation who they captured eat these parts before they kill them.

In the war booty, they do not have their principal, specific item, nor among themselves do they observe any policy; each one takes whatever he can grab. As soon as they have concluded the action and are loaded with the booty, they set fire to the settlement and march for theirs. Then, they walk with hurried steps day and night to avoid the possibility that those [survivors] who fled, and were able to join with those of other villages, might now pursue them on the path . . .

Seldom do these precautions serve for the Tupinambá to elude being attacked during the retreat by their enemies, and often they receive great harm and destruction because the escapees, united with their friends, follow them headlong into their retreat or come looking for them in their villages, where they surround the Tupinambá, who entrench themselves in their manner with good form. When they are fortified like this, the war does not end until the besieged or the besiegers are totally destroyed. In these conflicts, there are innumerable deaths, so that always they keep between themselves opposition and hatred, this condition being the work of Providence, without which their incredible propagation would not be containable in the world. While the conflicts last, the chiefs walk yelling and exhorting their people so that they will not lose enthusiasm for the credit of the nation and its glory, reminding them of the victories that they, or their ancestors, have already achieved against the enemies, and the rest that might occur for them, as an incentive for fury and rage.

The Tupinambá change their names as soon as they regroup at their houses, which they do with the following ritual. On the day designated for the change, he who has to change his name prepares his invitation and wine. The invited ones gather with their festive adornments at the feast, and the owner of the house receives them with the same adornment. When quite drunk and tired from folly and sensuality, they start making compliments to him, and sing praises with their songs and music. Referring to his feats, they beg him to say the new name he wants to take. He then declares it and goes to lie down in the hammock, where for a certain number of days, he exists without eating or drinking, as it is a bad omen to do otherwise.

When the Tupinambá grab some of their adversaries alive, they enslave them (although it is rare for them to pardon his life). He serves his master, to whom he is no longer in submission because he is occupied doing the same thing that the master or his sons do—which is to farm certain hours, cut wood, hunt, and fish; between master and slave, there is no division.

Ordinarily when they bring the captives, they bind them in a way so that they do not flee or [they] throw them into prisons of very thick cotton, which they call *mazaraca,* that they cannot untie because they tie them around the neck and waist. Secured by this method, they give the captives much to eat, a woman to enjoy, and every type of delight that facilitates his feeding and fattening. Imprisoned, he chooses the woman he desires; if she is married, the husband does not oppose him, and with her he amuses himself when and how he pleases, she having the careful-ness of serving and attending to him, putting ready for him whatever he asks. Sometimes it happens that the captive—being a young man, robust and well shaped and talented—wins a pardon from death and is sold to the Portuguese; however, ordinarily, he ends up in the following manner.

The master designates the day on which he has to eat him (and this is the greatest festivity among the Tupinambá); they celebrate vespers, in which they begin to practice gluttony, drunkenness, and lasciviousness. At this function, there is no stew lacking, no drink that might be missing, no sensual act that might not be executed, and all relatives and friends are invited, even those forty leagues distant. During the whole night, no one sleeps; all pass the night singing to the sound of their instruments. At dawn, all are prepared with their ornaments, which they have, and they come to the clearing at his order. Behind everyone comes the captive completely bent, and with his body smeared with honey, very content and adorned, and painted in various colors, with a garter around the waist and a wooden sword, and only distinguished from the rest by being bound around the neck with a cord of strong and long cotton that has two equal ends.

Reaching the clearing, they put the captive between two poles, already stuck in the ground and with two holes through which are passed the ends of the referred cord, [the captive] remaining with freedom for his actions and only bound by the neck in the middle of the cited two poles. Two robust Tupinambá hold onto the two ends of the cord, which they loosen or tighten according to their desire that he be more or less the master of his own actions.

The miserable one (being a content heathen) put in this position, they place at his head a pot of wine; all the onlookers drink from it to his health, and he also does it. This completed, the one who has to kill him arrives very adorned and painted, with his wooden sword, which is placed at the foot of the victim. He tells him that he might give an account of his life and the actions that he has performed; the captive begins to lecture, making from his life the discourse that he desires, concluding that now he is receiving revenge from whoever has to kill him because already he helped eat his [the executioner's] relatives or killed them, and it remains certain that his [the captive's] relatives have to avenge him. Concluding the lecture, the old women encircle him, and tell him that he might indulge in seeing the sun and saying farewell to it because soon he will die; he responds that he accepts with pleasure death for what he already did to their relatives, and what they received from his relatives.

This practice finished, they play instruments, sing, dance, and make a great racket and merriment; this concluded, the executioner places himself in front of the captive and tells him that he may defend himself, that he wants to kill him. Both draw their swords, and the ends of the cord are loosened. Liberty is given to the captive to block and defend himself from the first blows, and by this ability, it has not seldom resulted that, right off, he who must die very seriously wounds the executioner because the latter, confident that the lookouts with the cord would not give great freedom, approached the captive more than he should have and receives great blows, which his carelessness facilitates; and so he who must die, skillfully anticipates and makes use of the occasion. Ultimately, the pulled cords keep the captive choked between the poles, where the executioner hits him on the head and takes his life.

The captive, dead in this manner, is conducted by the followers to another place where, done in mouthfuls according to the quantity of dead bodies and invited people, he is distributed to everyone, who eats this baked or roasted meat. The executioner, judging this action as the greatest of honors, designates at this time another day on which he will give a feast and change his name, as already referred.

The First Wave

Warren Dean

In his posthumously published history of the Brazilian Atlantic rain forest, Warren Dean marshals evidence from Brazil's economic, physical, botanical, and geological history to make his somber case. The author was deeply pained by what he learned during the course of his study, and we cannot turn away from the implications of the impending destruction of this vast wonder of nature. "The last service that the Atlantic Forest might serve, tragically and forlornly," he wrote in his concluding chapter (p. 364), "is to demonstrate all the terrible consequences" of destroying the adjacent Amazon rain forest, today deeply threatened as well.

The provenance and date of the arrival of humans in the New World have come to be questioned lately. It still appears most probable that they reached South America via the Isthmus of Panama, although there are faint evidences of Asian and African contacts. There are datings at scattered sites as early as 50,000 years before the present, but they remain controversial. All other sites indicate human presence began as the last glacial episode was in retreat. Evidences of hunter-gatherers in the region of the Atlantic Forest are about 11,000 years old. Stone implements of that age are widespread in what was open country, at its southernmost reaches. Human remains 10,000 years old have been found in caves north of present-day Belo Horizonte, also in open country.

The adoption of agriculture utterly transformed the relationship of humans to the forest. What had been a residual resource, low yielding to hunter-gatherers, casually or accidentally burned when driving or attracting prey, now became their principal habitat. They found savanna soils too sandy, dry, acid, and aluminum-toxified to farm. Agriculture was much more viable on forest soils. From the beginning, farming in the region of the Atlantic Forest—indeed, throughout the lowland areas of the continent—required the sacrifice of forest. The technique was extremely simple: Near the end of the drier season, the underbrush in a patch of forest, a hectare more or less, was slashed so as to dry it out, and the larger trees were ringed with stone axes. Then, just before the coming of the rains, the area would be set afire, causing the enormous stock of nutrients stored in the forest biomass to fall to earth as ashes. A few of the largest trees that had resisted the fire would remain, scorched but standing. The rains washed the nutrients into the soil, neutralizing as well as fertilizing it. Planting was then carried out, with no tool save a digging stick. Forest that had never before been burned was not only marvelously fertile, but also free of the seeds of invasive plants and, therefore, little weeding was necessary.

After two or three seasons—manioc requires eighteen months to reach maturity—the patch was allowed to return to woods. In regions of sandy and highly leached soil, abandonment was necessary because yields quickly declined, but in the region of the Atlantic Forest, soils were generally fertile enough to permit longer cultivation. Abandonment of the cultivated patch was more likely to be caused by the invasion of weeds and pests. Weeds could be uprooted by hand, but there were no defenses against pests, which included, most formidably, the leaf-cutting ant. Abandonment also occurred when the village was relocated for reasons of sanitation, internal social conflicts, or insecurity in the presence of intervillage rivalry. All farming regimes represent a disturbance of a natural ecosystem. Indeed, they attempt to freeze natural succession at its earliest stage, introducing cultivated plants that in their wild state had been pioneer species. This kind of farming, called swidden or slash and burn, is the least intrusive because it imitates the natural scale of disturbance and, rather than freezing permanently the process of succession, merely exploits it temporarily.

Secondary, or successional, forest, what the indigenes called *capoeira* (formerly planted land), that eventually reclaimed abandoned fields was similar in structure and composition to growth that naturally repaired canopy openings caused by tree falls. Tree regrowth repaired the soil by raising subsoil nutrients and dispersing them through leaf fall, and by shading soil processes from direct sunlight and rainfall. Usually, farmers would not attempt a repetition of burning and planting in a given patch until the forest had grown back to a certain height. In practical terms, the delay was advisable to shade out completely weed growth, and to restore the balance between pests and their ambient predators. It is uncertain how long this interval might have been in the region of the Atlantic Forest, but twenty to forty years seems probable.

Swidden was very economical of labor, but it was not artless. The burning itself was a dangerous and problematic task. Its timing required a sixth sense, lest it be done too far or too little in advance of the rains. It could not be too intense, lest it burn the shallow, fertile layer of litter and its organisms. Swidden did not imply the loss of skills already acquired because these farmers had to continue to hunt and fish. Proteins still had to be obtained from animal sources because manioc lacks them and even maize provides only a few of them. Swidden farmers could not replace wild game with domesticates because their fields were not adequate to provide forage for larger animals, and they had no means of penning and protecting smaller animals or fowl. On the other hand, the planted patches, like any burned area, attracted game and thus served two purposes. To judge from observations of present-day swidden farmers, techniques slowly but continually improved. Shrewd associations of crops improved yields, speeded growth, and reduced infestations. The woodland fallow was not entirely abandoned, but was tended so as to exploit a variety of useful species common to secondary forest. Numerous "wild" trees were transplanted during the phase of cultivation and protected from competition as the forest recuperated. There were fruit bearers, among them guava, papaya, cashew, soursop, Surinam cherry—and lacking English equivalents because they were neither exported nor cultivated in the English-speaking tropics—*jabuticaba, grumixama, araçá, cambuçi, cambucá, sapucaia,* and *pacova;* fiber- and seed-bearing palms; canoe-wood trees; and the prized genipap and annatto, which yielded black and red skin paints that also repelled insects and blocked the sun's rays.

Slash-and-burn agriculture was stunningly reductive. Nearly everything live within the burned patches was reduced to ashes, and only the ashes were exploited. Perhaps the first farmers regretted this initial waste. There were, no doubt, episodes of burning that escaped control, as might happen occasionally in drought years on the wetter, windward side of the Atlantic Forest and more commonly in the drier, inland forest. Swidden farming, though more intensive than hunting and gathering, was more prodigal of the forest. It is likely that the interval allowed for woodland fallow was not long enough to restore the original forest to its fullest development. Under conditions of sufficient local human population pressure, it may not have been allowed even to reach its full potential height.

Agriculture, then, may have further reduced complexity and biomass over considerable areas of the Atlantic Forest during the 1,000 and more years it was practiced before the arrival of Europeans. To lend some concreteness to such an assertion, let it be supposed that farming was taken up by hunter-gatherers when their population reached 0.1 per square kilometer and that in response to the success of the new regime, average density soon grew, in the highland regions of the Atlantic Forest, to 0.3 persons per square kilometer; that is, one per 333 hectares. John Hemming's estimates of highland populations in this area at the time of contact—about 0.4 per square kilometer—are consonant with this supposition, if the populations of agriculturalists then continued to grow slowly as techniques were refined. Suppose further that the nutritional requirements of this population could be satisfied by clearing annually 0.2 hectares per person (based on an average yield of manioc of five tons per hectare, more than half of it lost to animals and pests or wasted). Then, if these farmers cleared nothing but primary forest, they would have burned about 50 percent of it at least once during that millennium, even if they never allowed fire to escape accidentally or maliciously and never practiced fire drives of animal prey.

Letter to Governor Tomé de Sousa

Manoel da Nóbrega

The Jesuit friar Manoel da Nóbrega arrived in Brazil in 1549 along with the colony's first governor, Tomé de Sousa. Over the next ten years, Nóbrega fought tirelessly in defense of Amerindians. Nóbrega saw them as ripe for religious conversion if placed under genuine Christian guidance. Isolating "heathens" in Jesuit-controlled aldeias, or villages, offered the best means for Christianization since contact with other Europeans put Indians at risk of moral corruption or, worse yet, enslavement. In this 1559 letter to Tomé de Sousa, Nóbrega refers to the difficult task of converting Indians, in addition to spelling out the improprieties committed by lay and clerical Europeans alike.

May the peace and love of Christ our Lord always be in your continuous favor and aid. Amen.

. . . [P]rimarily, I want to lament over this land and give you an account of the particular things that I most have in my soul . . . because I see the evil path that this land takes, always deserving from our Lord great chastisement, and punished for its sins, it wants other, greater punishments because it becomes ever more incorrigible and thrusts greater roots into its obstinacy.

Since I have been in this land, to which I came with Your Majesty, two desires will torment me always: one, of seeing the Christians of these parts reformed into good customs, and that there would be good seed transplanted in these parts, by that fragrance of good example; and another, to see a disposition in the heathens to be able to apprehend the word of God, and that they would become capable of grace and enter into the church of God . . .

From these two desires that I mentioned, others came to me, which were desires for the means of fulfilling the first two wishes, and from these means I chose two that seemed best: one was to seek a bishop, such as Your Majesty and I portrayed for reforming the Christians; and another, to see the heathens subjugated and thrown under the yoke of obedience to the Christians, so that there can be impressed in them all that we might want because the heathen is of a nature that, once subdued, the faith of Christ will be written very well in his understandings and desires, as was done in Peru and the Antilles, since the heathen appears in a similar condition as them; and we now are starting to see by the eye of experience, as below I will tell, if they leave him in his liberty and free will, as he is a brutal heathen, nothing will be done with him; as by experience we saw that during this whole time we expended much work on him, but without reaping more fruit from it than a few innocent souls that we sent to heaven.

Our Lord brought the Bishop Dom Pedro Fernandez, such a virtuous one, whom Your Majesty knows, and very zealous about reformation of the customs of the Christians, but as to the heathens and their salvation, he gave little of himself because your bishop did not believe in it, and they seemed to him incapable of the entire doctrine because of their brutishness and bestiality, nor did he consider them sheep in his flock, nor did he feel that Christ our Lord would see fit to have them as such; but Your Majesty helped me in this, to the praise of our Lord in his providence; to permit that he [the bishop] flee from the heathens and the land, having little desire to die in their hands, to be eaten by them, and as for me, I always desired this and asked our Lord for it, and also asked that he send me at the opportunity someone greater than the bishop; but this was denied to me. What I judge from this, seeing that I was not the counselor of our Lord, is that whoever did this perhaps wanted to pay the bishop for his virtues and great kindness, and punish him simultaneously for the carelessness and little zeal that he had for the salvation of the heathen. He punished him [Pedro Fernandes Sardinha, Brazil's first bishop, eaten by cannibals], giving him the death penalty, which he did not love [doing], and compensated him with the punishment, being as glorious as they now claim to Your Majesty that it was, given that he was in the power of the unfaithful with as many and as good circumstances as he did have.

The bishop, seeing that he was very zealous in the salvation of the Christians, did little because he was alone and brought with him some clerics as companions, who ended his example and badly used and dispensed the church's sacraments, giving them to everyone in perdition. . . . But as they came, they introduced into the land that clerics and dignities would cohabit with their [Indian] slaves, who for this end they chose the best and most expensive they found, with the begetting sin that they reconciled having whomever would serve them, and soon started to make children and propagate themselves . . .

They also started to use their orders and dispense the sacraments, and untied the cords with which we detained souls, to give jubilee in place of condemnation and perdition to the souls, giving sanctity to dogs and precious stones to pigs, who never will know how to leave the mire of their sins, by which not only the evil ones, but also some good people, if they reconciled it, took liberty of being that which their bad inclination demanded from them. Thus, the land is now in these terms, in which all the houses of the land are counted, in all we found full of moral sins, full of adultery, fornication, incest, and abominations, so much that I relieve myself from caring if Christ has anyone clean in this land, and scarcely are offered one or two who well preserve their condition, at least without public sin . . .

In all these captaincies, in addition to these sins that I have mentioned, I noted some that much more than others offend the divine Benevolence and throws more stones from the rostrum because they are against the charity, love of God, and the holy. And these sins have their root and beginning in the general hatred that the Christians have for the heathens, and they not only hate their bodies, but also hate their souls, and in everything they impede and shut off the paths that Christ our Lord opened for them to be saved, those that I will mention to Your Majesty, since I already started to give you an account of my pain . . .

Another sin also born from this infernal root is that the Christians teach the heathens to kidnap their own people and sell them as slaves. This custom, more than in any captaincy, I found in Espirito Santo, captaincy of Vasco Fernandez, seeing more of this occurring throughout the better part of the captaincy.

In São Vicente, those heathens, the *Topinachins* [*Tupinikins*], do not do this; but the Christians of São Vicente in Rio de Janeiro negotiated from the heathens of the Gato many females whom they sought as wives, giving their fathers some payment, but they [the women] will remain slaves forever. In Pernambuco, there also is much conduct of this sort, principally after the past wars that the Indians, although no longer capable, waged.

The same was introduced into Bahia in the era of Dom Duarte, because in the era of Your Majesty, none of this was yet accepted, and after the past war, from which the Indians emerged timid; and through fear and subjugation by the Christians, and also because of greed for the ransom, the Indians sell the most forlorn who are among them. Those of Porto Seguro and Ilheus never will sell themselves, but the Christians taught them that they might assault and sell those of the backlands who come to produce salt from the sea; and thus it occurs there, those of the sea sell those of the backlands as much as they can because the rapine that the Christians taught them seems fine to them.

And because this is the general conduct of everyone, it befitted me to shut off confessions because no one wants to do what is obliged in that [sacrament], and they have the entire other clergy who absolves and sanctions them.

From this same root is born that Christians were little disposed to the salvation of the slaves whom they had from the heathens, allowing them to live according to their law, with neither doctrine nor teaching, in much sin; and if they die, they will bury them in the dunghills because from them they do not intend more than service; and so that the Christians might have more of those who might serve them, they bring heathens into their houses, to content themselves with the female slaves, and thus the Christians are cohabiting with heathens.

I now have told Your Majesty the majority of my pain. . . . I beseech you through the charity of Christ our Lord to rescue this poor Brazil. . . . May he give you, through his mercy, his peace on earth and glory in heaven. Amen.

From Bahia, 5 July 1559
Speaker and servant of Your Majesty in Christ,
Manoel da Nóbrega

From the River of Jenero

Francisco Suares

In June 1596, the explorer Francisco Suares wrote a long letter to his brother, Diego Suares, in Lisbon telling of the lucrative trade between "Rio de Jenero [in] Brasill" and the Spanish viceroyalty of Peru, by way of the Rio de la Plata, in small ships. Trade of this kind was legal only during the years between 1580 and 1640, when the lack of a male heir to the Portuguese royal dynasty resulted in the merging of the Portuguese and Spanish crowns. Philip the first of Portugal (Felipe I) was one and the same as Philip V of Spain. After 1640, Brazil returned to its earlier isolation when Portugal regained its dynastic independence from Spain. Even so, smuggling in the Plata region continued.

(The imaginative [and inconsistent] spelling was typical of many books published before the eighteenth century.)

Sir, we set sail from Lisbon the fourth of April 1596 and arrived here in this river of Jenero the twentie seventh of June next ensuing. . . . I hired a ware-house by my selfe and landed my commodities. And now I am selling them as fast as I can, and sell them very well and to great profit: for I have solde all our hats. I would I had brought forty or fifty dozen, by reason of the great utterance of them up into Peru and into the new kingdom of Granada, by the way of the river Plate. For here is passage every three or foure months with barks of thirty and forty tunnes a piece, which are laden with sugars, rice, taffataes, hats, and other kindes of commodities of this countrey, which are caried up the sayd river of Plate in the sayd barks, and thence are conveyed up into Peru. And these barkes are but tenne or twelve dayes going up the sayd river to Peru. And within foure and five moneths after, the sayd barks come downe this river againe laden with reals of plate [silver] and bring downe from those places no other commodities but treasure. It is a woonderful thing to beholde the great gaine and profit that is gotten in this river and in this countrey. I am ashamed to write it, fearing that I shall not be beleeved. For the imployment of one hundred ducats in Spaine, being brought hither, will yield twelve hundred and fifteene hundred ducats profit. This trade hath been used but within this yeere. For wee can goe up to the mines of Potosi, which are the best and the richest mines in all Peru. If the merchants of Spaine and Portugall did know this trade, they would send nor venture so much merchandise to Cartegena as they doe. For up this river is a great deale the neerer way and the easier to go to Peru. For the Peruleiros or merchants of Peru, which dwell there, come downe to this harbour and river of Janero, and bring with them fifteene thousand and twentie thousand ducats in reals of plate and gold, and imploy it heere in this river in commodities: and when heere are no commodities to be had for money in this place, then these merchants of Peru are constrained to go to Baia and Fernanbuc [Pernambuco], and there to imploy their money. I would I had brought good store of silks and not these kinds of commodities which I did bring. For heere is more profit to be had a great deale then in the voyage of Angola.

The Sins of Maranhão

Antônio Vieira

The Jesuit priest Antônio Vieira, provincial of northern Maranhão, dedicated his life to attacking the practice of resgate—*slave-hunting expeditions in the interior—by prospectors, landowners, and other colonists. In 1652, following an investigation that he had undertaken, Vieira wrote that "the entire region of Maranhão has been worn down, depopulated, and reduced to one or two scanty villages, and vast numbers of people have been wiped out." The sermon below was delivered on the first Sunday of Lent in 1653, in São Luis, the capital of the province. His denunciation of the abuses committed against the Indians led to a new law in 1655 prohibiting enslavement, although it left loopholes and was not easily enforced. Reaction against the law, further, led to the expulsion of the Jesuits from Maranhão in 1684.*

At what a price the devil today buys souls compared to what he offered for them previously! There is no market in the world where the devil can get them less expensively than right here in our land. In the gospel, he offered all the kingdoms of the world for one soul; in Maranhão, the devil does not need to offer one-tenth as much for all the souls. It is not necessary to offer worlds, nor kingdoms; it is not necessary to offer cities, nor towns, nor villages. All he has to do is offer a few Tapuia Indians and at once he is adored on bended knee. What a cheap market! An Indian for a soul! That Indian will be your slave for eternity, as long as God is God. This is the devil's contract with you. Not only do you accept it, but you pay him money on top of it . . .

Christians, nobles, and people of Maranhão, do you know what God wants of you this Lenten season? That you break the chains of injustice, and let free those whom you have captive and oppressed. These are the sins of Maranhão; these are what God commanded me to denounce to you. Christians, God commanded me to make these matters clear to you, and so I do it. All of you are in mortal sin; all of you live in a state of condemnation; and all of you are going directly to hell. Indeed, many are there now, and you will soon join them if you do not change your ways.

Is it possible that an entire people live in sin, that an entire people will go to hell? Who questions this does not understand the evil of unjust captivity. The children of Israel went down to Egypt, and after the death of Joseph, the Pharaoh seized them and made slaves of them. God wanted to liberate those miserable people, and He sent Moses there with no other escort than a rod. God knew that in order to free the captives, a rod was sufficient, even though He was dealing with a ruler as tyrannical as Pharaoh and with a people as cruel as the Egyptians. When Pharaoh refused to free the captives, the plagues rained down on him . . .

The only disadvantage is that some of you will lose a few Indians. I promise you that they will be very few. But to you who question this, I ask: Do not some of your Indians die or flee? Many do. Will death do what reason will not? Will happenstance bring what a good conscience will not? If smallpox strikes and carries away your Indians, what will you do? You will have to show patience. Is it not better, then, to lose the Indians to the service of God than to lose them by punishment of God? The answer is obvious.

Minas Uprising of 1720

Anonymous

During the mid-1690s, Paulista prospectors fulfilled a dream that had hounded the Portuguese for nearly two centuries: they discovered rich gold deposits in what today is the state of Minas Gerais (General Mines). Minas's gold founded many personal fortunes, yet windfall tax revenues for the Crown (the quinto, *or a fifth of all the gold produced) proved elusive. Prospecting drew free spirits who were quite willing to take advantage of the weak official presence in the region. The result was widespread tax evasion. In an effort to enforce tax collection, the Crown mandated that all exported gold be smelted at royal facilities and restricted gold dust's usage as specie. The following report describes the miners' reaction to the new rules. Contained in the report, however, are several interesting subplots, such as the miners' resentment against merchants, the church's standing in the community, and the specter of a slave rebellion. Perhaps the reader will notice others.*

On São Pedro eve, during the night, a riot by armed people descended from the hill of Ouro Preto, and another riot arose in the area of Padre Faria, and together they attacked the house of the ordinary *ouvidor* [a justice or magistrate], doctor Martinho Vieyra; and only by leaving the house, he escaped the riot's rage and death. Some of these rioters, climbing up, destroyed everything that he had in the house, throwing from the windows the royal ordinances, the books of the Royal Treasury, and all the rest of the papers belonging to his ministry, while reading the sentences and rulings with mockery, and taunting the *ouvidor,* whose staff one of the rioters held; the latter shouted to the people that if they wanted him to do justice for them, then he was present; accompanying this action were some voices and words of dishonor against the said magistrate.

This first insult completed, they started to chant: *viva o povo, viva o povo*

The gold rush in the province of Minas Gerais in the eighteenth century. *(Bibloteca Nacional, Rio de Janeiro)*

[Long Live the People! Long Live the People!]. And thus, they added partisans joining them in that riot, some by willingness, others by force. . . . They soon joined together, and fortified themselves in the upper level of the house of the *Câmara* [assembly] and the Church of Santa Quiteria; there they elected a judge of the people, or head, in their language. On the following day of São Pedro, they sent a bulletin with some sections to the *Conde* [count] of Assumar, general of Minas, who with prudence responded to them that some things that they asked for were being resolved by Your Majesty in the letters that he would receive from the fleet, doing this so that they might calm down, because he treated paternally the most common of the people; and as to the rest, he had been summoning the *ovidores* for other business and, on the road, would propose to them his reasons for taking measures that would be agreeable to everyone.

On the following nights, until July 16, that entire village appeared an inferno with disorders, riots, and disturbances caused by some disguised people who descended from the hill of Ouro Preto, coming below accompanied by Negroes and mulattoes; breaking into houses; injuring, drubbing, and killing those who resisted them. Those of the villa of

Ouro Preto emptied the goods of their stores and hid them in the woods because of the fear of robbery, and the insults that the rioters committed with such stubbornness made them seem to be unleashed demons with the power to scatter the village and all its population. On the first of July, the count-general requested a Company of Jesus cleric for those present in his home, whom he intended to pacify the people, to persuade them well, and show them the impropriety that they had displayed with the riot; and that if they had some formal petition to make about the laws of Your Majesty, they should do it by a method respected and used by the people, which is that of the agents of the *Câmaras*. They, without admitting reason (omitted are other modes of impropriety with which they treated this cleric), wanted to restrain him [the cleric], drawing their weapons. And on the same day, the count-general dispatched from the villa of Ribeirão do Carmo the *tenente*-general with the pardon, which they did not accept, instead insulting the *tenente* and wanting to restrain him.

The count-general continued this business with paternal prudence, love, and kindliness, dispatching the *mestre de campo* [field marshal], Domingos Teixeira, who was found in Minas, whom he entrusted to labor a great deal, in the service of God and Your Majesty, to accommodate the people and make them capable of reason, and despite this diligence, the people neither ordered an end to this [rioting], nor were calmed with the pardon, nor with compliments satisfied; and incited the following morning to yelling that was heard from the hill, they marched to Ribeirão, having the previous night written to the count-general of the *Câmara* of Villa Rica that the people wanted the said count to go to Ribeirão, but that he could only go unaccompanied because the people would not be inflamed, worrying that he would go to punish them. Having requested to speak to the *conde*-general, who would wait for them until nine o'clock in the morning, they left Villa Rica for Ribeirão before daybreak.

On the second day of the month, they, in formation, marched from Ouro Preto to Ribeirão, bringing with them and obliging to join their gathering those whom they encountered, making their march horrific with shouts, clamoring, and cries of *viva o povo*. The count-general ordered religious officials and priests to the heights of Rozario (a small chapel on the highway to Ribeirão), so that they might detain the crowd with an urbane method and without the rattle of anger, much less of war, and for that reason he even sent the senate of the *Câmara* of this villa, with his raised banner, and accompanied by good men of the land, but this kindliness and moderation by the count-general was not enough to make the people reasonable. They arrived finally at the palace and they exposed publicly their intention and openly manifested the reason of the riot; they did not want to accept the *casa de fundição de quintos* [royal gold smelter and tax house] as a year ago Your Majesty ordered erected by a new law, and about which the people were informed throughout the interim regarding the consumption of gold dust, and how it had been accepted in one span, during which all the principal men of Minas had signed [in agreement]. And also, they did not accept the mint, which for relief of the same people, and by letter from the *Câmara do Ribeirão,* had been requested from Your Majesty. And at the completion of these principal points, they left with other petitions of so little significance that there might as well have been only two that encountered Your Majesty's orders. It was their entire deed and why they rebelled.

The count-general conceded to them what they requested, not wanting to shed the blood of the people whom he governed, and he ordered published for them a pardon in the name of Your Majesty for the crime then committed, by the method and with the conditions that they wanted, promising these things if they calmed down and did not continue the riot. It seemed that here ought to remain buried all the disturbances of Minas; but, the ultimate goal of this riot was rebellion, which they intended against the general of the sovereignty, not for another cause more than wanting to live without a governor and ministers of justice who might rule them, and perhaps without obedience to the monarchy; thus, little by little, their intention was discovered.

On the sixth of July, they started to riot again and asked the *Câmara* to order the doctor, the ordinary *ouvidor,* to withdraw; and the *Câmara* thus wrote to the count-general with indecent threatening phrases. The count-general ordered him [the ordinary *ouvidor*] to leave the *comarca* [judicial district]. However, not being satisfied with the oldest judge as *ouvidor,* as per law, in the absence of the proprietor [of the post] whom they ousted, they demanded with another nocturnal riot doctor Mosqueira for *ouvidor.* The count-general, to calm them, conceded a provision for such doctor to serve as *ouvidor;* so great was the count-general's patience in suffering the people by accommodating them, yet still anticipating that everything that the new *ouvidor* might do was null and void, hoping that at a better time reason would convince them of this absurdity. Becoming apparent that some of the people, but not everyone, wanted these things, they proclaimed the entire affair an uprising for the expulsion from Minas of the count-general, their governor, in order to unite the people of the suburbs of this village. And inviting more people from other settlements, they declared in a common voice that only after a general uprising would they calm down and that another governor would not enter Minas, nor justices appointed by Your Majesty. The rest of the settlements in Minas were observing the outcome of this uprising and rebellion at Ouro Preto, to thus declare themselves. The current danger, moreover, would make the impending and future one more dreadful, which was feared as a greater consequence. The people of Villa Rica experienced extortions, assaults, and the greatest insults by those who descended the hill with the evil thoughts of already criminal men: some were beaten up, others assaulted in their homes; they were robbed, and calling for justice, everyone asked the count-general for help.

The count-general ordered the arrest of those whom he prudently judged the cause, motive, and occasion for this uprising; and not even with these imprisonments was the rebellion calmed, but instead, was provoked further and inflamed with greater rage, and now with evident suspicion of greater ruin to Minas. On July 14, the riot that descended from the hill was so horrific, and with such vehemence, that they went to the home of the schoolmaster, the vicar of the jurisdiction of Ouro Preto, and made him get out of bed, so that he would open the door of the church for them, supposing that the rest of the people were in it, and where they went and indecently overturned even the alters. On this night, there were the greatest disorders, breaking the doors and windows of residents, and killing one man from the same hill, whom they supposed gave information to the count-general.

On July 15, they acquainted the count-general with the insolence already proclaimed in those uprisings, and of the ultimate goal and ruin coming from this rebellion; and rudely, they ordered him to say that he would take measures for leaving, because certainly they were expelling him from Minas. The residents of Ouro Preto, who now were appearing discouraged by that which they bore, insisted with supplications that the count-general help them, and free them from the oppression that they suffered. The residents of Padre Faria, as most opposed to those of the hill (and so much so that they always opposed the expansion of that settlement or encampment on the hill), suffered with more impatience these insolences, and were seen with such desperation on the first night of the riot that they wanted to climb the hill with war declared, killing each other with hostility, and destroy all the houses on the hill, going from place to place wielding weapons simultaneously with the uproar; and many fatalities would have followed with the confrontation of the two parties if the Reverend doctor Luiz Ribeiro had not dissuaded them from that action, telling them that they should seek the remedy for this oppression from the count-general.

The count-general—laden with reason, patience, prudence, and justice—finally decided to leave Ribeirão on July 16, a most happy day since it was the day of Our Lady of Carmo, patron saint of Ribeirão, and he marched to Villa Rica accompanied by dragoons and residents of this village, and with their slaves also armed, to confront the rebellion, which with so much prudence and patience he sought to quell. And entering Villa Rica, knowing for certain that on the hill the assassins, rioters, and rebels were still currently lodged, and that throughout the neighboring woods they had been placing armed people, either for an invasion or for defense of their rebellion (which they certainly would execute if the intention were not obstructed or cut off from them), the count-general seized the initiative to order burned the homes of the principal originators and agents of the uprising.

And thus he sent the captain of the dragoons, João de Almeida de Vasconcellos, to climb the hill, designating to him Sergeant-Major Manoel Gomes da Silva, Captain Antonio da Costa Gouvêa, and Second Lieutenant Balthasar de Sampaio, all residents of the hill, so that they would show him the houses of those who publicly and openly were rebels and agents of this uprising, and accomplices in this crime, and put fire to them. When the captain of the dragoons arrived at the hill with the men whom the count-general named to him, he asserted that by no manner would they entrust their consciences with any hatred or private passion, and only signal to him the homes of those knowingly actors, agents, and accomplices in the crime, which they thus did. And soon, the said captain of the dragoons, arriving at the house of the *mestre do campo,* Pascoal da Silva Guimarães, ordered a captain of the orderlies, whom he brought with him, to pull out the images and ornaments from the small chapel in the said house, and ordered him to hand over everything that pertained to the divine cult to the venerable vicar of the cathedral, Antônio Dias, according to the order of the count-general. When they started the fire, three neighbors came running to complain, imagining that fire was being set to all the houses, to which Captain Antonio da Costa Gouvêa replied quickly and assured them that the fire was only for the houses of the known originators [of the uprising], and that they might have calmed down, as some had done, and because of that they had saved their homes.

But since on the said hill, two thousand, or close to three thousand, Negroes mined, on seeing that spectacle of fire they were changed; and exiting the holes in the ground, from which they excavated gold, imagining that fire would be set generally to all the houses without distinction, the Negroes were entering those that they found deserted, and robbed and burned them. And Captain João de Almeida could not respond quickly to that because not only the fire and the rough terrain hindered him, but it was necessary, according to the order of the count-general, to be with his soldiers in formation while the home of Pascoal da Silva was being destroyed, because of the risk of armed people who were said to be in the neighboring woods and, thus, to avoid the danger of some unexpected assault. And moving on to execute the same order at Ouro Podre (another place situated on the same hill), this captain could put guards in a narrow passageway so that the Negroes would not mix with the soldiers; and that caused the order here to be executed only in a house of a guilty one, and with neither confusion nor ruin for those who were not guilty.

Smuggling in the Diamond District

George Gardner

The Portuguese Crown learned harsh lessons about law enforcement and tax collection at the gold mines of Ouro Preto. Thus, when diamond deposits were discovered in Minas Gerais during the eighteenth century, Crown officials vowed to impose tight controls. Authorities limited the number of legally sanctioned miners, closely monitored traffic to and from the mines, and mandated severe penalties for diamond smuggling. Nevertheless, people from all walks of life circumvented diamond regulations. In the following entry, George Gardner, an English traveler, relates one such episode in which the line of accomplices stretched from a slave, to a local merchant, and ultimately, to a broker in Rio de Janeiro.

The privilege of diamond washing, formerly a monopoly of the government, is now accessible to any individual who chooses to risk his time and capital in this labour, a privilege only conceded since Brazil has declared its independence; all that is required is that the adventurer should give notice to the *Câmara* [assembly] municipal of the exact spot where he intends working, a notice demanded in order to protect some of the virgin tracts still preserved as royal property. The greater portion of the inhabitants of the Cidade Diamantina who possess a few slaves employ them in the washings, which are generally chosen in places where the *Cascalho* [brittle rock] is near the surface and near the beds of the little mountain streams, which are so numerous in the adjoining locality. Many free blacks also work on their own account and thus obtain a precarious livelihood. The persons engaged in these adventures are generally a very improvident race, for even those who carry on the most extensive *Serviços*, as the workings are called, often run deeply in debt after a rich washing has been exhausted, before they succeed in finding another productive spot. I was assured by one of the most extensive miners in the district that the excitement produced by this kind of life is like that of a gambler; whoever enters on it, never renounces it.

The district that gives rise to this curious source of industry is comprised within the space of fourteen leagues square, and it is beneath the mark to state that 10,000 individuals subsist entirely on the product of diamonds and gold extracted from its soil. It is not, however, so much the miners as the shopkeepers who reap the greater share of profit from this source of industry, all of whom trade more or less in diamonds and gold dust, which they take from the miners in exchange for the supply of their own wants and those of their slaves. It is rare to meet with a miner who is not in debt to some shopkeeper, to whom he is bound to give in payment the product of his washings, at a lower rate than he could obtain if he had the advantage of offering them in an open market to the highest bidder. The life of a shopkeeper, although not so exciting as that of a miner, is one, however, less subject to risk; he generally soon grows rich, while the poor miner struggles on in poverty, his greatest source of happiness existing in hopes that are seldom realized.

Slaves are allowed to work on their own account on Sundays and holidays, not in the *Serviços* of their masters, but anywhere else, except on the royal preserves; and it was told to me as a remarkable fact that most of the largest diamonds obtained in this district have been found by slaves on these occasions; it is not, however, an unfair inference to conclude that as the blacks are most expert thieves, some of those stones at least have been stolen. Better opportunities now exist for more readily disposing of diamonds thus obtained than when the workings were entirely in the hands of the government. In those days, they were mostly disposed of clandestinely to contraband dealers, many of whom used to hide themselves in the mountains by day, and at night, visit the huts of the slaves to purchase the stolen property; even the shopkeepers were deeply engaged in these illicit transactions. The Justice of the Peace, who was during the period of my visit one of the richest merchants in the city, owes his fortune to the following circumstance. At the time that Brazil still remained under the dominion of Portugal, he was the proprietor of a small shop and occasionally made a journey to Rio de Janeiro to purchase goods. One evening, returning from one of these long journeys, having retired to rest earlier than usual, he heard someone knocking at

Rio de Janeiro, circa the eighteenth century. *(Bibloteca Nacional, Rio de Janeiro)*

his door, to which at first he paid no attention, concluding it to be only some customer; but as the noise continued, he at last arose, when he saw a slave who had come to offer a large diamond for sale that weighed about two pennyweights and a third. The price asked for it was 600 *mil-réis,* at that time equal to about £180 sterling, but not having so much money in his possession at the moment, he was obliged to borrow some for the occasion. Early next morning, he set off on his return to Rio de Janeiro with his purchase, stating to his friends that he had forgotten some important business that could only be settled by his presence. On reaching the capital, he found it necessary to use great caution in endeavoring to dispose of his prize; as all trade in diamonds was at that time contraband, anyone found dealing in them could be condemned to ten years transportation to Angola, on the coast of Africa, with his property being at the same time confiscated and sold for the benefit of the government. At last he was prevailed on to dispose of it for 20,000 *mil-réis,* about £6,000, which was paid to him in hard dollars; never having seen so large a sum of money, he was perfectly astonished at its amount when it was brought to him and, after regarding it for some time, asked with great simplicity if it all belonged to him. Shortly afterwards, the individual who bought the diamond sold it for 40,000 *mil-réis,* and when Juiz learned its great value and found that he might have sold it for at least a third more than he received, his mortification, it is said, was so great as to affect his mind. He has long, however, recovered from his chagrin, and is now one of the most active as well as most extensive gold and diamond merchants in the district.

Decree Elevating Brazil to a Kingdom

João VI

Carnival in Rio de Janeiro in the late colonial period. *(Bibloteca Nacional, Rio de Janeiro)*

The Napoleonic invasion of the Iberian Peninsula drove the Portuguese royal family from Lisbon in 1808. Under British naval protection, they sailed for Brazil, moving the seat of royal power across the Atlantic. After Napoleon's defeat, the Portuguese Côrtes (parliament), as well as the leaders of the vic-

torious nations at the Congress of Vienna, demanded that the monarchy return. On December 16, 1815, after thirteen years in Brazil, Prince Regent João VI issued a decree elevating Portugal's New World colony to the status of a kingdom. João delayed his departure for another five years, but finally returned to Portugal in 1821, leaving behind his son, Pedro, as regent.

D. João [VI], by the grace of God, Prince Regent of Portugal and the Algarves, in Africa and Guinea, and of the conquest, navigation, and commerce of Ethiopia, Arabia, Persia, and Indian, etc., make known to those to whom this present letter of law shall come, that there being constantly in my royal mind the most lively desire to cause to prosper those states that the Divine Providence has confided to my sovereign rule; and giving, at the same time, its due importance to the magnitude and locality of my domains in America, to the copiousness and variety of the precious elements of wealth that it contains; and knowing besides how advantageous to my faithful subjects in general will be a perfect union and identity between my kingdom of Portugal, the Algarves, and my dominions of Brazil, by raising them to that grade and political class, which, by the aforesaid proposition, they ought to aspire to, and in which my said dominions have been already considered by the plenipotentiaries of the powers that form the Congress of Vienna . . . my kingdom of Portugal, the Algarves, and Brazil, shall form from henceforth one only and united kingdom under the title of the United Kingdom of Portugal, Brazil, and the Algarves.

II

Imperial and

Republican Brazil

Modern Brazil was shaped not only by the nation's Portuguese colonial heritage, but by its subcontinental vastness, as well as by its continuing slave economy, which is treated in the third section of this anthology. The country, Peter Flynn notes, "may indeed be a fast-changing, 'modernizing' society, but it is easy to be misled by some of the more dramatic features of population growth and shift, the manifold problems of recent industrialization and the growth of modern technology."[1] Brazilian life, then, has deeply set roots. Not only have many social conventions survived to the eve of the twenty-first century, but the country's retention of its monarchy after independence under the same dynastic family as ruled during colonial tutelage acted to ensure that basic things in Brazil did not change at all, even after the empire gave up the ghost and Brazil became a federal republic in 1889.

Brazil under Pedro I, the regency that followed his abdication, and his son, Pedro II, was governed by a highly centralized order that required the rotation of officeholders and officials from place to place, lest they grow too attached to their area of service and so lose the ability to carry out the wishes of the imperial administration. Centralization extended to higher education: until 1889, outside of the military academies, only four university-level schools operated in all of Brazil. Two were in law, in São Paulo and Recife, and two more in medicine, in Salvador and Rio de Janeiro. Most of the graduates of these four schools practiced neither law nor medicine; the large majority went into public service, forming over

time the imperial (and early republican) governing elite, becoming legislators, police officials, governors, and cabinet ministers. The principle of
geographic rotation was so firmly established that many students started
out in one school, then transferred to another, thousands of kilometers
away. Most came from elite families, but not all. Even though the size of
the *turmas* (graduating classes) was very small—usually under 100 from
each school—each class had a sprinkling of orphans and youths from
families that today would be called the middle class, and other students
from far-flung regions of the country.

At the top of the imperial pyramid sat the emperor, his court, and the nobility, created in one fell swoop at the outset of Brazilian independence.
While Brazil's neighbors read the writings of Jean-Jacques Rousseau and
Thomas Jefferson, the Brazilian monarchy installed dozens of viscounts,
barons, dukes, marquises, and counts. The titles rewarded property hold-
ers and blue bloods, while others were granted to successful merchants.
The monarchy celebrated its durability with pomp and ceremony, although the boy emperor Pedro II, as he grew older, preferred to wear business suits, to take and develop photographs, and to read republican authors
like Victor Hugo. It is true that when Pedro assumed his majority at the age
of fourteen in 1840, the monarchy underwent national consolidation under
its constitutional monarch. The emperor appointed all members of the
senate for life, and his control of what was termed the moderating power of
the executive branch countered parliamentary principle. With suffrage
limited to propertied males, government was not responsive to the public
will, even if the public had outlets to express its opinions, which it did not.

Yet the sovereign's concrete powers were more limited than might have
been imagined. The emperor could (and did) dismiss cabinets (and close
the bicameral parliament when his advisers told him to), although there
was little difference in outlook or socioeconomic origins between the
two national political parties; most of the country's regions carried on under a kind of autonomy dictated by great distances and the thinness of the
apparatus of the imperial government. Some regions, particularly on the
periphery of the country, bore grudges about what they considered to be
imperial neglect and struggled to break away from the Brazilian union.

Life under the Empire (1822–1889) and Republic (1889–1930) was
marked by population growth and modernization in the major cities,
and by endless conflicts at the regional and local level. These involved dis-
putes between incumbents and their opponents, between local landowners and their rivals, between warring family clans, and between *coronéis*

(local chieftains, who could be ranchers, agriculturalists, merchants, or even priests) and their competitors. With public education not a government priority and the large mass of the population illiterate, members of the elite found it convenient to withhold any real participatory democracy, although the new republican constitution in 1889 created a shell of representative institutions that, in fact, were not democratic at all. Fewer than 3 percent of the adult population voted in national elections through 1930, and all elections—down to votes for town councils, police chiefs, and judges—were subject to manipulation, misrepresentation, intimidation, and the outright buying of votes. Brazilian government ran behind a facade of checks and balances, but power remained in the hands of the landed elite and its allies in incumbent provincial machines, as well as the small, emerging cadre of industrialists, agents of foreign capital, and professionals linked to the patronage machines at every level of government. More than anything else, oligarchy dominated the Republic, just as it had done under the Empire. Republicanism, which took root during the 1860s and grew in influence in every succeeding decade, advocated government by an educated elite, but not democracy, which republicans considered inefficient. Republican ideas spread in the country's two law schools and among the officer corps of the armed forces.

The role of the military changed as the nineteenth century progressed. Unlike Spanish America, where military leaders fought for their nation's independence and thereafter remained firmly in power in most of the new countries, in Brazil, the leaders of the armed forces remained loyal to the Portuguese Crown. After independence, the 1824 Brazilian Constitution gave the military the right to intervene at the request of the monarch, and a national guard was established in 1831 to strengthen the central power. But until the Paraguayan War of 1864 to 1870, the military stayed out of politics. After the war, in which tens of thousands of Brazilians, many of them slaves fighting to win their freedom, died, the unwillingness of the civilian government to replenish the armed forces' budgets and to pay for needed modernization set into motion the ominous tendency—nurtured for more than a century—whereby the military acted as an independent political force, threatening intervention frequently and overthrowing constitutional governments twice before 1930. On both occasions, in 1889 when it ousted the monarchy and in 1930 when it ended the federal republic, the insurrectionary military leadership allied with sympathetic civilians, but in any event, it was military, not civilian power that accomplished the goal.

Despite pressures and threats from many sides, Brazil remained unified through its language and culture. Social mores were remarkably consistent from north to south. The pattern of kinship organization was universally distributed, as Linda Lewin observes,[2] across all parts of the Empire and Republic. As for the emerging new institutions wielding power—*coronelismo* during the Empire, the family-based expression of oligarchy, in addition to chambers of commerce and agro-industrial associations in the late nineteenth century, and the "politics of the governors" under the decentralized Republic—they were, in many ways, adaptations of earlier forms that went back to the colonial period.

The Constitution of 1891 enacted a form of federalism so extreme that each of the former provinces—now called states—could raise revenue by taxing exports not only abroad, but also in interstate commerce. The stronger states of the Center-South—São Paulo, Minas Gerais, and Rio Grande do Sul—prospered, as did the national capital, Rio de Janeiro, which was a commercial and banking center, but the rest of the country languished. Although the national government was not helpless, it remained dominated by the republican elites of the two most powerful states, São Paulo and Minas. The only time contested elections occurred was when these two states could not agree on a candidate for the presidential succession. In 1930, this disagreement was exacerbated by the heavy impact of the Great Depression on agricultural prices, especially coffee, which had fueled São Paulo's economic boom. When dissident military officers sympathetic to the 1922 nationalistic *tenente* movement allied with civilians opposed to São Paulo's crude attempt to control the presidency in defense of its own interests, the Liberal Alliance coalition of civilians and army officers seized control of the government on October 3, 1930. Thus, the defeated presidential candidate, Getúlio Vargas, came to power as head of a provisional government that was both centralized and authoritarian.

Notes

1   Peter Flynn, *Brazil: A Political Analysis* (London: Ernest Benn, 1978), p. 6.
2   Linda Lewin, *Politics and Parentela in Paraíba: A Case Study of Family-Based Oligarchy in Brazil* (Princeton, N.J.: Princeton University Press, 1987), p. 15.

Declaration of Brazilian Independence, 1822

Pedro I

The demands of the Portuguese Côrtes *[parliament] for Prince Regent Pedro to follow his father to Portugal (and for Brazil to revert to its former status) prompted some Brazilians, led by Pedro's tutor, José Bonifácio de Andrade, to imitate Brazil's Spanish American neighbors in search of independence. Pedro himself preferred to stay in Brazil and reacted with growing displeasure at the pressure from Lisbon for him to return. In January 1822, he announced that he indeed would remain and, on September 7 of that year, while riding on the banks of the Ipiranga River in São Paulo, made the final break. The following description was written by a priest, Father Belchoir Pinheiro de Oliveira, who was present. Pedro's declaration of independence, however, was not based on democratic principles; he quickly became an authoritarian monarch and forced José Bonifácio into exile. Becoming increasingly unpopular with his Brazilian subjects, he abdicated in 1831, returning to Portugal and leaving his five-year-old son Pedro behind as regent, just as his father had done with him.*

The prince ordered that I read aloud the letters transported . . . from the *Côrtes* a letter from D. João, another from the princess, another from José Bonifácio, and still another from Chamberlain, the secret agent of the prince. The *Côrtes* demanded the immediate return of the prince, and the imprisonment and trial of José Bonifácio; the princess recommended prudence and asked that the prince heed his minister. José Bonifácio told the prince that he must choose one of two roads to follow: leave immediately for Portugal and hand himself over to the *Côrtes,* as was the situation of D. João VI, or remain and proclaim the independence of Brazil . . .

D. Pedro, trembling with anger, seized the letters from my hands and crumpled them. He threw them on the ground and stomped on them. . . . D. Pedro walked silently toward our horses at the side of the road. Suddenly, he halted in the middle and said: "The *Côrtes* is persecuting me, and calling me an adolescent and a Brazilian. Well now, let them see their adolescent in action. From today on, our relations with them are finished. I want nothing more from the Portuguese government and I proclaim Brazil forevermore separated from Portugal."

The Baron of Parnaíba

George Gardner

For most nineteenth-century Brazilians, relevant political power revolved around local potentates and not the imperial court in Rio de Janeiro. Known as coronéis, *these bosses controlled provincial and municipal politics through the deft application of benevolence and violence.* Coronelismo, *or boss rule, especially flourished in economic backwaters such as Piauí, which drew little national attention except at election time. In the following entry, George Gardner portrays one coronel, the Baron of Parnaíba, who controlled a rustic, impoverished region in the north of Brazil.*

As I brought several letters of recommendation with me to the Barão de Parnaíba, the president of the province, I made inquiries for his house on entering the city and was directed to it by a soldier. The Palacio, as it is called, is situated on the most elevated part of the town, is of one story, and has a very ordinary appearance. On arriving at the door, I found it guarded by a sentinel, one of the most abject-looking beings that can be imagined. He was a young mulatto, dressed in the uniform of the troops of the line, which seemed as if it had not been off his back for the last six years: his cloth cap was old and greasy; his blue jacket one half patches and the other half holes, was open in front, displaying his naked breast, for he could not boast the possession of a shirt; his trousers were a little better than his jacket; and his bare feet were thrust into a pair of old shoes, down at the heels and open at the toes. Had it not been for his musket, and his upright position, I should certainly have taken him for a beggar. There was a pavement a few feet in breadth in front of the house, on which, when I stopped, my horse's forefeet rested, and before I had time to speak, the sentinel started forward, seized the bridle, and turned him off into the street. I then dismounted and was about to proceed to the door, but no sooner had I put my foot on the pavement, than I was served in the same way as my horse had been and told that no one was allowed to enter the palace with spurs on. These I instantly took off and, having asked if anything else was necessary to be done, I was at last allowed to enter.

On reaching the lobby, I was met by a sergeant, who asked me if I wished to speak with his Excellency and who, on being told that I had letters for him, said that it was his duty to deliver them. After waiting about a quarter of an hour in the lobby, I was shown into a large room containing two small tables, a sofa, and a few chairs. Here, I had not been more than five minutes when his Excellency made his appearance with my letters in his hand. He told me to excuse him while he read them, as also to pardon his undress, which he wore, he said, on account of the great heat of the day. The dress he had on was certainly one of a very light nature, but was that generally worn in the house by the inhabitants of this province. It consisted of a thin, white cotton shirt hanging loose over a pair of drawers of the same material, which reached but a short way below his knees; his legs and feet were bare, the latter being thrust into a pair of old slippers; around his neck were several rosaries, with crucifixes and other appendages of gold attached to them.

While he was looking over my letters, I could not help scrutinizing the appearance of an individual whose name is more celebrated than that of any other in the north of Brazil and whose despotic government of the province of which he is president has gained for him the appellation of the "Francia [Paraguayan dictator] of Piauí." He was low in stature and strongly built, though not corpulent, and his looks bespoke considerably more activity, both of body and mind, than is generally met with in persons of his age in Brazil, for he was then about seventy years old; his head was remarkably large, and according to the principles of phrenology, was pretty well-balanced before and behind, but deficient in the region of the moral sentiments, and was of considerable breadth between the ears. In conversation, his countenance had a sinister, unpleasant expression, notwithstanding that it was generally covered with a half-formed smile. After finishing the letters, all of which he read over very carefully, we entered into a conversation respecting my visit to the province, but I could not make him understand that my collections were for any other purpose than that of being converted into medicine or dye stuffs. That the productions of nature were studied for any other purpose than as regards their mere utility to man, he could not form the slightest idea. As soon as he learned that it was my intention to remain for some time in the city, he sent a person to procure an empty house for my use, and as it was not furnished, he was kind enough to send me two chairs, a table, and a large earthen pot to hold water . . .

. . . The province of Piauí sends two members to the national chamber of deputies in Rio, but in all that relates to its internal government, the Barão de Parnaíba rules with despotic sway. He has been its president ever since the establishment of the independence of the Empire, with the exception of one short period, when another person was sent to supersede him, but he did not hold his appointment long, dying suddenly and under suspicious circumstances. Since that period, although the presidents of all the other provinces are changed every two or three years, he has remained constantly in office. He is more feared than respected by the mass of the population, and on an emergency, can command among his own friends and dependents more than 2,000 staunch supporters; he has always at his call those who are both ready and willing to execute his orders, of whatever nature these may be. By the firmness of his government, he has acquired many enemies, especially by the enactment of some provincial laws, respecting which, it must be confessed in their favor, their tendency is always to benefit the poorer classes of the inhabitants; among others, he has forbidden that beef and farinha, the two principal articles of food, be sold in the city above a certain fixed price, and that a very low one. He has, however, always taken care that his own cattle be sent to Bahia and other distant, more profitable, markets, having abundant facilities for such arrangements. Although generally ill-informed, he possesses a great share of shrewdness and cunning, qualifications highly requisite for the maintenance of the despotism with which he has hitherto governed the province, under which it can certainly boast of a greater amount of peace and quietness than almost any other province in the Empire. It is not a little strange that notwithstanding his many enemies, only one attempt has hitherto been made to assassinate him, and that so late as the year before I arrived there.

On January 17, 1838, on returning from one of his fazendas and when about half a league from the city, he was fired at from behind some bushes; the shot only wounded him in the right shoulder. The assassins, for there were two, fled immediately, and one of them appeared among the first to congratulate the Barão on his arrival after so fortunate an escape. Parties were instantly dispatched to scour the woods in pursuit of the delinquents, and a black man, who was found hidden among some bushes and could not give a good account of himself, was taken to the city, and on being interrogated, confessed that although he was one of the parties, he did not fire the shot, the person who did so being one Joaquim Seleiro, a mulatto saddler who lived in the house of the Barão. This man was said to be of a very vicious disposition and of strong passions; and it was well known that a few days before the occurrence, he had been ill-used in some manner by the Barão, without just cause. At the time he was denounced, he was leading a party in the woods in search of the assassins and was not a little astonished on his return to find himself a prisoner. He strongly denied the crime of which few deemed him to be innocent; since the laws of the country do not inflict the penalty of death for a mere attempt at murder, he was therefore committed to prison, where he died twenty-six days after the perpetration of that crime, under circumstances that have given rise to suspicious reports.

Uprising in Maranhão, 1839–1840

Domingos José Gonçalves de Magalhães

Independence brought few guarantees that the Brazilian kingdom would remain politically intact. Immense distances and forbidding terrain, by themselves, handicapped the state's power. Meanwhile, several regions, because of their unwillingness to exchange Portuguese authority for an equally foreign one in Rio de Janeiro, pressed for autonomy. Intraregional politics, itself commonly settled with violence, added immeasurably to Brazil's political instability. As a result, between 1822 and 1848, no fewer than five regional revolts threatened Brazil's political disintegration. As the following account shows, however, national and regional political conflicts might easily transform into vicious class and race wars. Known as the Balaiado, the Maranhão uprising of 1839–1840 taught national and regional elites that they could wage political battles only at the risk of social upheaval. Therein lies one of the keys to Brazil's political stabilization by 1850.

Before telling this history, it is necessary to know the men, classes, practices, and customs of the country that draws our attention, because such things are of great importance for the weighing of facts and understanding of many things, which without this previous knowledge would seem, at first view, inexplicable. The population of this province is computed at 217,000 souls, among them whites, mixed peoples, and Negroes, scattered over an area of more than 800 square leagues. Its land, although fertile, as that of the entire Empire, is little cultivated; copious rains wet it from December until June, and in this pluvial time, which only for that reason they call it winter, the weeks are linked without the intermission of one dry day; the fields are deluged, the rivers grow, of which there are many; and the flooded highways become difficult transit. Such a pestilence of fevers develop at the beginning and end of the rains that only those accustomed to the humid and hot climate can resist them.

The principal types of cultivation are cotton and rice, and for these they employ numerous arms of African slaves, those who are treated with such barbarous rigor, that even the necessary sustenance they [the landlords] deny to them; one ear of corn is their lunch, rice and manioc meal the dinner, scavenging and hunting furnish the rest for them; they walk naked or embraced with a small loincloth, except for few exceptions; and for that reason, the slaves seek to withdraw from the yoke of the landlord.

The plantation owners appropriate everything that is harvested without fretting over the land with means of industry, hardly careful to improve the cultivation; and for that reason, the province is dotted by plantations raising bovine cattle, in whose care and in the salting of meat and hides are occupied throngs of lazy men, without steady homes, for the most part a race crossed by Indians, whites, and Negroes, whom are called *cafusos:* those who are very fond of this semivagrant life, little interested in other trades, and much in scavenging and hunting, distinguishing themselves only from the savages by the use of our language. They are men of cruel temperament by the habit of herding and killing cattle, consuming the rest of life in laziness or brawls. From this brute people, there are great emigrations from this province, and thus the people of Piauí and Ceará are similar to them in practices and customs. Many of the plantation owners, in imitation of the old barons, live without any respect for the authorities, avenging by their own hands particular insults and harboring on their lands the criminals who seek their shelter, and who together lend themselves to their [the landowners'] reprisals. By such people, they [the landowners] are escorted and become feared, and it is as easy for them to arrange a murder as to deny a debt, or at least not to pay creditors, who at their opportunity, if they can, do not hesitate to employ the same means for their own good. This is the people who incited war against us; it is they who compose the army of the rebellion . . .

This province was found in peace when Senhor Vicente Thomaz Pires de Figueredo Camargo took possession of the presidency [of the province] on March 3, 1838. . . . Strong opposition was manifested against the administration of Senhor Camargo, opposition in part malicious, because those who then composed the party of the government, before rising to the public offices, as oppositionists, had been strongly attacking the government of Senator Antonio Pedro da Costa Ferreira, a person dear to the party that now, in getting even, waged war against them [the people now in office]. A small newspaper with the title of *Bemteví,* written in popular language, attracted a broad party; it attacked the president and the law of the prefects, a new creation that, with the president's indication, had passed in the provincial assembly . . .

. . . The population was divided into two rancorous parties, the *bemtevís* [hummingbirds] and *cabanos.* (*Cabanos* was the name applied, in Maranhão, to the people of the interior, or those living in cabins and huts. It denoted a rustic and fierce people.) Into the arms of the second [party], the government offered itself, although it ought to have remained neutral and balance them [the parties]. Partisan government is always unjust. The repercussions from the complaint in the province had reached the *Côrte* [the capital], and was repeated by the journalists. All this anger by the parties was excited more by the ambition for power and positions, and by the desire to triumph in the elections; those who were on top because of the party's influence did not want to descend; the others wanted to rise, and insults were traded, until at last the cry of rebellion and civil war succeeded the infamous war of words.

On December 13, 1838, in the village of Manga, situated on the left bank of the Iguará River, in the *comarca* [judicial district] of Itapucurú, there appeared a certain Raymundo Gomes, a man of sufficiently dark color, accompanied by nine of his race; they broke into the village jail and freed the criminal inmates. There existed in the village twenty some troops under orders of the subprefect and those who were tempted by the same spirit joined Raymundo Gomes. This rebel soon started to apprehend commissioners, and to proclaim against the prefects and the president, whom he planned to topple and in his place elevate the vice president, known as an oppositionist. That a hidden hand directed this drama cannot be doubted. Raymundo Gomes was incapable of making by himself such a resolution, although by his habits he was very appropriate for executing it. Born in Piauí and son of that race crossed by Indians and Negroes that we described, raised in the country among cattle that he herded, offering his knife to his own and others' vengeances, inexperienced in the human letters, only known for some murders from which he lived unpunished, stained by the perversity of the customs that we related and the ineffectiveness of the laws, he would not commit himself to disturbing the public tranquility for political motives without an outside impulse; and when he might dare to, he would abandon his boldness at not finding the decided support, which was incontestably given to him. Stupid instrument of a blind party that imagined to be able, when it might please them, to close the dike of popular rage, Raymundo Gomes, the cowboy assassin, was converted into chief of the *bemteví* party, and those who lifted him from the earth's dust shamed themselves by their deed . . .

Caxias, formerly Aldêas-Altas, was the flourishing emporium of the interior of Maranhão and Piauí, the richest and most commercial city of the province after the capital, notable for the luxury of its inhabitants and the lack of good manners of many, and still more notable for being the theater of continuous vengeances and murders. Resting on the right and eastern bank of the Itapucurú, sixty leagues to the southeast of the capital, it faces on the opposite bank the parish of Trezidella, which dominates it. In all the long extension of this principal river are discovered properties, plantations, towns, and villages; and as the land that it penetrates is the most fertile and much cut by its branches, which they call *igarapés,* it is also the most populated and richest area of all Maranhão. The slaves alone are computed at around 20,000 Africans, which often threatens the public tranquility as some of them, withdrawing from the landlord's yoke and hiding out in the forests, go in sorties to rob the surrounding plantations, and armed force is necessary to capture them. This was not one of the smallest ills of the present rebellion, since the fleeing plantation owners left to the mercy of the rebels their houses and slaves, and the latter made use of the opportunity to escape the labor of the plundered fields, and went to find shelter in that area of the coast between the sandbar at Tutoya and Priá, where in a number exceeding 3,000 and commanded by the Negro Cosme, considered a witch doctor, they made great havoc. In a more appropriate place, we will address these people, who for the time being were accumulating in that area without attracting the attention of the government, which was totally occupied in matters of greater cost.

Caxias, the city of crime, refuge of criminals, the domain of minor pashas who at their will determined others' lives, was accustomed to seeing murders every day. Pious souls portended for it a great disgrace as punishment for its crimes, and God wanted it to be the bloody theater for all the horrors of the rebellion, perhaps as a correction for its depraved customs and its future improvement.

Everything in Caxias attracted the rebels; its very central position, its riches, munitions, sympathies, and immorality invited them to besiege it . . .

The journalists in the national capital started to occupy themselves seriously with the business of Maranhão, which was poorly weighed at the beginning, as always happens, and they gave it no value. Particular reports, cities and villages captured, plantations devastated, continuous horrors, and the ineffectiveness of the provincial government frightened the people and exposed to the ministry the impossibility of pacification of this part of the Empire, if it would continue in the hands in which it was found. Also, the general government recognized the necessity of entrusting to a single man the presidency [of Maranhão] and command of the armed forces, to avoid by this maneuver delays and intrigues observed currently and in other identical circumstances . . .

Colonel Luiz Alves de Lima was thus named president and commander of the armed forces for Maranhão . . .

Those who already were familiar with his name and reputation cheered him happily, and the newspapers of the province, to which the eminent qualities of the new chief were not secret, disposed themselves in his favor; and from now on we will note that they never made the least opposition or censure against his government, instead always exalting him, and in this each party always wanted to outdo the other. There is so much certainty that the great man, who in the execution of his sacred duties, did not aim at any other end, that it imposes silence even on jealousy and intrigue. On great occasions, great men stand out while small ones disappear.

We have said that our expeditions did not cease, and it would be verbosity to cite more than thirty gunfights monthly from which there resulted rebel deaths and prisoners, and great losses of their mounts . . .

With these continuous reversals, the insurgents started to become discouraged and only cared about fleeing, seeing certain harm and death everywhere; and as they deserted and turned themselves in to our forces, they were immediately armed and employed against their own comrades, sorely reducing the insurgents' ranks and invigorating ours.

Raymundo Gomes, appearing so badly spiritless and distrusting his forces, sent a delegation designated by some caudillos asking for a pardon, but nevertheless demanding certain conditions unworthy of attention. The president returned it to him with a proclamation that served as a response, ordering them, without any condition, to lay down all arms in order to be pardoned, and otherwise he would continue to pursue them until exterminating them. Sending this response, at the same time, he made a force from the third column march to uphold it . . .

Raymundo Gomes, however, who because of his crimes doubted the pardon, escaped without weapons, without baggage, without followers, and almost naked, and went to offer himself to the Negro Cosme, who put him in an iron collar [to chain him to a post], and discovering in him [Gomes] the ability to make gunpowder, employed him in that exercise, always under guard. The Negro Cosme, the criminal fugitive from the jails of the capital, then started to be the important figure who most frightened the plantation owners, since he was found in the leadership of 3,000 slaves stirred up to rebellion by him. He signed his name "Dom Cosme, guardian and emperor of the *bemtevi's* liberties." He proclaimed against slavery, he gave titles and posts, he established a school for reading and writing, and hidden in the headwaters of the Rio Preto, *comarca* of Brejo, on the plantation of Lagôa Amarella, he had forward patrols, and he sent parties to rob from and incite insurrection at the surrounding plantations . . .

Through an emissary, the president knew that Francisco Ferreira Pedrosa, boss of 1,700 criminals harbored on Bella-Agua, desired to turn himself in because he now could not maintain his position and feared not being pardoned, and he [the president] sent assurance to him that he would accept him with the condition of first doing some service in return for having taken up arms against the government; that he would beat the Negroes and later turn himself in. Thus, he acted; the Negroes, in disarray and fleeing after the attack on Lagôa Amarella, ran toward Bella-Agua supposing there to find support, and they found death and subjugation. It was always the policy of the president to impede the joining of the rebels with the slaves, rendering the first averse to the second, which certainly was a joy for the province. Raymundo Gomes, who found himself imprisoned at Lagôa Amarella under the power of Cosme and who, by him, would be in the end sentenced to death, found an opportunity to escape on the same day that, as he later narrated, he ought to have received the punishment for his crimes at the hands of that other criminal; his fate, however, wanted that on that day the Negroes would be attacked; they, as he, only sought in headlong flight to cheat death, and from there he went to hide out in Miritiba . . .

Then the president continued to Miritiba, where Raymundo Gomes hid, and through an escort, ordered him to seek his presence. Insignificant was his figure—almost Negro, which we call *fula*, short, stocky, bowlegged, long and flat forehead, timid and shifting eyes, hardly polished with reason, low and meek voice, no boldness of the conspirator—and although he might have been chief of the insurgents, he obeyed more than he ordered and never marched in front of his forces at the moment of battle, and he kept himself in the rearguard, always ready to flee and avoid dangers. Out of all of them, he was not even the most criminal and cruel; instead, compared to the others, he seemed humane. Before him, the old Matroá turned himself in, all bent over with the weight of 120 years of age and crime, dragging a long sword, however, bold and boasting of having entered every great and minor revolt of the North during his life; this old man died one month after turning himself in. In Muritiba, more than 700 rebels laid down arms, all of them naked and without munitions for war, except weapons. The number of surrenders in all our points reached 3,000, and when the period given [for a pardon] expired, there was still captured in the *comarca* of Brejo a band of 300 bandits, who had remained in a hostile attitude.

To complement the pacification of the province, there was imprisoned in the place named Calabouço, a district of Miarim, the infamous Negro Cosme and the rest who accompanied him. Some fifty died because of the tenacious resistance that they offered. Cosme was delivered to justice, and Raymundo Gomes, after amnestied, pledged an eight-year term of exile from the province, São Paulo being designated for him as his residence.

On January 19 [1841], the president ordered announced the pacification of the province.

A Paraíba Plantation, 1850–1860

Stanley J. Stein

Brazil soon gained renown for its exports. In the sixteenth and seventeenth centuries, Brazilian sugar set international standards. During the eighteenth century, Brazilian gold helped finance Britain's industrial revolution. No sooner were gold deposits depleted than Brazil became the world's dominant exporter of coffee, one of the nineteenth century's booming agricultural commodities. In many circles, Brazil and coffee were synonymous, and this identity often shaped Brazilians' attitudes about each other and their land. Social status flowed from coffee, and this, in turn, depended on the strong backs of African slaves and the incessant clearing of virgin forests. Nearly a half century ago, Princeton's Stanley J. Stein studied Brazil's Paraíba Valley, home to many nineteenth-century coffee barons. His portrait of the coffee plantation remains unsurpassed.

An abandoned Vassouras fazenda, which still dazzles the eye with its coat of deteriorating whitewash [and] its imperial palms standing sentinel-like over the entrance way, reflects a permanence, solidity, and strength that recent decades have not eroded. Dating from 1850 as a rule, these impressive, sprawling structures were not the first buildings on the site. They developed from more humble beginnings, when the hills were covered with clearings of corn, beans, and cane, and small gardens of coffee, and when the pioneer *fazendeiro* (landowner) could see virgin forest from the earthen terrace of his modest establishment.

Engrossed in clearing patches of forest to plant foodstuffs and in trying a new crop, coffee, the pioneer planter had little leisure to look beyond immediate necessities. Once his crops were sown, his next preoccupation was getting a roof over the head of his family, his slaves, his water-driven machinery, and his harvests. The nearby stream served for drinking water; he planted his crop of cane along its banks; from it, he diverted the water to drive his primitive processing equipment, a *moinho de fubá* (gristmill) and a *monjolo* (pounding mill). If he prospered at the spot, he added a small waterwheel to run a mill for grinding cane. Once these tasks were finished, he planted along the roads and on the borders of his fields rows of fruit trees—oranges, bananas, and others—including, too, an orchard for the "enjoyment and recreation of himself and his family."

In the midst of forest that encroached on all sides, in touch with the outside world only when travelers stopped for the night, the early fazendas were more than the way stations surrounded by tiny clearings typical of the years before 1800. They were nuclei of settlement. From these pinpoints of population, there went out each day the free and the slave to clear the forest, to plant, and to harvest. In exchange for coffee and other products sent to Rio, they received iron for implements worn out in the siege with the forest and slaves to wield them; also cotton goods and salt. In common with all pioneer plantations, everything was temporary; the essential job was to feed, clothe, and house the people of the settlement.

Early fazendas, like the later ones, were planned as a functional square. Living quarters for the free were set up against the base of a hill with dwelling units located over an incomplete ground floor or cellar partially dug out of the hill. Around the square were aligned the *senzalas* (slave quarters), the storehouses, the cribs, mule sheds, stables, and the pigpens. In the center of the square, there was nothing but a wide expanse of beaten earth called the *terreiro,* dusty in the winter sun, a quagmire in the torrential summer rains. This nucleus of buildings was known as the *sede* of the fazenda. Since most of the fazendas were situated near falls on the streams where a marked drop could supply waterpower for the primitive fazenda machinery, the sound of the falls was constant. For this reason, so many of the fazendas were called *"Cachoeira"* (waterfall) or *"Ribeirão"* (stream). Others were named after the patron saint of the founder, after a topographical feature, or after one of the awe-inspiring forest giants growing in the neighborhood.

These early structures were utilitarian, primitive to an extreme. Walls were made of wooden corner-posts, rough-hewn, the spaces filled with uprights of *palmeira* wood across which were tied strips of the same wood. As metal was hard to come by, and had to be laboriously and expensively hauled in by mule, a wirelike liana (*cipó de São João*) was used to tie the *palmeira* crossbars to the poles. Over this framework was thrown mud, producing the mud-and-wattle construction common to this day in the Brazilian interior. All construction was roofed with *sapé,* a common grass. Bare earth was the floor, for time and labor could be diverted only to flooring storage bins to keep crops from moisture and rats.

Primitive surroundings and the need for self-sufficiency produced the mentality characteristic of frontier psychology. During this period of expansion, 1800–1830, each small improvement in the standard of living, each modest luxury, received careful attention. Inventories of the time are filled with minutiae: the number of squared logs; the precise weight of copper pans; the three-legged stools; the wooden bowls of all sizes; the billhooks; axes, digging sticks, and hoes available; the implements of the fazenda's smithy; the contents of the fazenda's chapel; the number of doors and windows in the dwelling house of the fazendeiro. Perhaps strangest of all, each roof tile burned in the fazenda's kiln (olaria) was counted; a typical inventory stated that the roof of the dwelling house had 5,200 tiles. Seldom are wheeled vehicles of any type mentioned, for the narrow trails offered passage over long distances only to mules. This was the period of small-scale cultivation carried on by a few slaves when coffee was slowly, hesitatingly adapted to the highlands, when fazendeiros learned the agricultural know-how that they were to follow for the rest of the century.

In the development of techniques, fazendeiros had few manuals, and such as they had were based on inadequate practice and poor theory. Even those few were restricted in influence, for the number of literate fazendeiros was small. Consequently, the methods used by early coffee growers were those of trial and error. Fazendeiros probably saw their neighbors receive a few seedlings (mudas) from muleteers on their return from the lowlands. Within three or four years, new mudas sprouted beneath the first bushes and these were given to the fazendeiros of the neighborhood, whose interest was aroused by the high prices paid for coffee and its lighter weight in shipping compared to that of other crops. Coffee planting was tried in various types of soil and terrain, at first probably being put into former corn and sugar fields until experience taught that virgin soil and well-drained land were essential to its profitable cultivation. Such experiments took a toll in worn-out land and prematurely aged or unproductive bushes. Inventories of many fazendas of this early period report coffee bushes with no value, usually near the dwelling house. Sometimes, these bushes were pruned to within inches of the ground in the hope of saving them.

But planting went on, the profits of the successfully grown bushes returning to the fazenda in the form of more slaves to undertake ever-greater plantings. Fazenda self-sufficiency—coupled with cheap, plentiful land and a growing labor force—placed a floor under the experiment, and soon coffee took its place beside sugar and subsistence crops as a pillar in the growing economy of the county (*município*).

By the middle thirties, coffee cultivation was no longer a haphazard venture. In Vassouras, as in the neighboring *municípios,* the number of coffee trees had become the measure of a planter's wealth and was a clear indication of his other form of wealth, the number of slaves in his labor force. By the fifth decade of the century, as the taste for coffee grew among Europe and America's growing urban populations, the demand for slaves and the hunger for virgin forest grew among the coffee planters of the Paraíba Valley.

In response to the demand, African slaves by the thousands were openly smuggled into Brazil between 1840 and 1850, and found their way to the plantations of the Paraíba Valley. Vassouras fazendeiros with ample land and credit made enormous additions to their labor forces in these years.

At the same time, as coffee production grew, the large plantation emerged as the dominant producer of the crop, tending to absorb in its land-hunger small- and medium-sized holdings. This tendency was to be intensified in the succeeding decade of the fifties, years of unprecedented prosperity for the *município,* but which were to eliminate many a small-scale planter (*sitiante*).

The decade of the 1850s was the golden age of coffee and the society based on it in Vassouras. These were years whose fears and failures were forgotten in the nostalgia they evoked but three decades later, when only their optimism and exuberance were remembered . . .

During the boom years, certain external features of fazenda life were transformed. A few fazendas had been established on poor locations, near bottomlands or on badly drained terrain that left stagnant water near the living quarters. To the fazendeiros who would not recognize the evils of such conditions, one observer wrote that because of such negligence, many fazendeiros "suffer immense damage not only to their slaves, but also to their cattle." On other fazendas, owners had allowed tile roofs to deteriorate, and under heavy rainfall, unprotected mud-and-wattle walls rapidly disintegrated.

There were motives other than the purely economic for changing a fazenda site, or adding to and remodeling older buildings. The more sophisticated children of well-to-do planters were more aware than their parents of isolation and primitive surroundings. Said Luiz Peixoto de Lacerda Werneck of his position as administrator of a Vassouras fazenda, which he had undertaken on behalf of his debt-ridden mother-in-law: "In accepting the proposal, I had to move from Rio de Janeiro to the Fazenda, abandon and perhaps lose a commercial, financial, and political career that had been well begun, and go into exile with my family to a *roça* [farm] far from the nearest hamlet, beset with all the burdensome tasks of agriculture, without distractions or rest and far from schools where I could educate my children; all of which, without becoming immodest, is not an insignificant sacrifice on my part."

Notwithstanding the opinion of Luiz Peixoto, the larger fazendas of the time of his writing in 1862 were an improvement over those of the previous quarter century. It had been difficult to change fazendas in the forties, when eyes were riveted on the expansion of cultivation and the purchase of slaves. But in the fifties, the opulence of Vassouras and neighboring coffee centers drew Portuguese craftsmen—carpenters, stonemasons, cabinetmakers, as well as an occasional French artisan— who found employment on the fazendas and in the towns that were rapidly developing a civic consciousness and the "arts of civilization." Small furniture shops sprang up in Vassouras at this time, and slaves became skilled in the art of woodworking . . .

Fazenda interiors also underwent expansion and elaboration in this period. Aside from the added ells, however, basic changes in floor plans were limited by the location of the walls that sustained the heavy tile roof. The principal rectangle of the house was generally divided into three parallel sections, subdivided by thinner walls.

From a small veranda approached by wooden stairs or granite steps with wrought iron railings, the visitor might enter a large room or antechamber (*sala de espera*), from which doors opened to the right and left onto other rooms, which usually included a formal reception room, a chapel, and another small room (*quarto*). In the rear, doors led to rooms of the central section, usually windowless alcoves, and to a corridor leading to the third section, a large dining hall with rooms at each end and doorways leading to the ells. The dining room looked out on the *páteo* [patio], which the ells also faced. One ell might include a number of sleeping rooms off a corridor; the other might house the kitchen and various storerooms. In the shed that closed the fourth side of the *páteo,* various ovens and open-air cooking facilities were located. Kitchens of this period were paved with red bricks. Other rooms of the house had plastered ceilings and wooden floors.

In the mid-fifties, a few inventories of well-to-do fazendas still revealed the humble furnishings that the early settlers had brought with them or made on the spot: wood-framed, rawhide-covered trunks, wooden chests for storing food and clothing, and heavy baskets; rough-hewn tables and benches, three-legged stools, simple cotlike beds, and an occasional wardrobe; and the appurtenances of the chapels. To these elements was now added furniture of Regency and Directoire inspiration. Though more elaborate and finished than those of the earlier period, these pieces embodied a simple elegance in the gracefully curved arms and backs of the chairs, sofas, and *marquesas,* and in the austere caning that suited the furniture of a warm climate. Unfinished hardwoods were used: heavy jacaranda, mahogany, the light-brown textured *vinhático* bordered with strips of dark-brown *cabiuna*—timber from the nearby *derrubadas* [clearings] transformed by slaves or itinerant carpenters. Dining tables were often called "elastic" to indicate that there were as many extra leaves as there were chairs available to accommodate guests and family—anywhere from ten to thirty. Bathrooms were not a feature of most fazendas, but tublike "basins for baths" and countless urinals "with" and "without covers" suggested the affluence of a particular household.

Fine porcelain, a mark of distinction, also made its appearance in purchases of English china, and porcelain tea and coffee services, which replaced the older chocolate services. Lettered with the initials of the newly created rural aristocrat, *comendador* or *barão,* these services, kept for gala occasions when everyday white stone china was put away, sometimes showed the fazendeiro's recognition of the close tie between his title and the soil, for the initials of the fazenda often replaced his own. Glassware and silverware were other indications of affluence in this period of difficult transport; wine glasses in large numbers often appear in inventories. The total number of luxury items even in the more elaborate households was not large, however; the mechanics of fazenda life still moved on a very simple plane.

Impressive structures, yes; but first and foremost, these isolated establishments were centers of activity. For the fazenda was more than a unit of commercial agriculture: it was above all a way of life. The railroad had not yet arrived to draw wealthy families even temporarily from their fazendas to the capital in Rio. Extremely poor roads limited travel to trips made to neighboring fazendas or to the town of Vassouras or Paty, where rich fazendeiros built and maintained town houses for the use of their families between Christmas and Holy Week. During the remainder of the year, the family lived on the plantation, surrounded by a large number of household slaves. In addition to the shops organized for basic maintenance, carpenters, a smith, a tailor, and a stonemason, a large unproductive slave personnel hovered around the *sede:* "*pagens,* waiters and waitresses, cooks, stable-boys and body servants for the free men and women," according to [a Mr.] Ribeyrolles, who traveled through Vassouras and neighboring coffee areas at the end of the fifties. He concluded that the fazenda household resembled that of the Roman patriarchate.

In front of the house could be seen the activity of the *terreiro.* From his shaded veranda or a window of the house, the fazendeiro watched his slaves clean the *terreiro* of sprouting weeds or, at harvest time, revolve the drying coffee beans with wooden hoes. Until the hot sun of midday drove them to the shade, bare-bottomed black and mulatto youngsters played under the eye of an elderly slave "aunt," and often with them, a white child in the care of his male slave *pagem.* In the corner of the *terreiro,* slaves might butcher a pig for the day's consumption, while some older children threw stones at the black buzzards that hovered nearby. Outside the *senzala,* a decrepit slave could be found performing some small task or merely warming himself in the sun. The *senzala* itself had changed little in the face-lifting of the fazenda: a tile roof, perhaps a cooling outside corridor enclosed by strong wooden bars, never any flooring. The narrow, windowless cubicles of the mated slaves—the single men and women slaves lived in separate, undivided *senzalas*—contained the few possessions a slave could have: a bed or *tarimba* of boards supported on two sawhorses, covered with a mat of woven grass, and perhaps a small wooden chest; and on the wall, a few pegs and *cuias* or gourds for storing beans, rice, or pork fat. From the *engenho* came the thumping sound of the *pilões* [pistons] and the splash of water cascading from the large waterwheel. In the shade of the *engenho,* an old slave wove strips of bamboo into mats and screens, while other slaves were apparently occupied with the minor details of the day's unhurried routine.

Behind the main house, the *páteo,* enclosed on all sides, offered a shelter from outsiders' eyes, a place to be at ease (*à vontade*). Here and in the rooms around it, the lives of the free and slave women blended together. Laundresses chatted or sang as they dipped their arms into the granite tank in the center of the *páteo* or stretched washing to bleach on the ground, and through the door of the kitchen, slaves occupied with the unending process of food preparation could be seen at long, wooden worktables. Flies hovered everywhere, outside and in. From a small porch opening on the *páteo* or from the dining room window, the mistress of the house, wrapped in a dressing gown, leaned on the railing and watched the goings-on, maintaining a flow of gossip (*bate-papo*) with her slaves or reprimanding one or another of them. Yet, despite the close contact between free and slave, the locks on the doors of pantries and cupboards, and the barred windows of both, gave mute testimony to the faith of the mistress in her slaves.

The dining room, with its close relation to kitchen, *páteo*, and sleeping rooms, was probably the general place of family congregation on those fazendas that did not have special sewing and sitting rooms. Bedrooms were small and sparsely furnished, and in the case of alcoves, entirely dark. In the house, the younger women and maiden aunts sewed and embroidered, gossiped and made delicacies for feast days, while the mistress of the household took a direct hand in the management of affairs. Slave women made beds, arranged disorder, swept, and moved dust from one point to another with feather dusters, while nursemaids took charge of the younger children and wet nurses satisfied squalling infants.

At meal times, which occupied a large part of the day, diners sat on both sides of the long extension table, the fazendeiro sitting at its head. To his right and left were the visitors invited to join the family. When guests were present, talk was largely between them and their host, while the children and dependent relatives ate in silence, speaking only when addressed. A demitasse of coffee closed the meal, which was followed by the inevitable toothpick taken from a silver holder. While the free retired to their nap, the household slaves gossiped and yawned through their work, unless the mistress or master in an exigent mood kept them busy with small biddings.

The arrival of a relative, friend, stranger, priest, or even a *mascate* (peddler) broke the monotony of living and often brought welcome news of events outside the fazenda. Drawn to the interior by the new wealth of Vassouras, the *mascates*—at this period mainly Portuguese—tramped the roads with small trunks strapped to their backs and measuring rods hidden in walking sticks. Wisely, they concentrated on the fancies of the female members of the family, first displaying their eye-catching textiles, ribbons, shiny jewelry, and notions. Some, however, carried diamonds and the decorations newly created barons could wear in their lapels.

When the parish priest came to baptize or to say an infrequent mass, the indoor chapel was opened to all. Usually located to the left of the main entrance, the household chapel contained a simple altar covered with white, lace-trimmed cloths, where there was the wooden, hand-carved *santo de confiança* (saint of the fazenda), flanked by vases of fresh flowers. There was usually a baptismal bowl in the same room; occasionally, one wall of the chapel opened partially to reveal the *tribuna,* a small compartment where the women could hear mass intoned.

For those who did the work of the fazenda—the slaves, men, women, and children, many of them recent arrivals from Mozambique, Angola, the Congo, and Benguela—Saturdays and saints' days were eagerly awaited. First, the permission of the fazendeiro was sought, and perhaps the slaves of a nearby fazenda were invited. Many came, too, without formal invitations. On the wide *terreiro,* wood from the *derrubadas* was piled. After the last chore had been completed, the fire in the early evening was lit to warm the body and the spirit. The fazendeiro, watching from the house, often sent word to his overseer to distribute a small ration of rum (*cachaça*).

Two or three slaves played the drums placed near the fire, where they could be heated when necessary. The slaves—men in white pants and striped shirts; women in blouses and wide, gathered skirts, kerchiefs on their heads—danced separately near the drummers, moving in a counterclockwise circle. A master singer sang the first line of a riddle (*jongo*), and the assembled slaves repeated the refrain. If no person could sing the answer to the riddle, a new one was sung. In the mixture of African tongues and Portuguese, the Negro slaves mocked their masters and themselves. There were other dances mentioned by contemporary observers, the *lundú* and the *batuque.* Often the dances continued far into the night with little thought of the early hour at which [the] fazenda routine was resumed . . .

"Neither man nor his land rested." This is the way the restless cycle of transient coffee agriculture was described, the cycle of tearing from the virgin soil as much as possible in the shortest possible time to move on to new clearings. But just as the older plants furnished seedlings for new plantings, so reaching the plateau of prosperity brought the first signs of the decline that was to shadow the years that followed. Foremost among these were the reduction in the available supply of land, the aging of slave labor and its increased cost to fazendeiros, and the end of former fazenda self-sufficiency.

It was at the close of the prosperous decade that there appeared a recognition of the approaching end of virgin forest. For the first time, land evaluations began to discriminate between *mata virgem* (virgin forest), secondary growth, and pasture. The disappearance of virgin forest was by no means restricted to the small- or medium-sized fazendeiros. Wrote the Baroneza do Paty in 1862 of the immense holdings left her and her children by the Barão do Paty do Alferes: "The absolute shortage of land for planting coffee did not allow me to increase any plantings. . . . Regretfully I must report that on all our fazendas, which cover an area equal to 21,104,000 square *braças* or almost two and a half square *legoas*, . . . we do not have 200 square *braças* of virgin forest of first quality."

Under such conditions, many fazendeiros saw their agricultural techniques—characterized by the use of poorly chosen seedlings, insufficient maintenance of coffee groves, and careless harvesting by slaves—return to plague them: the short life of the coffee trees threatened the economic basis of their society. The estimates of the life span of a coffee bush were various in this period. While Domingos de Barros, writing before the cultivation of coffee had spread throughout the highlands of the Paraíba Valley (1813), estimated that a bush lasted from twenty-five to forty years in good soil, Ferreira de Aguiar, basing his assertion on observations in Vassouras somewhat later (1836), claimed that it gave little fruit after twenty years. "When they reach the age of twenty to twenty-five years, they are considered old," wrote Rodrigues Cunha in 1844. Jean-Jacques Burlamaqui in 1860 dropped the figure lower: "It's not worth picking after fifteen years." New plantings and the exclusion of subsistence crops as competitors for virgin soil could alone compensate for the inevitable drop in coffee production.

Tied closely to the problem of reduced forestlands was that of the aging and high mortality of slave labor, a key factor in a society based entirely on the slave. It was especially serious to those fazendeiros who had stocked their plantations with slaves in the thirties and early forties. The period of maximum productivity in the life of a slave was relatively short, from eighteen to thirty years of age, and fazendeiros had never enjoyed what they considered an adequate labor force even during the busiest days of the slave trade. After 1850, the constant complaint of the fazendeiros concentrating more and more on coffee became the "lack of hands for fieldwork."

Stemming from the increasingly evident disappearance of virgin forest and the diminishing supply of labor was the end of fazenda self-sufficiency. Before the early 1850s, both large coffee fazendeiros and small agriculturists had grown foodstuffs for personal consumption, with the surplus going to the local markets. Attracted by high coffee prices in the early fifties, and alarmed by the diminishing labor pool now partially drained by the road-building and maintenance companies that sprang up after 1850, large fazendeiros had reduced foodstuff acreage and concentrated their labor force upon coffee. This concentration was natural because planters' credit depended solely upon the arrobas of coffee shipped to the *comissário* (agent) in Rio, and because coffee alone left a handsome profit after paying costly transport by mule. Erroneously, fazendeiros believed that the previous abundance and low price of foodstuffs would endure. When they reduced their acreage in subsistence crops, however, even the slightest variation in their harvests forced them to turn to the formerly bountiful local market, which had been supplied in recent years principally by the small agriculturalists. These—*sitiantes, arrendatários,* and *agregados*—had been unable to compete with the big planters in producing coffee, which demanded abundant labor, land, and credit . . .

Despite the storm warnings, however, from the vantage point of the 1860s, the Vassouras planter surveyed a half century of remarkable progress. The establishment he had founded and supplied with an expensive labor force had grown phenomenally. Some luxury goods had arrived from abroad to soften the essentially primitive life of the *sedes*. It seemed clear that a new generation, the sons of the founders, would take over the establishments that had sunk roots into the soil of the steep slopes. There was little doubt in the successful future of large-scale agriculture, "which is and will be for many years the principal source of public and private wealth, the most efficient auxiliary of our progress, cooperating in all the evolution that has brought us to the present state of civilization." On the momentum of this success, the economy of Vassouras rolled on toward troubled times.

The Paraguayan War Victory Parade

Peter M. Beattie

On July 10, 1870, Rio de Janeiro's English-language Anglo-Brazilian Times *announced Brazil's triumphal parade celebrating the nation's victory in the Paraguayan War (1864–1870) as "The Official Rejoicing." Emperor Pedro II and the parliament commissioned special review stands and the celebration of a* Te Deum *mass. Authorities distributed 8,000 invitations to "respectable" citizens, convoking them to demonstrate their patriotism for this special occasion. Why then, when the emperor arrived at the appointed time for the parade, did the review stands remain "utterly quiet"? Why did Rio de Janeiro's "respectable" citizens "contemptuously abstain" from what, in most nations, would mark a moment of stirring nationalism? After all, the increasing influence of social Darwinism internationally led many to consider victory in war a clear demonstration of the superiority of a nation or, more specifically, a national "race." Reportedly, only 200 of those invited attended.*

Public resentment toward the war sprang from many sources. Some complained of the debt Brazil mounted in foreign banks to fund the campaign and the consequent rise in taxes. Others pointed to government corruption and the windfall profits made by unscrupulous entrepreneurs who produced shoddy war goods—even the review stands built for the parade were so rickety that police and army inspectors found them to be dangerously unstable, and ordered them reinforced. Still others complained of the emperor's abuse of his political powers to wage an unpopular war. But perhaps foremost among these sources of frustration was the coercive recruitment methods used to fill ranks on a distant and insalubrious front. In peacetime, coercive recruitment or impressment targeted men who did not conform to elite ideals of "honorable" manhood. The police provided the army with most of its recruits, drawing mostly from the "unprotected" poor: men who lacked a national guard post, a skilled occupation, a certifiable marriage, the capital to pay for an exemption, or an influential patron to shield them from impersonal authority. Men who failed to maintain a fixed residence and regular employment, or who violated social mores by abandoning a spouse or deflowering a virgin (seducing a young woman with false marriage promises), were sometimes summarily sent to serve as enlisted men as punishment. Thus, authorities tended to press migrants, the un- and underemployed, rogues, orphans, and ex-slaves. Vulnerability to recruitment marked a lack of status that distinguished the unprotected poor from the "honorable" poor. While most officers came from more privileged backgrounds, the bulk of enlisted men came largely from what their superiors considered the dregs of society.

The Paraguayan War mobilized four times more troops than any previous Brazilian campaign. The demand for soldiers fell heavily on the shoulders of the unprotected poor, but it also affected the protected poor, eroding traditional thresholds of status. For instance, the state called up national guardsmen (protected from recruitment in peacetime and never mobilized for war on so grand a scale) as first-line troops, and recruitment dragnets nabbed many poor freemen who, in peacetime, probably would have been able to exempt themselves from service. The phrase "club-and-rope recruit" became commonplace, describing the crude methods used to raise troops. Parliament also established a special corps, the Volunteers of the Fatherland, promising those who signed on a number of benefits, including land grants, on demobilization—what would be an unprecedented government effort at homesteading for native Brazilians. Still, these efforts failed to produce adequate recruits. Although many men did volunteer in fits of patriotic fervor, most were pressured or physically coerced into service. To expedite mobilization, the state purchased and urged the donation of hundreds of slaves manumitted on the condition that they serve at the front, and officials pressed scores of convicts. Unlike the United States, where even the Union army only hesitantly incorporated black soldiers and then segregated them from white ones, in Brazil, the low status of soldiering impeded the use of a color bar. There were many white and black soldiers in military regiments, but most army soldiers were of mixed race.

Impressment and the pressure on elites to cooperate with war mobilization were particularly fierce in the nation's capital. Rio de Janeiro was the seat of the army and navy's largest garrisons, which provided support for police in conducting impressment. The capital district contributed one of every eight troops [soldiers] mobilized even though its population represented less than one in thirty-three Brazilians. It also logged the highest total of slaves donated for military service, indicating that elites in Rio de Janeiro were under more pressure to contribute to the war effort. One Rio de Janeiro newspaper lampooned this "patriotism" by depicting a slave owner with African features donating two slaves for the war. The slave owner sarcastically addressed an Afro-Brazilian veteran who had lost an arm in the campaign: "You want to be decorated only because you lost an arm? Then what can I say who will lose no less than four," *Arlequim* reported. These mobilization practices were far from the ideals of universal male conscription and the citizen-soldier that were taking hold in Europe and North America, and formed part of increasingly strident militarist and nationalist ideologies. Impressment upset the lives of common and privileged *cariocas* (Rio residents) by causing men to take to the hills during collection sweeps. A cartoon in São Paulo's *O Cabrião* showed the city full of wild beasts, displaced by men hiding from recruitment agents in the wilderness. These disruptive tactics affected the work forces of merchants, artisans, and businesses in Rio de Janeiro, fueling resentment to the emperor's war policy.

Thus, more-elite *cariocas* snubbed the emperor's patriotic fest for a variety of reasons, but it is likely that many found distasteful the idea of honoring the services of enlisted men with such lowly social origins. Instead, it was the city's poor, many of whom likely had relatives or friends in the enlisted ranks on parade, that partially filled the vacant stands. While foreigners found the spectacle laughable and clucked that Pedro II was a poor organizer of patriotic events, but an excellent Carnival director, a small portion of Paraguayan War veterans had the brief satisfaction of marching in a commemorative parade.

The fates of most enlisted veterans, however, was not enviable. Few ever laid hands on the promised land grants. Because these military colonies were situated on distant and often unfavorable sites, most titleholding veterans preferred to sell them to land speculators for a fraction of their worth. Only veterans with a powerful patron who could grease the wheels of the bureaucracy could hope to enjoy the promised benefits and pensions. Some veterans disabled by the war were accepted into regiments known as the "Invalids of the Fatherland." Rio de Janeiro's invalid regiment was eventually symbolically housed near the city's garbage dump on the island of Bom Jesus in Guanabara Bay. On the fiftieth anniversary of Brazil's martial triumph, one journalist scorned the treatment of aged Paraguayan War veterans at Bom Jesus whose pensions and meals were so parsimonious that most were forced to beg or seek employment on the mainland to sustain themselves and their families. Even after this embarrassing exposé, little changed for these veterans. Indeed, decades later, the government forced disabled veterans out of their lodgings on Bom Jesus to make space for political prisoners from more privileged backgrounds.

The government's disregard for war veterans was possible largely because of their lowly social origins. Widespread impressment allowed officials to dismiss the services of veterans, even though many volunteered, by emphasizing the tradition of the "club-and-rope recruits." This contrasts starkly with the treatment of Civil War veterans in the United States. Government pensions for veterans and their families became America's first experiment with social welfare programs, and the Republic Party used these benefits as an effective instrument of political patronage and voter mobilization. However, restrictive voting rights in Brazil and the relatively smaller size of its wartime mobilization prevented Paraguayan War veterans from becoming an effective political force. Even though similar kinds of veteran benefit legislation was debated, the Brazilian government never implemented any. Thus, as during the 1870 parade, most of the more privileged preferred to ignore the services of veterans. As Benedict Anderson argues in *Imagined Communities,* nationalism requires a certain imagined homogenization and leveling of a populace to take hold. As the 1870 victory parade indicates, it was difficult to sustain such imaginings for many Brazilians. Brazilian nationalist sentiment could be stymied by the inequalities of slavery, the racial prejudice undergirded by the empirical bigotry of social Darwinism, military impressment, restrictive voting rights, and traditional concepts of honor and status. An imperfect implementation of leveling bureaucratic practices in Brazil, like universal male military conscription, that emphasized the obligation of all able-bodied male citizens—rich or poor, black or white—to serve for national defense, would come only after the demise of slavery and challenges to the biological determinism that labeled Brazil's African and indigenous populations a hindrance to national progress, and with the massive international mobilizations required by the world wars.

A Vanishing Way of Life

Gilberto Freyre

Soon after returning from the United States in the early 1920s, Gilberto Freyre embarked on a lifelong campaign to popularize his view that because the traditional slave masters had enjoyed sexual relations with slave women, the institution of slavery in Brazil was therefore more benign than elsewhere. Born to an elite sugar family in Pernambuco, Freyre broke with tradition by attending Baptist schools in Recife, then at Baylor University in Waco, Texas, and finally at Columbia University, where he studied anthropology and history. His interpretation is not widely accepted today because careful social science research has found many of his arguments faulty, but before his death in 1980, Freyre's thesis had successfully contributed to the more or less official interpretation of Brazil's past. This selection makes Freyre's case for the world of the small sugar mill, which he believed was kinder and more humane than the industrial sugar factories that replaced them during the late–nineteenth century.

Whoever knows Pernambuco, Alagoas, the south of Paraíba . . . who knows this region of Brazil not superficially but in intimacy, knows the enormous distance that separates the old *senhor de engenho* [sugar producer] from the modern *usineiro* [sugar industrialist]. Not that I want to depict the old *senhores de engenho* as saints. But there is no doubt that under the patriarchal system employed in the old sugar mills, more help was given to the labor force than is the case at the great majority of sugar factories today. There was, no one can deny, harshness and even brutality in the ways that the whites from the Big House treated their slaves. But the slave owner usually helped the blacks in the slave shacks more than the *usineiro* today helps his employees; he would keep on, for example, old or sick blacks, supporting them. In the majority of the old *engenhos*, life was sweeter and more humane than it is today in the sugar factories. The festivities—Saint John's Day, the pastoral days, at the folklore celebrations—frequently created moments of fraternization between the owners and their workers. These moments virtually do not exist today. There almost never is fraternization. The sugar factory owners fraternize at a distance—in Recife, in Boa Viagem [Recife's beach], in Rio, in Paris, in Buenos Aires.

A few of them [though] preserve the old habits of the *senhor de engenho.* Their sons, or they themselves, when they are feeling frisky, still deflower mulatta girls and immediately abandon them. The girls then are forced to come to Recife, Maceió, Paraíba, to Fogo Street, to the Pateo do Carmo, to the Rosario Street, adding to the volume of prostitution in the cities. The new nobility do not traffic with them. The chic thing is to spend money on foreign women. These frisky *usineiros,* imitating gentlemen, prefer blondes, but they deflower mulattas.

The *usina* separated the owners not only from their labor force—that was the second family of the *senhor de engenho*—but from the pastoral countryside. . . . The social and psychic distances became greater and greater. They became immense. Virtually all of the lyricism in the relations of man with nature, with the forest, with animals, with rivers, with plants, with the earth, with other men, has disappeared. We have arrived at the dramatic point where either we reestablish this equilibrium between man and nature in the sugar region of the Northeast or man will become degraded to the ultimate extreme. Not only are workers affected, but the large property owners as well. Today, you cannot compare any *usineiro* from Pernambuco, Alagoas, or Paraíba—people who don't even read newspapers—with the Pernambucan *senhores de engenho* of the last half of the nineteenth century, among whom Herbert S. Smith found so many readers of French books and even English books, and subscribers to the *Review des Deux Mondes.* The most refined *senhores de engenho* were educated by priests, who were their uncles in the private schools of Recife, and at times, in Europe . . .

A Mirror of Progress

Dain Borges

Euclides da Cunha's Rebellion in the Backlands (Os Sertões, 1902) is an epic chronicle of the punitive military expeditions that massacred Canudos's millenarian community in 1897. It barely mentions central national events, such as the abolition of slavery in 1888 or the republican military coup in 1889, yet it became the most enduring comment on Brazil's progress from monarchy to republic. It persuaded readers in 1902 that da Cunha had diagnosed the nation's illness—dangerous social dualism and splits, a schizoid soul—through scrutiny of an obscure symptom. Though no longer scientifically convincing, Rebellion in the Backlands *is still compelling. It declares themes, such as the need to awaken the people, that have preoccupied Brazilian radicals throughout the twentieth century. Its themes and stark images—desert and water, death and resurrection, saints and bandits—have been adapted and challenged in forms such as Glauber Rocha's visionary film,* Deus e o Diabo na Terra do Sol (Black God, White Devil, 1964), *and the Peruvian Mario Vargas Llosa's political novel,* The War of the End of the World *(1981).*

It might seem that the political transition from the Empire to the Republic would leave the countryside apathetic. By mid–nineteenth century, Brazil's small farmers, big planters, and central government had worked out a conservative patronage deal that immobilized politics. Tensions over issues such as military recruitment for the Paraguayan War (1864–1870) and even the reform of slave labor (1871–1888) apparently did not break it. In the dry backlands, or *sertão*, of the state of Bahia, those who cared about politics played it as a sport of connections, schemes, and bloody election brawls.

But the republican coup of 1889, following three years of escalating abolitionist protest, did catalyze rural conflicts. In the far southern state of Rio Grande do Sul, the Republic unleashed a murderous civil war between factions in rural counties, in which some participants declared themselves monarchists. In Bahia and neighboring northern states, the republican regime's separation of church and state in 1889–1891 reopened old grievances about government interference in religion. Protest there took the form of pilgrimages, miracles, and prophecies: "In 1898 there will be many hats and few heads."[1]

A ragged lay preacher, Antonio Conselheiro ("the Counselor"), settled hundreds of his followers on an abandoned ranch called Canudos in 1893. At first, the community may not have been millenarian, but simply a penitential retreat, tolerated by priests. As it grew, Conselheiro became a local political boss, made some allies and many enemies, denounced civil marriage and other satanic republican reforms, and in 1896, was tricked into defying new taxes. "We have the law of God, they have the law of the Hound." The Canudos war began when military police were sent to arrest his followers.

Euclides da Cunha thought this conflict was the inevitable outcome of long-standing cleavages in Brazil. Trained as a military engineer, he analyzed Canudos according to then-prevailing (though not undisputed) sociological theories of the determining force of climate and race. At every level in the backlands, even on the scale of geological time, da Cunha finds imbalance, opposition, and conflict. He argues that the rugged, chaotic landscape itself constitutes "the remnants of a centuries-old conflict between the seas and the earth." The climate oscillates between killing droughts, when plants lose their "mute battle" with the sun, and sudden rains, "when the tropical flora revive triumphantly, in a transforming apotheosis." The people of the Bahian backlands, *sertanejos,* were formed by the impact of this unbalanced climate on their mixed-race bodies. They are mostly of Indian and Portuguese descent—a slightly more promising mixture, da Cunha thinks, than the mixture of African and Portuguese blood that predominates in coastal Brazil. He cares less about the traits of ancestral races, however, than about the mixture itself. The entire Brazilian nation, he believes, is a half-formed "body in fusion." The elements of ancestral races are "a play of antitheses" within each Brazilian; each Brazilian carries on a civil war inside his own body. Unlike national races with a uniform type, such as the Dutch or British races, Brazilians "have no race." Thus, in the struggle for life and in imperialist wars between national races, Brazil is at a malleable, vulnerable phase of its evolution.

The typical Bahian *sertanejo* is a cowboy, "condemned to life" in this volatile environment, prepared from childhood for struggle, "strong, cunning, resigned, and practical." If he is sometimes "incorrigibly indolent," he is also scrupulously honest in cattle deals and admirably resigned in droughts. The best one could hope for, da Cunha argues, is that the backlanders would abide tenaciously underneath modern Brazilians, like archaic strata in stable rock. Unfortunately, *sertanejos* add to their climatic and racial chaos a bizarre religious culture, a jumbled mix of medieval Catholicism with Indian and African superstitions. And like an earthquake, the republican revolution of 1889 disturbed the layers along this fault line. At Canudos, historical and environmental forces impelled the *sertanejos* to turn an unbalanced man into their prophet, in a process neither he nor they quite understood. "It is natural that these deep layers of our ethnic stratification would rise up in an extraordinary anticline— Antonio Conselheiro."

Revisionist historians in recent years have not only discarded da Cunha's unconvincing racial diagnosis, but have also interpreted Canudos as a normal community. They have found evidence that it grew quickly from its founding in 1893 to a thriving small city—perhaps, at times, as large as 20,000 people. It was not "centuries remote" from Bahia's capital, Salvador, but rather close: overnight to the Queimadas railway station, then two days by mule to Canudos. Pilgrims came from a cross section of the rural population: ex-slaves, paupers, cowboys, farmers, and merchants, as well as malcontents and bandits. Some came for refuge or the hope of work on nearby ranches; most came to repent and scourge their sins. Conselheiro apparently brokered their labor and their votes like any other rural godfather.

Da Cunha imagines Canudos growing as a morbid, "sinister *civitas*." He draws on new French psychological theories about urban mass politics and manipulated crowds. Antonio Conselheiro must be a degenerate borderline paranoid (like agitators in republican Paris). His influence over the people must be the sort of hypnotism that can operate on vulnerable, "mixed" people, fusing them into a criminal crowd: "his gaze— dazzling sparks. . . . No one dared look at him. The crowd, succumbing, lowered its eyes in turn, fascinated, under the strange hypnotism of that formidable insanity." The people at Canudos became "an unconscious brute mass, growing without evolving, without specialized organs and functions, through mere mechanical addition of successive stages, like a human polyp." The *sertanejo* transformed into the backlands thug, the *jagunço*.

The diagnosis of contagious mob spirit and this image of a crazed city spoke to da Cunha's own experiences of "the cyclical progress of political disease" in Rio de Janeiro from 1880 to 1897, sordid experiences that made him wary of both democracy and military government. Born in 1866, da Cunha studied engineering at the Rio de Janeiro military academy. His post–Paraguayan War generation of cadets were a new breed, educated in geometry, positivism, and contempt for civilian politicians. Their senior officers were defying the government. In 1887, they declared that they would not perform police duty by chasing runaway slaves; this encouraged slave mutinies and mass escapes, and accelerated the declaration of abolition in May 1888. Months later, da Cunha was expelled from the academy for a republican provocation: breaking his saber while on parade review. In November 1889, senior officers, conspiring with disgruntled former slave owners, overthrew Emperor Pedro II. Of course, the military academy reinstated da Cunha, now a republican hero. But he found that when his classmates came to power under the second military dictator, Marshal Floriano Peixoto (1891–1894), they behaved less as scientific patriots than as opportunistic pseudoradicals. And he thought their civilian partners in the nationalistic Jacobin movement were agitators and assassins, "ambitious mediocrities," "cavemen in kid gloves." He denounced government repression during the feverish 1892–1895 civil war, was transferred out of Rio, and resigned from the army.

When the campaigns against Canudos began in 1896, however, da Cunha wrote two patriotic newspaper columns comparing Canudos to the Vendée revolt of monarchist, Catholic peasants during the French Revolution. This won him assignment as the paper's war correspondent—back among his classmates—in the last weeks of the siege, in 1897. At first, he sent back stirring propaganda pieces; then he reported sympathetically on prisoners; then his dispatches stopped. He was keeping silent, while taking notes, about atrocities he would denounce in *Rebellion in the Backlands*, five years later.

Most of *Rebellion in the Backlands* is a dramatized (and in places, fictionalized) narrative of the campaign, contrasting the tactical incompetence of the army to the cunning and courage of the millenarian guerrillas. In November 1896, a crowd from Canudos, singing hymns, routed 100 mounted military police coming to arrest them. Weeks later, *ser-*

tanejo sharpshooters ambushed a second, hastily organized column of 500 soldiers under Febrônio de Brito. The army "subordinated its tactics to the rigid framework of classic war doctrine" and didn't adapt its geometrical formations to the tangled terrain of thornbush, "which fought for the *sertanejos.*"

For da Cunha, the most indicative episode is the defeat of the third army expedition, led by Colonel Moreira Cesar, which approached Canudos in February 1897. Moreira Cesar's republican career was a twisted version of da Cunha's: knifing a journalist in 1884, executing prisoners during the civil war in 1893. He was the model modern military demagogue, popular with the Jacobin crowds of Rio de Janeiro. "Our political fetishism needed idols in uniform. They chose him as their new idol." Da Cunha portrays him as the republican double of Antonio Conselheiro, an epileptic mad genius who mixes "clashing monstrous tendencies and superior qualities, both in the highest degree of intensity, . . . a protean soul bottled up in a fragile organism."

Advancing too fast into the outskirts of Canudos, Moreira Cesar was ambushed and killed. His army of more than 1,500 lost its discipline and stampeded, turning into a crowd, "a knot of men, animals, uniforms and carbines." *Sertanejos* strung up the mutilated corpses of officers in trees. The common soldiers, "most of them mestizos, made from the same clay as the *sertanejos,* shocked by the counterblow of the inexplicable reversal in which their supposedly invincible chief had fallen, came under the suggestive spell of the marvelous, invaded by supernatural terror aggravated by outlandish rumors."

Not only soldiers at the front, but also the people of "civilized" Rio de Janeiro panicked at rumors of monarchist hordes (armed by Britain!). In Rio, mobs assassinated monarchist politicians and burned newspapers. Here again, da Cunha argues that Canudos is significant as the mirror in which Rio de Janeiro can see its own savage face. The bonfires show that the fashionable Rua do Ouvidor—with its newspaper offices, tearooms, and shops—"was no better than some trail through the scrub." Republican democracy was nothing but crowd hysteria. Like other failed adventure stories written at the same time—Joseph Conrad's *Heart of Darkness* (1899) or James Mooney's *The Ghost Dance Religion and the Sioux Outbreak of 1890* (1896)—*Rebellion* uses an imperialist encounter to question and ironically reverse the values of "savage" and "civilized," backwardness and progress.

More carefully then, the government organized the fourth expedition, in April 1897. It eventually took more than 6,000 soldiers, at least a third of the Brazilian army, and cost thousands of casualties. The war minister himself supervised a slow buildup of supplies near the front. Howitzer bombardment, sticks of dynamite, kerosene, and hand-to-hand fighting finally accomplished the siege. By the time da Cunha arrived at the dusty, filthy trenches, the battle was in its last days. Antonio Conselheiro had died; unburied corpses fouled the ground; a group of starved women and children, "human rubble," had surrendered; but the surviving men fought to the death. In describing them, da Cunha's sympathies, moved by the bravery of the fanatics, overcome his prejudices. "The bedrock of a nation was being chiseled. We were attacking the deep, living rock of our race. So, dynamite was called for. . . . It was a consecration."

Soldiers looted the charred shacks of the city, dug up Antonio Conselheiro to photograph and preserve his head in a jar, and—either under orders or with the tacit permission of their officers—slaughtered the few male prisoners they captured. Da Cunha describes one black prisoner as coming "from the last and lowest rung of our racial ladder. . . . His halting, infirm step, his woolly head, his shrunken face, flat nose over thick lips parted by bent and twisted teeth, his tiny eyes burning red in deep sockets, his long bare swinging arms—all gave him the hideous appearance of an aged orangutan."

Officers didn't even bring him in their tent. "He was an animal. It wasn't worth the trouble to interrogate him. Brigadier General João da Silva Barbosa, from the hammock in which he was recovering from a recent wound, gestured. A corporal, assigned to the engineering staff and famous for such deeds, divined his meaning. He approached with the noose. Being short of stature, however, he found it difficult to set it around the condemned man's neck. This man, however, helped him calmly; undid the tangled knot; ran it through his own hands, noosing himself. Nearby, a lieutenant from the General Staff and a fifth-year medical student contemplated that scene.

"And they saw the unfortunate man transmute, as soon as he took his first steps toward execution. From that blackened and repugnant frame, barely standing on the long, shriveled legs, there suddenly emerged admirable lines—terribly sculptural—of a splendid physique. A masterpiece of sculpture, modeled in mud.

"Suddenly the black man's stooping posture straightened up, showing off, vertical and rigid, in a beautiful pose that was unusually haughty. His head set itself on shoulders which squared back, expanding his chest, and raised itself in a defiant gesture of aristocratic scorn. His gaze, in a manly glare, lit up his face. He moved on, impassive and firm; mute, his face immobile, his wasted muscles in sharp relief against his bones, in impeccable indifference. He turned into a statue, an ancient statue of a Titan, buried for four centuries and now emerging, blackened and mutilated, in that immense ruins of Canudos. It was an inversion of roles. A shameful antinomy."

Da Cunha argues pessimistically that the macabre and criminal episode of Canudos—the army's homicidal fury, the *sertanejos'* suicidal fanaticism—is the symptom of fatal antagonisms everywhere within Brazil's soul. He fears a twentieth century in which unified imperialist armies will invade and conquer a divided Brazil. Yet he insinuates that Canudos might be justified as a sacrifice for the nation, if it demonstrated transfigurations that could unleash the nation's energies. In peacetime, he had seen slack-faced *sertanejo* cowboys squatting in the dirt "in a posture of unstable equilibrium," apparently apathetic and inert. But a stray calf or "any incident that demands that he unchain his sleeping energies is enough. The man transfigures. He straightens up, showing new lines in his stature and in his gesture. . . . From the common figure of a clumsy peasant, there emerges, unexpectedly, the domineering visage of a coppery and potent Titan, in a surprising unfolding of extraordinary force and agility." He leaps to his horse and gallops off, "threading rapidly through the inextricable labyrinths of thornbush." Da Cunha's belief that the Brazilian people were only awaiting schoolteachers, missionaries, or inspiring leaders to lift them from apathy to vitality, from the Middle Ages to the modern age, became an enduring theme of Brazilian populist nationalism.

Note

1 I have consulted *Rebellion in the Backlands,* trans. Samuel Putnam (Chicago: University of Chicago Press, 1944), but all quotations are my own loose translation from Euclides da Cunha, *Os Sertões: Campanha de Canudos,* 35th ed. (Rio de Janeiro: Francisco Alves, 1991).

Drought and

the Image of the Northeast

Gerald M. Greenfield

Drought long has stalked the Brazilian Northeast, a region often described in terms of persistent poverty and resistance to change. Northeasterners see drought as both a cause and symbol of their region's relative underdevelopment, and claim that this reflects a long-standing pattern of government favoritism toward the South. In this view as well, the Northeast has been exploited by southern business and financial interests, drained of both its people and capital. Outside the region, however, the derisive terms "drought industry" and "drought industrialists" capture a widely held belief that northeastern politicians and elites have shamelessly taken advantage of droughts to provide patronage for their cronies, waxing rich off the misery of the backward masses. This conception also suggests that the persistence of poverty facilitates the maintenance of traditional patterns of a patriarchal, elite dominance. In this polemic, the term drought *does not merely describe a climatological phenomenon, but rather, serves as a capacious metaphor summarizing a complex of features popularly associated with the Northeast. Drought includes such stock characters as impoverished, ignorant backlanders prone to religious mysticism and fanaticism, and avaricious local bosses who readily employ violence to achieve their corrupt ends. Further, it invokes an older, less-developed, and more traditional Brazil. The Northeast, as popularly understood, refers to these characteristics rather than to a specific set of boundaries. Hence, Bahia, officially part of the "East," conceptually belongs to the Northeast.*

Despite numerous recorded instances of drought dating as far back as the 1500s, in the mid–nineteenth century, cattle ranches and sugar plantations stood as the area's dominant symbolic representation. Drought remained simply an unfortunate fact of nature that affected various parts of the nation's vast interior, including the backlands of the "southern" province of Minas Gerais. Similarly, while questions of development and modernity held importance at that time, the issue was framed largely in national rather than regional terms.

The contemporary regional identity of the Northeast, then, is a social construct, an artifact of human imagination whose origins lie in the latter portion of the nineteenth century. The Great Drought of 1877—still recalled as the worst such occurrence in the region's history—played a major role in this process of definition. It created a conceptual context and discursive repertoire for interpreting all subsequent droughts. The other key event in the emergence of a Northeast was the reduction of Canudos in 1896–1897, which transfixed the nation at the time of its occurrence, and powerfully influenced generations of Brazilians' (and foreigners') central understandings regarding the nature of the backlands and its peoples.

The prominence of the *cangaceiro* (bandit) in the early decades of the twentieth century also contributed to the evolving image of the Northeast, as did the continued incidence of devastating droughts and failed government initiatives. The rise of northeastern regionalism in the 1920s, and the subsequent popularity of the "new northeastern novel" in the 1930s, accelerated both the completion and dissemination of this specific representation of the Northeast as a land of hardship, poverty, exploitation, and mysticism.

Demographic and economic trends further contributed toward characterizing the Northeast in these pejorative terms. At the time of Brazil's 1872 census, the Northeast held the greatest percentage of the nation's population. In a trend that would continue throughout the next century, it began losing population relative to the Southeast. In part, this reflected out-migration due to the continuing incidence of drought, and the fact that foreign immigrants tended overwhelmingly to settle in the Southeast. But these population movements, at heart, were a result of the economic dynamism of other regions. In the course of the nineteenth century, coffee became Brazil's most important export. Over the latter decades of that century, coffee cultivation increasingly concentrated in the fertile red soils of São Paulo, and the economic axis of the country definitively shifted south. At the same time, the rubber boom, which began in 1870 and peaked in 1910, contributed to the identification of the

Amazon as a region, a "new" North as distinct from the older Northeast still largely wedded to its colonial economy of sugar and hides. Coinciding as it did with the pattern of droughts, millenarianism, and banditry, the relative economic decline of the Northeast suggested an obvious link between regional backwardness and the inherent qualities of the land and its people. Who would anticipate anything other than decline from a primitive, ignorant, tradition-bound people who lived in an almost barbarous fashion?

The Great Drought gripped the backlands or *sertão* from 1877 to 1880. Desperate for food and water, the backlands masses, the *sertanejos,* streamed out from the parched area. More favorably located settlements, especially those along the coast, soon reeled under the impact of thousands of drought refugees, generally called *retirantes,* but also referred to as *flagelados,* the "scourged" or "afflicted." The national government ultimately expended enormous sums of money on drought relief, much of it ostensibly earmarked to provide work relief for the displaced backlanders. In the National Legislative Assembly, senators and deputies waxed eloquent about the suffering of the displaced backlanders, and acknowledged that both conscience and the nation's Constitution mandated a compassionate public response. But they also pointed to the superiority of work relief as opposed to government handouts, and soon decried a relief effort rife with corruption, fraud, and inefficiencies. The lazy *sertanejo* and profiteering politico emerged as key elements in the problem of drought.

Several national learned societies held special meetings to discuss the causes and possible prevention of drought, contributing to a lively polemic in newspapers and folios that stressed the need for rational, scientific approaches to the problem. Many of these modernizers pointed to the backward nature of the *sertão* and its peoples, and saw the drought as sad proof of the distance that separated Brazil from the advanced nations of the civilized world. The barbarous living conditions of the *sertanejos* and their inertial resistance to progress also received wide commentary. Policy discussions that linked drought and underdevelopment stressed the need for large-scale public works to improve the region's water resources and transportation infrastructure.

Successive governments would continue to seek a solution to northern drought by funding scientific studies and public works projects, the so-called hydraulic or technocratic approach. In 1906, the first national government agency officially designated to combat the problem of regional drought appeared, the Superintendency of Studies and Works against the Effects of Drought. Known more widely by its subsequent acronym, IFOCS (Inspectoria Federal de Obras Contra as Secas-Federal Inspectorate of Anti-Drought Works), this agency arose in response to both the 1906 drought and the legacy of the great droughts of 1877–1880 and 1888–1889.

Dom Pedro the Magnanimous

Mary Wilhelmine Williams

Ordinary Brazilians revered Emperor Dom Pedro II, although his unfailing support of the interests of the elite meant that he was responsible for little material improvement in the lives of the vast majority of his subjects. During the 1930s (when the book from which this selection is taken was published), some chose to remember Dom Pedro in the same worshipful, larger-than-life manner as they saw dictator Getúlio Vargas. The biographer's breathless conferring of near-sainthood to her subject is balanced by her acknowledgment that as an intellect and an emperor, Pedro was little more than ordinary.

The Beginning

One afternoon in April 1831, Rio de Janeiro was festively decked and was stirred by unusual excitement. From windows and balconies hung gay damask draperies; flags and pennants of green and gold waved in the breeze. Crowds of people—black, brown, and white—were making for the large *praça* [square] in front of the imperial City Palace on the margin of the bay. Some of them carried green branches of the "national" croton shrub in yellow bloom. The military guards were drawn up in front of their muskets with glossy sprigs from coffee trees spangled with starry blossoms and green and red berries. Also in the square were the municipal officers, on horseback and wearing ancient ceremonial uniforms. Presently, from vessels in the harbor and fortresses on the hills, came the boom of cannon. The crowds shouted joyfully, "Long Live Dom Pedro II, Emperor of Brazil!"

On a second story balcony of the palace was their sovereign, surrounded by his sisters and his ministers of state, who were likewise splendid in the imperial green and gold. The tiny emperor, little more than five years old, was standing on a chair, that the people might more easily see him. He was a delicate-looking child, with light golden hair, fair skin, and German blue eyes, and with a slightly projecting lower lip that betokened his Habsburg ancestry. In almost gay wonder, he gazed on his cheering subjects and responded to their vivas by waving a handkerchief.

Aspects of his Reign

Dom Pedro had ruled for more than thirty years when he first saw other lands from the vast, underdeveloped one of his birth. . . . He had read extensively, and had so combined understanding and sympathy with knowledge as to be something of a world citizen, mentally and spiritually, even before he set foot on alien shores.

By 1871, Brazil was at peace within and was free from vexing foreign problems. In February of that year, his daughter Leopoldina died of typhoid fever in Vienna, leaving four little sons. This, and the fact that Dona Thereza, long in delicate health, was now ill and needed climatic change and expert medical care, caused the emperor to plan to go to Europe. He obtained from Parliament permission to absent himself from the country and arranged to have the princess imperial act as regent during his absence. . . . The chamber of deputies wished to vote a large sum for the expenses of the emperor's trip and to have him escorted to Europe by a Brazilian squadron, but Dom Pedro refused both. His civil list was enough for his expenses, he said, and he wanted to travel simply, like a private citizen, and incognito, untroubled by formal etiquette. It was, therefore, arranged that he and Dona Thereza should sail on a regular transatlantic steamer, the *Douro,* accompanied by only a small suite of ten persons. Among these were Dom Pedro's childhood friend, Luiz Pedreira, now Barão de Bom Retiro, and the Condessa de Barral, former governess of Princess Isabel. The party also included Rafael, the black friend and servant of the emperor's infancy, whose only service during later years had been to clean his master's boots.

The End

On [November 23, 1891, in Paris exile] he attended a session of the Academy of Sciences, which he greatly enjoyed, but when he emerged onto the street, he became chilled by the sharp air. . . . Influenza developed. . . . His sixty-sixth birthday [in early December] found him very weak, though he received some friends who called to congratulate him. By the 3rd, it was apparent that he had pneumonia of the left lung. . . . His breathing, very faint toward the last, ended a little after midnight on December 5, 1891.

Although mentally, Dom Pedro was well above the average, he had no marks of intellectual genius. Yet, he was one of the most notable people of his century. While not original or creative in his work as emperor, he did his utmost to bring to his people the best results of human thinking throughout the world; and in view of the national and constitutional handicaps against which he struggled, he should rank among the wisest and best rulers of the period. As a personality, he was, however, more original than as a sovereign; as a man, he was far more notable than as an emperor. He was greater for what he was, than for what he did. His modesty, simplicity, and democracy; tenacity of high purposes; devotion to duty as he saw it; unwearied enthusiasm for learning; subordination of material values to intellectual and spiritual ones; and his integrity, magnanimity, understanding pity, and Christlike kindness, made him one of the finest personalities of modern times.

Solemn Inaugural

Session of December 24, 1900

Congress of Engineering and Industry

The young Republic owed much of its ideological inspiration to Auguste Comte and positivism. According to Comte, empirical sciences would guide material and social development during humanity's highest stage. His influence was such that even those Brazilians with only a passing interest in positivism associated scientific achievement with their country's economic development, social harmony, and entry into the ranks of advanced civilizations. In short, positivism became one of the cornerstones of twentieth-century Brazilian nationalism. Understandably, engineers and physicians now grabbed much of the national prominence formerly reserved for men of letters and law, the bacharéis. *In 1900, engineers commemorated the quadricentennial of Brazil's discovery with the following affirmation of their patriotic service and nationalist spirit.*

Dr. Osorio de Almeida, president of the congress, declares open the solemn inaugural session and pronounces the following speech:

Most excellent president of Brazil and most excellent gentlemen:

Twenty years ago, some engineers and industrialists met in a small chamber of a building on Alfandega Street and formed the Engineering Club, having as an objective the study of all questions that interested the development of engineering and industry in our dearly loved fatherland. A simple program in its enunciation, it is, however, among the most complex that can be offered to human endeavor because it renders concrete everything that contributes to the building of a country's civilization. The science of law strengthens the principles of order and justice; medicine discovers the laws of preservation of the individual. Engineering and industry, however, are what furnish, at first, the power that constitutes the ratification of law and, secondly, the means of protection against the destructive action of natural forces, and even transforms them into factors of comfort and well-being for humanity.

The defense of our frontiers and ports from attacks against the country's integrity, the weapons with which we can maintain our liberty, only are obtained with the aid of engineering and industry. It is to that aid that we also owe the projects for draining our swamps, building sewers, supplying water; in short, the works of sanitation that avoid the handicaps that result from the agglomeration of the populations for the preservation of the individual. The roads, highways, railroads, navigation—all those means of communication between people that are so many other instruments of solidarity in the sublime task that was entrusted to humanity, and that even contribute powerfully and effectively to the equitable distribution of nature's gifts, unequally produced by the enormous variation of the soil, heat, and humidity that our planet presents—all that is the fruit of engineering and industry. [*Cheers*]

Intellectuals at Play

Olavo Bilac Collection

Young men in the upper classes cultivated bohemian airs and reveled in their self-importance. The behavior of university students was often appalling, involving attacks on passersby, the overturning of trolley cars, and sometimes provoking riots. Cultural and literary life exhibited a playful side, as illustrated by this staged photograph dating from the 1890s from the collection of poet Olavo Bilac. The tableau reconstructs Rembrandt's painting The Anatomy Lesson.

Intellectuals at play. *(Academia Brasileira de Letras, Rio de Janeiro)*

City of Mist

Manoel Sousa Pinto

Brazilians, and especially Paulistas (residents of the exuberant city of São Paulo), basked in pride at the rapid civic improvements in their midst. Under the Republic, state governments negotiated for loans from foreign banks for the purpose of reconstructing their major cities to be as progressive (that is, European) as possible. The Republic saw massive gains in transportation, sewage treatment, the construction of port facilities, office buildings, viaducts, and streetlighting. This reminiscence by Manoel Sousa Pinto, published in 1905, describes his return to the city after many years. Sousa Pinto (1880–1934) was a Brazilian who had grown up in Portugal, where he took a law degree at the University of Coimbra. His career in Brazil included art criticism and newspaper work.

Arriving in the city, we called for street taxis; the driver, using gestures typical of the Neapolitans, drove through the streets, muttering in an Italian of ill origins. At dinner, we were served *minestra* and *rizzotto*— Italian foods, no doubt about it, the Italy of saffron rice and grated cheese, with the day's newspaper on the table with the name *Fanfulla*.

In the lettering and names on the retail stores one sees an insistent mixture of Italian and Portuguese, and once in a while, signs in other languages. *"Bottiglieria alla Ponte dei Sospiri,"* a bombastic message appears, and *"Aux 600,000 paletots."* There is also a *"Rotisserie Sportsman,"* as well as Brazilian restaurants and a beer house calling itself *"O Chopp."* It is a consortium of languages, a little Babel, with names repeated over and over again in monstrous commercial hyperbole. More than in Rio, I have the impression here in São Paulo of cosmopolitanism, of confusion, of the penetration of foreign ethnic groups.

The Italian, for now, predominates. There are Italian bankers, industrialists, physicians, attorneys, and large and small businessmen, not to mention the Italians who pull carts, carry things, are maids, workmen, trolley conductors, peddlers, shoe shine boys, and so on.

I don't know if it comes from the Italian influence here, but without doubt, São Paulo's building boom impresses us agreeably. This city presents an artistic air, a sense of generally good taste, in its monuments and residences, in its houses and its mansions, in its architecture in both the public and the private sphere—it is an attractive city, handsomely filled with buildings . . .

Swift, inexpensive, and extremely comfortable streetcars take us through the city, running on regular schedules . . . bringing the good impression of a modern city, clean, recently constructed, fresh appearing, still awaiting completion, with a sense of progress and respect for art. . . . There is much to admire here and much to learn. Riding around gives the impression of leafing through the pages of a picture book displaying the best of modern architectural construction.

São Paulo's climate is characteristic of a European city, with the small inconvenience of brusque changes in temperature and the threat of a kind of foglike, persistent, fine mist in the air that they call *garoa*. There is good reason, then, for an observer like myself, enamored of new ways to call things, to dub this "the city of mist."

It is to be expected that in hundreds of different varieties of houses— the variety of the facades is one of the most enchanting aspects of these lovely tree-lined streets—one encounters the good as well as the bad, the reasonable and the exaggerated, the pretty and the perfect. There is something for all tastes—Norman structures, the sinuous and illogical arabesques of art nouveau, even English cottages and little Alpine snow chalets. There are Spanish-style mountain villas, Oriental minarets, the covered verandas of northern Europe, the gracious Italianate manors, Renaissance-inspired galleries, baroque exaggerations, rustic Swiss lodges, even the horrible pockmarked symmetry of the Pombaline style of Portugal, heavy and brutish, ready for earthquakes.

All around, thanks to the talented work of skilled artisans, native-born and immigrant, São Paulo passes by like pages of an album. There are sumptuous public buildings, like the Ipiranga Museum, various state government palaces, and excellent school buildings—São Paulo has turned its attention lovingly to the question of education—all transforming, enhanced by its tree-ventilated and landscaped avenues, making traveling through the city a pleasure. It must be delightful to live in this city and to go to sleep during the misty nights, cozy in this lovely and gentle city.

For it is here that I have lost myself in curiosity, getting about on foot or by tram, fulfilling an errant pleasure of familiarizing myself with the city's varied districts, the contrasting aspects of Bexiga, Hugienópolis, the Elysian Fields, the neighborhood called Paradise, enjoying the shade of the Public Garden, where exotic animals play eccentrically—seeking out panoramic views, admiring this or that . . . being surprised on foggy nights by the curious shadows of the streetlighting on the Tea Viaduct, a point of dreaming.

The Civilist Campaign

J. R. Lobão

Burying Rui Barbosa's *civilista* campaign. (Cartoon by J. R. Lobão, *O Malho*, Rio de Janeiro, 2 April 1910)

Civilian candidates only fared well during the Republic when they were supported by the political machines of the leading states. This cartoon, from Rio de Janeiro's O Malho, parodies what it depicts as the burial of the 1910 "civilist" campaign of the Bahian jurist and orator Rui [old spelling: Ruy] Barbosa, who ran against (and lost to) the war minister, Hermes da Fonseca, the nephew of the first military president of the Republic, Deodoro da Fonseca. Barbosa flitted between government and journalism, and in 1907, represented Brazil at the Hague Peace Conference. Barbosa's defeat led to punitive action by Hermes to oust entrenched civilian state oligarchies. The president's interventions, collectively known as the salvacões, *failed to accomplish far-reaching changes, since the new state governments quickly reverted to the abusive patronage system. Although Barbosa's campaign failed, it was Brazil's first "modern"-style campaign taken to the public. The irreverent cartoon—alleging electoral fraud as well as chicanery—demonstrates the extent to which political discourse was addressed to the newspaper-reading public. This atmosphere was closer to the 1930s, when the Republic would be toppled, than 1889, the point of transition from a monarchy to a federal republic.*

Gaúcho Leaders, 1923

Photograph

Political bosses from Rio Grande do Sul skillfully cultivated their state's gaúcho image. In June 1923, heads of some of the most powerful family clans gathered together to discuss politics. They included Oswaldo Aranha (far left), Laurindo Ramos (second from the left), Flôres da Cunha (fourth), and Nepomuceno Saraiva (fifth), all of whom would have leading roles in the coming 1930 revolution. No longer considered marginal players with folkloric affectations, by the early 1920s, gaúchos were prominent in the exploding tenente movement and increasingly important on the national political scene.

Gaúcho chieftains in 1923. *(Robert M. Levine Collection)*

Factory Rules, 1924

Abramo Eberle Metalworks Management

Although agriculture still dominated the economy, many Brazilians earned their living in industry by 1920. Brazilian textile manufacturers and food processors, players in the domestic market since the turn of the century, gained some momentum when World War I curtailed imports. Adjuncts to coffee production, such as rail and port facilities, also engaged Brazilians in industrial trades. Along with these symbols of progress came threats to the social hierarchy from an often militant, urban working class. Major strikes in 1917 and 1919 added substance to those threats. The following regulations were posted in the Abramo Eberle Metalworks in Caxias do Sul, in Rio Grande do Sul. As they suggest, the factory floor was the front line for the enforcement of social order, vigilance, and discipline. The fines may seem small, but workers rarely earned more than the equivalent of $1 per day.

ARTICLE ONE

Hours are the following:
October 1 to February 28, work will start at 7:30 until 12 noon, and at 1:15 until 6:15; March 1 to April 30 and August 1 to September 30, 7:30 until 12 noon, and 1:15 until 5:45; May 1 to July 31, 7:45 until 12 noon, and 1:15 until 5:15.

Workers of both sexes will start and finish work in accord with the signals from the bell. Workers' entry into the factory is not permitted after the above hours, except with express permission from the foreman and by means of explanations that, in the judgment of the same person, are satisfactory. No worker can be absent from work without previous *notice* and, if lacking this, will be subject to the fine of Rs.2$000 [25¢] for the first time, Rs.3$000 [37¢] for the second, and Rs.5$000 [62¢] for the third, after which, at the first reoccurrence, he will be dismissed for lack of discipline at work, there being exemptions for such cases as illnesses, family misfortunes, etc., which, however, will need to be proved *without lies under penalty of the proof not being accepted.*

ARTICLE TWO

No journeyman, worker, or apprentice shall exit the factory, *or the section in which he works,* without first asking permission from the foreman, explaining the reason: The same fines already referred to above and, with the reoccurrence, the same final penalty as in Article One will be applied to this infraction.

ARTICLE THREE

It remains strictly prohibited: To sing, whistle, or talk during working hours, except in the line of service. In cases of infractions committed by the nonobservance of this article, the same fines included in Article One will be applied.

ARTICLE FOUR

It is not permitted to prepare for leaving (washing, etc.) before the quitting signal is given. The use of latrines will be permitted, at the maximum, three times per day and, needing more, it is necessary to ask permission from the foreman, gatherings in the urinals being expressly prohibited. He who, because of sickness, needs to use the latrine more than three times per day, ought not to come to work. It is advised that the use of the latrines and urinals will be rigorously inspected by people who are going to be expressly employed for this purpose.

ARTICLE FIVE

Once per week, in the afternoon, the section foreman will order the cessation of work, in the sections that he might judge appropriate, a few minutes early, so that the workers might clean their machines for their good preservation, each one by himself remaining responsible for his own machine and, for each group of machines in each section, the respective foreman [remains responsible]. The foreman of each section will give a report to each worker about the tools that each one receives for his exclusive use, and for the disappearance of any tool, the worker remains responsible. It is prohibited for any worker to use tools delivered to another without previous consent from the latter. It behooves workers to return to the crib the tools that, for a temporary usage, they received from the same immediately after their use, during which they remain responsible for them. If they might not be in perfect condition and might have been ruined because of neglect, their value will be charged to him. The specialized tools from each section will be delivered to the care of the respective foreman, who will remain responsible for them.

ARTICLE SIX

During break time as also during working hours, it is prohibited to perform any work not ordered by the respective foreman. Each worker is responsible for the bad results of his labor, and from each section, the respective foreman [is responsible]. The latter is charged with making the worker pay for losses that he caused, either by neglect or carelessness, and failing to do this, it falls on the foreman to pay the said loss, if he does not indicate another responsible person. The foremen will be obligated to observe and note the fines, and if they do not, they will in turn be fined double for nonobservance of the rule. Any doubts that are raised between workers and foremen ought to be resolved by the general foreman and, according to the seriousness of the case, by one of the factory managers.

ARTICLE SEVEN

The cases not foreseen in these regulations will be resolved as follows, in this order:
   • by the section foreman;
   • by the general foreman;
   • according to the case, by one of the factory managers.
Penalties not provided for noncompliance with the regulations will be resolved in accordance with Article One, but according to the seriousness of the case and with the maximum recourse, the immediate expulsion of the worker from the factory. The product of the fines will be

delivered to a commission of four members, who will name a treasurer, who with this product, will open a current credit account in the firm, to which will be paid 8 percent interest annually, and the sum of money collected will revert, at the commission's discretion, in behalf of extraordinary needs of the workers.

ARTICLE EIGHT

The use of weapons of any type in the factory is rigorously prohibited, and whoever might enter armed, will be immediately dismissed.

ADDENDUM TO THE FACTORY RULES

All workers who do piecework remain obligated to the same rules as those who do daywork. As a consequence, they cannot:

· leave work without previous permission from the section foreman or, in addition, the general foreman;

· enter after the start of work or interrupt work before the bell rings; or

· pass, during working hours, from one section to another and converse either with pieceworkers or dayworkers.

Transgressors breaking these clauses will be fined.

III

Slavery and Its Aftermath

During the first phase of the Portuguese development of Brazil, natives were used as slaves. The transition to a predominantly African slave force occurred gradually, over the course of the second half century after discovery. As late as the 1560s, there were virtually no African slaves engaged in northeastern sugar production.[1] Once Africans began to be imported in large numbers, they were set to the hardest tasks in the fields, leaving to Indians the lighter duties of cultivation. By the mid-1580s, Africans comprised about one-third of the slave population in Pernambuco, the most prosperous sugar-producing captaincy. But the Portuguese perceived that Africans could be worked harder and taught more difficult skills. Records from 1572 show that an African was sold for twenty-five *réis,* whereas an Indian with the same skills brought only nine *réis.* By the mid–seventeenth century, the importation of slaves from Africa increased significantly. During the 1700s, tens of thousands of slaves were disembarked in Atlantic port cities, with as many as 86,400 arriving between 1701 and 1710. Because profitability from sugar production was in decline owing to competition from the West Indies, many landowners sold their slaves south, especially to Minas Gerais, 400 kilometers inland from the coast, where alluvial deposits of gold and diamonds had been discovered. The eighteenth-century gold rush attracted thousands of Portuguese settlers and adventurers, and shifted the focus of economic development south. This was reflected in the 1763 move of the royal capital of Brazil from Salvador in Bahia to Rio de Janeiro. The demand for slaves in the mining region was so high that 60 percent of the slaves arriving in Salvador were reexported to the gold mines of the interior.[2]

The transatlantic slave trade flourished. High levels continued until the early 1820s, when disruptions caused by the European conflicts that led to Latin American independence, and opposition to the slave trade from the British caused a decline in the trade. The British and American trades ended after the first decade of the nineteenth century, and slavery was legally abolished in the English colonies in 1834. Most of the new Spanish American republics outlawed slavery as well. Only Brazil, Cuba, and Puerto Rico continued to import slaves from Africa as the nineteenth century progressed.[3]

Two-thirds of the inhabitants of Brazil at the dawn of the nineteenth century were African-born slaves or their descendants. During the colonial period, slaves had been imported in vast numbers to work Brazil's mines and plantations. Conditions were brutal, and many slaves risked their lives to run away. As many as 20,000 escaped slaves lived for years in a fugitive slave encampment at Palmares before it was weakened by internal divisiveness and finally destroyed by royal forces in 1694. We now know that there probably were hundreds of *quilombos*—runaway slave settlements—throughout colonial Brazil, although most did not last very long and were ruthlessly suppressed. Some of these settlements may have been aided by local Indians; some even existed in urban areas, including Rio de Janeiro. Violent resistance to slavery in urban areas, however, was limited to acts by individuals or small groups, whereas in Bahia, for example, many slave revolts occurred.[4]

Brazilian slaves, on the whole, came from four distinct points of origin. Most came from West-Central Africa, either from Congo North (or Cabinda), Luanda, or Bengeula, the latter two both being ports in Angola. The majority of the Africans imported after 1840, as part of the illegal slave trade with Brazil, came from Cabinda because the British were blockading the Angolan ports. The second major source of slaves was East Africa, from today's southern Tanzania, northern Mozambique, Malawi, and northeastern Zambia. Additional slaves came from Madagascar and from West Africa, along the present-day Gold Coast and Guinea, including Dahomey (now Benin), Ghana, western and eastern Nigeria, and the Bight of Biafra. Some of these peoples were Muslims, possibly from present-day northern Cameroon.

The slave trade was unspeakably cruel. Thomas Ewbank, who visited Brazil in the 1850s and published a journal in 1856, described the sufferings of slaves in urban Rio de Janeiro, where—according to Gilberto

Freyre—slavery was supposed to be fairly benign. A few members of the elite (and a number of free mulattoes as well) became fervent abolitionists. The most eloquent voice against slavery was that of Joaquim Nabuco, who spent much of his career in the diplomatic service in Great Britain and the United States, and who, more than anyone else, is associated with raising the consciousness of Brazilians of his class about the intrinsic evil of slavery. The "Golden Law" (*Lei Aurea*) signed by Princess Isabel in the absence of her father, the Emperor Pedro II, who was abroad, culminated the gradual process of emancipation that had started in 1871. In that year, parliament enacted the Law of the Free Womb (*Ventre Livre*), which declared all children born to slaves to be free, although owners were given the option of freeing children at age eight (in exchange for government compensation) or keeping them in service until the age of twenty-one without compensation. The law had the effect of prolonging slavery and dampening abolitionist pressures, but since the slave trade had effectively been brought to a halt in 1850 owing to British naval intervention, slavery was on its way out. In 1885, a second antislavery act, the Saraiva-Cotegipe Law, declared free all slaves at the age of sixty. Cynics noted that this benefited slave owners, since the laws relieved them of legal responsibility for slaves who had, in most cases, grown too old to work. On May 13, 1888, the empress finally abolished slavery completely. Slave owners were angered and withdrew their support from the monarchy, which fell a year later.

Emancipation brought little respite from hardship for the former slaves. The abolitionist movement died, and government authorities took steps to keep former slaves from wandering into towns and cities in desperate search of work. Many places enacted vagrancy laws transparently aimed at controlling the movement of ex-slaves. In the countryside, there were few opportunities for work, and virtually no schools or opportunities for training. The vast Northeast languished in economic depression throughout the nineteenth century, and the coming of the agro-industrial sugar factories (*usinas*) in the sugarcane-growing regions of the Northeast and the State of Rio de Janeiro made it possible for producers to hire day laborers for a pittance and, if they wished, to drive the families of ex-slaves from their properties. The neglect of the former slaves amounts to one of the bleakest chapters in Brazil's long history of governmental insensitivity to the needs of its underclass, largely black and of mixed race.

Notes

1 Stuart B. Schwartz, *Sugar Plantations in the Formation of Brazilian Society: Bahia, 1550–1835* (Cambridge: Cambridge University Press, 1985), p. 65.
2 Herbert S. Klein, *African Slavery in Latin America and the Caribbean* (New York: Oxford University Press, 1986), pp. 67–68.
3 Schwartz, *Sugar Plantations,* p. 343; Klein, *African Slavery,* p. 150.
4 Mary C. Karasch, *Slave Life in Rio de Janeiro, 1808–1850* (Princeton, N.J.: Princeton University Press, 1987), pp. 323–24.

The War against Palmares

Anonymous

I. Governor's Report, 1675–1678

Early on, Portuguese Brazil set a pattern that would endure throughout the Americas for parts of four centuries: lucrative sugar exports and African slavery traveled hand in hand. The northeastern captaincy of Pernambuco, the world's richest sugar producer during the sixteenth and much of the seventeenth centuries, earnestly began importing African slaves after 1570, and almost immediately, some captives fled to the wide-open frontier where they formed quilombos, or runaway slave communities. With slave owners in Pernambuco and neighboring captaincies distracted by Dutch invaders between 1630 and 1654, quilombos swelled in size and number. The most famous ones united into the Republic of Palmares, or simply Palmares. Palmares offered African slaves (and even impoverished Europeans) an alternative to the harshness of the plantation. Perhaps most troubling to Crown officials, an independent Republic of Palmares might ally with European rivals in an attempt to expel the Portuguese from Brazil entirely. The following report underscores the peril that a well-organized and armed Palmares presented.

The captaincies of Pernambuco have been returned to the dominion of Your Highness and are now free from the foreign enemies who came to conquer them. Our weapons are powerful enough to beat that enemy who oppressed us for so many years, but were never effective in destroying the opposite enemy who infested us internally and who inflicted losses just as great. Neglect did not cause this failure, because every governor who lived in Recife carefully engaged in this campaign. However, the difficulties of the terrain, the ruggedness of the roads, and the impossibility of transportation made the campaign unrealistic for those lacking prowess. The best commanders in the ranks and the most battle-tested soldiers were occupied in these levies, and the labors that they endured were not trivial, but they reaped very little fruit.

To prove the uniqueness of these campaigns, I will briefly recapitulate the information that I discovered through experience. Extending through the upper reaches of the Rio São Francisco is a chord of untamed forest that bounds the *sertão* [backlands] of Cabo de Santo Agostinho, running almost north to south, paralleling the coast. The *palmares agrestes* [wild palms of the region] are the principal trees and gave the region its name. The trees are so richly endowed that people use them to make wine, oil, salt, and clothing. Their leaves serve as roofing, the branches for supports, and the fruit for sustenance. And the texture that covers the stalks in the trunk makes string for all types of bonds and rope. These *palmares* do not run so uniformly that other forests with diverse trees do not separate them, and within a distance of sixty leagues are found distinct *palmares*. To the northwest, sixteen leagues from Porto Calvo, is the *mucambo* [hiding place for runaway slaves] of Zambi; five leagues north of that is Arotireui; a little east of that are the two *mucambos* of the Tabocas; fourteen leagues northwest of these is Dambrabanga; eight leagues to the north is the walled city called Subupira; six more leagues to the north, the royal walled city called Macaco; five leagues to the west is the *mucambo* of Osenga; nine leagues northwest from our settlement of Serinhaem, the city of Amaro; and twenty-five leagues northwest from Alagoas is the Palmare of Andalaquituxe. These are the largest and most defendable, but there are others of less importance and with fewer people. These *mucambos* are various distances from our settlements, according to the direction, because they are spread out over forty or fifty leagues.

The area is naturally rugged, mountainous, and wild, supporting all varieties of known and unknown trees with such thickness and entangled branches that, in many places, it is impenetrable by light. A diversity of thorns and creeping, harmful plants and intertwined trunks impedes passage. Spread out among the hills are very fertile plains for cultivation. To the west of the *sertão* of Palmares stretch extensive, infertile fields useful only as pastures.

In this uncultivated and natural refuge are gathered some Negroes to whom, either because of their crimes or the stubbornness of their masters, Palmares seems less punishing than what they fear [as slaves]. With so much imagination, they felt more secure where they could be more at risk. The open pastures of cattle ranches facilitated their escape. By taking prisoners and persuading others with hopes of liberty, they started to spread out and multiply.

People think that once Negro slaves arrived in these captaincies, Palmares started to have inhabitants. When Holland occupied Recife, the number of inhabitants increased since the same disturbance for the masters was a release for the slaves. Over time, Palmares grew, and the nearness of settlers made them deft with arms. Today, they use all types of arms. They make bows and arrows, but steal and purchase firearms. Our assaults have made them wary and experienced. They do not all live in the same place, so that one defeat will not wipe them out. Distinct functions exist in Palmares as much for sustenance as for security. There are great workers who plant all the land's vegetables, and prudently store fruits for the winter and times of war. Their main sustenance is coarse corn, from which they make various appetizing foods. Hunting provides much food because those forests are abundant.

They wage all forms of war, with all the superior commanders and inferiors, as much for victory in battle as for assistance to the king. They all obey the one who is called *Ganga Zumba,* or in other words, Great Lord. As the king or lord, he enjoys everything produced in Palmares in addition to imported goods. He has a palace and a royal cloak, and is attended to by guards and officers who are accustomed to royal houses. In all respects, he receives a king's treatment and the ceremonies proper for a lord. People immediately kneel in his presence, applaud him, and affirm his excellence. They speak to him as His Majesty and obey him out of admiration. He lives in the royal city called Macaco, a common name for death, which they associated with an animal [the monkey]. This city is the metropolis among the rest of the cities and settlements. It is fortified entirely by a wall of wattle and daub, with openings aimed so that the combatants might harm your safety. The area outside the wall is entirely planted with iron spikes, and such clever traps that even the most vigilant will be imperiled. This city occupies a wide area and is composed of more than 1,500 houses. Among the residents are ministers of justice for the necessary execution of laws. They imitate everything found in a republic.

Although these savages have completely forgotten bondage, they have not entirely lost recognition of the church. In this city, crowds have recourse to a chapel and entrust their worries with images. At the chapel's entrance is a very perfect image of the child Jesus, and others of Our Lady of Conception and Saint Bras. They choose one of the smartest to revere as the priest who baptizes and marries them. However, baptism does not follow the form determined by the church, and marriages are not the special events that the law of nature still demands. Lust is the rule for selection of mates, and each has the women he desires. Some Christian prayers are learned and documents of faith compatible with their abilities are observed. The king who lives in this city was accompanied by three women, a mulatta and two *crioulas* [dark-skinned minors]. By the first, he had many children, but from the others none. Their style of dress is the same as observed among us: more or less clothed according to the possibilities.

This is the principal city of Palmares and the king who dominates it. The rest of the cities are the responsibility of sovereigns and superior commanders, who govern and live in them . . .

This is the enemy who lasted for so many years within these captaincies, who defended the area, who perseveres. Our injuries from this enemy are innumerable because they endanger the Crown and destroy the settlers . . .

Vassals are destroyed because the enemy wrecks havoc on life, honor, and possessions. Regarding the latter, they demolish property and rob slaves. As for honor, women and daughters are irreverently treated. As for life, vassals are always exposed to sudden assaults. Furthermore, the roads are not free and journeys not safe, so that one only travels with troops who can repel the enemy.

II. Agreement with Domingos Jorge Velho
for the Conquest and Destruction of Palmares, 1693

Palmares survived for over sixty years despite repeated Portuguese military offensives. Peace appeared imminent when, in 1678, the Portuguese negotiated a pact with Palmares's leader, Ganga-Zumba. However, a younger generation of Palmarinos rejected the compromise, and when Ganga-Zumba died shortly thereafter, possibly at the hands of the dissenters, leadership passed to the hard-liner Zumbi. Meanwhile, settlers from the southern captaincy of São Paulo, the bandeirantes, *were building a reputation as frontiersmen and fighters. During their expeditions in search of gold and Indian slaves, the* bandeirantes *explored some of South America's most forbidding regions, thereby justifying Portuguese land claims well beyond the limits previously agreed on with Spain. After decades of frustrated Crown efforts against Palmares, Governor João da Cunha Souto Maior quite naturally turned to the* paulista *leader, Domingos Jorge Velho. Their 1693 agreement was concise, yet fully expressed the Crown's profound wish that Palmares be annihilated once and for all. Although Domingos Jorge Velho triumphed, Palmares and Zumbi remain fundamental to Brazilian lore and national identity.*

CONDITIONS ARRANGED WITH THE GOVERNOR OF THE *PAULISTAS*, DOMINGOS JORGE VELHO, ON AUGUST 14, 1693, FOR THE CONQUEST AND DESTRUCTION OF THE NEGROES OF PALMARES

Articles and conditions that the Governor João da Cunha Souto Maior concedes to Colonel Domingos Jorge Velho to conquer, destroy, and suppress totally the rebellious Negroes of Palmares with his people and officers who accompany him, and the governor is obliged in these articles to execute the inferred [conditions] . . .

1. The governor gives to the said colonel 200 kilograms each of powder and lead for the first expedition.

2. The governor will order given to him 600 *alqueires* (measures) of flour . . . placed in the villa of Alagôas, and the said colonel is then obliged to transport it with his Indians.

3. The governor gives more than 1,000 *cruzados* (units of currency) from the public treasury, contributing firearms and other supplies for the campaign.

4. The governor relinquishes to the colonel the prisoners' jewels and the *quintos* (tax revenues), which they took from Your Majesty, so that the said Colonel Domingos Jorge Velho can divide everything between himself and his officers as he sees fit.

5. After suppressing the said Negroes, they cannot use their services in these captaincies, and he, Domingos Jorge, will be obliged to have all the prisoners put in the plaza in Recife, from there to sell them to Rio de Janeiro or Buenos Aires . . . and only the Negro children of Palmares from seven to twelve years of age can stay in these captaincies, some who will be sold according to their value for the account of the said colonel and his people.

6. The governor will give to the said conquerors land grants in the

same Palmares region, so they can populate and cultivate the land as their own, living as subjects and with the same lands under the dominion of Your Majesty, whom God watches over.

7. Said Domingos Jorge is obliged to prevent any Negro from fleeing his master to the said lands and settlements; instead, he will quickly return them to their masters.

8. From now on, neither the governor nor the said colonel can pardon the Negroes since the governor does not want . . . the Negroes, in any manner, to become free from captivity on account of the terrible consequences that would follow against the people.

Slave Life at Morro Velho Mine

Sir Richard Francis Burton

Great Britain invested heavily in nineteenth-century Latin America. Since this was especially true in Brazil, the British sent emissaries who might accurately assess investment opportunities while charming their hosts. And who better to fill such a position than the famous adventurer, Sir Richard Francis Burton? Burton arrived in Santos as the new British consul in 1865 and soon impressed Emperor Dom Pedro II with his knowledge of Portuguese. Eighteen months later, he set out for Minas Gerais to survey its mineral wealth. While there, Burton visited Morro Velho, a British-operated gold mine. Although the British had pressured the Brazilians into banning slave imports less than two decades earlier, Burton leaves no doubt as to the labor regimen at the British enclave. His comments remind us that even in the midst of suffering, tragedy, and rigid social control, slaves might carve out moments of reprieve.

A peculiar sight, and very fit for a photograph, is the muster of the blacks that takes place every second Sunday. When we were there, about 1,100 out of 1,452 attended in the "compound" fronting the "*casa grande.*" Both sexes were barefooted—everywhere in Brazil, a token of slavery. The women, fronted by a picket of twelve young girls, were ranged in columns of six companies. They were dressed in the "sabbath" uniform: white cotton petticoats with narrow red band round the lower third, cotton shawls striped blue and white, and a bright kerchief, generally scarlet, bound round the wool. On the proper right, perpendicular to the column, are the "good-conduct women." The first year's badge is a broad red band round the white hem, replaced by narrow red stripes, one for each year, till the mystic number seven gives freedom. We saw ten women and as many men officially apply for the preliminaries to manumission.

Ranged behind the women, the men are clothed in white shirts, loose blue woollen pants, red caps—Turkish or Glengarry—and cotton trousers. The "jacket men," as the "good conducts" are called, stand on the proper left of, and at right angles to, the battalion of Amazons. They wear tailless coats of blue serge, bound with red cuffs and collars, white waistcoats, overalls with red stripes down the seams, and the usual bonnets; each has a medal with the Morro Velho stamp, the badge of approaching freedom. Children of an age to attend the review are clad in the same decent, comfortable way; a great contrast they offer to the Negrolings that sprawl about the land.

The slaves answer to the roll call made by the heads of the respective departments. This done, the superintendent, followed by the manager and assistant manager of the blacks, and the two medical officers, walks down the companies and minutely inspects each individual. I observed that almost all the "chattels" were country-born; there was only one Munjolo [African tribesman], distinguished by the three scars of his race; the other "persons held to service" call him "Papagente" or man-eater.

After inspection, a pay table was spread before the door, and the girls and small children received their allowance of pay and soap. The three coppers of former days have been raised to six to eight for those employed on the spalling floor, and the stone carriers get twelve "dumps" of "obligation." By extra earnings and overtime, the pay will increase to sixteen to twenty coppers. Each takes per week half a pound of soap. The men and married women are paid at the Public Office. The former anciently received four coppers, now they get double and, by industry, may gain from eight to ten *patacas* [Brazilian coins] each of eight coppers.

Muster over, both sexes and all ages are marched off to church. The day is then their own. The industrious will look after house and garden, pigs and poultry; they will wash and sew, or fetch water, wood, or grass for sale. The idle and dissolute will keep the day holy in African fashion: lie in the sun, smoke, and if they can, drink and smoke hemp, like the half-reclaimed savages of "Sã Leone." Dinah here and elsewhere is proverbially fond of trinkets and fine rags. Parade over, she will doff her regimental attire, and don a showy printed gown and a blazing shawl, the envy of all beholders.

Once the Negroes showed us what in Hindostan is called "*tamasha*," in Spain and Portugal a "*folía*," in Egypt and Morocco a "*fantasíyah*," and here a "*Congáda*" or *Congo-ry*. A score of men, after promenading through the settlement, came to the *casa grande*. They were dressed, as they fondly imagined, after the style of the Agua-Rosada house, descended from the great Manikongo and hereditary lords of Congo land. But the toilettes, though gorgeous with coloured silks and satins, were purely fanciful, and some wore the *Kanitar* or plumed headgear, and the *Arasvia* or waist fringe, and carried the *Tacape* or tomahawk belonging to the red man. All were armed with sword and shield, except the king, who in sign of dignity, carried his scepter, a stout and useful stick. The masked old man—with white beard, trembling under-jaw, *chevrotante* voice, and testy manner—was cleverly represented by a young black from Sabará. On his right sat the captain of war, the premier; on his left, the young prince, his son and heir, an uninteresting Negrokin. Of course, the buffoon of the Dahoman court was there, and the fun consisted in kicking and cuffing him as if he were one of our clowns or "pantaloons."

The "play" was a representation of the scenes that most delight that mild and amiable Negro race: orders for a slave hunt; the march, accompanied with much running about and clashing of swords, which all handled like butchers' knives; the surprise, dragging in prisoners, directions to put to death recreant ministers and warriors, poisonings and administering antidotes—in fact, "savage Africa." His Majesty freely used his staff, threshing everybody right regally. The speeches were delivered in a singsong tone; the language was Hamitico-Lusan, and there was an attempt at cadence and rhyme. Slaughtering the foreman and drinking his blood were the favourite topics, varied by arch allusions to the superintendent and his guests. After half an hour, they received their *bakshish* and went to show their finery elsewhere.

The ceremonies of the Sunday ended with five couples bringing up as many newly baptized bits of black, to receive the reward of fertility. Payment for progeny is a good idea; as a rule, the Brazilian slave girl says, "What has a captive to do with children?" At Morro Velho, on the contrary, Negresses desire issue because they are temporarily taken off work. Unfortunately, when the second babe is to be born, the first is neglected, and the doctor is rarely sent for till death is at hand. It is an object to nurse only one child, and to be ready for bearing another when required. Thus, the hospital books for the first six months of 1867 show that the death rate of Negroes has doubled the birthrate: with a total of 1,452, 16 were born and 32 died.

The sires of "occipital race" are in a state of wonderful grin—"*patulis stant rietibus omnes."* The mothers, in marvelous gold chains, are marshaled by a big black Meg Merrilies, who seems omnipotent over her sable flock. Each matron receives a *mil-réis,* a bottle of wine, and a bit of the best advice from the superintendent. When the ceremony ends, the scamp of the party—he is ever foremost on such occasions—proposes three cheers and a tiger for Mr. Gordon, and all depart in high feather.

A slave muster is also held daily in the great hall of the "Blacks' Ranch," which is lighted up during the dark season. The bell sounds at 5:00 A.M.; half an hour afterward, the Brazilian assistants, in the presence of Mr. Smyth, call out the names, first of the men, then of the women, and lastly of the newcomers, who being sometimes rebelliously inclined, are being broken to harness. Breakfast is cooked overnight, and each labourer carries off his meal.

I also visited the hospital, which is under the charge of Mrs. Holman, the matron, and inspected the reports, transmitted monthly and yearly to the directors. The building is as well situated as any other, and is clean and new, spacious and convenient; the medical men live close by. Yet the blacks have, like sepoys, an aversion to it, and prefer to die in their own huts; consequently, many of them are brought in only when moribund. There is a white ward, but Englishmen are usually treated at home, and they get sick leave, if absence from work be deemed necessary . . .

. . . Women about to become mothers are taken off work and sent to hospital in the fourth month. After confinement, they are relieved from hard labour and sometimes work for half a year in the sewing department. Those familiar with the condition of the Lancashire "bloomers," of the Cornish women who assist in dressing the tin ores, and of the English agricultural labourers' wives generally, will own that the slave mother is far better treated at the Morro Velho mines. The young children, tended by an elderly woman, play under a large tiled shed in the great square of the Bôa Vista quarters. But the Negro in Brazil is an exotic, he is out of his proper ethnic centre; it is difficult to keep him alive, as the next quarter century will prove, and when young, he requires every attention from the parent. The Brazilian planter who would not see the number of his slaves diminish, allows the children to be with their mothers, and the latter to be off work for two and even three years.

Scenes from the Slave Trade

Logbook Entries; João Dunshee de Abrantes

At least 3,600,000 black slaves were brought to Brazil alive, while thousands more perished aboard the ships traveling from Africa to Brazil. Between 1800 and 1852, during the period when some European nations began to turn against the institution of slavery and pressure slave traders to cease, more than 1,600,000 slaves arrived in Brazil. In Africa, slaves were captured, branded, placed in heavy iron manacles, and transported on voyages that sometimes took as long as eight months to reach their final destination. The international trade was outlawed in 1830, but slave ships continued to journey to Brazil. By the 1840s, the British were seizing ships carrying slaves and freeing their captives, although when slavers saw hostile naval vessels approaching, they often threw their human cargo into the sea to avoid fines and the confiscation of their ships. The first two selections were written in logbooks aboard British naval ships in February 1841. The third passage was written by João Dunshee de Abrantes, a Brazilian abolitionist, in the northern port of São Luiz [Luis] do Maranhão.

I. Logbook from the Warship *Fawn*

The living, the dying, and the dead, huddled together in one mass. Some unfortunates in the most disgusting state of smallpox, distressingly ill with ophthalmia, a few perfectly blind, others living skeletons, with difficulty crawled from below, unable to bear the weight of their miserable bodies. Mothers with young infants hanging at their breasts, unable to give them a drop of nourishment. How they had brought them thus far appeared astonishing: all were perfectly naked. Their limbs were excoriated from lying on the hard plank for so long a period. On going below, the stench was insupportable. How beings could breathe such an atmosphere, and live, appeared incredible. Several were under the soughing, which was called the deck, dying—one dead.

II. Logbook from the British Hospital Ship *Crescent*

Huddled together on deck, and clogging up the gangways on either side, cowered, or rather squatted, 362 Negroes, with disease, want, and misery stamped on them with such painful intensity as utterly beggars all powers of description. In one corner . . . a group of wretched beings lay stretched, many in the last stages of exhaustion, and all covered with the pustules of smallpox. Several of these, I noticed, had crawled to the spot where the water had been served out, in the hope of procuring a mouthful of the precious liquid; but unable to return to their proper places, lay prostrate around the empty tub. Here and there, amid the throng, were isolated cases of the same loathsome disease in its confluent or worst form, and cases of extreme emaciation and exhaustion, some in a state of perfect stupor, others looking around piteously, and pointing with their fingers to their parched mouths. . . . On every side, squalid and sunken visages were rendered still more hideous by the swollen eyelids and the putrid discharge of a virulent ophthalmia, with which the majority appeared to be afflicted; added to this were figures shriveled to absolute skin and bone, and doubled up in a posture that originally want of space had compelled them to adopt, and that debility and stiffness of the joints compelled them to retain.

III. Captives

Removed from the ship into barges, they came in neck chains, or *libambos,* leashed to one another to stop them from running away or throwing themselves into the water. Often, they had already been divided into lots before leaving the ship. And they were delivered in bunches to the merchants or the bush captains, representatives of the planters of the interior of the province. Since, in certain seasons, the ships remained two or three days in view of the harbor entrance without being able to enter, the buyers went out to meet them in boats to complete the transactions. The traffickers did everything they could to land those horrible cargoes at once. And after a certain number of years in the business, their service was perfected, and usually only sick slaves or those of a weak constitution set foot on the soil of San Luiz. These were sold at any price, while the other unfortunates, descended from good races, were haggled over and high offers were made.

Cruelty to Slaves

Thomas Ewbank

In his 1947 book, Slave and Citizen, *Frank Tannenbaum—drawing on the work of Gilberto Freyre—suggested that Brazilian slavery had been more humane than the North American version. His thesis sparked a debate that occasionally engages scholars even today. In many ways, however, the argument has become superfluous. Historians such as Eugene Genovese and Emilia Viotti da Costa, an American and a Brazilian respectively, have shown that benign slavery never existed in the Americas. Undoubtedly, they based much of their opinions on firsthand accounts by foreign travelers like Thomas Ewbank, who visited Brazil in the 1850s. The tortures described in his travelogue vividly attest to Brazilian slavery's dehumanizing character. One of the contemporary lithographs reproduced here, on the other hand, while depicting the use of the iron mask on slaves, renders the encounter between the two fettered slaves in a picturesque way, thereby draining it of its shock value. The other drawing, of the face mask apparatus itself, at first glance looks more like a Carnival costume than a device for punishment.*

It is said slaves in masks are not so often encountered in the streets as formerly, because of a growing public feeling against them. I met but three or four, and in each case, the sufferer was a female. The mask is the reputed ordinary punishment and preventative of drunkenness. As the barrel is often chained to the slave that bears it, to prevent him from selling it for rum, so the mask is to hinder him or her from conveying the liquor to the mouth, below which the metal is continued, and opposite to which there is no opening.

Observing one day masks hanging out for sale at a tin and sheet iron store, I stopped to examine them, and subsequently borrowed one, from which the annexed sketch is taken. Except a projecting piece for the nose, the metal is simply bent cylinderwise. Minute holes are punched to

Two slaves depicted as appearing to chat happily, even as they are bound by eighteenth-century devices of restraint: a mask to prevent eating, and chains at the ankle and around the neck. (Bibloteca Nacional, Rio de Janeiro)

admit air to the nostrils, and similar ones in front of the eyes. A jointed strap (of metal) on each side goes round below the ears (sometimes two) and meets one that passes over the crown of the head. A staple unites and a padlock secures them.

At most of the smiths' shops, collars are exposed, as horseshoes are with our blacksmiths; at one shop in Rua das Violas, there was quite a variety, with gyves, chains, etc. Most of the collars were of five-eighths-inch-round iron, some with one prong, others with two, and some with none except a short upright tubular lock.

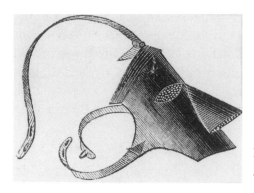

Detail of a face mask. *(Bibloteca Nacional, Rio de Janeiro)*

Here, too, were the heaviest and cruelest instruments of torture—shackles for binding the ankles and wrists close together, and consequently doubling the bodies of the victims into the most painful and unnatural positions. Had I not seen them, I could hardly have thought such things were [possible]. While making a memorandum of their form and dimensions, the proprietor or his adjutant, a black man in his shirt sleeves, came from the rear, and handling them, spoke by way of recommending them, supposing I was a customer. They were made of bar iron, *three inches wide and three-eighths of an inch thick!* Each consisted of three pieces, bent, jointed, and fastened, as shown in the margin [of his journal]. The large openings were for the legs, the smaller for the wrists. A screw bolt drew the straight parts close together. . . . The distance from joint to joint was two feet.

Such are the tortures that slaves privately endure in the cellars, garrets, and outhouses of their masters. T____, a native merchant, says another common punishment is to enclose the legs in wooden shackles or stocks. Some owners fasten their slaves' hands in similar devices, and some again, retain relics of the old thumbscrews to lock those members together. In the northern provinces, he says, the slaves are much worse used than in Rio; that it is no uncommon thing to tie their hands and feet together, hoist them off the ground, and then "beat them as near to death as possible." A heavy log fastened by a chain to the neck or leg of a slave who has absconded, or who is supposed to be inclined to run away, is a usual punishment and precaution. He is compelled to labor with it, laying it on the ground when at work, and bearing it under his arm or on his shoulder when he moves.

I observed one day a slave wearing a collar, the largest and roughest of hundreds I have seen. . . . Of inch-round iron, with a hinge in the middle, made by bending the metal of its full size into loops, the open ends flattened and connected by a half-inch rivet. The upright bar terminated in a *death's head,* which reached above that of the wearer, and to it another piece, in the form of the letter S, was welded. The joint galled him, for he kept gathering portions of his canvas shirt under it. Rest or sleep would seem impossible.

A Bahian planter, the brother of an ex-councillor, dined with us one day and spoke with much freedom on slavery. Like most men, he thinks the land can never be cultivated in the northern provinces by whites. The city slaves of Bahia, he said, are principally Minas (from El Mina on the West African coast). Shrewd and intelligent, they preserve their own language, and by that means, organize clubs and mature schemes of revolution that their brethren of Pernambuco have repeatedly attempted to carry out. Some write Arabic fluently and are vastly superior to most of their masters. In the interior, he remarked, the slaves are badly fed, worse clothed, and worked so hard that the average duration of their lives [after enslavement] does not exceed six years. In some districts it reaches to eight, while the number that see ten years after leaving Africa is small indeed. Deceptions are played off on foreign agents of the slavery commissions. These visit the *engenhos* once or twice a year. The planters, informed when they set out, have their slaves decently garbed and *well oiled,* to make them look supple and in good condition. On a late visit, the examiners were so highly gratified that one left and wrote home a flattering account of the treatment of the helots. The other continued his inquiries, came to a fazenda where he was not looked for, and there beheld what he did not expect—a Negro about to be *boiled to death* for some act of insubordination. His owner had incited, according to custom in such cases, neighboring proprietors to witness the tragedy.

From the little I have seen, I should suppose the country slaves are the worst off. Every morning, while nature was enshrouded in the blackness of darkness, did I hear them driving wagons through the thick mist, and as late as ten at night were they shouting at the oxen as the jolting and groaning wheels rolled by. (This was, however, in the busiest season.) I often wondered how they found their way over the horrid roads, how their naked feet and limbs escaped unharmed, and how they then worked in the fields, unless their pupils had the expansile and contractile powers of night animals.

On large estates, a few days' rest are given them every three or four weeks during the sugar season, but on smaller ones, where owners commonly have difficulty in keeping out of debt, they fare badly and are worked to death. Staggering into their huts, or dropping where their labors close, hardly do their aching bones allow the angel of sleep to drive away the memory of their sorrows, than two demons, lurking in the bell and lash, awaken them to fresh tortures. To say these poor creatures are better off than when ranging their native lands is an assertion that language lacks the power justly to describe. It may be true, if the life of an omnibus hack is better than that of a wild horse of Texas. I would rather, a thousand times, be a sheep, pig, or ox, have freedom, food, and rest for a season, and then be knocked on the head, than be a serf on some plantations. I say *some,* because there are in Brazil, as in other lands, humane planters.

Suicides continually occur, and owners wonder. The high-souled Minas, both men and women, are given to self-destruction. Rather than endure life on the terms it is offered, many of them end it. Then they that bought them grind their teeth and curse them, hurl imprecations after their flying spirits, and execrate the saints that let them go. If individuals are ever justified in using the power that heaven has placed in their hands to terminate at once their earthly existence, it must be these. Those who blame them for putting the only barrier between them and oppression could not endure half their woes. And how characteristic of human frailties! Here are slave dealers who weep over the legendary sufferings of a saint and laugh at worse tortures they themselves inflict; who shudder at the names of old persecutors and dream not of the armies of martyrs they make yearly; who cry over Protestants as sinners doomed to perdition and smile in anticipation of their own reception in the realms above . . .

Slavery and Society

Joaquim Nabuco

Joaquim Aurélio Nabuco de Auaújo (1849–1910), the son of a powerful imperial landowner and senator, hated slavery from the first time he saw it and spent most of his life working for its eradication. A diplomat, he was posted to England and the United States, permitting him to maintain contact with antislavery groups. An unreconstructed monarchist, he retired from public life after the fall of the Empire in 1889 and dedicated himself to writing his memoirs. He was an eloquent orator and wrote fiercely, condemning every aspect of the institution of slavery, mincing no words during a time—in the mid–nineteenth century—when society expected criticism to be indirect and subtle. Nabuco wrote the book from which this excerpt is taken in London and paid for it to be published in Portuguese by a local printing firm. He believed that independence could only be consummated by abolition, when "Brazil would be raised to the dignity of a free country before America and the world."

When slavery penetrates modern societies, it destroys a large portion of their moral justification. . . . Only one looking at these societies blinded by passion or ignorance will fail to see how slavery has brought degradation to many modern populations, to the point that they are no better than corrupted populations of past times. The use of slave labor not only hinders to the point of stagnation material development, but it deadens the moral progress of civilization, including knowledge, the arts, science, letters, costumes, government, people—in all, progress . . .

Every dimension of our social existence is contaminated by this crime: we grow with it, and it forms the basis of our society. From where does our fortune come? From profits produced by slaves. Our state of liberty was rooted in this criminal activity, and now, when we want to free ourselves from it, it holds us fast. . . . Slavery corrupts everything, robbing working people of their former virtues: diligence, thrift, charity, patriotism, fear of death, love of liberty . . .

From the womb: The slave, while still a fetus, feels the contortions of the mother under the lash. Its blood becomes corrupted. When one feels its pulse, one senses the horrible treatment of the poor black woman. In this situation of [advanced pregnancy], so grave, so much in need of assistance, she is afforded no respect, not even rest. The owner is compromising two lives. The mother rises to perform service, works; she suffers the pull of the infant on her breast, on one side, and the whip on the other . . .

Who is the father? The mother disappears or is ready to disappear as soon as nursing ends; the father remains unknown. There is no fidelity in this nameless promiscuity because there is no love. . . . There is no future, no affections, no notion of honor or duty; they must live for the present, nothing more. Food is rationed; there is nothing left to chance. Lovemaking is a union of an instant; marriage a relationship of a few days: slaves have family instincts, not feelings of sentiment. Instinct makes a child, sentiment produces a son; one makes a woman feminine, the other a wife. For these reasons, in the midst of all these men, it is impossible to know who the father is. No one has any awareness of being a father.

The feeding hour arrives. The mother has already gone back to work. The infant goes to her breast while she continues to work the soil. The lash continues to fall. Who has traveled to the interior of our provinces and has not seen lines of black women with infants at their breasts, under the heat of the sun, working ten hours at a time? This accelerates the development of the infant: the contact with the sun's rays and the mother's breast. The child gains strength: it is a natural way of creation, a savage one, rooted in milk, exhaustion, and heat. Night and day, bonded together in this same way, at the breast, one who has suffered everything, the other who is starting the process of suffering.

When the time comes to stop breast-feeding—and this time comes quickly—the child stays tethered to the mother [just] three or four days more . . .

Abolition Decree, 1888

Princess Isabel and Rodrigo Augusto da Silva

It took nearly four decades after the end of the slave trade to emancipate the remaining slaves. Owners increasingly found it difficult and costly to retrieve fugitive runaways, and the slave population was growing old. For these reasons, the imperial decree of abolition, issued while Dom Pedro was in Europe for medical treatment, was a measure that could no longer be avoided.

The Princess Imperial Regent, in the name of His Majesty the Emperor Dom Pedro II, makes known to all subjects of the Empire that the General Assembly has decreed, and she has approved, the following law:

Art. 1. From the date of this law, slavery is declared abolished in Brazil.

Art. 2. All contrary provisions are revoked.

She orders, therefore, all the authorities to whom belong the knowledge and executive of the said law to execute it, and cause it to be fully and exactly executed and observed.

The secretary of state for the departments of agriculture, commerce, and public works, and *ad interim* for foreign affairs, Bachelor Rodrigo Augusto da Silva, of the council of His Majesty, the emperor, will cause it to be printed, published, and circulated.

Given in the Palace of Rio de Janeiro, May 13, 1888, the sixty-seventh year of independence and of the Empire.

Princess Imperial Regent. Rodrigo Augusto da Silva

Laws Regulating Beggars in Minas Gerais, 1900

Legislature of Minas Gerais

Slavery was abolished as a legal institution in 1888, but nothing was done to provide for the welfare of emancipated slaves. Following abolition, most ex-slaves stayed in the places where they had been owned, eking out livings as sharecroppers or doing odd jobs for the landowning class. Others were driven by drought or lack of employment to migrate in order to avoid starvation. Fearing large influxes of poor people, most of whom were black, many Brazilian states (called provinces until 1889) promulgated laws defining vagrancy as a crime. Begging was regulated as precisely as any craft or trade, and officials were given the authority to expel anyone who did not conform to the new laws.

Decree No. 1,435 of December 27, 1900: Beggars

Art. 1: All persons who are unable to earn a living through working, who are destitute, who lack relatives or means to provide sustenance, who live by asking for alms, are considered beggars in the eyes of the law.

Art. 2: No one may ask for alms within city limits without first registering in the mayor's office as a beggar.

Art. 3: This may be either voluntary or coercive, if the police wish it. Only persons fulfilling these requirements will be eligible to beg:

    a. When the person is destitute and has no relatives to support him; and

    b. When the person was born in the city or has resided there for more than two years.

Art. 4: Any person found begging without having registered officially will be taken to the police station to be examined by a physician.

a. If he is found capable of working, he will be dealt with accordingly;

b. If he is seemed not capable of working, he will be registered as a beggar unless he is a resident for less than two years, in which case, he will be sent to the place of his former residence.

Art. 5: All physical disabilities and ailments will be noted by the Office of Hygiene.

Art. 6: Each beggar who meets the legal requirements will receive an official card to be displayed on his chest in a visible form.

Art. 7: Registered beggars are subject to the following regulations:

a. No begging outside of zones designated for this purpose or on days on the calendar not specified for begging;

b. No begging without display of the person's identity card;

c. No begging without display of the person's papers;

d. No begging using someone else's papers;

e. No cursing or saying offensive things to persons unwilling to donate alms;

f. No singing;

g. No displaying of deformities or wounds; and

h. No persons except a husband or wife, a mother or father, or small children, may accompany the beggar to the designated location for asking for alms.

IV

The Vargas Era

Getúlio Vargas came to power in 1930 at the head of the military-backed Liberal Alliance coup that its partisans called a "Revolution." If so, Vargas was, in Antonio Gramsci's phrase, a "passive revolutionary from above." The losing candidate in the national election earlier in the year (an election marked by fraud on both sides), he remained in power as head of state until 1945, and governed as elected president from 1950 until his death by suicide in 1954. Vargas's government transformed Brazil, for better or worse. An advocate of safe but bold change, he grafted new constituencies and new rules were grafted onto traditional political practices. Although his career spanned three constitutions and enormous changes in the political climate, his pragmatism always prevailed. He was willing to take risks, a trait that explains not only his political longevity, but also the miscalculations that led to his ouster in 1945 and later drove him to suicide. He was able to adjust to changes in national and international circumstances, but he fundamentally left unaltered much of the fabric of Brazilian life. Some things endured throughout his decades in power, including the readiness of the armed forces to intervene and the elite's tenacious hold on privilege. Brazil's distribution of income remained among the least equal in the world, but Vargas did not perceive this as a problem that needed to be solved.

In 1930, he had stood at the center of forces united in their demand for change and sharply divided over what results they sought. Because of this, Vargas needed to devote almost all his energy to negotiating among factions and keeping himself in power. Indeed, he was more concerned with staying in office than in holding to any firm purpose. Only in 1932, when São Paulo revolted to restore the old system, did he show that he could act decisively and with the use of force. He believed in granting regulated citizenship without disharmony, that is, without the freedom to dissent. Putting a good face on Vargas's regime in the early 1940s, a visiting political scientist called it "despotism mitigated by sloppiness." Corruption remained a national institution; little could be accomplished without bribes to expedite action.

Vargas's style was rooted in the tradition in which supplicants sought personal intervention from officials to cut through red tape or bestow favors. An irony of Vargas's legacy, therefore, was that although he championed a merit-based civil service program, the old style of personal favors not only survived in the states, but increased at the national level as a result of the government centralization. Brazilian archives are filled with personal requests to cabinet ministers (and to Vargas himself) for jobs for relatives, favorable treatment in granting contracts, or to overrule regulations—all in violation of what Vargas said he was trying to accomplish. The more government bureaucratized state employment, moreover, the more power individual administrators accumulated, and it was never certain that they would act in the interest of their constituencies. Consequently, many of Vargas's reforms ended up—intentionally or not—*para inglês ver* ("for the English to see"). His corporatist framework also encouraged authoritarian decisions, since Vargas believed that the needy would otherwise continue to be ignored.

In making himself the chief of state of all Brazilians, Vargas limited the potential for competitors to emerge. During his first government, he logged 90,000 miles visiting every corner of the country. His fame spread by word of mouth and was transferred to popular culture. Due to Vargas's unrivaled popularity, the communists had to ally with him and the political organizations he left behind after 1945, and at the same time, compete with them. Vargas also confounded his enemies by continually experimenting: during the to-be-dashed 1937 presidential campaign, for example, he had Labor Ministry officials truck in workers from government-sponsored unions to political demonstrations.

He did not hide his admiration for persons secure in their wielding of power. Goiás's state boss Pedro Ludovico recalled an encounter between Vargas and a Carajás chieftain during an excursion to a reservation in his region. When the tribesman presented Vargas with a petition, Vargas asked him by what authority he spoke for his people. "Because I have the most power," came the reply. When Vargas asked him, affably, how long he would continue to hold this power, the chief replied, "As long as I'm alive." Vargas laughed, because this was his outlook as well.

His most far-reaching goal was to modernize the country yet preserve its national independence. While this overall aim evaded him, his achievements in this regard yielded more "revolutionary" change than any other policy. The effort also usurped great resources. Government centralization was costly: funds for such massive projects as the Paulo Affonso hydroelectric station on the São Francisco River, for example, could never have been raised by states, given their constant bickering and depleted credit ratings. As a result of World War II, just as Vargas and other nationalists had feared, Brazil had become more dependent on the United States and influenced by its culture—through advertising, movies, consumer goods, and the direct effect of the behavior of the thousands of American servicemen stationed at Brazilian bases during the war.

Vargas's constant shifting produced different reformist streams. Since practicality came first, he was able to play political poker by dealing from different hands. He reorganized civil society, bringing benefits to many (but not all) urban employees and workers. The 1930 Revolution ended the more blatant abuses of the old "politics of the governors" by renewing interventionist powers that the national executive had lost in 1889, but it placed patronage and coercive powers in the hands of his interventors, and after 1945, created a hybrid form of backroom brokering involving partisan politics. The regionalist dimension of politics might have survived even more than it did had not the *paulistas* been pragmatists as well, suppressing their resistance because they agreed with Vargas's social corporatism and his measures to intervene in the economy. In the other outlying states, Vargas's interventors replaced the clans in power before 1930, but in most cases, new oligarchic alliances emerged; in the decades after Vargas's death, prominent local elites continued to dominate state politics in the old ways.

An assiduous politician and manipulator, Vargas ostracized the Left by winning over centrist nationalists in the armed forces command. Soon, he turned his attentions to the problem posed by São Paulo, the country's most powerful state, still smarting from its political defeat in 1930. São Paulo demanded a return to constitutional rule—in other words, to the pre-1930 system by which São Paulo dominated the federation. The bold measures taken by the state's leadership and the unprecedented support from ordinary *paulistas* is captured by Cristina Mehrtens's essay in this section on the "Gold for São Paulo" campaign in 1932.

Vargas ignored the countryside, even though he himself was a man of the rural frontier. The photographs of rural life in this section come from Vargas's own home state, Rio Grande do Sul. He left many institutions untouched, including Brazil's half-century-old Civil Code, a conservative legal document that reinforced patriarchal social relations, declaring husbands the legal head of their households and leaving married women virtually without rights. He left charity work in the hands of the private sector, although he turned them into semipublic agencies by giving them subsidies. During the 1920s, a number of *paulista* factories had pioneered the concept of the "workers' villages" (the Vila Operária Maria Zélia, for example), in which workers were given housing and provided with a comprehensive program of social benefits, including schools, infant-care centers, chapels, and soccer teams. The archdiocese of São Paulo maintained a Metropolitan Catholic Workers' Central, with local agencies in the working-class neighborhoods of Moóca, Penha, Bras, Barra Funda, Itaquera, Ipiranga, and Lapa. The organization built children's playgrounds, showed films, and sponsored classes for women on hygiene and domestic skills. Patrícia Galvão's novel, *Industrial Park,* excerpted herein, conveys the tensions of working-class life during the Great Depression, when Vargas and his officials attempted to squelch labor unrest by offering favored treatment to co-opted labor leaders, ignoring, in so doing, the harsh inequities of the workplace. This piece is followed by a photo essay, "Two Versions of Factory Life," which illustrates some aspects of this issue.

The collection of documents seized from members of the Brazilian Communist Party, a sampling of which are reprinted in this section, reflects the polarization in ideology that characterized the early Vargas years and the vacuum created by Vargas's decision to suppress the Left. They come from the now-famous Dossier 20 from the Political Police, opened under President Fernando Henrique Cardoso's policy giving access to historians of previously classified materials in government archives.

Vargas also tolerated the far Right, especially the fascist Integralist movement headed by would-be führer Plínio Salgado and the brains behind the movement, Gustavo Barroso, born João Dodt to a German family in the northern State of Ceará. Barroso played on Brazilian distrust for the State of São Paulo as well as anti-Semitic attitudes among the elite by accusing Jews of controlling São Paulo's financial markets, a laughable charge that did not gain many serious listeners. Francisco José de Oliveira Vianna was a more formidable voice from the far Right. A jurist and enemy of participatory democracy, he counseled Vargas privately to govern on the corporatist model: that is, to follow the fascist model of an all-powerful and all-knowing nationalistic state. Oliveira Vianna's contempt for democracy and his strange pride in his origins in the State of Rio de Janeiro's aristocracy is expressed in his obsequious letter, included in this section, to the author of a book extolling the virtues of Vargas's Estado Novo, the dictatorship imposed by the armed forces in November 1937. Reproduced here as well, Vargas's New Year's address of 1938 offers his reasons for overthrowing his own government and his plans for the country under corporatism.

Estado Novo officials aggressively announced that they were creating a new Brazil, as seen here in the propagandistic selection, "A New Survey of Brazilian Life." Outsiders viewed the Estado Novo more critically, as exemplified in two pieces. When U.S. General George C. Marshall came to Brazil in 1939 to encourage support for the allied cause, his wife, Katherine Tupper Marshall, recorded his impressions in a memoir. Scholar Bailey W. Diffie analyzed the Estado Novo in unflattering terms in his correspondence with officials of the Department of State.

The Estado Novo left a mixed bag of legislation, much of which promised major changes, but without adequate funding, failed to reach most Brazilians. Leading educational reformer Anísio S. Teixeira, whose lifelong vision for a free and high-quality system of public education was never realized, offers here an assessment of the failure of the government's efforts under Vargas. Vargas lauded public schoolteachers as the "little, overshadowed heroes of daily life," but he did little to improve their pitiful wages. At the secondary level, Brazil had fewer than a dozen no-tuition secondary schools. While Vargas's educational reforms varied enormously from state to state, his National Educational Plan, which called for free and semimandatory public education, was made part of the 1934 Constitution. In Rio de Janeiro, Teixeira took dramatic steps to professionalize education, expand matriculations, and improve schools, but he was fired as being too liberal. São Paulo achieved progress mostly under its own auspices, under the unwritten arrangement its elite had made with Vargas after 1932 to let the state carry out its own programs. The drive to modernize Brazil led Vargas to create free, comprehensive universities, but few nonelite youths who did not attend private secondary schools could hope to pass the rigorous *vestibularios* (entrance examinations).

Ousted from power by the military in 1945, Vargas regrouped during the late 1940s, capitalizing on his popularity among ordinary Brazilians. His social legislation, much of which remained in place until the late 1990s, had benefited the middle class through the creation of a vast number of bureaucratic jobs. Working-class Brazilians also benefited if they held regular jobs. When the minimum wage was introduced in 1940, eligible workers in Rio de Janeiro received the equivalent of $131 (U.S.) in 1998 value a month. This was a generous amount, although it is telling that workers continued to stay out of officially sanctioned labor unions, which not only guaranteed the minimum wage, but added benefits. The national monthly minimum wage rose to the equivalent of $252 by 1954, but thereafter went into free fall, bottoming out at $120 a month in 1992. The five personal testimonies reproduced toward the end of this section show to what extent Vargas did alter the lives of individuals; whether their stories are typical or not, however, cannot easily be verified.

Although popularly chosen in 1950 (the first time he had actually won a national election), Vargas's presidency in the early 1950s floundered. Inflation and rising expectations made it difficult for Vargas to deliver on his campaign promises, and his own supporters were divided over ideology and goals. In August 1954, confronted by an imminent military coup to oust him from the presidency, he took his own life. His suicide produced outpourings of grief that matched in intensity and scope the heartfelt shock experienced by most Americans at the death of Franklin D. Roosevelt in 1945. Even though Vargas had not provided very much, and even if the archaic hierarchical structure of the Brazilian oligarchy had remained completely intact, he was the first politician to extend dignity to the Brazilian people. In numerous places, many of the social initiatives of the 1930s (free milk for infants, water projects, inspection of meat, child care centers) were discontinued in the mid-1950s for lack of funding.

The contrast between the political spirit of the Old Republic, which despised the common people, and the uplifting rhetoric of Vargas's radio broadcasts, speeches, and public appearances even to the most remote reaches of the vast country, was striking. Vargas really had become the "father of the poor" in the minds of the mass of the population. And for nationalists, the stridency of his admonition against imperialism and foreign interests, which had dominated his suicide letter, confirmed that he was a prophet and seer. In some ways, Vargas's alarm paralleled his contemporary Dwight D. Eisenhower's warning to Americans about the "civil-military complex." Whereas Eisenhower was ignored, in Vargas's case, his campaign against foreign domination galvanized a certain sector of public opinion, even as it yielded to the developmentalism of the late 1950s, as well as the military regime of the 1960s and 1970s.

Educated Brazilians understood that the government's propaganda machine had inflated the concrete accomplishments it claimed. They also knew that their problems had not been solved, nor had their standard of living risen as far as the broadcasts and speeches promised. But Vargas had made them aware of Brazil's vulnerable place in the world, and from the first days of his Liberal Alliance presidential campaign in 1930, he had let them know that he cared about all Brazilians, not just the powerful. To the majority of the population with barely enough to eat, this mattered little in any tangible way, yet for many of these men and women, it was enough that Vargas had spoken on their behalf. Still, Brazil's "father" treated his children differently; those with darker skin and who lived in the countryside were benignly neglected in favor of those he considered to have the potential to carry out his dreams of national construction.

The Social Question

Platform of the Liberal Alliance, 1930

*Vargas campaigned for the presidency in colorless fashion, as if he expected to
lose, but his proposals for change represented a significant new direction for
Brazil. In contrast to the incumbent administration—which regarded organized labor as a matter for the police and ignored the plight of the millions of
impoverished Brazilians—Vargas's Liberal Alliance, borrowing from the exiled
tenentes, addressed social problems, as can be seen in this excerpt from their
platform. Once the successful October coup seated him as chief of state, moreover, Vargas reorganized the national government, creating new cabinet ministries to carry out some of the promises made while campaigning.*

One cannot negate the existence of a social question in Brazil as one of
the problems that will have to be dealt with seriously by public authorities. The little that we have in terms of social legislation either is not
applied or only in tiny measures, sporadically, in spite of the promises
that have been made by us as signers of the Versailles Treaty and of our
responsibilities as members of the International Labor Organization,
whose conventions and regulations we fail to observe. . . . The activities
of women and children in factories and commercial establishments in
every civilized nation are subject to special conditions that we, up to
now, unfortunately do not heed. We need to coordinate activities between the states and the federal government to study and adopt measures to create a national Labor Code. Both the urban and rural proletariat require instructional measures, applied to both, to address their
respective needs. These measures should include instruction, education,
hygiene, diet, housing, protection of women and children, of invalids
and old people, credit, salary relief, and even recreation, including sports
and artistic culture. It is time to think of creating agricultural schools and

industrial training centers, of making factories and mills safe, bringing sanitation to the countryside, constructing workers' villas, granting vacations, [establishing] a minimum salary, consumer cooperatives, and so forth.

Manifesto, May 1930

Luís Carlos Prestes

Between 1924 and 1926, Luís Carlos Prestes commanded a group of young, reform-minded military officers, the tenentes, *who traversed the Brazilian backlands hoping to stir a popular uprising. Although their mission failed, the* tenentes *captured the imagination of a public disenchanted with Brazil's traditional oligarchy. Many of these* tenentes *later resurfaced as members of the Liberal Alliance, the political coalition that seized power in 1930. Quite naturally, the Liberal Alliance sent overtures to the immensely respected Prestes in an effort to gain his endorsement. Prestes, who during his exile had visited Moscow and become a communist, replied with the following manifesto.*

To the suffering proletariat of our cities, to the workers oppressed by plantations and ranches, to the miserable masses of our backlands and very especially to the sincere revolutionaries, to those who are disposed to the struggle and to the sacrifice on behalf of the profound transformation through which we need to pass, these lines are directed.

Stripped of any rhetorical whims, they were written with the principal objective of clarifying and stating in detail my opinion with respect to the revolutionary Brazilian moment, and to show the necessity of a complete modification in the political orientation that we have been following, in order that we might be able to reach the coveted victory.

The last political campaign [the 1930 presidential election] ended adjourned. One more electoral farce, methodically and most carefully prepared by the petty politicians, it was brought to fulfillment with the ingenuous competition of many and by a great number of dreamers still not convinced of the uselessness of such efforts.

One more time, the real popular interests were sacrificed and all the people cheaply mystified by an apparently democratic campaign, but which in its depths, was nothing more than the fight between the op-

Rebel soldiers in the 1930 Revolution in the city of Recife. *(Robert M. Levine Collection)*

posite interests of two oligarchic currents, supported and stimulated by the two greatest imperialisms that enslave us, and to whom the petty Brazilian politicians deliver, with timid feet and hands, the entire Nation.

Making such affirmations, I cannot, however, cease recognizing among the elements of the Liberal Alliance a great number of sincere revolutionaries, on whom, I believe, I can still count in the frank and decided struggle that I now propose against all the oppressors. . . . Despite all this revolutionary demagoguery and despite saying that the liberals would stand up for the revocation of the latest oppressive laws, there was no one within the Liberal Alliance who would protest against the brutal political persecution by which the proletarian associations of the entire Country were victims during the last electoral campaign, and in Rio Grande do Sul itself, during the height of elections, there was initiated the most violent persecution against workers fighting for their own rights. The reactionary proposals of the struggling oligarchies are identical [to those of the Liberal Alliance] . . .

The heroes of the 1930 Revolution. (CPDOC Fundação Getúlio Vargas, Coleção Revolução de 30, Rio de Janeiro)

Heroes

of the Revolution

Composite Postcard Photograph

Most, but not all, of the leading figures of the Liberal Alliance Revolution of 1930 are included in this composite photograph sold as a postcard. It likely dates from 1932 or 1933. Luís Carlos Prestes is excluded, as is tenente *Siqueira Campos, who died in an airplane crash. João Pessoa is there, although it was his assassination in mid-1930 that propelled the revolutionary movement to its final stage. João Alberto Lins de Barros, the unpopular interventor in São Paulo, is absent, but Cardinal Sebastião Leme, a Vargas crony who played no known role in the coup, stands one photo removed from Vargas himself.*

The "Gold for São Paulo" Building, 1932

Cristina Mehrtens

Regional conflict was a main ingredient in the Liberal Alliance's coup d'état of 1930. Throughout the Old Republic, São Paulo state had dominated the Brazilian economy because of its huge coffee exports. Politically, paulistas had shared power with the neighboring dairy state of Minas Gerais, forming the well-known café com leite coalition. When the former violated that informal agreement in 1930, interests in Minas Gerais joined those from peripheral states and the military in the Liberal Alliance. São Paulo's fortunes might have appeared glum after the 1930 coup. The worldwide depression had wiped out demand for coffee. Meanwhile, the new president, Getúlio Vargas, imposed state governors, or interventors, who were openly hostile to São Paulo. The state, however, remained the wealthiest in Brazil and commanded a state militia that rivaled the national army. With those assets at its disposal, São Paulo revolted against the Vargas regime in 1932. The following article shows that even though São Paulo lost the brief civil war, it nonetheless secured important political concessions. Furthermore, the events of 1932 left paulistas with an invigorated identity that portended their state's meteoric development into Latin America's premier industrial and financial center.

São Paulo's insurrection, launched in defiance of the national government and its failure to return Brazil to the rule of law, exploded in 1932. It was led by conservative landowners and industrialists seeking to regain the power that they had lost when Vargas had come to power. Nearly all *paulistas* joined the struggle in support of the refrain, "for a civil and *paulista* government." The resulting armed conflict (from July to September) was backed and conducted by volunteers drawn from the upper and middle classes, as well as part of the working class. These groups reinterpreted the movement's ideals through their enthusiastic participation. This essay focuses on one of the most visible elements of the state's rebelliousness: the "Gold for São Paulo" building.

The "Gold for São Paulo" building. *(Drawn by Cristina Mehrtens)*

An initiative to raise money for the armed conflict, the "Gold for São Paulo" campaign was planned in a meeting of important *paulistas* in August 1932. It far surpassed its creators' expectations. Money poured in, much of it from anonymous donors, revealing the generosity of society's humble people, whose modest gifts represented everything they had. Those who could not volunteer for the battlefront—including foreign residents and women—embraced the cause by contributing money and playing a vital role in organizing campaigns. By September, the campaign for gold had received 87,120 wedding rings and many other gold articles. Part of this money was used to fund the civil war and, after its cessation, the rest—60 percent of the amount collected—was distributed to the Santa Casa da Misericórdia's hospitals. Each Santa Casa received

The state of São Paulo's flag.

the amount proportional to the contribution made by its city. In 1935, the Santa Casa da Misericórdia in São Paulo used its money to raise a building, a symbol of honor, the "Gold for São Paulo" edifice in the Largo da Misericórdia. The chosen location was, by itself, a traditional symbol of the city's past since it had housed the colonial Igreja da Misericórdia, one of the most prestigious institutions in the region. The architectural firm that was contracted to design and construct the building, Ramos de Azevedo, was Brazil's largest and most prominent one.

The firm's architects incorporated historical themes into their blueprints. The building's facade, incorporating the flag of the *paulista* "nation," evoked the Revolution's character. In turn, flags were used to mark the portable kiosks on street corners where people could bring their contributions and they seemed to adorn every window in the city as well. According to the modernist writer Oswald de Andrade, in *A Revolução Melancólica,* "windows waved with flags and walls with posters." The flag personified the people's identity. On the building itself, the flag's mast symbolized a collection of wedding rings and coins, arranged in a spire and crowned by a helmet, standing for the *paulista* warrior.

The flag, then, was literally emblazoned onto the side of the building. At twelve stories high, the building's windowsills portrayed the flag's twelve black-and-white stripes. Perhaps (or perhaps not) coincidentally, the civil war had lasted twelve weeks. Ramos de Azevedo's publicists explained that the building was "the synthesis and allegory of the heroic São Paulo people's love, wealth, and life"; they concluded by stating that the building "will be a mark that will, for good, symbolically represent an era, the most glorious historical moment accomplished by the Piratininga people. A singular monument that will restore to the people part of its sacrifice in the form of medical assistance by the most noble, altruistic institution." Through this building, never acknowledged by Brazilian architecture critics, the Revolution acquired an identity and form. The assertion that the *paulistas* had lost a battle but won the war— based on the fact that in spite of the defeat in the armed conflict, Vargas convened the Parliament and called for a constitution in 1934—assumed new contours here. The Revolution's ideals became a *paulista* motto, and the "Gold for São Paulo" Building interjected a new visual language into city life.

Where They Talk about Rosa Luxemburg

Patrícia Galvão

Artist and writer Patrícia Galvão (1910–1962), or Pagú, captivated the avant-garde elite with her flamboyant style and militancy. A member of the vanguard "cannibalist" literary movement, she married its leader, Oswald de Andrade, in 1930, and bore his son. Later, she traveled abroad as a journalist, became a communist, and on her return to Brazil, spent four years as a convicted subversive in prison, where she was tortured. When she was released, her health had deteriorated. Still, Galvão picked up her career as a social critic and defender of modernism, becoming a widely published journalist. This excerpt is from her 1933 proletarian novel, Industrial Park, *an attack on the dehumanizing impact of factory life in São Paulo.*

Otavia leaves the Dois Rios Colony for political prisoners almost consumptive. A six-month sentence for being a citizen. Alive because she's strong.

The second class on the night train that takes her back to São Paulo also carries the latest *carioca* sambas. The preoccupation with the social struggle has invaded popular songs:

> All Hail!
> All Hail!
> This samba's
> Going to land in jail.

On the black wooden bench, she reads an evening paper from Rio. The first paper she's read after such a long time. Carnival had been regulated. A lot of people collapsed in the streets from hunger. But there was plenty of champagne at the Municipal Theater. She glances over the other pages. "The Tragic Northeast." A drought victim, overcome by hunger, killed her little children. She was taken to jail. An immense portrait illustrates a fascist interview. Brazil needs order!

The Ministry of Agriculture at Boa Vista Estate will cost only 16,000 *contos*. The fantastic toilettes of the acting governor's daughter in Petropólis. Begging is on the increase! The Sino-Japanese conflict. Strikes intensify in Spain. In Greece of the poets! In Greece? Who would have thought? World agitation is a fact! Even columnists know it. At the bottom of a page, lost and fearful, a telegram about the building of socialism in the U.S.S.R.

—I see there are more of us, comrades . . .

The union is seething.

—A year's struggle, Otavia! Enough for a lot of proletarians to become disillusioned working for the bourgeoisie. To understand the class struggle. We expelled some intellectuals; others came in. You know one of them. He definitively left the bourgeoisie. Alfredo . . . he's transformed. But it was hard to change old habits . . . and his taste for the Hotel Esplanada. There he is!

—I already know.

—Otavia . . . you!

He embraces her ineffably.

—You really became a proletarian?

—I gave up two cows . . . the bourgeoisie and Eleonora . . .

Alfredo Rocha laughs in well-chosen poor clothes.

—Tell me about your exile . . .

Alfredo? Could she believe it? Could her companions be wrong?

She'll talk with him all her free hours to see if she can discover a false position, an opportunistic purpose, a shadow of bossism or opportunism. That great bourgeois from the Esplanada!

Everyone tells her that his political line is perfect.

On a cold Sunday, she enters her rented room, bringing a half-dozen yellow flowers picked on the way back from the street market.

Alfredo follows her, in an old overcoat.

Otavia puts on a checkered apron and gets water ready in a decanter for coffee. Her breasts bounce in her blouse. Alfredo glances at them by accident.

—You still don't believe me, Otavia!

The water murmurs. The aromatic coffee colors the one chipped cup. Alfredo bites quietly into a piece of cornbread. She smiles.

—I will believe one day.

At night, after the job she got at a bakery, Otavia walks through the streets trying to find one or another old companion from the factory.

She peeks into the ice cream shops and the bars. Schoolgirls pass by licking sherbets. She goes down Joly Street. The proletarian setting hadn't changed. The same Portuguese vendor's produce stand. She used to buy bananas there. On the corner, she almost crashes into the giant figure of her companion Alexandre, whom she had met thundering against the bourgeoisie at the union meeting. In a sleeveless striped shirt, talking with two foreign workers.

—Hi there, friend!

The four head for a bar. They sit down. The tables are filled with workers.

—This shit never was a revolution!

—As long as Luís Carlos Prestes doesn't come . . .

Alexandre breaks into the conversation.

—It would amount to the same thing . . .

—How's that?

—The same thing! He would just replay the black comedy that's out there!

—Then who will set it straight?

—Who?

—We, the workers! The exploited need to make the revolution happen.

A common worker comments.

—The revolution won't come about because most people are just like me! I confess that I'm afraid of the police. Whoever wants to can go ahead . . .

—They're many like you, shouts Alexandre. But my children who are still young already understand the class struggle!

Alexandre doesn't know how to read or write. But social reality, coming from his mouth, excites the crowds.

—It's the words of one worker to other workers!

The masses galvanize in the full union hall.

—What party should we support, comrades? The parties of the bourgeoisie? No! The P.R.P. [Republican Party] or P.D. [Democratic Party]? No! The lieutenants? No! All workers must come into the party of the workers!

The dissidents become quiet. The mighty voice dominates, spreads, registers an act of social revolution. Alexandre's house is near São Jorge Park. He says it's a house. Bourgeois neighbors, chicken coop. His two little Creoles, nine and ten years old, weren't baptized but are named

Carlos Marx and Frederico Engels. Marcos and Enguis, as their paralytic grandmother calls them from her dirty bed. From the flimsy mattress, made of patches, she sees the soup boil on a stove of kindling wood.

—Fire's almost goin' out!

The boys' mother was lost many years ago under a pile of sacks at the Santista Mill.

—Come see how pretty my poverty is!

Behind the black giant, Otavia and Alfredo appear. Almost night.

Poverty, yes. But what a revolt inside that poverty.

Carlos Marx didn't sell a single newspaper in order to nail red union manifestos onto posts in the early morning.

The tin plates fill with broth. The black eats out of a big bowl. Alfredo tries to like the simple and poorly prepared food. He feels happy. He doesn't find Brazil abhorrent, as before. He doesn't need to drown his individualistic irritability in any picturesque scenes, neither in the ovens of the Sahara nor in the glacial Arctic Ocean. He wants them to leave him in Braz. Eating that revolutionary food. Without longing for Cairo hotels or French wines.

Carlos Marx and Frederico Engels come running in to tell that the cook's baby right next door was kidnapped. The mother was at work. The six-year-old sister was taking care of her little brother.

—A well-dressed bourgeois lady thought he was cute in his sister's lap. She got out of her automobile and took him. . . . Yesterday afternoon.

Alfredo takes an interest, interrogates:

—Did they go to the police . . .

—The father went. But the deputy of social order said that the child is better off in the house of the rich!

Alfredo opens an evening paper that he had brought and looks for the report.

—Not here. There's never space to denounce these bourgeois in-famies. . . . But look at all this about Lindbergh's son. They say that his mother is the most pitiful woman in the world. The new Virgin Mary!

They smoke in silence. Alfredo tosses the paper. In the ashes, the last burning embers. An old cat shakes her burned paws. Frederico Engels studies. Carlos plays with a dark-skinned girl who comes in. Very dark. Endless scratches on her long, bare legs. They argue.

—Is it true, *Seu* Alexandre? I don't believe it . . .

—She said that Rosa Luxemburg never existed . . .

Otavia sits down on the ground with the children.

—Yes, she did exist! She was a German proletarian militant killed by the police because she attacked the bourgeoisie . . .

—Is the woman who kidnapped little Neguinho a bourgeois?

—Of course! Frederico explains, lifting up the top of the book that he's spelling aloud. If she were poor, the police would kill her just like Rosa Luxemburg.

Otavia explains that the bourgeoisie is the same everywhere. Everywhere they order the police to kill the workers . . .

Alexandre laughs. His immense voice breaks in.

—They kill the workers, but the proletariat doesn't die!

Proletarianization

Matilde had written to Otavia:

"I have to give you a little bad news. Just as you taught me, everything's great for the materialists. They've just fired me from the factory, without an explanation, without a reason. Because I refused to go to the boss's room. More than ever, comrade, I feel the class struggle. How I am outraged and happy to have this awareness! When the manager put me in the streets, I felt the full reach of my final proletarianization, delayed so many times!

"It's fate. It's impossible for the proletarians not to revolt. Now I have felt all the injustice, all the iniquity, all the infamy of the capitalist regime. The one thing I have to do is to fight ferociously against these bourgeois scoundrels. Fight alongside my comrades in slavery. I will leave Campinas day after tomorrow. And I'll look for you the day I arrive."

Otavia smiles. She wraps herself in a patchwork quilt. She has a book open on the pillow. The candle on the headboard flickers, ruining her eyesight in searching the tiny letters. She doesn't read. She thinks about the vast world in revolt for the class struggle. In the Brazilian sector, combat intensifies, enlarges.

So many people joining in! The scandalous allegiance of the great bourgeois who was Alfredo Rocha. Now, Matilde, who had hesitated so many times! The hesitant and even the indifferent are forced to confront the social question. No one is permitted to be disinterested anymore. It's a fight to the death between two irreconcilable classes. The bourgeoisie splinters, divides, crumbles, marches toward the abyss and toward death. The proletariat rises, asserts itself, becomes acculturated. Any militant understands and studies economic questions with the same facility that a bourgeois leafs through a stupid issue of *Femina*.

The bourgeoisie lost its meaning. The marxist proletariat found its way through all the dangers and fortifies itself for the final assault. While the bourgeois females descend from Higienópolis and the wealthy neighborhoods for orgies in *garçonnières* and clubs, their humiliated maids in hats and aprons conspire in the kitchens and gardens of the mansions. The exploited masses are fed up and want a better world!

In the shrill workshop, Alfredo takes the great unknown step of his life. He dons the dark shirt that he had always romantically yearned for, and that now his ideology and his economic situation authorize and direct.

Red fire drenches his body with laborious and happy sweat. Finally, he is a proletarian. He has left the moral filth of the bourgeoisie for good. If Eleonora only knew! Always dazed by alcohol and by the first male she danced with. The typical decadent. How he had deceived himself by marrying her! He had left her half of his fortune. Much was lost in a publishing venture. With the rest, he supported the struggle. As much as Eleonora tumbles through life, heading for catastrophe, the healthy figure of Otavia revives for him the strong companion, pure and enlightened, that he always wanted.

Two Versions of Factory Life

Photographers Unknown

One of the truths of the Vargas administration was that his Labor Ministry officials devoted more attention to creating bureaucracies than to enforcing the government's new labor laws. The first set of photographs depict the official view of the workplace: dynamic, hygienic, energetic. Men and boys, with a few women in the background, are leaving work; they are well-dressed, healthy in appearance, and the street is swept clean. Compare this to the second set of photographs, the first of which is dated 1941, the other dated "decade of the 1950s." The photograph of workers on the factory floor is dated 1941. It was taken at Abramo Eberle Metalworks in Caxais do Sul, the same factory whose posted rules are found at the end of the second section of this book. While the workshop is clean, the men wear neither gloves nor protective eyeglasses, although they are working with molten metal. Workers are standing in pools of floodwater; even after the flood subsided, conditions remained primitive and dangerous. The seated workers are manufacturing gold-plated religious objects in preparation for the Fourth National Eucharistic Congress held in São Paulo in September 1942. The other photograph shows a shoeless boy at a machine press at the same factory, in clear violation of both child labor laws and regulations requiring protective clothing.

A model factory in 1942 in Rio Grande do Sul. (Museu Antropológico, FIDENE / UNIJUI, Ijuí, Rio Grande do Sul)

Metalworks in Rio Grande do Sul in 1940. (Museu Antropológico, FIDENE / UNIJUI, Ijuí, Rio Grande do Sul)

Quitting time outside a factory in Rio Grande do Sul in 1940. (Museu Antropológico, FIDEN / UNIJUI, Ijuí, Rio Grande do Sul)

The interior of Abrams Eberle Metalworks in 1941 in Caxias do Sul, RS. (Museu Antropológico, FIDENE / UNIJUI, Ijuí, Rio Grande do Sul)

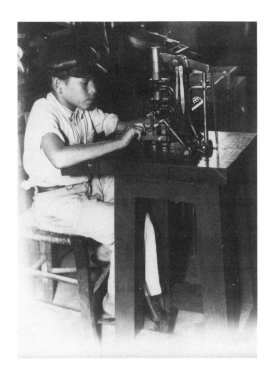

A shoeless child laborer, circa 1950s, in the Abrams Eberle Metalworks in Caxias do Sul, RS. (Museu Antropológico, FIDENE / UNIJUI, Ijuí, Rio Grande do Sul)

Seized Correspondence from Communists, 1935–1945

Dossier 20, Police Archives

These excerpts from letters sent by members of the Brazilian Communist Party and from party propaganda were held for years in the famous "Dossier 20" in the Security Police headquarters (DOPS), and only became available to researchers in mid-1997. "Condemned to Death" not only reveals the terrible conditions under which political prisoners were kept, but that Brazilians—in this case, imprisoned physicians—had hopes of reasoning with the authorities. The poem "Cavalier of Hope" shows the esteem in which Luís Carlos Prestes, the jailed communist (and longtime nationalist) leader, was held by militants on the Left. "The Open Letter to Integralists" displays the contortions the Brazilian communists were forced to undergo when the Moscow party line changed—here, after Stalin signed his short-lived nonaggression pact with Hitler, abruptly making allies of Brazil's communists and their bitter enemies, the fascist Integralists. The "Open Letter to Getúlio Vargas" followed Vargas's declaration of war on the Axis. Vargas's maneuver put him on the same side as the Soviet Union, forcing the communists, many of them still in prison, to praise the Brazilian dictator.

I. Condemned to Death

A petition from imprisoned physicians in the House of Detention,
December 3, 1936

The tragic penal colony of Dois Rios has received another shipment of some of the Brazilian people, many of them youths, kidnapped from

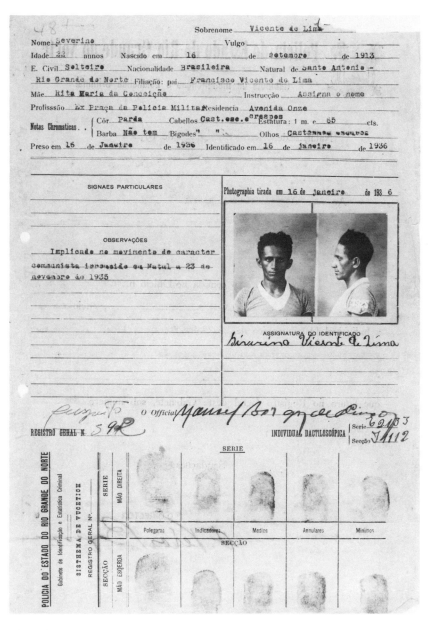

The police registry card for the prisoner Severino Vicente de Lima, arrested in 1936 for participating in the 1935 communist insurrection in Natal. *(Rio Grande do Norte State Police)*

their families by the treasonous government of GETÚLIO VARGAS. In this Siberia, placed in a wretched and dilapidated barrack, sleeping on a dirt floor covered with sand, miserably fed, exhausted by forced labor, afflicted by a barrage of humiliations, which include being forced to walk with crossed arms when not working, frequently beaten, a wave of epidemic disease is sweeping the place . . . pneumonia, dysentery, and so on. Some of the prisoners arrived with acute symptoms of disease—bloody spittum, colitis, difficulty in breathing. . . . We, as physicians, are horrified at what we have seen . . . some of them have been taken from the barracks and vanished, and we believe that they will never be seen again.

Political and Cultural Activities among Political Prisoners in Rio de Janeiro

Being a political prisoner is a fecund opportunity in the life of a revolutionary to learn more. This is what is happening among political prisoners all over Brazil. Following the November [1935] uprisings . . . conditions have been created for the invaluable exchange of personal experiences between thousands of prisoners, ranging from the revolutionary leaders to those caught up in the movement who were completely distant from what was happening. On the prison ship *Pedro I,* in the houses of detention, in the prisons, peasants, workers, soldiers, sailors, labor organizers, teachers from all levels, artisans, college graduates, physicians, engineers, armed forces officers, journalists, legislators, artists, in sum, representatives of all social groups, have taken advantage of the circumstances created by the repression to realize a gigantic educational endeavor to study and debate the conditions under which the country lives . . .

What we have done is to organize the life of prisoners, to make the most efficient use of time. We hold democratic elections among the general prison population, to select a "collective." We have started, ironically, the first people's university in Brazil. We offer courses in political consciousness and general culture. We produce theater performances, posters, musical concerts; we compose and sing revolutionary songs; we produce within the prison walls illustrated underground newspapers, which are passed from hand to hand. This educational work is a valuable part of revolution making. Our "arts commission" handles cultural activities. We teach prisoners to read Portuguese, French, English, German, Russian, and Esperanto; we teach geography, mathematics, history, physical and natural sciences, economic issues, courses in military tactics and strategy, Morse code, how to take apart motors, sexual education—in short, all of the things that can be imagined that can be taught in classes or lectures. Our revolutionary university stimulates interest, and encourages debate and discussion. We circulate books about prisoners. We offer daily classes in hygiene, and organize physical exercise and the practice of sports. Most important, of course, is our work in political consciousness-raising . . . in the ten months we have been imprisoned for our political beliefs, we have created the most effective schools for revolutionary training that Brazil has ever seen.

II. *Cavalier of Hope*

A poem written in honor of Luís Carlos Prestes by a prisoner at Maria Zélia prison, São Paulo.

Prestes, the gentle heart of our people
is filled with your presence; the hand that imprisons you
Knows that our struggle at your side will rise again
To fight again. The masses await you!

As long as you are imprisoned, the injury continues,
As long as you are imprisoned, the masses remain aware of your
    condition.
But after the day, happily, comes another day . . .

As long as you are in prison, our people remain enslaved.
We love you deeply, and we accompany your fortunes.
You are the flower of our race, the most pure and most brave,
Our oldest brother, our strongest brother.

People of Brazil, its persecuted people,
Who live without bread, who toil at work naked,
Maintain their vigilance with a sad and watchful eye.
The masses wait for you; you are our leader!

III. Open Letter to Integralists

From its founding in 1935, the most implacable enemy of the Communist Party's popular front, the ANL (National Liberation Alliance), was the fascist Integralist Party. After Stalin signed his nonaggression pact with Hitler in 1939, the communists abruptly changed their tune; they now viewed the fascists as potential allies against Vargas. This undated letter was issued after the Hitler-Stalin Pact by the Political Bureau of Brazil's Communist Party. It should be noted that, at the time, the Integralist leader, Plínio Salgado, had been permitted to find exile in fascist Portugal, while the communist leader, Luís Carlos Prestes, sat in jail in Rio de Janeiro.

For some time, communists and Integralists have been suffering ferocious repression at the hands of the government. The infested prisons of our country are filled with men whose only crime was to have fought for the interests of our great country, Brazil, seeking to create a more humane and just society.

The nefarious Getúlist Security Tribunal is ceaseless in its sinister work, hunting down and sentencing Brazilian patriots. Taken together, they have imprisoned men for combined sentences of thousands of years. And if the horrors of the existing prisons were not enough, they created the terrible penal colony on Fernando do Noronha Island, a place for political prisoners unequaled in the world for its isolation and distance from civilized society. The misery and oppression in which the Brazilian people live under the Estado Novo worsens each day. With the outbreak of war in Europe, conditions for our workers get more and more precarious. Salaries fall and living conditions worsen . . .

Without freedom of expression, of the press, and to associate, with labor unions transformed into miserable agents of the Labor Ministry bureaucracy and the police, we, communists and Integralists, sincere patriots, who love our country above all else, must form an inseparable bloc to fight for the good of Brazil, expelling the tyrant Vargas from the presidential palace.

Integralists! If we all unite, nothing will divide us.
Down with Getúlio and his rotten Estado Novo!
Long live Luís Carlos Prestes and Plínio Salgado!
Long live the Communist Party!
Long live the Integralist Party!

IV. Open Letter to Getúlio Vargas

This September 8, 1941, communication, authored by the Communist Party of Brazil in Rio de Janeiro, was distributed through the underground after Hitler's breaking of his pact with the Soviet Union's Joseph Stalin.

In the hour that we celebrate the anniversary of Brazil's political independence from the Portuguese yoke, the world finds itself the victim of ferocious aggression that threatens to submerge the forces of civilization in tyranny. Most of the people of Europe have fallen under the Nazi terror, suffering in need of human necessities and loving under abject moral degradation. Two great nations, however, Great Britain and the Soviet Union, are heroically resisting the furious Hitlerist wave. The Soviet Union, with its formidable Red Army, its air force, and its navy. Britain, with its Home Fleet and its Royal Air Force. Africa has been invaded; Australia and the Dutch East Indies are at war; there is blood in the China Sea, and America and Russia are threatened . . .

Meanwhile, the forces of the Nazi vanguard press are in our hemisphere through the work of Fifth Columnists, preparing the ground for the final assault on our continent, where Brazil, by virtue of its strategic position, stands as the first and most solid point of resistance against these forces.

The shots of the May 1938 Integralist "putsch," financed by the German Transatlantic Bank, still echo.

The Integralists still make propaganda through the thinly disguised "Campaign for a Strong Press," and the magazine *Rataplan,* widely distributed among soldiers under the direction of Colonel Cota, who is a member of the Integralist governing body, the "Chamber of 40. . . ." Nazi lies, agitation, and propaganda constitute a sixth arm of the Hitlerist war machine, and it is in full operation [in Brazil]. . . . The Fifth Column in Brazil is so well organized that [Minister] Francisco Campos was able to say, to friends, that whenever he wants to, Hitler can take Brazil by picking up the telephone. . . .

The moment has arrived, Mr. President, to adopt energetic measures against the Fifth Columnists, such as those carried out in the United States, in Cuba, in Mexico, and in practically all of the countries in our hemisphere. The moment has arrived to amnesty all progressive and liberal-democrat political prisoners. . . . Only this way can we build and fortify a national front against Nazism and consolidate the Brazilian Union.

The Paulista Synagogue

Gustavo Barroso

While Plínio Salgado played Integralist führer in a relatively statesmanlike manner, the movement's intellectual chieftain, Gustavo Barroso, openly admired the Nazis, and expressed contempt for Jews, liberals, and those he considered weaklings. As president of the Brazilian Academy of Letters, he wore a pistol in a leather holster when he addressed that august body. Barroso dared Brazilians to stand up to his bullying, but few did. Since there were so few Jews in Brazil, he depicted his enemies—in this case, paulista *bankers—as tools of an "international Jewish conspiracy." Not many Brazilians took Barroso seriously, but his vicious attacks were never challenged by anyone speaking for the government. Over time, they had a psychological impact, making educated Brazilians less open to foreigners and especially to Jews. Newspaper editors stayed silent, as did intellectuals and academics. The following selection comes from Barroso's* The Paulista Synagogue, *one of several anti-semitic books published by him—at prestigious publishing houses—during the 1930s.*

Brazil remains in the hands of a voracious colony of Jews, mysteriously aided in their fiendish business deals and moneylending by individuals in high positions nationally.

One group of São Paulo Jews, headed by the agent of international bankers Senhor Numa de Oliveira, holds great influence within circles at the federal and state level; [another is] the Jew Horácio Lafer, federal deputy from the same state, who carries out his activities in the anterooms of government ministries, conniving for favors . . .

What do the true *paulistas* of São Paulo say to this? On what basis [are the Jewish] parasites protected? We really have no reason to expect an answer, because we know that in such compromising cases, silence is a traditional Jewish tactic. People with scruples, decent people, provide all necessary explanations.

What took place in 1929, on the heels of the crash of coffee prices, was nothing more than the application by the Paulista Synagogue of the lessons taught by the [forged] *Protocols of the Elders of Zion*. . . . The insatiable Jews of the Paulista Synagogue, momentarily finding themselves in a contrary position to the 1930 Revolution, allied themselves with the rejected and ambitious politicians from São Paulo who cowardly poisoned *paulista* public opinion against the central government and the rest of Brazil, taking the state into a civil war in 1932. They persuaded the youth of the state to believe that Getúlio Vargas was an enemy of São Paulo, applying the Jewish tactic that [Henry] Ford calls "inciting feelings of hatred against those people they want to annihilate." Meanwhile, we Integralists know that the only enemies of São Paulo are the Jews who deceive us.

This was stirred up by an illusion created by the Jewish Satan. This demon does not employ whips or bitter potions; he offers delicious desserts, unheard of luxuries, beautiful women. All of this, meanwhile, hides the eternal abyss of everlasting pain, a ceaseless gnashing of teeth. The process employed by the International Jew is the same: to seduce and trick the Christian.

Why the Estado Novo?

Oliveira Vianna

Reactionary sociologist, law professor, and historian Francisco José de Oliveira Vianna (1883–1951), a proponent of statist authoritarianism, was an instrumental member of the inner circle around Vargas that successfully pressed for a move to the right. As he believed that individuals were subordinate to the higher interest of the national state, he supported the cancellation of civil rights in the name of national security and anticommunism, and counseled Vargas on his corporatist labor legislation, aimed more at social control than at delivering benefits to workers. The letter reproduced here congratulates Antônio Figueira de Almeida, a prolific (and minor) writer of textbooks, and in 1940, the author of a tract on the Estado Novo Constitution published by Vargas's Press and Propaganda Department (DIP). The letter praises Vargas's 1937 military coup and his imposed constitution, which borrowed unapologetically from the fascist charters of Salazar's Portugal, Pilsudski's Poland, and Mussolini's Italy. It also reveals Vianna's curious fixation with the brotherhood fluminenses—persons born in his state of Rio de Janeiro—despite his usual nationalist hostility to local and regional identity.

My Dear Figueira,

I read your book explaining the November 10th Constitution to the people. I note with pleasure that despite your many tasks as a professor and public servant, you, my dear friend, continue to uphold with dignity the name of your grandfather, the great *fluminense* Andrade Figueira, preserving in your blood his political sense, his zeal for the public interest, and civic vocation.

This political spirit and civic vocation, which you, my noble friend, have inherited, is what inspires the new Constitution. I well noted that the tradition in your blood has not let you dedicate yourself exclusively to your teaching, to your publication of excellent geography and history books, and your social and literary criticism. You knew that you had to publish, as well, your book about our political and constitutional issues.

On this point, you, my dear friend, are not merely a dignified inheritor of your grandfather's political and civil combativeness; but, as well, you are a good *fluminense,* loyal to the old traditions. Because we, *fluminenses,* have, as a characteristic trait of our collective psyche, a sense of public spirit, love for public life, in sum, a sense of the state, especially our duty to criticize it constructively.

Was it not we, in collaboration with the *paulistas* and *mineiros* [people from Minas Gerais], who constructed the Empire and, with it, the national polity, giving it its juridical organization and legal fiber . . . that has been up to now the guarantee of our public order, and the basis for all of our prosperity and impressive progress?

Groups from other regions brought to our national political life other principles: agitation, argument, political and parliamentary liberty. To us, then, falls the vital mission to construct and evolve the principle of political organization and public authority.

I understand, then, the gesture of my dear friend, in choosing as your subject the Constitution of 1937.

That Constitution comes to restore the authority of the national power, sacrificed by the "soi-disant" liberal spirit that dominated the two previous republican constitutions [1891 and 1934], both decentralized, distorted regionally, localist, and consequently, antinational.

The principle of the sovereignty of national power, happily, has been restored in the 1937 Constitution by a man of the state who came from the far South. . . . Under liberalism, we have the motto, "The king reigns, but he does not govern." Now we have the counter motto: "The king reigns, governs, and administers," something that inspired us throughout the political life of the Empire, in affirmation of the progressive consolidation of central authority.

It is with pleasure, then, that I send my congratulations to you, a son of the *fluminense* valley . . . [speaking with] the voice within the blood, one that is conservative, beckoning one to the side of the principle of authority and antisocialist tradition, a call to the sentiment of the nation.

—Oliveira Vianna

New Year's Address, 1938

Getúlio Vargas

Getúlio Vargas weathered numerous challenges during his first years as chief of state. They included a civil war in São Paulo, a communist-led uprising in 1935, the rise of the paramilitary fascist Integralist movement, the collapse of coffee exports, and Brazil's burdensome foreign debt. By late 1937, however, the country appeared stable enough to hold elections for a new president. Perhaps Vargas interpreted the situation differently or, perhaps, he simply craved power. For whatever reason, with the army's backing, Vargas overthrew his own regime in November 1937, canceled the elections, and promulgated an authoritarian constitution. Vargas justified the Estado Novo (New State) directly to Brazilians in his 1938 New Year's Day radio speech, in which he played the paternal protector, stern yet fair, optimistic yet fearful of disorder. Over the next eight years, Vargas would cultivate that image to the maximum.

At the dawn of the new year, when in the hearts and souls the call of hope and happiness is more lively and crackling, and we feel more strongly, and overwhelmingly the aspiration for victory, achievement, and progress, I come to communicate with you and speak directly to everyone, without distinction of class, profession, or hierarchy, so that united and in brotherhood, we might lift quite high the idea of an irrevocable vote for the greatness and happiness of Brazil.

I have received from the Brazilian people, in grave and decisive moments, unequivocal proof of a perfect communion of ideas and sentiments. And for that very reason, more than ever, I judge myself obligated to transmit to the people my word of faith, so much more opportune and necessary if we consider the responsibilities arising out of the recently instituted regime, in which patriotism is measured by sacrifice and the rights of individuals have to be subordinate to the obligations to the nation.

It was imperative, for the good of the majority, to change procedures and agree to a labor policy, consonant with our realities and the demands for the country's development.

The Constitution of November 10 is not a document of simple, legal regulation of the state, made to order, according to fashions in vogue. It is adapted concretely to the current problems of Brazilian life, considered in origins of formation, defining, at the same time, the directions toward its progress and enrichment.

The actions practiced, in these fifty days of government, reflect and confirm the decisive will to act inside of the principles adopted.

We are suspending payment of the foreign debt, because of the imposition of circumstances alien to our desires . . .

We are modifying the onerous policy followed in relation to coffee, and in the same manner the monetary regimen, which was in force for our trade . . .

Alongside these resolutions of an economic and financial character, there figured others of not lesser significance, in the political-administrative sphere. I want to allude to the acts of abolition of political parties, of organization of the national court, and regulation of pensions in the public, civil service.

By the first, there was had in view elimination of the interference from factious interests and groups in the solution of the problems of government. The state, according to the new order, is the nation, and because of that, ought to dispense with political intermediaries in order to maintain contact with the people, and consult their aspirations and needs. By the second, there were created national courts, causing the disappearance of organizational contradictions and anomalies in which we had as many courts as existing federated units. The codification of national law, already initiated, will come to complete these measures of notable reach for the strengthening of the ties of national cohesion. Just as a single flag supremely protects all Brazilians, the law also ought to assure, by a uniform method, the rights of citizenship in the entire national territory. By the last, it is fitting to refer to the law that prohibits accumulation of public offices. For more than a century, this provision challenged the legislators of good intention. The solution encountered is, without doubt, strict. It will bring about sacrifices to some people, but it represents a benefit for the collectivity and demonstrates, in an undeniable manner, the moralizing proposal of abolishing all situations of privilege. Permitting more equitable distribution for access to the public offices, it implicitly benefits more people and offers an opportunity to assure equivalent remuneration for services rendered.

We will persist in the willingness to eliminate the barriers that separate zones and isolate regions, so that the national economic body might be able to evolve homogeneously, and the expansion of the internal market might be done without restraints of any type . . .

In the regimen of the revoked Constitution, it was not possible to take these initiatives, nor assume the responsibilities of such heavy duties . . .

Until recently, our equipment for teaching was limited to the minimum necessities for individual competence. . . . There was an abundance of Ph.D.s and a lack of qualified technicians; the man competent in his trade was rare; artistic technique declined in front of the machine, without us being able to make free use of industrial workers.

The national government resolved to undertake, in this respect, a decisive task. In addition to modernizing the existing establishments, increasing their capacity and efficiency, it initiated the construction of large professional schools, which ought to constitute a vast network of popular teaching, radiating throughout the country. It will attend, also, to the initiatives of local governments, by means of auxiliary materials and technical guidance . . .

The sentiment of human solidarity is one of the most noble and highest manifestations of the Christian spirit. When the state takes the initiative of projects of economic assistance and supports the struggle of the worker, it is to attend to an imperative of social justice, giving an example to be observed by all, without need of compulsion . . .

The multiplicity of sectors in which the state acts does not exclude, but instead affirms, a fundamental rule: that of security for the work and achievements of general interest. The public order and tranquillity will be maintained without vacillation. The government continues vigilant in the repression of extremism and is going to segregate, in fortified military prisons and agricultural colonies, all those agitating elements, recognized by their seditious activities or condemned by political crimes. We will not permit that the struggle and patriotic dedication of the good Brazilians might come to endure turmoil and alarms originated by personalistic ambitions, or the ideological craziness of false prophets and vulgar demagogues . . .

Brazilians! In the hour of cheerfulness and promise, I bring to you my friendly greeting.

Like you, I believe in the high destiny of the fatherland and, like you, I work to achieve it. In the New State there will be no place for the skeptics and the hesitant, unbelieving in themselves and others. There are those who, at times, interrupt your journey's repose honestly earned, with the alarm of their fears and the rumor of slanderous negativism. With trustful heart and uplifted enthusiasm, you devote yourselves to the daily labor and to the cares of the home, where you have guarded the hopes of happiness and find the comforting shelter of dear ones.

To all those who live under the bright protection of the Southern Cross, I give, in this dawn of the new year, the best vows of good fortune and prosperity. And from all of you—Brazilians!—I ask and hope, at this moment, for the solemn promise to well serve the fatherland and to do everything for its enrichment.

Rural Life

Photographers Unknown

These photographs from the early 1930s are from the município *of Caxias do Sul, not far from Vargas's birthplace. The first photograph shows children at their first communion in the village of Galópolis. Many are immigrants or children of immigrants; there are very few children of mixed race in the Brazil of the far south. Two nuns—very rare in Brazil in the twentieth century—stand at the rear. The next photograph is the Fidelis Gomes family in Criúcia, in the same* município. *There are eleven children; the dark-skinned boy in the first row may be the child of a servant or neighbor. The photographs of farm life come from Ijuí in Rio Grande do Sul. Immigrant families stand next to thatched-roof shacks, which may either have been used for storage or have been their residence. A woman wearing wooden shoes holds a curved knife alongside a pulley devise and a primitive hoe. The men with the horse-drawn cart are harvesting wheat; the workers in front of the barnlike structure pose with their harvesting wagon, which is pulled by oxen. Agricultural workers attempt to combat swarms of locusts. In the absence of pest control, this is a futile endeavor. Lastly, two men prepare to butcher a hog, as a woman watches from the doorway of her hut.*

Children at their first communion in front of Galópolis Church in Caxias do Sul, Rio Grande do Sul, in 1933. (Museu Antropológico, FIDENE / UNIJUI, Ijuí, Rio Grande do Sul)

The Fidelis Gomes family from Criúcia, Caxias do Sul, Rio Grande do Sul, circa 1930s. (Museu Antropológico, FIDENE / UNIJUI, Ijuí, Rio Grande do Sul)

On a coffee plantation. (Museu Antropológico, FIDENE / UNIJUI, Ijuí, Rio Grande do Sul)

A farm woman. (Museu Antropológico, FIDENE / UNIJUI, Ijuí, Rio Grande do Sul)

A scene from agricultural life. (Museu Antropológico, FIDENE / UNIJUI, Ijuí, Rio Grande do Sul)

Workers pose with some of the tools of their trade. (Museu Antropológico, FIDENE / UNIJUI, Ijuí, Rio Grande do Sul)

Swarms of locusts plague workers. (Museu Antropológico, FIDENE /
UNIJUI, Ijuí, Rio Grande do Sul)

Two workers preparing to butcher a hog. (Museu Antropológico,
FIDENE / UNIJUI, Ijuí, Rio Grande do Sul)

A New Survey of Brazilian Life

Brazilian Institute of Geography and Statistics

Under Vargas, especially during the authoritarian Estado Novo (1937–1945), state agencies produced a constant stream of press releases, pamphlets, and books explaining their mission. Even the Brazilian Institute of Geography and Statistics, created to establish and evaluate statistical standards, issued books filled with self-congratulatory material. This excerpt is from a book published in English. Translations were also published in French, German, and once in a while, Spanish.

In no other sector of Brazilian life has there been such profound and significant achievements, in the last eight years, as in the field of social policy. Peaceful vindications have been liberally accorded by a continuous improvement of the social laws, based on the equilibrium and discipline of labor activities in Brazil. The new policy has also been relevant in its aims to make closer and closer the relations between the various classes and the public power, through a constructive system of mutual cooperation.

In summarizing the magnificent strides taken by Brazilian legislation in labor matters, suffice it to say that from October 1930 to July 1938, no fewer than 190 decrees were issued with the object of ameliorating social conditions and ensuring proper assistance to the working classes. Enactments have rationally regulated women's labor in industrial and commercial concerns, prohibiting night work, establishing the principle of equal remuneration irrespective of sex for every kind of work of equal value, ensuring the pregnant mother a period of rest without a loss of salary, fostering the institution of crèches, and providing other measures for protection of female labor.

Rules were laid down ensuring a hygienic environment to youngsters engaged in industrial work. Regulations enacted have ensured definite working hours and other favorable labor conditions for employees in houses of amusement, in pawnshops, in overland transports, banks and banking houses, barbershops, pharmacies, bakeries, warehouses, and allied establishments in the federal service.

Brazilian labor legislation ensures to all workers, irrespective of nationality, perfect equality of conditions and rights. The professional or trade association is free. However, only a syndicate legally recognized by the state has the right to be the legal representative of those who participate in the group of production for which it was constituted, as well as to defend their rights before the state and the other professional organizations, to enter into collective labor agreements, binding on all their members, to levy contributions, and to exercise toward them the function delegated by the public authority.

The Constitution of November 10, 1937, empowered the executive to issue decree laws. From that date on, twenty-six government acts were added in reinforcement to conform the labor legislation to the needs of the nation. . . . The Labor Justice is special and of an economic nature. It aims at social peace. It is within its province to take cognizance of all questions arising from work, healthy or unhealthy conditions of work, periods of rest, statutory leave (as in the case of pregnancy), compulsory reengagement, strike, and lockout (which, according to the terms of the Brazilian Constitution now in force, "are declared antisocial instruments, detrimental to labor and to capital, and inconsistent with the superior interests of national production").

General George C. Marshall's

Mission to Brazil

Katherine Tupper Marshall

It did not take clairvoyance to know that war was imminent in 1939. Therefore, the United States sought to shore up diplomatic relations with Brazil, a country rich in strategic materials, but also home to German, Italian, and Japanese colonies. General George C. Marshall visited Brazil that year and, according to the account by Katherine Tupper Marshall, his wife, helped secure the country firmly within the Allied camp. Her story, however, relates more than a diplomatic episode. Schoolchildren parading in neat uniforms were an Estado Novo mainstay that reflected Vargas's desire to inculcate youth with a nationalist ideology. Moreover, by including even foundlings in Marshall's tour, Vargas added not only to the American's but also his own popularity. Many of those youths would reach adulthood by 1950 and, almost certainly, a good share voted for Vargas's return to the Presidential Palace in that year's democratic election.

George had hardly reached Washington on his return from the West Coast when President Roosevelt sent for him to come to the White House. At this time, all those in authority were watching developments in South America with growing alarm. The Panama Canal was a decided danger spot—George had gone before the Military Affairs Committee in January asking for better antiaircraft and plane protection, naming Panama as a crucial point. Brazil was a particular source of concern. Its population in some parts included many Germans of second and third generations, and its army had been largely equipped with German materiel. Also, the State Department had gotten wind of the fact that General Góes Monteiro, chief of staff of the Brazilian Army, had been invited by Field Marshal Hermann Göring, at the direction of Chancellor Hitler, to visit Germany. He would be received "with open arms" and given the honor of leading a division of German troops in an impressive parade, to be staged in honor of the Brazilian Army.

The situation was a delicate one. It was hardly an opportune time for a Brazilian soldier to place himself at the head of a column of German troops. So it was immediately announced by the president that General Marshall, the newly designated chief of staff, would make a goodwill trip to Brazil. The upshot was that Chancellor Hitler was informed that General Góes would not go to Germany at this time; instead, he was to stay at home to welcome a distinguished American soldier who was coming to Brazil.

As to Hitler's reaction to this, nothing was known officially; but almost immediately, Mussolini announced that his daughter, Madam Ciano, would leave for Brazil on a goodwill visit. Madam Ciano's ability for intrigue and her political power were well known, but her charm seemed to be inadequate so far as Brazil was concerned, for in the goodwill competition she was decidedly the loser . . .

At Curitiba [capital of Paraná], the governor—or interventor, as I believe he is called—had arranged a parade of the schoolchildren for General Marshall. Some 5,000 participated. The uniform of the girls consisted of white middy blouses, blue pleated skirts, and sandals with bobby socks. The boys wore a more military-looking dress, and all presented an immaculate and persuasive picture. Each school was preceded by a small drum corps, and all the children marched with pride and precision.

This feature of the trip appealed very strongly to General Marshall as he is as deeply interested in children, I believe, as he is in grown-ups.

In the middle of the parade, there appeared about 200 little boys from six to twelve years old, dressed in blue overalls with pink piping, and carrying various farm tools. One little boy was pushing a hand cultivator in front of him. This group made quite an impression on my husband and, on inquiry, he discovered these children were members of a small agricultural school for foundlings, in which the governor was much interested. Consequently, after the parade, though it was very late and a formal dinner was about due, the governor took George a few miles outside the city to inspect this school. The pupils had just arrived in trucks from the parade and were filing in for their dinner. All the surroundings were neat and orderly, and the boys themselves seemed happy and very well cared for.

That night at the dinner, which was an elaborate affair and lasted from eight until midnight, George was turning over in his mind what he might do to repay the bountiful hospitality he was receiving on every hand. Returning hospitality by giving dinners does not greatly appeal to him, yet that is the usually accepted method in diplomatic procedure. Thinking over the events of the afternoon, he decided that a small gift to the foundlings would be much more appreciated than an elaborate dinner to dignitaries. As he had to leave by plane at eleven o'clock, he directed a member of his staff to start out early in the morning, as soon as the shops opened, and purchase a box of candy for each of the little agricultural students, and to take the candy out and present it to them that morning. This was done, and it not only made a profound impression on the little boys, but as a result of press reports, it seemed to make an even greater impression all over Brazil. Consequently, children were turned out en masse everywhere General Marshall went, and as their parents of course turned out to see their children, unusually large crowds resulted. At several places, as many as 20,000 children marched or lined the streets to receive General Marshall. When he returned to Rio where his program was completed, he was urged to visit the schools in the city. This he did.

In looking back on the reactions to his mission to Brazil, George felt that more good had resulted from the small presents to the children than from any other single factor. This story always amused Lord Halifax, and whenever we dined with him, he would press George to tell the other guests how he won out on his Brazilian mission with a "tin of taffy."

Comments on the Estado Novo

Bailey W. Diffie

Getúlio Vargas remains an enigma. On one hand, he built a popular political base by championing nationalism, economic development, and social welfare. Yet, during the Estado Novo (1937–1945), he entirely dispensed with democratic pretensions and ruthlessly eliminated opponents. Bailey W. Diffie, one of the leading scholars on the Luso-Brazilian world and a faculty member at the City College of New York, visited Brazil during the height of the Estado Novo. His correspondence with U.S. government officials portrays Vargas's sinister side.

According to information gathered here in the Argentine newspapers, Mr. Turner Catledge of the *New York Times* has discovered that Brazil is not a fascist country. Perhaps Mr. Turner Catledge is right. *Fascist* is a very indefinite and ambiguous term. We are not all in agreement as to the exact meaning of the term, so I shall not quarrel over a definition. But there are certain characteristics of the present regime that resemble far more those of Italy and Germany than those of the United States, England, or France. There is no liberty of speech in Brazil. People do talk loudly and at length, but the voices that can be distinguished over all others are those that are raised in praise of Getúlio and the present regime.

There is no freedom of press in Brazil. The newspapers print strong, denunciatory articles on politics; but they are strong against democracy and they are denouncing the democratic countries. The news of Brazil may be divided into three kinds: that sold to the papers by the American and English news agencies, that given to the papers by the French news agencies, and that published under direct subsidy by Italy and Germany, and perhaps Japan. Except for one or two of the morning papers, there is not a newspaper in Brazil that does not regularly print news that is the most obvious propaganda put out by the fascist powers. There is full freedom in Brazil to denounce the United States (although this is not very common), France, or England. There is no freedom to criticize Germany, Italy, or Japan. The name of Mussolini is sacred, and Hitler's almost so. The papers vie with each other in printing antidemocratic, antiliberal news and editorials. The socialists, the communists, the Russians, the French popular front, the Spanish Republicans, the Jews, the Masons (Masonic Order) are regularly attacked as menaces to Brazil and the world.

It is only too obvious after a short stay in Brazil that all of the propaganda of this kind is inspired and paid for by interested parties. On the other hand, to announce yourself as a democratic advocate, to side with China, to take the part of the Spanish people, to defend the Jews, or above all, to say anything against Mussolini (the Latin Messiah), is enough to land you in jail. Some few people do say the forbidden things, but they are few, they speak in hushed tones, and they are in danger of arbitrary arrest.

There is no liberty of teaching in Brazil. In fact, the idea of liberty of speech in the classroom is so alien to the thought of the Brazilian teachers that I found it impossible to explain what it signified in the United States. "We can teach anything we want to in Brazil, that is, anything that is not against the government," was the consensus of opinion of the teachers. I remember an occasion when I asked if there were any radical teachers in the Colégio Pedro II. I got the answer that "so-and-so used to call himself a socialist, but he will not do that anymore." This statement was accompanied by a malicious and smirking laugh that indicated the so-and-so knew very well what would happen to him if he professed socialism. Getúlio was not content with a bit of mere negative repression. He is busy now "purging" the school of undesirable elements; he is cleaning up the libraries of the schools so that all socialist or "liberal" literature will be taken out of them; and he is "revising" the texts so that the students will learn only what he wishes them to learn. I never discovered an idea in Brazil that had little enough liberality to escape the denomination of communism. Every conceivable form of progressivism is denounced as coming directly from Moscow.

Brazil has been turned into one organized, inspired Red hunt. The daily papers carry a constant series of announcements of the arrest of thirty communists here, of forty there, of ten in another place. Everybody and everything is considered as potentially dangerous. All foreigners are suspects. Among the things that are denounced as communist (if not by Getúlio himself, at least by those appointees with which he has surrounded himself) are: the communists, the socialists, the liberals, the democrats, the Spanish Republicans, all opponents of the Getúlian government, the Freemasons, the Jews (who are also involved in an international capitalistic plot), the Rotary Club, the YMCA, and Paul Muni, Bette Davis, Clark Gable, Robert Taylor, and Ed Wynn. Arbitrary arrests are common. No accusation, no proof, no explanation is necessary. The police suddenly discover a communist or a nest of communists. Soon after I arrived in Brazil, the papers made a big announcement of the discovery of a dangerous band of communists, whose headquarters were in an insane asylum. Perhaps there was method in their madness.

Over a period of four months, I had my hair cut by a Portuguese barber from Fall River, Massachusetts. Missing him from the shop, I asked about him. The man who was cutting my hair flourished his scissors, rolled his eyes in horror, and exclaimed: "He was arrested, he was a dangerous communist organizer; and to think that he worked side by side with me for four years and I never knew it." The news of such an arrest would spread to the entire community, of course, and terrify all . . .

Brazil is not yet an ally of Italy and Germany. Getúlio is a Brazilian nationalist, but he does not confuse nationalism with throwing Brazil into the hands of the fascist powers. If he has any idea except keeping himself in power, it is that Brazil must be for the Brazilians, not for the British bondholders, nor for the Americans, nor for the Italians of São Paulo (and Italy), nor for the Germans of Santa Catharina, Rio Grande do Sul (and Germany). But Getúlio is surrounded by men who are imbued with the fascist idea, who are conscious imitators of Hitler or Mussolini, who believe that Brazil should join the anticommunist front. If the time should come when Getúlio loses his balance, one of these men might take the direction of the state. There are strong possibilities in several members of his cabinet, particularly Francisco Campos.

Official propaganda, inserted in the Brazilian papers by the chief of propaganda, is all antidemocratic and profascist (or at least proauthoritarian). The gist of the government-inspired news is that democracy is a failure, the democratic powers are tottering, the new constitution of Brazil offers the only means of salvation, and it is time for Brazil to consider what her world friendships should be. Liberalism is labeled as the greatest evil of the age, the source of all trouble, a Jewish plot for the disruption of society, and a mask under which communism is parading. At the same time, the people of Brazil are assured that none of their "democratic" liberties have been removed. And since the Brazilians have no knowledge of democratic liberties, they accept this propaganda almost without question.

Getúlio has wiped out all of the Brazilian political parties. There was nothing much admirable about the political parties, of course. They were animated only by the ignoble desire to get into office, grab while they were in, and stay in by any means available. One of the reasons why Getúlio has been so successful in staying in is that he was opposing men whose political records left them without ardent supporters, except within their own clique. There is as yet no political party to take the place of those that were deflated. Getúlio is as near a one-man political machine as the world has ever seen. Just now, Brazilian politics is summed up in the words *Getúlio Vargas,* although his future road is by no means an assured one, and there are said to be three revolutions in preparation at this time. These three are supposedly: the Integralists, the Armandistas (followers of the ex-candidate for president, Armando Salles, and therefore almost synonymous with São Paulo), and the navy, within which there is a very strong Integralist influence. If these three should get together they might do something, but they have as a basis of cooperation only their dislike of Getúlio. And his policy of arbitrary arrests leaves them a difficult terrain in which to work. So, for the minute, we may say that Brazil is a country with universal suffrage exercised by the one and only voter who, like a priest at communion, says, "this is for your brother, and this for your sister," and then proceeds to discover that all the ballots have the one name, Getúlio Vargas.

And that is democratic, nonfascist Brazil. In order not to quarrel over terms, let us say that Brazil is a democratic country with one voter who always elects himself as savior, and then uses arbitrary arrests, red-baiting, a form of terror, censorship of the press, suppression of free speech, abolition of civil rights, nullification of academic freedom, and the systematic oppression of all forms of liberal thought and all advocates of liberal thought, as a means of perpetuating his one-man rule. If this is democracy, we have been very badly educated in the United States. If this is not fascism, then we are being pretty squeamish about the meaning of words.

Educational Reform after Twenty Years

Anísio S. Teixeira

Anísio Teixeira, Brazil's greatest educational reformer, started his career in his native state of Bahia, where in 1928 he oversaw extensive changes. Visiting the state in 1948, he did a follow-up study, revealing how much work needed to be accomplished; although Vargas's old education reform laws were still on the books, they were being enforced in ways prejudicial to the needs of ordinary people. The following was part of a speech given by Teixeira in Salvador on April 16, 1948.

Most of the state's educational efforts are performed by a cadre of primary schoolteachers centered in cities or dispersed throughout the interior, where in almost all cases there are no school buildings, only makeshift classrooms, and virtually no teaching materials. There are few state-funded secondary schools in Bahia, which lamentably is disorganized and congested, and only three institutions to train elementary-level teachers. Only one of them has adequate facilities. In spite of this strangulation and humiliation, there are still noble examples of teachers' devotion and persistence.

The school population reflects the conditions under which the children are forced to study. . . . This is not an exaggerated observation, and the problem cannot be expected to resolve itself under the current policy of laissez-faire educational administration. Things are worse now than twenty years ago. . . . Primary schools have been reduced to being inefficient places, for teaching reading and writing, and suffer a corresponding loss of social prestige. Middle schools have to perform the functions of elementary schools, and as a result, they are stigmatized. Secondary schools do little more than teach what primary schools should have done, and they serve mostly as gateways for the ornamental classes [elites] of the country to become public functionaries. Note the absurd situation in Salvador, the capital, with around 10,000 students in primary school and 5,500 in the two public secondary schools, evidence of the rapid disappearance of primary education and the inflation afflicting secondary schools. One municipality in the interior of the state has no primary schools at all, but has a near-luxurious secondary school.

Ordinary People:

Five Lives Affected by Vargas-Era Reforms

I. Life as a Cadet

APOLONIO DE CARVALHO

The life story of a youth from a military family who rose to be an army general (and as a young officer, a member of the Brazilian Communist Party and a volunteer for the Spanish Republican Army against Franco) illustrates the role played by the armed forces in providing career opportunities for those from nonelite backgrounds. These youths could not aspire to university educations, but they could apply to the government-run military schools, where training was rigorous, and for the most successful, they could rise within the ranks unimpeded by class or social distinctions. Given that the armed forces dominated Brazilian political life for much of the period between 1930 and 1954, and again from 1964 to the early 1980s, many of Carvalho's classmates rose to national leadership positions, although his leftist credo subjected him to persecution.

I was born in Corumbá, in Mato Grosso. My father was a northeasterner from Sergipe, a career military officer transferred from place to place. My mother was a *gaúcha,* from Bagé. I am, as they say, very Brazilian . . . with blood from north to south. In terms of my birthplace, I could say that I am an (im)prodigal son of Mato Grosso, because I left there sixty years ago and never returned.

I spent my childhood there. I started my schooling in Campo Grande; then I went to the Realengo Military Academy in Rio de Janeiro. I was commissioned as an officer. As a youth from the interior, I brought with me distinct perceptions of seeing things, different from those born in the big, modern, cosmopolitan cities. In Realengo, people were from all over, and this produced a fertile learning experience for us cadets as we learned together. The cadets were, for the most part, from the middle class, with modest economic backgrounds. Some were almost poor, but

Getúlio Vargas's presidential campaign in Juiz de Fora, Minas Gerais, in 1950. (CPDOC, Rio de Janeiro)

they brought with them personal aspirations to improve their standing in society. In Brazil, unlike other countries, we do not have a traditional military class. My father, for example, was the son of poor agriculturists who became a worker, then took the entrance exam for the Praia Vermelha Military Academy, finally becoming an officer . . .

In military school, I learned to read more and to study. At the same time, I became involved in intellectual and political issues. This was a slow process, very slow. In the beginning, I was simply an observer, someone curious. Gradually, I caught on to what was happening in Brazil, coming to understand its social problems. I brought something with me as well: my family was proud of its dislike of authoritarian regimes, of imposed force, of corruption. Both my father and my older brother were supporters of the *tenente* movement [in 1930], believing that it would bring democracy. There were between 750 and 800 of us in military school, all more or less from modest origins. We were from what you might call the "people," although we were not from the lowest class. For this reason, we had a collective predisposition to understanding the problems of the mass of the population.

Our curriculum was very professional. We studied ballistics, military strategy, topography, military history, mathematics up to integral and differential calculus. We also received a general education, learning about health, the exact sciences, the humanities. We had excellent teachers. The nonmilitary curriculum was weaker, however, so I learned on my own. I studied about history, about the evolution of society, about the debates over the transformation and destiny of peoples, some things about how politics worked. I was at Realengo at a propitious time, between 1930 and 1933, and I learned about the relationship between the military and society. . . . There was a sense of political openness and a democratic atmosphere within the academy. We discussed intensely all the problems of the time. We had a student magazine where we expressed our opinions, and I took advantage of this, writing articles, reading others to debate with colleagues, helping to produce dialogue . . .

In a way, my own social history started in 1930, when I came from Mato Grosso, still rather naive, without any real notions of Brazilian politics. I soon came to have contact and was challenged by what I saw in the federal capital. During this time, the armed forces were in the middle of political life, as an extension of the nationalistic movements of the 1920s. . . . [But] when I left the school in 1933 as a lieutenant, I was still somewhat confused. I knew that society was complex, made up of social contradictions, and I had to learn to deal with them. I knew of the existence of positive forces seeking concrete changes, in favor of the people and the nation, but that also there was a dominant class reluctant to yield its power . . .

II. Life of a Rural Schoolteacher

GERALDO VALDELÍRIOS NOVAIS

The 1930 Revolution committed itself to improving public education, which was second-rate and negligible prior to Vargas's victory. For the first time, government funding permitted the opening of public schools in the countryside; young teachers, mostly men and often with little formal training themselves, were hired to work in these new schools. One of the first was Geraldo Valdelírios Novais, from Lorena, in the coffee-growing zone of the State of São Paulo.

My name is Geraldo Valdelírios Novais, the son of José Batista Novais and Ana Rosa do Prado Novais. I was born in Lorena, São Paulo, on December 21, 1912.

My father was an artist who made his living as a carpenter, the profession of Saint Joseph. My mother took care of our home. . . . I studied at the Salesian parochial school in Lorena, a secular school run by the Salesian fathers . . . so famous that it received students from other countries, Bolivia and Paraguay. Most of the students came from land-owning families, many from other Brazilian states.

We had excellent books and excellent teachers. We studied French, English, Latin, Portuguese . . . we studied religion in depth. It is one thing to be religious, quite another to understand the fundamentals of religious faith, to have a solid foundation. We received instruction in morality and civics; we learned the rights and responsibilities of citizens; about elections and the rules of eligibility for voting. . . . I graduated in the same year as Vargas's Revolution, 1930. I stayed at home the next year, thinking about what I might do with my life. In those days, there weren't as many opportunities as today. I came from a modest family and had to wait for some favorable occasion to get a start. . . . I wanted to study law, become a judge, or enter the diplomatic corps. Be a judge, a consul, ambassador, these things. But it didn't work out. I left school at a time of economic depression and political upheaval. There were few jobs. Things only began to improve after 1933.

Of my parents' seven children, six became teachers. In the end, it was my only option . . . as it was for my three sisters and two brothers. One of them finished only after great difficulty, because he had to work, and only graduated after he was married. One took ill with rheumatism and had to stop studying. He ended up working in a pharmacy. One brother died of influenza in the 1918 epidemic; I caught it, too, and almost died, but a medical student, one of those drafted by the government to help, saved me. He warned me that my lungs would always be weak, but he was wrong: [so far,] I have lived into my eighties.

Because of a change in regulations put into effect in 1932 by the federal education ministry, I was able to enroll in the Taubaté Normal School for Teachers when the teachers' school in Guaratinguetá was filled. It was a state-run school and it was free. Most charged tuition then. Later, I transferred back to Guaratinguetá. But classes were suspended when the 1932 civil war broke out in São Paulo, and the city was punished because it housed *paulista* troops. São Paulo lost, but its moral position was so strong that, in 1933, Getúlio called elections for a constituent assembly. . . . The students at the teachers' school supported the 1932 Revolution; we wanted to participate in it. . . . My older sister volunteered to sew uniforms for the soldiers. Others volunteered in the coffee fields in place of soldiers called up to fight. . . . I served as well, in the hospital in Lorena. I was a kid, eighteen years old, and I carried wounded men from the wagons in which they were delivered up the steps of the hospital. . . . There was an outpouring of support, a sense of quiet solidarity. People donated rings, bracelets, necklaces, jewelry to pay for the war effort.

Classes started again in November after the Revolution ended. We took the final examinations and most of the students passed. I ended up studying only six months to be a teacher; everything else I learned on my own. As a result, I developed some of my own teaching methods, like explaining the rules of grammar.

After graduation, I applied for several teaching openings but was unsuccessful. The old pre-1930 ways carried over. Teaching as a career fell under the 1933 national educational reforms. Before that, many teachers lacked formal training; they prepared themselves one way or another, and then got their jobs through political influence. The only way to get a teaching job was through connections. I did have a letter from someone influential for a position in Sorocaba, but another applicant had one from someone more important, and he got the job. Eventually, the open competitions through examinations gave everyone equal opportunity. The number of points you got depended on your score and your previous experience. . . . Getúlio Vargas supported this because he was in favor of educational reform. He forced the states to adhere to national standards. As a result, at the end of 1933, I got a provisional job at a primary school in Riberão Bonito, in the Paraíba Valley. . . . in the following year, I was named a French teacher at the São José Normal School in Lorena. I taught for a year. Then, in 1936, I started working for the State of São Paulo and continued to do so for thirty-five years, until 1971. I was a primary schoolteacher, then school director, and ultimately supervisor of education.

My first job as a state employee was at a boy's school in the coffee-growing region, in São João da Bocaina, near Jaú. . . . It was isolated, rudimentary, in a building with only two rooms. There were three teachers, one in the morning and two in the afternoon. [In spite of the name of the school] some classes were for boys; others coeducational. Students of all ages were mixed. Conditions were very modest. The schools were usually on the grounds of an agricultural property. When the landowner felt like helping, things went all right. But when he didn't care, the teachers faced adversity. Some landowners ordered the share-croppers on their property to send their children to school, while others did not. . . . When harvest time came, fathers pulled their children out of school. The students, poor things, came without shoes, dressed rag-gedly, almost never able to buy pencils or notebooks. Many of us spent our entire salaries providing assistance to these pupils.

We lacked equipment and teaching materials. Many times, we had to make our own things or pay for supplies out of our own pockets. Trans-portation was difficult. There were no buses. Some teachers rode on horseback to their schools. Some landowners gave rides to teachers in their cars. It was difficult to find a place to live. Some owners let the teachers live with them in their houses. Others set up boarding arrange-ments for teachers. Once in a while, a landowner provided housing for teachers.

In this school, I earned about 300 *mil-réis* [$26] a month, a pittance. But I lived in a boardinghouse in Bocaina, took the train directly to work, and still had something to send home to help my family . . . today this would hardly be possible. During the 1930s and 1940s, teachers were not well paid, but we earned enough to maintain our families. This is not true today for teachers. When you sign a contract to teach today you are signing a vow of poverty.

At one point, the State of São Paulo established a program to help rural schools and offered specialized training for teachers who would be as-signed to rural areas. This included instruction in agricultural methods, planting, and so on. It was a very good program, but after some time, the program was terminated.

III. Life of a Bricklayer

FREDERICO HELLER

This is the story of Armando, written in 1942 by Frederico Heller. Armando's father was Italian and a bricklayer by profession. Recently married, he and his wife emigrated to rural São Paulo in 1908. He worked for a year and a half on a plantation in rural Alta Paulista. When his wife became pregnant, they moved to the state capital. His son, Armando, was born in 1910 and attended school until eleven years of age. In the selection below, he constantly talks about the cost of things. Money was always in chronic shortage and poor people's lives were deeply affected by small increases in prices.

The boy distinguished himself above all in arithmetic and design. At first, his father nourished the idea of registering his son in a professional school for mechanics because there was not adequate opportunity to learn, thoroughly, the family's traditional trade: that of bricklayer. The father desisted, finally, from this plan in the hope of gaining through working as a team—he as a mason, his son as a hod carrier—ownership of their own house. In 1929, the great dream became a reality: the family owned, in a suburb of the *paulista* capital, a house with two bedrooms, a kitchen, a shower, and a shed in which to keep the material, scaffolding, and tools.

Armando's parents were satisfied, and also, his fifteen-year-old sister, whose marriage possibilities increased with the family's social ascension. The only discontent was Armando. As a result of the paternal labor system, his professional instruction was being neglected. The father was accustomed to accept projects in a type of piecework by which the payment was by thousands of bricks laid. Thus, he lacked the time to transfer to his son more solid knowledge of the trade. In the end, the son asked his father to stop sacrificing the needs of his career to the economic interests of the moment. He also complained of never having received so much as a nickel for a salary. Thus, family disagreements arose in which Armando always displayed a certain lack of energy.

Influenced by a girlfriend, he left, in 1930, his parents' home and started to work as a mason's helper for the salary of a hod carrier, learning the trade in a very short span of time, although, as was natural, a bit superficially.

The work no longer being as lucrative as before because of his son's desertion, the father mortgaged the house and opened, "because he already had worked enough," a shop for construction materials.

Armando, however, loved the daughter of a proprietor of some small houses, president of a sports club, and "leader" of the parochial center. The young lady's family did not nurture great friendliness for Armando, who seemed to them an intelligent lad, but with little energy. Still, after certain hesitations, they did not oppose him because their daughter already was twenty-three years old and, as a result, had few possibilities to arrange a marriage in accord with the ambitious desires of her father.

In 1931, at twenty-one years of age, Armando married the young lady, moving to a house belonging to his father-in-law and whose rent was raised a little earlier. "If that lad were not my son-in-law, I would never give him the house . . . ," is the argument with which the father-in-law sought to justify the increase in rent. But Armando did not just pay for the honor of being tied to that family of great social prestige in the neighborhood with an exaggerated rent and with hardly spontaneous presents to diverse family members: he also received some material advantages from this kinship. To gratify the family and show his boss his dedication, Armando carried out renovations on many of his neighbors' houses. Such renovations were numerous because of the dismal state of the majority of the houses, which were over forty years old, and because of the hygienic demands of the prefecture, which started to become interested, during this era, in the sanitary conditions of the neighborhood, until then left out of the general progress of the *paulista* capital.

In his heart, the father-in-law was convinced that his son-in-law did not merit preference from many proprietors, but despite this, he felt honored by the fact that even its most humble members would share in the family's prestige.

Two years after his marriage, Armando already constructed houses for some residents of the suburb related to his wife's family. By not being a licensed builder, difficulties emerged, which the father-in-law solved with his connections. The father-in-law could remove certain difficulties and make it so that Armando would obtain the title of "licensed builder," but not wanting to let him leave the sphere of his protection and dependence, he did nothing of importance in his favor. In 1935, the father-in-law unexpectedly died; thus, important financial losses arose for Armando. The family prestige tended to decline, and in virtue of this, the number of the customers also diminished. In addition, demands and expenses increased in arranging for a licensed builder who would sign the ground plans and "lend" his placard. After asking, in vain, for an abatement in rent from his mother-in-law, disagreements with his wife's family soon were accentuated.

However, the small commercial house of Armando's father went bankrupt, resulting in the loss of the mortgaged house. The fall in status of the wife's family and the consequences for his own professional career induced Armando to become closer to his father, employing him as a construction foreman. This attitude, motivated by sentimental reasons and not by a cold rationality, was from the monetary point of view counterproductive, since Armando's crew—two bricklayers and two hod carriers—by no means needed its own foreman, better paid (by 30 percent) than a common bricklayer. In addition, the father did not recognize his son's authority, demoralizing in this way the entire crew.

The fact of not possessing his own license involved a reduction of 8 to 12 percent in the liquid profit of each construction. The employment of his father, with the better-paid salary sometimes for inferior services, and also rainy days produced an additional diminution of the liquid profit, which amounted to 3 to 5 percent in the construction of new houses, and 5 to 7 percent in cases of renovations and repairs.

From 1935 to 1937, Armando worked only to earn rent, food, and clothing, and also to pay expenses related to the birth of a son. In the beginning of 1938, a small grocer in the neighborhood negotiated with Armando the construction of two identical houses, conceding to him very liberal conditions. The project gave Armando a liquid profit of six *contos de réis.* Armando purchased, with the money earned, scaffolding material (until then, expensively taken on loan) for 2 *contos de réis,* a bicycle for 600 *mil-réis,* two suits and other clothes for 800 *mil-réis,* and furniture for 1 *conto de réis.* The father received 400 *mil-réis* for the deposit on a house recently rented. Four hundred and fifty *mil-réis* were spent on dresses and 900 *mil-réis* on dentures for his wife. An illness of the son cost 400 *mil-réis.* Finally, Armando spent 300 *mil-réis* on a fishing trip made in the company of two friends. Thus, there remained a "deficit" of 850 *mil-réis,* augmented by the fact that there existed an overdue debit of 300 *mil-réis* at the grocery store and another in the amount of 280 *mil-réis* at the hardware store. He added an appreciable elevation to his standard of living.

At the end of 1938, Armando accepted the construction of an elegant, multilevel home. Contrary to the earlier construction, the owner was not from Armando's social class or a close social companion. Contrary to the earlier project, the contract did not stipulate advanced payment of installments. The builder could receive the diverse installments only after having entirely terminated the respective phases of the construction, since the contract ought to guarantee the interests of the proprietor, who risks his money, while Armando is unable to give any guarantee.

In order to receive as soon as possible the amount of the first installment, Armando wanted to expedite approval of the ground plan by the prefecture; he fell into the trap of a dishonest shipping clerk and spent, in the end, for the approval that ought to have cost, with the inclusion of the fees for the licensed builder, 1 *conto* and 300 *mil-réis,* nothing less than 2 *contos* and 100 *mil-réis.* More and more, the conditions of the contract obliged Armando to purchase all the material for the construction on credit at a small store in the suburb specializing in dealing with small "contractors" without their own capital. This dependency raised the prices by 15 to 20 percent for sand, bricks, whitewash, cement, and wood for the floor and the roof, and likewise doors and windows. The plumber who also depended on the small store charged, for each meter of pipe put in place and the sanitary fixtures, almost 30 percent more than a plumber who receives and pays in cash. To complete the predicament, misunderstandings arose with the proprietor over the interpretation of some of the contract's clauses. What does it mean to say, for example, "first quality" in the case of plaster, ornamental tiles, windows, and paints?

The interpretation did not depend exclusively on the legal and technical rules; it was, in great part, a question of local usage, just as good or bad faith. Until then, when a misunderstanding arose, the settlement was made in the ambiance of a bar on equal footing on the basis of the same economic possibilities and the same social level, but now the case was different: the proprietor had all the trump cards in his hand. But to avoid any appearance of arbitrariness, he consulted an official appraiser, an architect from the city, a man very correct and above any suspicion of partiality, but beforehand hardly friendly to "this small fry who only knows how to toil more or less, and bungles all the prices."

The architect agreed with the proprietor much more than the latter would have imagined; Armando had to acquiesce completely to the friendly advice of the appraiser and the enduring demands of the proprietor. Delivering, at last, the construction finished according to the desires of the owner, his total financial loss mounted to 8 *contos de réis,* in addition to the lost profit.

Armando sold the scaffolding for 1 *conto* and 500 *mil-réis* and took 2 *contos* borrowed from a friend. To save her quite-threatened family prestige, his mother-in-law gave, after much discussion, a bond to the hardware store, for which he was responsible to pay 4 *contos de réis* within two years. The interest was 12 percent annually.

All these complications, exaggerated by some malicious scandalmongers, jolted Armando's commercial reputation, whose earlier situation already was delicate owing to the lack of his own capital. No one any longer wanted to risk anything advancing him money for the acquisition of material, since the mother-in-law's bond included only the debt. Furnishing new material, the store calculated an increase over the common prices never less than 20 percent. In this anguishing situation, Armando dismissed his father, and his wife started to sew for people outside the family. With superhuman efforts, which furthermore helped to consolidate the marriage, until then hardly happy, both succeeded in reducing in two and a half years the debts to 2 *contos* and 600 *mil-réis*.

However, the neighborhood has developed rapidly. Armando is not able to benefit much from this circumstance because of the lack of capital or, at least, the lack of credit at reasonable interest. One other difficulty is that of not being a licensed builder. Those interested in construction, attracted by the relatively modest prices for land in this neighborhood, do not place much trust in the somewhat rustic builders and masons from the semirural settlement. Armando is one of these disqualified outcasts: he does not wear fine clothing, he does not make use of a modern office, and he owns, instead of the latest model automobile, just a bicycle.

On the other hand, the number of renovations of old houses is increasing. Without economic and sentimental relations with the new residents of the neighborhood, and in opposition to them, there is produced in the original center composed of homeowners, artisans, and clerks, a unity of interests and points of view until then unknown. As a result of the social disparity [between new and old residents], the sports rivalries between the two local clubs, and even the national resentments between the old Portuguese and Italian immigrants, are disappearing.

These economic and mental transformations improved Armando's professional possibilities a bit. The rise in prices for material at the beginning of 1941 signaled a new setback for him and all the other small contractors. Because of a lack of capital and, sometimes, foresight, they could not save themselves from the effects of scarcity and speculation. In June of the same year, Armando arranged, for the first time since the disaster at the end of 1938, the construction of a house. This time, execution of the project obeyed a more efficient pattern. The profit of 4 *contos* was spent on the renovation of some of his mother-in-law's shacks, having already settled the remaining debit at the hardware store. In February 1942, Armando began to employ his father, since he finds that he is "morally obligated" to that.

IV. Life of a Railroad Worker

MAURÍLIO THOMÁS FERREIRA

Looking back on his life nearly a half century later, Maurílio Ferreira, who was born in 1915 in rural Espírito Santo, recognized that obtaining a job with the railroad had been the turning point. Regular employment meant school for his children, a future. To be a railroad worker meant security and a pension. Perhaps because he understood that so few other workers received these benefits, Ferreira idolized Vargas, considering him his personal benefactor. He would have scoffed at social scientists writing that Vargas's labor measures were enacted to control the labor force. As long as Ferreira belonged to the union, his wife would buy food at reduced prices at the union-run store. He would receive protection from arbitrary dismissal, and his children would be eligible for scholarships available to families of union members. This would have been impossible were it not for the social legislation of the 1930s and early 1940s.

My full name is Maurílio Thomás Ferreira. I had a whole bunch of brothers, five or six. Most of them were older. I even have a photograph of them. Three were drafted into the guard (*Tiro de Guerra*), all at once, and they had to go even though they were married and had small children. . . . Before the Vargas government things were out of hand. . . . We lived on my father's land he had bought . . . everyone in the family had a little house and a small plot. . . . He distilled *cachaça* (rum) from sugarcane. . . . I had four sisters also. My father was angry because he now had to take care of his three daughters-in-law and their kids. My father had to pay for their uniforms, shoes—in the countryside, you had to provide everything yourself.

I attended a rural school, very rudimentary. After primary school, I studied with a teacher my father hired for all of us. Getúlio regulated lots of things. Before that things were disorganized. I was now the oldest boy living at home. My father decided to send me to the army, too, to get it over with, so I lied about my age. . . . I served in the army in 1930 when I was fifteen. . . . I was sent first to Vitória and then to Rio de Janeiro, to the Praia Vermelho barracks. I got out in December. I returned to work with my father and, when I was twenty-two, I got married, in 1937. I grew corn, potatoes, and coffee beans, and raised pigs. There was no place to sell things, so I had to transport my produce, and this was expensive. We made very little money. Things grew well; my father sometimes harvested 10,000 sacks of coffee. But we had too little land for all of my broth-

ers and their families. All of my family were *crentes* (evangelical Protestants). There was a church in Córrego Rico. We went. I directed a choir.
We were baptized. I met my wife there, when she was twelve years old.

[In 1942] I decided, all of a sudden, to leave. We had two children
already. We went to [the town of] Muniz Freire and bought a house with
my savings. I had no job, nothing. I worked as a barber but didn't make
very much; the town was too small. I worked for the mayor's office. I got
one job through one of my brothers-in-law, who was a driver for an Arab.
I became foreman on his farm, but he didn't pay me. I stayed for a year
and then left for another foreman's job. Then I got a job with the railroad. I got it [in 1945] when I went to Cachoeiro to sell chickens. A fellow
I sold them to told me to try and get a railroad job, that they were hiring
many people. He introduced me to some officials of the Leopoldina
Railroad. They hired me. I liked the idea of living in Cachoeiro because
there was a school there my kids could attend. My children all studied,
one as far as the fifth grade, the others to high school. And railroad
workers were eligible for pensions; [we were] one of the first. . . . When
I started working, they registered me in the railroad pension institute.
There was an enormous union building in Cachoeiro. The union sold
provisions and merchandise to us at cheaper prices. Later on, the union
gave a scholarship for my youngest son to study at high school.

Starting in 1945, my wife and I always voted in elections, every year. . . .
I joined the PTB . . . and became active in the union. . . . I admired
Getúlio Vargas, always voted for him. . . . He named the state interventors. . . . He was leading Brazil forward. . . . When he killed himself, it
was an enormous shock. . . . I kept his photograph [which the union had
given to us] and a copy of his suicide letter, to remind me of what he did
for poor Brazilians. . . . He was the chief organizer of this country.

V. Life of a Factory Worker

JOANA DE MASI ZERO

*Joana de Masi Zero, the daughter of Italian immigrants, joined the ranks of
millions of urban Brazilians who loved Vargas in spite of his flaws. Her testimony explains how his social reforms improved her life.*

My name is Joana de Masi Zero. I was born in São Paulo on October 23,
1916, in the district of Mooca. In those days, Mooca wasn't like it is today.

There were few houses; you could walk around. There wasn't much movement, although the streetcar passed by Ipanema Street . . . you catch it and were downtown in ten minutes.

We lived on Guarapuava Street. The houses there were simple, like all of the ones on old streets, close together. Ours was a duplex, with large rooms with high ceilings. The privy was outside. Later on, we built one inside, but the old outhouse remained in use, too. Our yard was ample, with many plants, including guavas, oranges, and even a pear tree. We kept chickens in the back of the yard. We also had Angora cats, who jumped over the wall and ran around everywhere, but they didn't get close to the chickens . . .

My sister Carmela and I stayed by the front door; when neighbors passed by we would chat with them. My mother didn't let us go out alone because we were girls and it could be dangerous. When Carmela and I and our friends did go out we all would hold hands; sometimes we walked singing. I only went through primary school. It was a good school; I started when I was eight. In those days, you started then and went until you were twelve.

I studied in a private school, Sete de Setembro, and then went on to another. My sister Carmela and I finished, but our older sister had to stop and go to work. In school, boys and girls had separate classes. No one mixed in those days, even during recess. The boys stayed on one side and the girls on the other. The school yard was divided so that no one could have contact with anyone from the other group. They entered on the left side and we on the right. The boys' teacher was very energetic. Boys are more rebellious; sometimes the teachers punished the boys right in the corridor. We wore uniforms. On regular days, we had blouses with the school emblem embroidered on it. On special days, we wore uniforms of white linen, pleated skirts, and white blouses. We wore white pants for physical education. . . . Everyone was neat and well groomed.

We studied many things: Portuguese grammar, arithmetic, history, geography, science, sewing, singing, gymnastics, everything. We studied four hours each day, from eight to noon . . .

My family worked hard. My father was a textile supervisor. In those days, they earned a good living . . . 200 *mil-réis* a month in 1920. This was good money. Salaries weren't meager, like today. You could buy what you needed at home. My mother even saved a bit. We built our house and paid it off fairly quickly, but then my father had an accident and died. He was handling a machine when it injured him. He hung on for a month. On his death certificate it said he died of pneumonia, because he couldn't breathe. My mother wanted to give him medicine against infection, but he refused, saying, "I'm not going to take anything!" He said his blood was good, that he didn't need anything.

I was five when my father died. My grandfather came to live with us, but he died, too. Only the women remained, my mother, my grandmother, and we three sisters.

The house was my mother's, but the rest? For food and clothing we had to work. First, my mother went to work in a chicken coop; later, she started to sew men's clothing at home. My oldest sister started working when she still was a girl. She was the first, when she was twelve. Then I went to work, and finally Carmela. At first, she stayed at home, doing chores: she would prepare lunch and keep house. My older sister worked in a textile factory, going from one to another. It was she who taught Carmela how to do textile work. My first job was sewing carpets by hand. I was twelve. I worked for a year and a half. It was in a private house, and they hired girls to work. Then I went to a factory, the Santa Madalena, on Bresser Street. When I went to work there my mother had to get me a work permit because I was still a minor, fourteen years of age. Actually, I was younger; I started in July, but my birthday was in October. Only then I worked legally. Only my sisters and I left school. Our other friends continued because their parents could afford it. . . . When I was fifteen, I moved to a more difficult machine in the factory. You earned more . . . forty-five *mil-réis* a month if you produced up to your daily quota . . .

I went from factory to factory . . . finding different jobs. . . . I worked in one factory for twenty-five years. Getúlio was president. Many people said that he was a dictator, but he did many things for us workers. His labor laws were good. There were no strikes, at least never at places where I was working. Sometimes, to avoid strikes, the bosses dismissed us early, saying to us: "You go home; we're going to stop the machines so we won't have any fights at the door." They meant with the militants. All the laws we have today were thanks to [Vargas]. . . . The first minimum wage was forty *mil-réis* a month. Then they started to withhold payments for pensions—three *mil-réis* a month. Everyone paid whether they wanted to or not. It was taken out of your pay envelope. Later, this system changed for the worse; retirement paid almost nothing. Every time the politicians changed the laws they took more from us. Getúlio's time was good; later, I don't know. We earned well and prices didn't go up. You went out to buy milk, for example, and the price was always the same. We didn't live in luxury; we made our own clothes—we knew how to sew—we were well dressed, we had money to go to the movies every week, sometimes twice. We ate well, we lived well. They say he was a dictator, but for us he was good.

But when the factory moved to Mooca, with new machinery, production didn't go well. We earned little at the beginning . . . our salaries were affected. But then the law required that the employers give raises of 35 percent. My employer said that he couldn't, that he couldn't even pay 5 percent more. . . . He didn't even want to negotiate. We went to the union, and the union officials took our case. Unions worked well then, at least ours did. It had a lawyer who worked for it, Dr. Paranhos. We could talk to him about any problem we had. The complaint took more or less a year to be decided, and in the end we won. So the boss left Mooca and moved the factory to Vila Maria, because he wanted to cheat us. He hired others and paid them less. On the whole, though, our bosses were decent, human. They came to visit; my mother invited them into the living room. They always asked about how my mother was.

When Getúlio died it was like a death in the family. People were sad. No one talked; everyone was quiet. It was a really sorrowful day, especially for the workers. Things were closed for, I think, three days.

I retired when I turned sixty-five. The first month I earned the same as I had made when I was working, and after that, for a while as well. Then they began to take a little here and there, and the government took more and more, and now I earn almost nothing.

Vargas's Suicide Letter, 1954

Getúlio Vargas

Vargas's death by his own hand in the presidential palace came hours before a military coup would have ousted him from the office to which he had been elected democratically in 1950. From 1930 to 1945, he had governed as a dictator, only to be removed once before by the generals. His suicide stunned the country and revealed deep-seated affection from ordinary citizens. The following piece from August 24, 1954, which may have been written as a farewell speech rather than intended as a suicide note, was likely edited by journalist J. S. Maciel Filho, Vargas's closest aide, as the political skies darkened. It shows indignation and sarcasm, lashing out at "interests" Vargas considered to have backed him into a corner.

Once more the forces and interests against the people are newly coordinated and raised against me. They do not accuse me, they insult me; they do not fight me, they slander me and refuse to give me the right of defense. They seek to drown my voice and halt my actions so that I no longer continue to defend, as I always have defended, the people, and principally the humble. I follow the destiny that is imposed on me. After decades of domination and plunder by international economic and financial groups, I made myself chief of an unconquerable revolution. I began the work of liberation and I instituted a regime of social liberty. . . . I was forced to resign. I returned to govern on the arms of the people.

A subterranean campaign of international groups joined with national interests, revolting against the regime of workers' guarantees. The excess-profits law was held up in Congress. Hatreds were unleashed against the justice of a revision of minimum wages. I wished to create national liberty by developing our riches through Petrobrás [the state petroleum company], which had scarcely begun to operate when the

João Goulart, who would assume the presidency in 1961, at Vargas's wake in Rio de Janeiro in 1954. (CPDOC, Rio de Janeiro)

wave of agitation clouded its beginnings. Electrobrás [the power utility] was obstructed to the point of despair. They do not want workers to be free. They do not want the people to be independent.

I assumed my government during an inflationary spiral that was destroying the rewards of work. Profits by foreign companies reached as much as 500 percent annually. In declarations of goods that we import, frauds of more than 100 million dollars per year were proved. I saw the coffee crisis increase the value of our principal product. We tried to maintain that price, but the reply was such violent pressure on our economy that we were forced to surrender. I have fought month after month, day after day, hour after hour, resisting constant, incessant pressures, unceasingly bearing it all in silence, forgetting everything and giving myself in order to defend the people that now fall abandoned. I cannot give you more than my blood. If the birds of prey wish the blood of anybody, they wish to continue to suck the blood of the Brazilian people. I offer my life in the holocaust. I choose this means to be with you always. When they humiliate you, you will feel my soul suffering at your side. When hunger knocks at your door, you will feel within you the energy to fight for yourselves and for your children. When you are scorned, my memory will give you the strength to react. My sacrifice will keep you united and my name will be your battle standard. Each drop of my blood will be an immortal call to your conscience and will uphold the sacred will to resist.

To hatred, I reply with forgiveness. And to those who think that they have defeated me, I reply with my victory. I was a slave of the people and today I am freeing myself for eternal life. But this people, whose slave I was, will no longer be slave to anyone. My sacrifice will remain forever in your souls and my blood will be the price of your ransom. I fought against the looting of Brazil. I fought against the looting of the people. I have fought bare breasted. The hatred, infamy, and calumny did not defeat my spirit. I have given you my life. I gave you my life. Now I offer you my death. Nothing remains. Serenely, I take my first step on the road to eternity and I leave life to enter history.

V

Seeking Democracy

and Equity

Vargas's efforts to promote national integration, industrial development, and benefits for skilled workers sped Brazil's maturation as a modern nation. The influx of migrants from the depressed hinterlands accelerated urban growth: by 1960, most Brazilians lived in cities. Expanded transportation and communications made distances shorter, at least for those who could afford air tickets, automobiles, telephones, and television sets.[1] A former leftist, Vice President João Café Filho assumed the presidency after Vargas's suicide, although the armed forces leadership considered ousting him. Juscelino Kubitschek, the governor of Minas Gerais, won the 1955 presidential election on a platform promising national development and democracy. Buoyed by foreign investment, Kubitschek oversaw the construction of the new national capital of Brasília, spurred the growth of the automobile industry, and shepherded the country through a maze of growing pains. When Kubitschek stepped down in 1960, however, the country faced an enormous foreign debt and labor unrest. The 1960 election was the first in Brazilian history where the incumbent turned over power to the opposition party, led by *paulista* reform candidate and Governor Jânio Quadros. Quadros's victory came less from party strength than from his personal popularity, as well as his promise to sweep Brazil clean of corruption and inefficiency. His principal opponent was Marshal Henrique Teixeira Lott, Kubitschek's war minister. While Lott was defeated at the polls, his vice presidential candidate, leftist João Goulart, won election.

During the months prior to his inauguration, Quadros departed on an extensive trip abroad, stopping in Cuba just one year after Castro's revolution. Journalists, who had been sympathetic to him during his campaign, began to emphasize his personal eccentricities.[2] Moreover, Congress balked at his proposed reforms, none of which were enacted. He applied an austerity program to stabilize the currency, an unpopular measure. Guanabara (Rio de Janeiro) Governor Carlos Lacerda, who had supported Quadros, began denouncing him angrily, in the same tone as Lacerda had attacked Vargas in 1954.

Seven months after he had taken office, the mercurial Quadros abruptly resigned. It is speculated that he hoped that Congress and the armed forces would seek his forgiveness, giving him additional powers to deal with the growing crises around him, but the country remained silent, and Quadros forlornly flew out of the country into exile. Goulart, more outspokenly leftist than Quadros and therefore an anathema to the military, was in the People's Republic of China when Quadros resigned, but he was permitted to return and take the oath of office as part of a deal that made him president under a parliamentary system that limited his executive powers. The first part of Goulart's presidency was rather successful. He assumed a moderate posture and worked quietly behind the scenes to restore the presidential system.[3] Voters in 1962 restored the presidential system by a five-to-one margin.

But the economic situation deteriorated ominously, exacerbated by runaway inflation and Goulart's efforts to keep workers' wages on par with the soaring cost of living. To stabilize the economy in a long-term manner, Goulart would have had to enact austerity measures similar to those that had helped bring down Quadros, and the militant labor unions and left-wing press would not allow him to do so. This united the rich and the upper-middle class against him, and his efforts to mobilize the mass of the population failed. By mid-1963, armed forces officers were beginning to conspire against him, with the full moral support of influential property owners, industrialists, bankers, and the U.S. State Department, since 1959 vigilant against another Castro-like takeover in the hemisphere. These were the years of the John F. Kennedy–Lyndon B. Johnson Alliance for Progress, and much of its funding was channeled to Brazil's Northeast to combat poverty and the influence of Francisco Julião's Peasant Leagues, which sought to take unproductive land from wealthy owners and give it to landless peasants. There were seventy-six million Brazilians in 1963, and many feared that the masses might be stirred by demagogic promises to abandon their traditional posture of docility in the face of hardship. Although most of the population was under twenty-five years of age, by 1960, the electorate had been enlarged to encompass almost one-quarter of the population.

During 1963 and early 1964, Goulart moved steadily further to the Left. Radicals took control of the leading labor unions, combating the regime's efforts at fiscal stabilization. He began to attack multinational corporations and what he called the imperialist activities of the United States. What stood in Goulart's way was what political scientists have dubbed the "system." Oliveiro S. Ferreira shows how "although it has no clear-cut constituents, it is comparable to an organism which reacts as a whole, as though by reflex, when one of its vital organs is threatened."[4] Philippe C. Schmitter deftly puts the definition in more academic terminology:

[D]espite obvious differences in interest and attitude, the *sistema* was formed by sedimentation, not by metamorphosis. Inter-sectorial flows of capital and entrepreneurial talent, inter-élitist family contacts, generalized fear of the enormous latent potential for conflict of such a weakly-integrated society, heterogeneity within the rural, commercial, industrial, and proletarian classes—all have helped seal the compromise. The success of this non-antagonistic pattern in turn ensured a continuity in the political culture and a reinforcement of those attitudes stressing the avoidance of conflict, dialogue, ideological flexibility, tolerance, and compromise.[5]

According to this view, the "system" reacted in self-defense when Goulart violated the rules of the compromise and attempted to appeal directly to the masses. When noncommissioned officers led by sergeants mutinied in Brasília in September 1964, he refused to condemn it, infuriating the military command. Araken Tavora's account of the repercussions within the armed forces, published in Brazil in English, is included toward the start of this section. Governor Carlos Lacerda, whose vitriolic attacks on Goulart grew in intensity, forged an alliance against Goulart with the governors of the other two most powerful states—São Paulo's Adhemar de Barros and Magalhães Pinto of Minas Gerais.

Starting on March 31 and ending on April 1, 1964, the military ousted the president and drove him into exile in Uruguay. The coup, which its makers called a revolution, drew almost no opposition, although it was bitterly received by university students, progressive intellectuals, and labor officials. The middle and upper classes, however, welcomed the declaration by the military leaders of the coup that they would stay on until national reconstruction was achieved. Strikes were banned, a censorship apparatus put into place, arrests were carried out (at first, only of active militants; later, of many people simply suspected of being leftist). The military leadership remembered that "the armed forces had withdrawn after intervening in 1945, 1954, 1955, and 1961, only to see the old Vargas crowd come back; they were determined never to let it happen again."[6] A Swiss analyst put it more bluntly: "The Army, tired of the incoherence of the political successors of Getúlio Vargas, the father of 'populism' in Brazil, seized power and, departing from the traditional role of guarantor given to it by the Constitution, decided to assume the responsibilities of power."[7]

The first military president, Marshal Humberto Castelo Branco (1964–1966), projected an image of being a democratic man, and was not unpopular. The son of a career army officer from northern Ceará, he articulated the rationale for the coup in reasonable language, and was warmly received abroad. One of his first moves, however, was to remove from office 55 deputies, 7 state governors, 122 military officers, and 4,500 government employees. Leading politicians linked to Goulart, including Quadros and Kubitschek, were stripped of their political rights.[8] Other figures, like progressive Archbishop Dom Helder Câmara, became "nonpersons," kept out of the newspapers and media, and under surveillance. Because Goulart was considered an heir to Vargas's populism, even the late president-dictator, still popular among older Brazilians, became a nonperson of sorts.

With the opposition in Congress purged, the military realigned with remaining legislators into two new party blocs, the right-wing ARENA and the moderate Brazilian Democratic Movement. Wags called them the "Party of Yes" and the "Party of Yes, Sir!" The military-era Congress did little but rubber stamp what the military wanted, including the 1967 Constitution, whose authoritarian provisions are recounted in this section. The chilling warnings hammered home in the government's propaganda campaign against dissent, and in favor of patriotic loyalty, come through loud and clear in the selection titled "The Maximum Norm of the Exercise of Liberty."

Under the military presidency of Artur Costa e Silva (1966–1969), the repression worsened. Left-wing militants had taken to the streets, robbing banks and kidnapping prominent persons (including the U.S. ambassador, who was freed with others in exchange for the release of political prisoners). The political police and intelligence agencies of each of the armed forces carried out mass arrests, often using torture on its prisoners, and drove thousands of others from their jobs or into exile.[9] As ever, whether one was tortured, murdered, or simply allowed to leave the country depended on one's personal and family connections; it helped to have a cousin or brother-in-law who was a colonel. While Brazil's repression was not as savage as under the military dictatorships in neighboring Argentina and Chile, it was terrible for those caught up in it, and it influenced the emergence of a generation of apolitical university students and intellectuals. The essays in this section by Christopher Dunn and Elizabeth Ginway address the issue of cultural life under the dictatorship.

Abandoning Goulart's populist nationalism, the military regime welcomed foreign investment back into Brazil. Enforced labor peace, coupled with generous tax and other concessions, produced an industrial boom praised by economists as Brazil's "economic miracle." The affluent classes, who for the most part endorsed the military regime, showed their willingness to sacrifice the apparatus of representative democracy for guided economic development and prosperity. Only a handful of attorneys and spokespersons for the Catholic Left protested the cancellation of the right of habeas corpus, although individual acts of savagery by the regime—such as the murder of a popular São Paulo journalist, Vladimir Herzog—brought thousands into the streets in protest. Still, some argued that the Brazilian people were not ready for democracy. Indeed, democracy was not restored until 1985, more than two decades after tanks rolled through the streets of Brazil's major cities.

Notes

1 See Robert Wesson and David V. Fleischer, "The Authoritarian-Democratic Background," in *Brazil in Transition* (New York: Praeger, 1983), p. 14.
2 See Wesson and Fleischer, "The Authoritarian-Democratic Background," pp. 18–19; Georges-André Fiechtner, *Brazil since 1964: Modernization under a Military Regime* (John Wiley and Sons: New York, 1972).

3 Wesson and Fleischer, "The Authoritarian-Democratic Background," p. 19.

4 Oliveiro S. Ferreira, "Uma Caraterização do Sistema," *O Estado de São Paulo* (17 and 24 October 1965), cited by Fiechtner, *Brazil since 1964*, p. 9.

5 Philippe C. Schmitter, *Interest Conflict and Political Change in Brazil* (Stanford, Calif.: Stanford University Press, 1971), p. 378.

6 Fiechtner, *Brazil since 1964*, p. xii.

7 Cited in Wesson and Fleischer, "The Authoritarian-Democratic Background," p. 25.

8 Wesson and Fleischer, "The Authoritarian-Democratic Background," p. 27.

9 See the Archdiocese of São Paulo, *Torture in Brazil, 1964–1979*, 2d ed., translated by Jaime Wright (Austin: University of Texas Press, 1998). Based on the project, "Brazil, Never Again," more than 2,700 pages of testimony documenting close to 300 forms of torture employed during the military dictatorship.

Rehearsal for the Coup

Araken Tavora

When left-leaning Vice President João Goulart rose to the presidency after the abrupt resignation of Jânio Quadros in 1961, the political atmosphere became more polarized than ever. Goulart, the heir to his mentor Getúlio Vargas's Labor Party, attempted to dislodge from power the archconservatives in the armed forces, as well as in state and local governments. In turn, Goulart's opponents, led by the fiery governor of Guanabara, Carlos Lacerda—a communist as a youth, but a convert to the anticommunist cause by the late 1950s—maneuvered to block Goulart's controversial (but legal) moves. Newspapers screamed charges and countercharges in their headlines; strikes broke out almost daily. This story of the growing crisis is told by a twenty-eight-year reporter for Manchete *magazine and Lacerda's* Tribuna da Imprensa, *Araken Tavora.*

The first formal warning came on June 5, 1962: in a letter to War Minister General Segadas Viana, the commander of the Fourth Military Region covering the State of Minas Gerais, General Rafael Souza Aguiar denounced increasing communist infiltration among the troops under his command. But no one listened to him. The war minister declared that the army was not involved in politics. Yet, at the same time, leftist General Osvino Fereira Alves, Goulart-appointed commander of the First Army, was trying to persuade trade unions to force Congress to name Foreign Minister San Tiago Dantas as the new prime minister. Congress, however, did not yield to the pressure: an old labor politician and former schoolteacher, José Brochado da Rocha, was elected.

In the first half of July, another political crisis developed. In a cabinet shuffle, new military ministers were appointed: for the War Ministry the choice fell on a seasoned general known for his democratic convictions. The name: Nelson de Mello, an army brigadier general who after his return from World War II had played an important role in the military coup that ousted dictator Getúlio Vargas in 1945, and who was to play the same part in the revolution that was to oust João Goulart. [To counter de Mello's choice] Goulart appointed a leftist admiral, Araújo Susano, as navy minister. Similarly, in the air force, Reinaldo de Carvalho, a lieutenant general loosely identified with Goulart, was appointed. Susano's appointment only increased the crisis, and eleven admirals immediately resigned. Uneasiness grew in the air force, too. For his turn, War Minister Nelson de Mello asked the businessmen of Brazil to get together and join in the fight against the growing communist threat.

These events brought the political tension throughout the country to a new peak. Then, the intention of Goulart's government became known: a coup was being carefully planned. Goulart intended to call up the armed forces to "restore peace," to take over the State of Guanabara, arrest conservative Carlos Lacerda, and then establish himself as dictator. Goulart's cabinet met twice to discuss military intervention in Guanabara, both times in the face of strong resistance on the part of the war minister. General de Mello finally prevailed, and the crisis cooled down.

The Brazilian trade unions then started a nationwide campaign to force Congress to abolish the parliamentary regime and give back full power to João Goulart, who claimed to be fettered by parliamentarianism, a system, said he, "that had been imposed on the country by a group of dissatisfied military men and reactionaries." The situation deteriorated rapidly during August, becoming worse by mid-September when the Military Club, whose members are all army officers, refused to pay homage to João Goulart. The navy plunged into a new crisis precipitated by the appointment of leftist Admiral Cândido Aragão as commander in chief of the marines, and the dismissal of some admirals and naval officers. In the army, uneasiness also grew as some notorious leftist officers were promoted by the president, and the war minister's opposition to João Goulart was brought out into the open. On September 14, the cabinet fell when the president tried to oust War Minister Nelson de Mello, whose democratic convictions constituted a barrier to his dictatorial aims.

From then on, the army chiefs became convinced that President Goulart's true objectives were to clear the way for communism and dictatorship. His tactics included the elimination of all democrats from key positions in the administration and the stimulation of subversion. Based on these convictions, six army generals, including Nelson de Mello, Ulhôa Cintra, Alves Bastos, Mourão Filho, and Dario Coelho, as well as Admiral Sylvio Heck and Air Force General Grum Moss, led by General of the Army Oswaldo Cordeiro de Farias, began to plan an armed coup to oust President João Goulart and save Brazil from what was now clearly taking shape—an immense communist conspiracy supported by the federal government.

While the communists increased their control of key posts in the administration, and other subversive organizations (such as the illegal General Command of Workers, which united all communist-ruled trade unions in the country to carry out politically inspired strikes) were created to spur unrest, the planners of the revolution redoubled their activity within the armed forces. Goulart's opponents found new receptivity for their ideas in the country's most responsible circles, and in the army, navy, and air force, since the majority of the military personnel was becoming increasingly convinced that if the president were not stopped in time, Brazil would inevitably fall into the hands of communism.

The U.S. blockade of Cuba in October 1962 was to show the extent of communist infiltration in the armed forces. Alleging the need for a change in key posts of the ground forces, the government removed democratic officers from command of the most important and well-equipped units throughout the country, and substituted for them notorious leftist officers.

In December, the new minister of war, General of the Army Amaury Kruel, revealed that a coup against democracy was being prepared in Brazil. Politically inspired strikes were declared in the country's most important centers as a communist response to the war minister's warning. In the State of Guanabara, tension mounted daily. There were indications that the federal government was about to take over the state, and Guanabara's Governor Carlos Lacerda announced that he would only leave the palace as a dead man.

The crisis cooled when War Minister General Amaury Kruel sent a message to the governor: "Put all the agitators in jail and you may count on my full support."

The return to a presidential form of government after a plebiscite on January 6, 1963, led automatically to the fall of the cabinet. When the new cabinet was formed, the former military ministers kept their posts, as did all the leftist officers who had previously been appointed to other key military posts. As a result, the unrest in the navy ranks increased. General Osvino Alves and Admiral Cândido Aragão were bitterly criticized for knowingly permitting lack of discipline and communist infiltration in the troops.

The heaviest opposition to Goulart came from Guanabara and São Paulo, whose governors were again threatened with federal intervention. The movement to depose Goulart gathered force as more political and military figures reluctantly agreed that revolution was the only solution. And in Congress, even the Social Democratic Party, the traditional ally of Goulart's Labor Party, began visibly to divorce itself from the government.

The president then started a new move: the country needed structural reforms. Some basic reforms, especially land and tax reforms, were announced. But the measures—many of them unconstitutional—through which such reforms would be put into effect were clearly designed to appeal to the ignorant masses rather than to accomplish anything. At that time, there was a visible deterioration in Brazil's economic and financial situation. The cost of living increased more than 70 percent, while the rate of inflation neared 6 percent monthly. The country faced innumerable and serious problems, of which rising inflation and poverty were the main issues.

The Military Regime

Antonio Pedro Tota

The political-military coup d'état of March 1964 was the result of several previous attempts. This time, the conspirators triumphed because they received important help from the urban middle classes and large portions of the business sector. The coup implanted a military government that consolidated itself in power. In December 1968, because of what amounted to a coup within the military government itself, a new authoritarian state was born, taking control of all aspects of Brazilian life by means of the repression of democratic freedoms and the neutralization of potential opposition. Antonio Pedro Tota, a professor of history at São Paulo's Catholic University and author of a popular textbook on Brazilian history, offers an analysis from the perspective of one who lived through the military period.

With the ouster of João Goulart, the presidency was taken over by the then-president of the Chamber of Deputies, Ranieri Mazzilli. In reality, power was exercised by the Supreme Revolutionary Command, composed of officers from the three military branches: General Artur da Costa e Silva, Admiral Augusto Rademaker, and Brigadier General Francisco de Mello. These military men were responsible for the Additional Act #1 (AI-1) that canceled direct elections of the presidency, substituting, in its place, indirect elections. It was on the basis of AI-1 that the National Congress elected Marshal Castello Branco, one of the most important military leaders involved in the movement that overthrew Goulart. The military men who took power belonged to at least two distinct factions, which jockeyed for leadership of the movement. The first were the Castelistas, the so-called Sorbonne group, influenced by General Golbery do Couto e Silva, and dedicated to combating through repression communism, the Brazilian Labor Party, and the Left. They also favored modernizing the national economy. The second were the "hard-liners," led by Costa e Silva, who believed that the campaign against communism and subversives should be harsher. To attain this goal, they established the Police Military Inquiry to investigate suspects linked to popular-based movements from the Goulart period.

Both groups were responsible for the climate of fear that gripped the country. Many prominent figures had their political rights taken away, including ex-president Juscelino Kubitschek. Many people were jailed and seized simply for suspicion; books that were considered subversive were burned by the agencies of state repression. The Castelistas believed that this repressive phase should be brief and that the country should gradually be returned to normal conditions. They also carried out reforms to modernize the state administrative apparatus . . .

[But the hard-liners fought back]. The National Congress was closed for a month in 1966 because it did not agree with the actions to strip people of their rights. It was necessary to occupy the Congress with army troops to back up the decree. The dictatorship consolidated its power. [Congress reopened] in January 1967 to work on a new constitution for Brazil. The candidate selected to be the next president was army minister, Costa e Silva. This signaled the defeat for the Castelista faction. Before transferring power to Costa e Silva, President Castelo Branco put into effect additional measures that gave even greater powers to the executive branch: the Press Censorship Law and the National Security Law . . .

Anxiety filled the air. Promised reforms to move the country in the direction of democratization never materialized. Opposition groups on the Left—including students, labor leaders, and members of the Communist Party—turned to clandestine means of opposition. The tension exploded in March 1968 when the police killed Edson Luís, a student, during antiregime protests in the streets of Rio de Janeiro. The wave of protests grew: parades, rallies, clashes with police troops. The moderate political opposition (MDB), intellectuals, and priests manifested their support of the protesting students and organized a "March of 100,000," in which diverse sectors of society were represented. The student movement linked up with labor activists. Strikes followed . . .

The government responded immediately. It decreed the Institutional Act #5, which hardened the dictatorship. The government would maintain order by any means. The president of the republic assumed near absolute power. Repression was broad-based. Congress was closed, and almost half of the MDB party were either deprived of their rights or imprisoned. Many professors, intellectuals, journalists, and even some military officers were dismissed from their jobs. All means of communication were subject to state censorship. Anyone could be charged with treason on the basis of national security. Many musicians and artists were forced to leave the country . . .

Excerpts from

the 1967 Brazilian Constitution

Acting on the premise that internal enemies threatened national security, Brazilian generals seized power from the legal government in 1964. During the next twenty-one years, the military would not only abrogate democracy, but it would commit and condone widespread human rights violations. When democratic opposition did surface, such as during the October 1965 gubernatorial elections, the generals quickly decreed a fresh series of repressive laws. In 1967, they institutionalized the laws promulgated since the coup by embedding them in a new national constitution. As the following excerpts show, the Constitution gave extraordinary and arbitrary powers to the armed forces in the name of national security.

National Organization—The Union's Jurisdiction

Art. 8—It behooves the union . . .

III—to decree a state of siege . . .

VII—to organize and maintain the federal police for the purpose of providing . . .

c) investigation of penal violations against national security, political and social order, or detrimental to the union's property, services, and interests, as well as other violations, the practice of which has interstate repercussions and requires uniform suppression, as provided by law;

d) censorship of public entertainment . . .

Political Rights

Art. 142—The electors shall be Brazilians of more than eighteen years of age, registered in accordance with the law.

Par. 1—Registration and voting are obligatory for Brazilians of both sexes, saving the exceptions established by law . . .

Par. 3—The following may not register as electors:

a) the illiterate;

b) those who do not know how to express themselves in the national language;

c) those who have been deprived, temporarily or permanently, of political rights.

Art. 143—Suffrage is universal, and the vote is direct and secret, saving in the cases provided in this Constitution; proportional representation of the political parties is assured in the form the law may establish.

Art. 144—Besides the cases provided in this Constitution, political rights:

I—shall be suspended:

a) for absolute civil incapacity;

b) by reason of criminal conviction, while its effects shall last . . .

II—shall be lost . . .

b) for a refusal, based on religious, philosophical, or political conviction, to perform a duty or service imposed on Brazilians in general . . .

Par. 1—In the cases of item no. II of this Article, the loss of political rights determines the loss of elective mandate, and public office or function; and the suspension of these rights, in the cases provided in this Article, entails the suspension of elective mandate, public office, or function, for as long as the causes that determined the loss shall last.

Par. 2—The suspension or loss of political rights shall be decreed by the president of the republic in the cases of Article 141, I and II, and of this Article, no. II, "b" and "c"; and, in the others, by a judicial sentence, ample defense being always assured to the defendant.

State of Siege

Art. 152—The president of the republic may decree a state of siege in case of:

I—grave disturbance or [dis]order, or threat of its outbreak . . .

Par. 1—The decree of martial law shall specify the regions to be included, appoint the persons entrusted with its execution, and the norms to be observed.

Par. 2—Martial law authorizes the following coercive measures:

a) obligation to live in a given locality;

b) detention in buildings not destined for persons accused of common crimes;

c) search and arrest in homes;

d) suspension of the freedom of assembly and of that of association;

e) censorship of correspondence, of the press, of telecommunications, and public entertainment;

f) temporary use and occupation of the property of autonomous government enterprises, mixed-economy companies, or concessionaires of public services, as well as the suspension of the exercise of an office, function, or employment in these entities.

Par. 3—In order to preserve the integrity and independence of the country, the free working of the powers and the practice of the institutions, when they are gravely threatened by factors of subversion or corruption, the president of the republic, after hearing the National Security Council, may take other measures established in law.

Art. 153—The duration of martial law, except in the case of war, shall not be greater than sixty days and may be extended for an equal length of time.

Par. 1—In any event, the president of the republic shall submit his act to the National Congress, together with its justification, within five days.

Par. 2—If the National Congress is not assembled, it shall be immediately convened by the president of the Federal Senate.

Art. 154—While martial law is in effect, and without prejudice to other measures provided in Article 151, the National Congress may also, by means of law, determine the suspension of constitutional guarantees.

Sole Par.—During martial law, the immunities of federal deputies and senators may be suspended, by secret vote of two-thirds of the members of the house to which the congressman belongs.

Art. 155—Martial law ending, its effects shall cease and the president of the republic, within thirty days, shall send a message to the National Congress with a justification of the measures adopted.

Art. 156—The nonobservance of any of the provisions relative to martial law shall render the constraint illegal and shall allow victims thereof to appeal to the judicial power.

Tropicalism and Brazilian

Popular Music under Military Rule

Christopher Dunn

Following the 1964 military coup in Brazil, the dictatorship quickly suppressed labor activism, banned student political organizations, and restricted political opposition. In the short run, however, the regime tolerated a leftist subculture in the major urban centers as long as it remained separated from urban and rural working classes. A young, educated urban milieu, known as the esquerda festiva *[the festive Left], actively produced and consumed a redemptive protest culture perceived as a vehicle for political resistance.*

The populist aspirations of the progressive national bourgeoisie contradicted its real alienation from a politically significant mass constituency.[1] The dilemmas of Brazilian politics had a particularly strong impact on the field of popular music. By the mid-1960s, urban popular music had divided into at least two camps: The first group, identified with an eclectic "style" known as Música Popular Brasileira (MPB), claimed to defend "authentic" Brazilian music and positioned themselves against the second faction, the international rock movement and its followers in Brazil called the Jovem Guarda (Young Guard), led by its avatar, Roberto Carlos. Debates surrounding the relative merits of cultural nationalism versus pop internationalism were often cast within the logic of resistance or accommodation to military power. In this context, important figures of MPB—such as Chico Buarque, Elis Regina, Edu Lobo, and Sérgio Ricardo—claimed the moral high ground over the Jovem Guarda, which they regarded as politically and culturally "alienated."

Although the Jovem Guarda enjoyed tremendous success in the expanding music market for urban youth, MPB artists dominated the tele-

Tempo negro. Temperatura sufocante. O ar está irrespirável. O país está sendo varrido por fortes ventos. Máx.: 38°, em Brasília. Mín.: 5°, nas Laranjeiras.

A dire weather report. (*Jornal do Brasil*, Rio de Janeiro, 14 December 1968)

vised music festivals, which were enormously popular in São Paulo and Rio de Janeiro between 1965 and 1969. As the local and national authorities further restricted popular participation in civil society, these music festivals seemed to offer young collegiate studio audiences a forum for revolt. By 1967, the festivals had become hotly contested events during which composers and performers were either enthusiastically applauded and consecrated or mercilessly jeered and rejected.[2]

Caetano Veloso and Gilberto Gil, two young composers from the northeastern state of Bahia, first gained national media attention in 1967 at the Third Festival of Brazilian Popular Music sponsored by TV Record of São Paulo. In distinct ways, each produced innovative fusions of international and local musical forms that undermined prevailing notions of "authenticity" and "alienation" in Brazilian popular music. Soon after the festival, the so-called "universal sound" of the Bahian group was dubbed as Tropicalismo in the Brazilian press. Tropicalismo only coalesced as a movement in the field of popular music, but related to a broad panorama of cultural production in film, theater, the visual arts, and literature.[3] Led by Veloso and Gil, the Tropicalista group included Tom Zé, Gal Costa, Torquato Neto, and José Carlos Capinam—most of them also from Bahia—along with Os Mutantes, an experimental rock group, and vanguard composer-arrangers Rogério Duprat and Júlio Medaglia, all from São Paulo.

The Tropicalista group conceived of regional and national affirmation not as a rejection of foreign styles and technologies, but rather, as the ability to engage with these symbolic and material products on the basis of their own position as composer-musicians on the periphery of national and international centers of capital. To this end, the Tropicalistas updated the metaphor of *antropofagia,* first outlined in Oswald de Andrade's *Cannibalist Manifesto* (1928), which advocated "devouring" the cultural heritage of dominant nations and creating a radical anticolonialist blueprint for Brazilian cultural production. They were assailed by many left-wing artists and critics for using electric instruments, and appropriating elements of foreign musical styles such as rock, soul, bolero, and rumba. Yet Veloso and Gil also drew heavily from traditional Afro-Brazilian music, and their lyrics frequently referred to the experience of migrants from the underdeveloped northeast.

The Tropicalistas formulated a view of Brazilian popular culture that was both heterogeneous and transnational. Meanwhile, both the military regime and its left-wing opponents continued to defend a narrow idea of national patrimony—the former for the purposes of social control and national unity, and the latter for the promotion of radical anti-imperialist cultural politics. The Tropicalistas produced allegorical songs that underscored the historical contradictions of their society by juxtaposing images of violence and poverty with familiar national mythologies associated with the idea of Brazil as a tropical paradise.

From the beginning of the movement, critics noted the Tropicalistas' use of allegory, a representational strategy that was particularly well suited to the type of cultural criticism they were developing.[4] Roberto Schwarz was the first to analyze the use of allegory in Tropicalismo in his 1970 essay, "Culture and Politics in Brazil."[5] For Schwarz, the Tropicalista allegory was painfully revealing—"like a family secret dragged out into the middle of the street, like treachery to one's own class"—but also hopelessly absurd. According to Schwarz, Tropicalismo posited an "atemporal idea of Brazil" in which its historical contradictions were fatalistically rendered as emblems of national identity. In other words, the aberrant disjunction between modernity as a cultural project and modernization as a socioeconomic project was simply rendered as a new form of cultural originality—as if the absurd itself was claimed as national patrimony. While skeptical of the political efficacy of this cultural strategy, Schwarz conceded that the Tropicalistas were able to "capture the hardest and most difficult contradictions of present intellectual production."

Veloso's allegorical song-manifesto, "Tropicália," featured on his first solo album from 1968, was no doubt a primary referent for Schwarz's critique. The song lyrics assemble a fragmentary montage of events, emblems, icons, musical and literary citations, and popular sayings, to construct a "mythic image of Brazil, grotesquely monumentalized," in the words of Celso Favaretto.[6] Its most immediate referent is Brasília, the once-promising symbol of national development and modernization that became the political and administrative center of the military regime. "Tropicália" alludes to Brasília's symbolic trajectory—from a utopian monument to national progress and high modernist architecture, to a symbol of military power and the failure of a democratic modernity. "Tropicália" is also an ironic monument to Brazilian culture, mixing references to consecrated literary figures like Olavo Bilac and José de Alencar with "low-brow" pop icons like Carmen Miranda and Roberto Carlos.

The contrast between the ultramodern and the archaic serves as the binary opposition that structures the entire song. In the first refrain, Bossa Nova—the sophisticated "finished product" associated with national developmentalism—rhymes with *palhoça*—the ubiquitous mud huts of the Brazilian backlands. In subsequent stanzas, the imagery becomes increasingly disturbing as the exalted monument is revealed to be a mere artifice of "crepe paper and silver" inhabited by a "smiling, ugly, dead child" who seems to beg with an outstretched hand.

Another key song-manifesto of Tropicalismo and the parodic tour de force of the group's concept album, *Tropicália, Panis et Circencis* (1968) is "Geléia Geral" by Gilberto Gil and Torquato Neto.[7] The song satirizes patriotic discourses by portraying a pompous official poet of the Brazilian belle epoque who praises Brazil's natural beauty and the modern poet-singer who then deconstructs this idealized image.[8] The heart of the song contains an interlude featuring an inventory of quotidian sayings, clichés, and kitsch objects from Brazilian popular culture. Commenting on Gil's vocal style, Gilberto Vasconcellos notes that he discursively "proclaims" the verses, as if he were "a populist deputy exalting the so-called relics of Brazil."[9]

> sweet wicked mulatto woman
> an LP of Sinatra
> passion fruit in April
> baroque Bahian saint
> superpower of the compatriot

Formica and anil skies
three hits of Portela
dried meat in the window
someone who cries for me
a real carnival
hospitable friendship
brutality garden

These emblems of *brasilidade* conform to Nestor García-Canclini's formulation of popular culture at the intersection of "complex hybrid processes using elements from different classes and nations."[10] The popular modernist rendering of the "sweet wicked mulatto woman"—so reminiscent of the characters of Jorge Amado novels—is juxtaposed with "an LP of Sinatra," a foreign cultural icon adored by the Brazilian middle class. The carnivalesque inventory of emblems of Brazilian popular culture relativizes the notion of national authenticity. Further down, a grandiose patriotic stock phrase describing Brazil's natural beauty—*céu de anil* (anil skies)—is coupled with a banal industrial product—cheap Formica. The satire of *brasilidade* turns mordant in the final two lines, which juxtaposc *hospitaleira amizade*—an evocation of Brazilian "cordiality" as described by Sérgio Buarque de Hollanda in *Raizes do Brasil* (1936)—to *brutalidade jardim*—a line from Oswald de Andrade's *Serafim Ponte Grande* (1928) alluding to violence and repression in a "tropical paradise."

More explicit allusions to political violence in Brazilian society appear in another important hit, "Divino Maravilhoso," written by Gil and Veloso, and recorded by Gal Costa on her first solo album from 1969. The song urges listeners to "pay attention" to the dangers of the historical moment without being overcome by fear, while maintaining a critical attitude toward culture and media:

pay attention
to the stanza to the refrain
to the curse words
to the slogans
pay attention
to the exultant samba

The last lines denounce oppositional poles of Brazilian cultural politics: *palavra de ordem* (slogan) usually alludes to left-wing orthodoxy, while *samba exaltação* refers to the exultant, patriotic sambas first promoted by the Estado Novo, and favored by the military regime.

The final stanza points to the very real dangers of armed conflict between the authorities and the opposition:

pay attention
to the windows up high
pay attention
while stepping on the asphalt swamp
pay attention
to the blood on the ground

By calling attention to the "windows up high," the song alludes to police agents and sharpshooters who often took positions in the high-rise buildings of downtown Rio de Janeiro during the famous protest marches of 1968. The next line places this conflict within Brazil's social and structural context. The distance between the ideals of modernization and the reality of the nation's precarious infrastructure is suggested by the opposition asphalt / swamp. The aftermath of political violence—"blood on the ground"—serves as stark testimony to the official repression that was a daily part of urban life in Brazil during the late 1960s.

"Divino Maravilhoso" provided the namesake for a short-lived and extremely controversial musical program hosted by the Tropicalista group for TV Tupí in late 1968. By this time, it had become clear to the military authorities under Castelo Branco's hard-line successor, Artur Costa e Silva, that the Tropicalistas' critiques of Brazilian society were potentially subversive. Soon after the promulgation of the draconian Fifth Institutional Act on December 13, 1968, Gil and Veloso were arrested in their São Paulo apartments, and later exiled to London.

Despite its short duration, Tropicalismo was arguably the most significant and influential cultural movement in Brazil during the second half of the twentieth century. The Tropicalistas renovated Brazilian popular music, while simultaneously making incisive critiques of the political and social dilemmas of Brazilian society. It still serves as a key reference point for artists interested in formal experimentation and creative engagement with cultural products from abroad. Contemporary groups such as Olodum, Chico Science e Nação Zumbi, and Paralamas do Sucesso, as well as composer-performers like Arnaldo Antunes, Carlinhos Brown, and Marisa Monte, all claim deep affinities with Tropicalismo.

The original group members—Caetano Veloso, Gilberto Gil, Gal Costa, and Tom Zé—continue to produce innovative popular music and they all still embrace the Tropicalista experience.[11]

Notes

1 See Heloísa Buarque de Hollanda, *Impressões de viagem: CPC, vanguarda e desbunde, 1960/70* (Rio de Janeiro: Rocco, 1992), p. 33.

2 Augusto de Campos et al., *Balanço da Bossa e outras bossas* (São Paulo: Editora Perspectiva, 1968), p. 128.

3 The Tropicalistas were deeply inspired by the film *Terra em transe (Land in Anguish)* by Glauber Rocha and the theater production of Oswald de Andrade's *O rei da vela (The Candle King)* by the Teatro Oficina. In separate ways, these two cultural events of 1967 critiqued imperialism, authoritarianism, and economic dependency, but also addressed the contradictions of the national bourgeoisie.

4 See Walter Benjamin's discussion of allegories in *The Origin of German Tragic Drama*, translated by John Osborne (London: NLB, 1977), p. 178.

5 Roberto Schwarz, *Misplaced Ideas: Essays on Brazilian Culture*, edited by John Gledson (New York: Verso, 1992), pp. 140–44.

6 Celso Favaretto, *Tropicália: Alegoria, Alegria* (São Paulo: Ateliê Editorial, 1996), p. 56.

7 The notion of *geléia geral* (general jelly) was first proposed by concrete poet Décio Pignatari following an argument with the modernist poet Cassiano Ricardo, who predicted that one day they would lose their vanguardist rigor. Pignatari, referring to the undefined, almost amoebic character of Brazilian culture, reportedly exclaimed, "[I]n the Brazilian *geléia geral*, someone has to exercise the function of spine and bone!" The lyricist, Torquato Neto, appropriated the trope, recycling it in an ironic and ambiguous fashion.

8 Favaretto, *Tropicália*, p. 94.

9 Gilberto Vasconcellos, *Música Popular—De olho na fresta* (Rio de Janeiro: Graal, 1977), p. 30.

10 Nestor Gárcia-Canclini, *Hybrid Cultures*, translated by Christopher Chiappari and Silvia L. López (Minneapolis: University of Minnesota Press, 1995), p. 205.

11 In 1993, for example, Veloso and Gil commemorated the twenty-fifth anniversary of the movement with a brilliant CD entitled *Tropicália 2*, which revisited and updated many of the movement's original concerns.

Literature under the Dictatorship

Elizabeth Ginway

Most literary critics agree that the military regime in Brazil had an impact on an entire generation of writers because of its use of censorship and its protracted hold on power for over twenty years (1964–1985). The technocratic outlook and training of the Brazilian military led its officials to believe that both tight political control and economic development were keys to maintaining long-term stability and national greatness. The Brazilian regime legitimized its power by implementing a series of economic policies that became known as the Brazilian "economic miracle." While economic growth was high, it mostly benefited the wealthy, thereby exacerbating discontent among students, labor, and the poor segments of the population. Resistance took the form of guerrilla activities, strikes, and popular demonstrations, and to stem the tide of unrest, the military cracked down on civilian rights, and secretly began the systematic use of torture and institutionalized censorship. This takeover by the military hard-liners in 1968, or the "coup within the coup," had a dramatic impact on Brazilian society, and the years 1969 to 1974 are remembered as the darkest of the dictatorship.

The crackdown by the military served to sharpen the virtuosity and sophistication of Brazilian writers, who took aggressive and satirical stances against political repression, as well as the supposed benefits of technology and development. Three main currents predominate in the fiction of the dictatorship: experimental political novels, dystopian fiction, and documentary or testimonial novels, all of which denounce the military regime. In retrospect, critics have questioned the originality of literary production under the dictatorship precisely because of its direct link to a historical period. Some critics have argued that literature loses its imaginative qualities when it is reduced to a mere reference to politics, while others point out the social value of having intellectuals as active members of society, willing to debate national issues. The readership of the novels published during the military regime was often politically active, and included journalists, professors, and middle-class readers. We must bear in mind that, in general, literature has been an elite activity in Brazil, and that illiteracy rates even in 1970 ran at over a third of the population of those age ten and over. Most literature of this period was directed at a university-educated, politically engaged audience that was clearly adept at picking up on the social criticism of these works of fiction, which could not be dealt with in the regular press. While the military targeted groups such as journalists with harassment, imprisonment, torture, and even death, the worst suffered by Brazilian writers was detention, exile, and censorship, mainly because works of literature criticized society in a way that did not mobilize mass opinion or threaten the military's hold on power in a direct way.

At the same time, Brazilian writers coming of age after 1964 under the dictatorship did not pander to their audience, and their controversial topics and styles provoked censorship. Censorship of literary works in Brazil was uneven, however; sometimes the military objected to political statements and, in other cases, it censored works for obscenity. To understand some of the inconsistencies of censorship in Brazil, a discussion of author Rubem Fonseca will be illustrative. An ex-police officer, Fonseca effectively captures the violence at all levels of Brazilian society and writes to jolt the reader's sensibilities. Fonseca has been widely read and translated, and his success has made him controversial among literary critics. His first novel, *O Caso Morel (The Case of Morel)*, published in 1973, depicts a case of sadomasochism and murder, and is written in an experimental, nonlinear form in comparison with the directness of his short fiction. In the novel, the shocking violence done to the young upper-class woman by her lover and the ambiguity in the police investigator / murderer / narrator's versions of events provoke considerable confusion on the part of the reader. By putting the reader in an uncomfortable position to judge the evidence, the novel is meant to denounce the absence of truth and of viable ethical choices under a dictatorship. While this novel was published without any government interference, the military censored Fonseca's collection of short stories from 1974, *Feliz Ano Novo (Happy New Year)*, citing it as pornography. The collection opens with a brutal story in which criminals invade a New Year's Eve party in Rio de Janeiro, and humiliate, mutilate, rob, and rape several elite party-goers. For sheer savageness, both the novel and the story are equally disturbing, and the decision to suppress one of Fonseca's works over the other demonstrates the arbitrary nature of censorship in Brazil.

Other novels that suffered censorship referred overtly to the military government by portraying Brazil's political situation from a leftist perspective, or by alluding to specific guerrilla activities. Authors also began to restrain themselves and, for example, avoided naming the actual perpetrators of violence within the government for fear of reprisal. On the other hand, some documentary novels that described police brutality often went uncensored. To explain this paradox, critic Flora Süssekind has theorized that realist novels that describe human misery are part of a long literary tradition in Brazil obsessed with portraying "Brazil as nation." In Süssekind's view, as long as documentary novels offered a sociological portrait of Brazil, even a negative one, their form and general message fit in with the growing pains of building a great nation. For this reason, certain novels that would seemingly threaten the regime by denouncing the consequences of development went uncensored. Another path chosen by several authors to avoid censorship was the use of elaborate literary techniques to distract the censors, while still portraying the disillusionment of an entire generation.

Literary experimentalism and sophisticated allegory were strategies that also appealed to the educated, middle-class readership. However, not all experimental novels escaped restriction. Completed in 1969, the novel *Zero* by Ignácio de Loyola Brandão went unpublished for some five years because Brazilian publishers feared retaliation by the military government. It was first published in Italy in 1974, where it was well received, then in Brazil in 1975, where it garnered several literary prizes. Censored by the military a year later, public protest returned it to the best seller list when it was finally released in 1979. *Zero* is a shocking and unflattering look at the social inequities between the rich and the poor during the so-called "economic miracle." The text is like a collage, incorporating advertisements, snippets from newspapers, and other graphics. These create a visual chaos in the novel that reinforces its theme of social chaos. This perspective on Brazilian society, along with its portrayal of the systematic violence by the government, made the novel disagreeable to the military. The experimental novels written in Brazil under the dictatorship tend to use chronological fragmentation, thus becoming puzzles for the reader to solve. These political novels denounce the dictatorship and its policies by portraying the activities of guerrilla groups, by recounting the practice of torture and the anguish of imprisonment, and by using the metaphor of insanity to capture people's frustration and sense of powerlessness after the harsh crackdown on all political activities after 1968.

Another prime example of an experimental political novel is Ivan Ângelo's *A Festa (The Celebration)* from 1970, also of interest because, like *Zero*, it found its way into English translation by Avon, a mainstream publishing house. Its fragmented construction evokes the social and moral turmoil of the era of the dictatorship by alternating between several intersecting story lines: the struggle of landless peasants, the dissatisfaction of the middle class, the activities of the Left, and the self-questioning of the author/narrator, who includes much speculation about the writing of the novel itself. These various novelistic threads are linked by events that come to a head on a date set for a party, and the celebration becomes an ironic testimony to the political failure and sense of alienation suffered by many under the dictatorship. Despite their diverse themes, political novels in Brazil depict social fragmentation through aesthetic experimentation, and criticize the political repression that destructures both society and the individual. In their nonlinear form, these novels require an active role on the part of the reader, who must reconstruct the text to achieve meaning and reexamine the nature of fiction in contemporary society.

Whereas experimental novels require a high degree of literary knowledge—and are, for the most part, geared toward a more sophisticated public—a more accessible form of social satire was the anti-utopian or dystopian novel that satirized the military government's policy of economic development. Such works usually portrayed a highly regulated society whose technocrats enforce the new "progressive" order with sinister results. For example, singer-songwriter Chico Buarque had been repeatedly censored by the military in the realm of popular music, where he had a large influence on the public. Buarque turned to fiction in 1974 with the dystopian novel *Fazenda Modelo (Model Farm)*, which protests the regulation of all aspects of society by the regime. Because of the author's fame, the novel became a Brazilian best seller. Similar to George Orwell's *Animal Farm*, this novel depicts an imaginary country where a herd of cattle is suddenly subjected to a rigorous new breeding program that effectively regulates sexuality and reproduction, all in the name of technological progress and international recognition. This allegory parallels the Brazilian military's imposition of an economic program that would give Brazil international fame as a model for progress among developing nations. The novel ridicules the military by satirizing its rhetoric and its attempt to control the most intimate aspects of reproduction. In a similar vein, Ignácio de Loyola Brandão's 1981 dystopia, *Não verás país nenhum (And Still the Earth)*, imagines the Brazil of the future as an ecological disaster. The Amazon has turned into a desert, and constant drought makes the heat of the cities unbearable. Pollution has transformed large segments of the population into mutants, and the "Militech" rulers maintain order with rubber bullets and a constant flow of propaganda about the country's progress.

A subcategory of this dystopian current, the fiction of the fantastic, also presents the idea of society gone wrong. José J. Veiga's 1968 collection, *A Máquina Extraviada (The Misplaced Machine)*, and several of Murilo Rubião's stories in the collection, *The Ex-Magician and Other Stories*, portray the disruption of development in monstrous or absurd situations that capture the effects of new technology on Brazilian society. Set in an ominous future, these depictions suggest the chilling consequences of a dictatorship gone unchecked, but unlike Orwell's sinister novels, they use humor and parody to undermine the authoritarian government's ultimate control. The authors of dystopian fiction convey the sense of powerlessness and suspicion associated with new technology by forcing readers to actively reflect on the similarities and differences between these nightmarish fictional worlds and their own reality.

The most accessible and widely read literary form during the dictatorship was documentary fiction. This type of fiction revealed what the newspapers could not tell: the human costs of modernization in abject poverty, police brutality, and moral bankruptcy. Documentary fiction in Brazil consists of both journalistic and testimonial novels (among them several best sellers), and most clearly describes the culture of resistance, as well as the public's need to reconstitute a collective memory during and after the years of strict censorship. The open style of journalist-turned-novelist José Louzeiro, for example, attracted a public that was anxious for news that could not be reported by the media. Louzeiro's main goal was to inform readers about topics such as abandoned children, death squads, police violence, and crime reports that were censored or distorted by the mainstream press. These novels had an immediacy that appealed to readers aware of the actual events articulated in fictional form. Brazilian readers also decoded journalistic fiction as denunciations of the penal system, and consequently, as attacks on political repression and torture, or as allegories of the violence and corruption of the judiciary system and of Brazilian society under the dictatorship. While part of their allure is the tabloidlike treatment of sex and violence, these novels nonetheless remain among the most important documents of the dictatorship because of their wide popularity and connections to actual events.

Another kind of documentary novel is testimonial fiction, associated with the process of *abertura,* or political opening, in Brazil that began in 1979. In that same year, journalist Fernando Gabeira, who had been tortured and exiled for his participation in the kidnapping of the American ambassador to Brazil in 1969, wrote *O Que é isso, Companheiro? (What's This, Buddy?),* recounting his prison memories in novelistic form. The book went on to become one of the best sellers of 1980 in Brazil and exemplified the power of testimonial literature. Gabeira's work generally avoids self-aggrandizement or exaggerated martyrdom, and denounces the use of torture by the military and the horrors of imprisonment in a simple and direct style that appealed to those middle-class readers who needed to inform themselves, yet also allay their guilt for their passivity under the dictatorship. The publication of testimonial literature represented a literary catharsis for Brazil and signaled the beginning of the end for the military. Indeed, as the dictatorship drew to a close in 1985, one nonfiction book documenting torture, *Brasil: Nunca Mais (Torture in Brazil),* sold more than 100,000 copies in ten weeks (whereas the usual print run of a nonfiction book at the time was 3,000 to 5,000 copies), further evidence attesting to the important cathartic function of documentary fiction and nonfiction in this period.

While other currents in Brazilian fiction during this era include more existential and introspective themes, it is clear that experimental, dystopian, and documentary fiction will be recalled as the literature of the dictatorship. Interestingly enough, the dictatorship had an unforeseen impact on literature in Brazil. In its rush to industrialize, the regime changed Brazilian reality in a definitive way. The fiction of the dictatorship, in turn, supplanted the pervasive image of Brazil as either a tropical paradise or a model of development, and substituted a dystopian image of a nation gone awry. If we read between the lines, however, we see a country that uses literature as a source of national conscience, and its fiction combines a good dose of realism, irony, and creativity as it struggles with the dilemmas of late industrialization.

Pelé Speaks

Edson Arantes Nascimento da Silva

In 1958, as a seventeen year old, Edson Arantes Nascimento da Silva, known universally as Pelé, electrified Brazil by dominating play at the Sixth World Cup, helping to establish a dynasty that won an unprecedented four world championships in the next forty years. As the most famous Brazilian of his generation, Pelé broke some barriers for blacks, although when he married a white woman, he chose to hold the wedding in Germany. Criticized by some for his conservative outlook, he rarely opened up to the press. The two exceptions were interviews given by Pelé to the Brazilian edition of Playboy *magazine, the first one in 1980, when he was thirty-nine years old; the second, thirteen years later in 1993, was conducted in his suite of the Ouro Verde Hotel in Rio de Janeiro, with his two security guards watching. Under President Fernando Henrique Cardoso, Pelé became the first black appointed to a cabinet position when he was named the minister of sport, a post created for him.*

August 1980

Playboy: . . . There are those who accuse you of having set a bad example when you asserted [during the military dictatorship] that the Brazilian people are not ready to vote in free elections.

Pelé: Everything I say is twisted and incorrectly interpreted. What I wanted to say was that the Brazilian people need to take voting more seriously, not to vote for Careca, for Pelé, or for Zico [soccer stars], because this will get Brazil nowhere. I doubt if any Brazilian has made as much good publicity outside the country as I have. And I want the best for the Brazilian people. I want to say this, but they changed what I said, claiming that I said that Brazilians are burros, that they do not know how to vote. What I still think, though, is that casting blank ballots or destroying ballots is a stupid way of protesting.

Playboy: Don't you think that if the government gave more opportunities for people to vote, they would become, over time, better prepared to use their vote?

Pelé: Sure. Before 1964, according to people who understand these things, there was democracy in Brazil, and if we came to change this it is because we were not choosing the right kind of people to lead us. And now that everyone is fighting for a return to civilian rule, it is a good thing that the people are prepared for this.

Playboy: You also made a polemical statement to a foreign journalist, saying that racial discrimination does not exist in Brazil. Do you confirm saying this or was it another case of being misunderstood?

Pelé: I believe that in my field, sports, there is no racial discrimination. I never had problems playing soccer with whites; I attended school with whites and never was discriminated against. I think that in Brazil the problem is social discrimination. This exists in truth, and is a big problem. Racial discrimination exists in the United States and in South Africa.

1993

Playboy: Someone or another always has attempted to exploit your fame, no? [Can you] talk about the pressure that the regime of General Geisel applied to you when he wanted you to play for Brazil in the World Cup in Germany in 1974?

Pelé: Actually, [General] Geisel's daughter, Amália Lucy, called me; also the Education Minister Jarbas Passarinho. They pressured me, they cajoled me, they did everything they could. But at that time, I had begun to become aware of the barbarities practiced by the dictatorship, the tortures, the people who disappeared. I learned that while we were winning championships many injustices had taken place, and I stayed firm; I didn't give in. I think it was my way of protesting. First, because I had formally left the Brazilian team. And then, because relatives of some of the people who had disappeared had sought me out, and I began to feel embittered by what I learned. After that, they made veiled threats that I'd better be careful with my income tax returns, these things. I ignored them.

Playboy: You really hadn't known about the tortures carried out in Brazil?

Pelé: No, I heard some things. On trips with the Santos team, with the Brazilian team, we had some contact occasionally with exiles. Even the mayor of Rio, César Maia, the other day thanked me because I received him once, in Chile. But I was kind of vague about these things, I didn't talk about politics. For this reason, I thanked the struggles of (musicians) Chico Buarque de Holanda, of Gilberto Gil, of Caetano Veloso, or Geraldo Vandré, those that figured things out before I figured things out, because I was traveling around the world playing soccer for Brazil, for my people. I was somewhere else; this is true. I wanted to honor those who tried to teach us and who also were persecuted.

Playboy: Is it true that you are in favor of the death penalty for corrupt politicians?

Pelé: Without a doubt. With all of my religious training, I think that those who embezzle even from school funds deserve the death penalty. These things aren't possible. They want the death penalty for an unbalanced person who commits a heinous crime, for a crazy person who rapes someone, for someone who kills out of insatiable jealousy, yet nothing happens to anyone who damages all of the people? There are people kidnapping businessmen, ignoring that these men provide jobs, that they are agents of progress. The industrialist who is kidnapped becomes embittered, wants to leave Brazil, doesn't want to invest any more.

Playboy: You're not proposing that they start to kidnap politicians?

Pelé: I'm not proposing anything. I'm only saying that if the guy has stolen money, you have to steal from who steals. Thieves who steal from thieves received a 100 years of forgiveness, right? I was amazed at the types who ran into the streets yelling for the impeachment of President Fernando Collor de Mello for corruption. But they don't have to pay. We need to insist that politicians take university courses, at least a year study of public administration. Really, I've never seen a politician sacrifice anything—but they ask that the people do it, sacrifice. It's revolting. We need a moral pact in Brazil.

Playboy: Is there any politician who merits your admiration?

Pelé: Juscelino Kubitschek, for example, was a great man, steadfast. Today, we have Tasso Gereisati, the former governor of Ceará. The current one also, Ciro Gomes. Even with so few resources, in a state so poor. I also admire Leonel Brizola. Because everything he does, with demagoguery or not, focuses on education, something I have defended for many years. . . .

Playboy: We've had twenty years of dictatorship, with politicians on the sidelines, and even with this, the country's situation didn't improve. Could the problem be with the egoism of the Brazilian elite?

Pelé: No, because during the period that the army was taking care of things, things weren't so bad. It wasn't what the people wanted, and there was a good deal of barbarity, but we made great advances, like in communications, for example. The education system wasn't so bad, either, and inflation wasn't so bad. When the army took over, everything was really awful. When the civilians got back into the government, things got worse.

Playboy: Does this mean that you think that without a good dose of authoritarianism, none of Brazil's problems will be resolved?

Pelé: I think not.

Playboy: And then?

Pelé: Politicians have to give space to free enterprise. Politicians have to take care of education, food, housing, everyday needs. The rest can be handled by the private sector . . .

The Maximum Norm

of the Exercise of Liberty

Grupo da Educacão Moral e Cívica

The military government emphasized the fostering of nationalism, using propaganda to encourage patriotic feelings among citizens. All schools were required to teach civismo *(citizenship education); similar campaigns were disseminated over television and radio, in the press, and on billboards throughout the country. Bumper stickers were distributed with slogans like, "Brazil: Love It or Leave It." The campaign frowned on dissent, and preached unconditional loyalty to the country and its military leaders. The selection below is excerpted from material used at the secondary school level, and also handed out to newspaper and magazine offices in 1973, nine years after the armed forces took power. The final part of the essay is eerily reminiscent of the corporatist ideology of the 1930s. Exposure to this sort of propaganda, and the carrot-and-stick techniques used by authorities to reward cooperation and squelch dissent, made the generation of youths who became adults in the 1970s cautious. It lacked the stimulus and experience needed to mobilize political concern.*

Brazil, to us in 1973, in the tenth year of the Revolution, is an enormous land distinguished by its greatness among the nations of South America; it is a land of hope, destined for power and for world leadership. Its population of 110 million forms a Western people who are united in pride and bravery. We are known for our generous character and Christian values; we love this country because it is ours; we triumph in its progress. We speak the same language and are united behind the same flag. Our history has been made by exemplary men, lovers of their country, who shed their blood to defend it.

[We possess] resources of prodigious wealth. Here, there are no volcanoes, hurricanes, cyclones. We have land in abundance, mineral and petroleum wealth, enormous rivers to produce electric power, forests, raw materials to contribute to industrial progress. Seventy-five percent of our population is less than twenty-five years of age. We have abundant human resources, labor, and managerial talent. The very map of Brazil appears in the shape of a human heart. It is a heart that encompasses treasures of rich natural resources above and below the ground. Through its great rivers—the São Francisco and the Amazon—circulate its lifeblood; extensive networks of highways form its arteries. It is a virgin heart, trembling with hope, a heart that incorporates blood from the Indian, Latin, and African races. The heart palpitates with future greatness for a powerful Brazil, seeking courageous solutions, fiery and spiritual, a country that brings to a tired and aging world a new vision of strength. This is my country; I am proud to call myself Brazilian.

The security of every Brazilian and the safety of every Brazilian institution is guarded by the nation's armed forces. There are two missions: defense against foreign aggression and vigilance against internal subversion. Brazilians do not seek territorial aggrandizement. Our people love peace. But the armed forces stand vigilant to repel any external threat. There stand other enemies within our midst: terrorists, subversives, and militants of communistic ideologies. The armed forces combat this menace, and remind us of our obligation for hierarchy and discipline.

We Brazilians know that teamwork is more effective than individual effort. Teams prepare us for dialogue and increase our capacity for efficiency. The social order is best served by liberty, justice, love, truth, and solidarity. Man in his process of self-improvement deals with other men. Thus, responsibilities are not simply individual, but social as well. Social order results from the perfect interrelationship of necessities and freedom, the middle ground for which is responsibility. To subordinate our own freedoms to the common good is the maximum norm of the exercise of liberty in the social order.

Families of Fishermen

Confront the Sharks

Paulo Lima

Jangadeiros (rafters) from the northeastern state of Ceará are renowned for their skills at ferrying cargo and fishing on the high seas. In addition, Brazilians will forever remember the jangadeiros who, by refusing to transport slaves in 1881, inspired Brazil's first successful, provincial abolitionist campaign. Today's jangadeiros perceive threats to their livelihood and way of life as a result of Ceará's expanding tourist and fishing industries. Their response, described by Paulo Lima in Sem Fronteiras, combines the independence, resourcefulness, and maritime skills that made their forebears legendary.

What does Prainha have? The answer is on the tip of the tongues of the residents of this community in the littoral *município* of Beberibe, 120 kilometers from Fortaleza. They have, as demonstration, a singular experiment in community organization and rational exploitation of fish.

In Prainha do Canto Verde, as the name itself says, the sea is green, and also very gentle and warm. The fish still have not lost the battle against the tourist industry, nor has the streetlight given way to neon. Windmills dispersed like flowers throughout the white, fine sand pump the freshwater that spurts from the ground a few meters from the beach. A sign at six kilometers from the village advises the visitor: ecological coast.

In the struggle against the invasion of its lands by Ceará businesspeople, the community extracted from the prefecture the legal guarantee by which, in Prainha do Canto Verde, no real estate will be sold to outsiders. It is the way found by the fishermen to preserve the enchantment of the locale, that fills with pleasure the eyes of whoever lives there and whoever passes through, and also to guarantee work and survival for the families who have lived there for a long time.

The initiative counted on the support of the Pastoral Association of Ceará Fishermen. Inevitably, the experience ran swiftly from beach to beach. "Other littoral communities, also threatened by real estate speculation, became excited about doing the same," recounts Rosa Maria Ferreira, one of the coordinators of the organization.

Since the 1980s, the Ceará Sea has not been for fish, nor for lobster. A fishbone choked the families that lived from the sea: predatory fishing. "That is our number one enemy," openly complains Master Zé Ramos, president of the association. "The predatory fishing placed in risk the income of 100,000 Ceará fishermen," he says, and shows off his new, almost completed *jangada* [a fishing raft]. It is his breadwinner.

It is because of these conditions that, in April 1993, the fishermen of Prainha do Canto Verde resolved to plunge once and for all into the struggle for citizens' rights. In partnership with the community of Redonda, in Icapuí, they launched into the sea the *jangada SOS Sobrevivência* [*SOS Survival*] for a long trip, from Ceará to Rio de Janeiro.

The objective was to draw a cry of alert throughout the Brazilian coast, making public opinion, the authorities, and the fishermen themselves conscious of the importance of conserving and protecting the lobster and defending artisan fishing.

The demands from the fishermen until now have not been considered, but the men of the *jangadas* do not regret what they did. It was beautiful. "It was worth it to risk danger," defends Master Mamede, the head of the famous expedition. He remembers the emotion of the departure and arrival. The fisherman was showing the entire world that he wanted a better life.

It is with this same energy, and tired of the promises from the governor, Tasso Jereissati, that the community of Prainha united in search of alternatives to improve life. For this, it counted on the support of the Pastoral Association of Ceará Fishermen and other organizations that came to help.

One of these is the Terramar Institute, which was founded in July 1993 by a group of Ceará fishing engineers. In April of last year, with the technical assistance of the institute, the fishermen decided to innovate: in *mutirão* [cooperative labor], they fabricated what are called artificial attractors of fish, which were set up at sea four hours by *jangada* from the coast.

The traps are modules of fifteen tires each, tied to the sea bottom. With time, marine algae attach onto this submarine construction, creating a food chain that ends up attracting fish. The technique, which was not unknown to fishermen, is also being used in Japan and the United States.

"Life improved for our side," observes Zé Ramos contentedly, because today production is stably maintained at around 120 kilos of fish per month. He hazards to guess that with the implantation of the attractors, fish production increased 40 percent. The master's optimism has a basis: the number of *jangadas* also grew, totaling fifty craft for 180 fishermen—a case probably unique among the littoral communities of the state.

Earlier, in an attempt to guarantee good production, the *jangadeiro* was obliged to navigate for up to nine hours, to pass the night on the high seas, and to return only on the following day. With the consolidated attractors, the *jangada* goes to sea and returns the same day.

René Schärer, who exchanged Switzerland for work at the Terramar Institute and for three years has aided the community, reveals a simple thesis about artisanal fishing: "Sustainable development is possible, although there should be respect for the rules of the game." In general, the fisherman is exploited at the time of selling the fish. Without counting on the help of warehouses, transport, and ice mills, the fisherman ends up at the mercy of the profiteers. This is what happens in almost 100 percent of the cases in the State of Ceará. At Prainha do Canto Verde, however, things are different. In addition to counting on abundant fish, the fisherman control 60 percent of the commercialization of the catch, guaranteeing for themselves and the consumer the best price for fish along the coast of Ceará.

There are more new developments. At Prainha do Canto Verde, the health station and the community center—which houses a nursery, a center for the association, and a dance hall—use solar energy. Also recent—and unprecedented in Brazil—is the installation of an ice mill fed by aeolian energy [produced by wind]. The daily production capacity is 750 kilos of ice. Until then, the community faced serious problems with the preservation of fish, a highly perishable product. Now, with the possibility of selling at more distant supply stations, the accounts can increase up to three times.

On the fourth of April, to commemorate the third anniversary of the protest voyage *SOS Sobrevivência,* the fishermen of Prainha do Canto

Verde and other fishing communities will embark for Fortaleza. In one of the neighborhoods of the capital's periphery, they will distribute free fish to the residents. The gesture has the flavor of solidarity in the struggle for citizenship. But it is also a protest against the complete disregard by the state government toward the problems of the fishermen.

The Reality of the Brazilian Countryside

Landless Movement (MST)

Unlike the United States, where homesteading laws encouraged common folk to own small farms, Brazil has always leaned toward large landholdings, or latifundia. Colonial land policy favored large grants to a few well-placed families. During the Empire, land laws practically forbade small landholdings. More recently, the 1964 military coup occurred as rural tensions and calls for land reform intensified. The military dictatorship curtailed serious land reform, but it never extinguished the essential conflict between landlords and rural workers. Shortly after democracy's return, therefore, a dynamic new organization, the Landless Movement (MST), began challenging Brazil's historical pattern of rural development. The following description of rural life and the accompanying manifesto appeared on the MST's Internet sites in 1998.

In light of the characteristics of agricultural development occurring in the country, it can be affirmed that serious agrarian problems exist in Brazil that need a solution.

However, this situation is characterized as a problem only by the working class. For the dominant elite, for those who benefit from this type of development, agrarian problems do not exist; on the contrary, it represents a greater opportunity for profit and well-being.

Land ownership in Brazil is concentrated in the hands of a minority, characterizing one of the highest indices of concentration in the world. About 1 percent of the owners hold around 46 percent of all land. And the concentration of land brings concentration of the means of production (machines, improvements, etc.), economic power, income, and political power in the rural environment. This is reproducing a society permanently in conflict between a minority of owners, and an ample layer of the population that has its labor more and more exploited.

The manner in which the land is utilized does not represent the interests of society as a whole and, much less, of the workers. The enormous potential that these available natural resources represent is not employed for the economic progress and well-being of the entire population. The overwhelming majority of lands are idle, badly utilized, underutilized, and destined for extensive cattle grazing, or simply, for speculation and reserve wealth. The best lands are destined for monoculture exports, such as sugarcane, coffee, cotton, soybeans, and oranges. Meanwhile, the production of basic foods for the internal market is practically stagnant.

As a result, there exists a poor distribution of agro-cattle production, and the Brazilian population is not fed according to the basic necessities. Thus, 32 million people go hungry every day, and another 65 million are fed less than the necessities.

The migration of rural populations to urban agglomerations is a natural and constant process in all societies, and accompanies civilization. However, in the Brazilian case, the velocity and volume of people who have to migrate from their rural communities of origin is appalling, being expelled from the countryside and having to search for cities as the single possibility for survival.

There is also an intense internal migration in which thousands of families are dislocated from one region to another in search of work. And more than 500,000 people migrated to Paraguay, Bolivia, and Argentina in search of rural work. Today, the majority of them wish to return to Brazil.

The conditions of work, and the relationships of domination and exploitation imposed especially on the rural wage earners, are an affront to human dignity. Many wage earners are treated like slaves. The labor and social rights established in the Constitution are completely disrespected, and unknown by the workers themselves.

The salaries paid in the rural environment are always below the minimum requirements of nutrition.

The labor conditions in the establishments using family-based production are also inhuman, involving children and the entire family, in shifts that reach up to fourteen hours daily.

There was an improvement in living conditions for the rural population in some regions, especially in the South and Southeast. But the immense majority of the rural population continues on the fringes of the benefits of economic progress and the advance of productive forces. The social indicators in the rural regions concerning the consumption of electric lighting, electric appliances, levels of literacy, infant mortality, level of education, number of doctors, and income per capita are alarming and equal to the poorest regions in the world.

Among the people who live in the countryside, those who most suffer the wretched living conditions are, without doubt, the women and children. The women perform a double work shift, dedicating themselves to domestic activities and labor in production. The majority receive nothing for their labor. They do not participate in the decisions about the family economy. The women are who most suffer a lack of health care for themselves and their children.

The result of the concentration of landownership, the means of production, production, income, and economic power by a minority that dominates the rural environment translates into a political regime of permanent exploitation and domination of the rural workers, submitted to all types of injustice and discrimination. Democracy, liberty, and the rights of citizenship are unknown to the immense majority of rural workers.

There is also an ideological and cultural domination by the elite over the workers that projects antisocial values, ridiculing the local culture, creating a situation of prejudice and discrimination against the values cultivated by the workers.

The means of mass communication and the alienating character of the practice of some religions contribute to this cultural domination.

Manifesto from the Landless to the Brazilian People

1. We are landless. We are workers and dream of a better Brazil for all. But in Brazilian society, the right to a dignified life is currently denied to the people.

2. Our situation has historical causes in the exploitation of the people by the greedy elite. And now it has been aggravated by the neoliberal economic policy of the FHC [Fernando Henrique Cardoso] government.

3. We have been suffering persecutions, false accusations by conservative politicians, the government, and the latifundia owners. But we are firm. Our cause is just. For that reason, our movement grows and has the support of society.

4. We will continue mobilized, utilizing all forms of pressure possible. Struggle is the weapon of the poor. And it is legitimate.

5. We fight for agrarian reform in order to work, produce, and guarantee abundant food on the table of every Brazilian.

6. With agrarian reform, we are going to improve the living conditions of everyone. The people need low-cost food, better wages, education, shelter, and health. We want to reconstruct Brazil without unemployment, rural flight, and youth thrust toward crime and prostitution.

7. Do not delude yourselves with the propaganda from the FHC government. The policy that would benefit foreign capital and the financial system is that which generates unemployment, the bankruptcy of national industry and agriculture. And it is the responsibility of that government.

8. We are going to vote against the government in these elections. We are going to vote for candidates who might have firm positions in favor of the people's interests. We do not want alms, but rights and dignity.

9. We want a better Brazil. A Brazil for all. With attention to the people's basic necessities, with the democratization of land, wealth, and power. Where there might be hope, a future for our people and pride in constructing a nation for Brazilians.

10. Workers, intellectuals, small entrepreneurs, retirees, housewives, and students, everyone, we need to unite in order to construct a new project of development for Brazil. A PROJECT FOR THE BRAZILIAN PEOPLE.

The "Greatest Administrative Scandal"

Seth Garfield

Ridding the nation of subversion and the government of corruption served as an oft-repeated justification for the military in seizing power in 1964. The federal Indian bureau, the Indian Protective Service (SPI), established in 1910, would be indicted by the military as a symbol of all that was rotten in the state of Brazil before the coup. The SPI's mission had been to "protect" the indigenous population and oversee its integration into Brazilian society. Nevertheless, the agency fell short of its goals, a victim of inadequate funding, mismanagement, and regional elite opposition. Furthermore, as was no secret, bureaucratic malfeasance and corruption long plagued the SPI. In addition to the agency's numerous internal investigations, the Brazilian Congress carried out a special inquest into the Indian bureau's misdeeds in 1963. Nonetheless, all such measures came to naught.

With the onset of the military coup, not only had the will to effect policy and administrative reform changed, but so, too, had the means afforded to an authoritarian state. Indeed, the military's decision to impugn the SPI conformed to its overall goal to disband populist politics, centralize state power, and intensify the settlement and development of the Amazon. To safeguard private capital investment in the Amazon, the military sought to defuse interethnic land conflicts through increased intervention in indigenous affairs. Signaling its commitment to national development and moral regeneration, the military showcased the crimes of the past and the promise of the future. Nevertheless, to the military government's chagrin, not all would go according to plan.

In 1967, Attorney General Jader Figueiredo was commissioned by the minister of the interior to investigate corruption in the SPI. That same year, a mysterious fire at the Ministry of Agriculture in Brasília destroyed the SPI's archive, with its correspondence and financial records. The

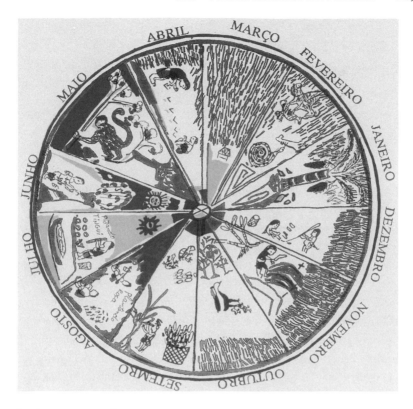

Calendar. (Drawing by José Mateus Itsairu Kaxinawá, *Commissão Pro-Acre*)

investigation continued, however, and after months of inquiries, interviews, and visits to Indian posts, Figueiredo held a press conference in
March 1968 to publicize his 20-volume, 5,115-page report.

Evidence had been found not only of massive corruption, landgrab-
bing, and labor exploitation, but of massacres, enslavement, rape, torture, and biological warfare against Indians.[1] The crimes stemmed from
the dereliction and, at times, collusion of SPI officials. The attorney
general concluded that the SPI had "persecuted the Indians to the point
of extermination, the lack of assistance being the most efficient means of
committing murder."[2] Likewise, the Rio de Janeiro newspaper *Correio da
Manhã* charged "[that what] incompetent authorities executed in Brazil
for years in the Indian sector has a name: genocide." Of the 700 SPI
employees, 134 were charged with crimes; 33 would be removed and 17
suspended. The military dismantled the SPI and, in December 1967, cre-

ated a new Indian bureau, the Fundação Nacional do Índio (FUNAI), entrusted with demarcating Indian lands and overseeing socioeconomic integration.

Observers have questioned why the military government did not muffle, rather than publicize, its shocking findings. One reason, I propose, was that the Figueiredo Report, with its cast of unscrupulous bureaucrats and helpless Indians, staged the perfect morality play to gain support for purges in the SPI and, by extension, other state agencies from the populist era. Yet, in divulging such heinous crimes, the military government risked—and would succeed in—tarnishing Brazil's name in the international community. Why did the military miscalculate?

Paradoxically, military officials believed that in denouncing the crimes perpetrated against Indians, they would convey the image of a government committed to salvaging Brazil's dearest legend—racial harmony— which, they would show, had become endangered under the populists. Indeed, according to the *Jornal do Brasil,* one month after the release of the Figueiredo Report, the Ministry of Interior impressed on the Ministry of Foreign Relations (Itamarati) that repudiating the atrocities "could only strengthen, in the exterior, the Brazilian image, with respect to racial democracy," and demonstrate that the "Revolution of 1964 [was] incompatible, in its inspiration, with the process of degradation of the human being."

The military's strategy backfired. "The greatest administrative scandal of Brazil"—in Figueiredo's words—would hound the government for years, as denunciations of genocide continued to reverberate in the international arena. Notwithstanding the military's sanctimoniousness, few believed that long-neglected Indian rights were suddenly being safeguarded by the most unlikely of heroes—a regime set on the rapid development of the Amazon. The demon that the government itself first conjured up now refused to go away. Buried under an avalanche of international censure, an embarrassed and offended Brazilian government would spend years fending off meddlesome foreign critics and human rights organizations.

In an effort to assist bedraggled diplomats to respond to the glowering accusations, circulars to Brazilian diplomatic missions from Itamarati highlighted government measures to defend indigenous rights; the U.N. delegation was enjoined to combat any resolution that might arise accusing the Brazilian government of genocide. The furor, however, refused to subside, straining foreign relations. Scathing exposés on Brazilian Indian policy blanketed the European press; the most notable was Norman Lewis's article in the London *Sunday Times,* "Genocide—From Fire and Sword to Arsenic and Bullets, Civilization Has Sent Six Million Indians to Extinction," published in February 1969.

The Brazilian government rankled at such accusations. The raison d'être of the Brazilian Indian bureau had always been to instill (or reawaken) civic pride and nationalistic feelings in the Indians. The state had to protect its primordial citizens from the machinations of foreign governments, missionaries, and interlopers—all armed, allegedly, with ulterior motives in tending to the Indians. What an unacceptable turn of events now for outsiders to dictate to Brazil how to treat its indigenous population!

In fact, more mundane factors motivated the government's critics. Politicians from the Movimento Democrático Brasileiro (MDB), the sole legal opposition party in Brazil, were among the first to pounce on the Figueiredo Report. They threatened to denounce the military government at the United Nations and to call for an international wardship system for the Indians—one of the regime's most dreaded nightmares. For the regime's opponents, shackled by an authoritarian system, the scandal offered an opportunity to discredit the military and enlist foreign support. The egregiousness of the crimes and the impotence of the victims ensured a large audience.

Finally, the Indians—less than 1 percent of the Brazilian population—found themselves in the eye of a political hurricane and exploited the government's vulnerability. For example, it is perhaps no coincidence that in April 1968, one month after the Figueiredo Report surfaced, two Xavante Indians announced to the press that white invaders were forcibly relocating by airplane a large group of Xavante from a nearby village. The airlift of a Xavante community from a cattle ranch to a Catholic mission—where 90 of the 280 Indians would perish in a measles epidemic—in fact, had occurred two years earlier. To secure assistance from a government facing international censure, the Indians undoubtedly reissued and updated their complaint.

The SOS for the Indians did not go unheeded. In 1970, a delegation from the International Red Cross undertook a three-month fact-finding mission to twenty different Indian tribes as well as government ministries in Brazil. The mission had been prompted by Red Cross concern with charges of genocide, along with the Brazilian government's efforts to clear them. Other foreign delegations would follow: in 1972, representatives from the London-based Aborigines' Protection Society would visit Brazil, later issuing a report on the indigenous population.

Seeking everything possible to "remove the indigenous problem from the headlines of Brazilian and foreign newspapers," Minister of the Interior Albuquerque Lima met in July 1968 and April 1969 with the Xavante, Bororo, Karajá, and various Xingu communities to reiterate the government's determination to protect or recover indigenous lands. In June 1969, it was President [General] Costa e Silva's turn. In the footsteps of Getúlio Vargas–who nearly thirty years earlier, had come to the region to popularize the state-backed "March to the West"—Costa e Silva visited Bananal Island, where he met with a delegation of Xavante, Karajá, Kayapó, and Kamaiurá Indians.

As on Vargas's trip in 1940, the Indians entertained the president with "traditional" song and dance. But things were not quite the same. The president's pan-Indian audience was a telltale sign of how much had changed since Vargas's visit, when the Xavante were still "unpacified" and the mortal enemies of the Karajá. So was the response of the Xavante, who two decades earlier, were at war with the Brazilian nation-state, but now summoned up the rhetoric they had been fed by state officials and missionaries to strike a responsive chord. In the "name of all the Xavante tribe," Humberto Waomote, an Indian from the São Marcos mission, saluted the president as well as the "authorities and brotherly people" for their efforts to "improve the life of the Brazilian Indian."[3] In April 1969, *O Estado de São Paulo* newspaper reported that a Xavante from the Catholic mission at Sangradouro proclaimed to the minister of the interior, "We are all Brazilians. We, the Xavantes, arrived first."[4]

The Xavantes' discourse bespoke awareness of their cultural identity as "Indians" and their rights as Brazilian citizens—lessons they had learned from whites since contact. Over the following decades, the Xavante and other indigenous groups would repeatedly remind the Brazilian government that, as those who "arrived first," they were entitled to larger reservations than the military intended. And with the aid of foreign and domestic allies—many of whose interest in indigenous affairs had been fired by the "greatest administrative scandal of Brazil"— some indigenous groups would score impressive victories.

Notes

1 Shelton Davis, *Victims of the Miracle* (Cambridge: Cambridge University Press, 1986), pp. 10–11.

2 "Inquérito Administrativo Referente a Apuração de Iregularidades no Extinto SPI," FUNAI-DOC, Processo 4483–68, vol. XX (Figueiredo Report).

3 *O Estado de São Paulo,* 20 June 1969.

4 *O Estado de São Paulo,* 25 April 1969.

Life on an Occupied Ship

Marçal João Scarante

Democracy's return in 1985 foreshadowed the termination of economic and social policies dating from the Vargas era. The ongoing sale of state-owned steel mills, mines, oil reserves, telecommunication services, and electric utilities to international investors represents a shift from nationalist development strategies to economic liberalism. At the same time, both public and private enterprises view the state's retreat from corporatist labor relations as a green light to slash payrolls by any means. Their methods include layoffs, cuts in real wages, intensified production routines, relaxation of safety rules, and de-unionization of the workforce. Although the tide is currently against them, many workers and union officials adamantly resist those changes. The most tragic case to date occurred in 1988 when three men died after the army opened fire on workers protesting new policies at the Volta Redonda steel complex. In April 1997, workers feared another tragedy after longshoremen in Santos occupied two ships docked at a Cosipa (Paulista Steel Company) wharf. Cosipa's hiring of nonunion labor had sparked the confrontation. Two of the longshoremen, whom the police detained unharmed after nearly two weeks aboard the ships, issued the following statements on the ninth day of the occupation, April 11, 1997.

Marçal João Scarante, director of the Checkers' Union,
on board the Maltese-flag ship, *Vancouver*

The people are in a ruinous living condition. Bathing only from the faucet, we sleep underneath stairs, on top of mooring ropes; we go about improvising. The cold is strong at night and we have had some problems. Yesterday, April 10, one of the comrades, Sebastião, had a nervous ulcer attack and had to be removed from here by ambulance. But, in the mind, we are all fine. Now, we are eleven stevedores and one checker. Here, the captain (Greek) has collaborated and the Philippine crew treats us well, in the same way that we treat them. They can do little, but they help us in the measure possible. The report is good. The people who remain very apprehensive have families there, outside. The people know that they are worried. I have four children and work fifty shifts per month. All the personnel here have their children, their responsibilities, and work very much to survive. But we are with elevated morale and raised heads. It seems that today some negotiation opened; even if it does [not] succeed for us immediately, now there is dialogue. We want to negotiate. This process of modernization started with [President] Collor and, since then, every president said that the workers would not be harmed, including Fernando Henrique [Cardoso]. This is not what is happening. The worker understands that the court has to be obeyed, but even reaching compliance with the court, it is necessary to seek the truth. Justice is being applied without the truth being sought. We have given qualified labor for thirty-two years. We are prepared and trained, and nevertheless, we are being exchanged for people unprepared, brought from Minas Gerais, which does not even have a coastline. Modernization, in this sense, is a fantasy. The worker still does not have active participation in the process of modernization, and that is what we want.

Mr. Soares, director of the Stevedores Union,
on board the Brazilian-flag ship, *Marcos Dias*

We are sleeping outdoors because we do not have access to anything here. We sleep on the deck, on the cold floor, or on newspapers and cardboard. At night, the temperature drops much here, and now we have various comrades with respiratory problems, with the possible assistance, which is little. Food has been arriving, but it is a problem because Cosipa has made it difficult to allow the food to arrive on the normal schedule. We have been eating dinner at two in the morning, lunch at four in the afternoon and later. It [Cosipa] tries to debilitate us. We know that it is deliberate. But the determination continues. We want negotiation. We have concern for the personnel who are in the Cosipa port and the families outside. That ought to be the concern of the judge who gives a decision about these things. We are competent, qualified by the navy, and the Law of the Ports says that manual labor has to be sought among those registered. Therefore, it does not make the least sense to replace prepared and trained workers with people unprepared and unqualified for the job, who come from a place that does not even have the sea itself. Will that be modernization? Will it improve the quality of the work? Therefore, modernization seems a deception viewed from here on the deck. We wanted to negotiate and we did not get it. But, the certainty is that we are going to resist until the end. Already, we have been here nine days and we are not going to desist. The situation that Cosipa created is unjust, regardless of any judicial decision. We want, therefore, justice, before anything else. Our worst moment was when the assault came. They tried to board ship and throw some gas bombs in the hold. Only they did not succeed in finding us. Later, the situation calmed down, but the apprehension always remains, because heads are hot. The people are worried, too. But we know that the struggle is just, and we know of the national and international support that we have received. We know that we are not alone.

A Letter from Brazil

Juliano Spyer

Brazilian police not only earn dismal salaries, but the government often falls months behind in issuing their paychecks. Since they can act with impunity, police officers commonly supplement their salaries by extorting money from slum dwellers. The world learned of this practice after a photographer secretly videotaped police officers committing murder during an extortion operation in a São Paulo slum. When the videotape appeared on international television, the whole world sensed why poor Brazilians often trust neighborhood gang leaders over the police. Shortly after the videotape aired, Brazilian Juliano Spyer issued a passionate, international statement via electronic mail.

Date: Fri, 04 Apr 1997 02:13:12−0800
From: Juliano Spyer ⟨spyer@internetco.net⟩
To: global.friends@concerned.citizens.com
Cc: várias
Subject: A letter from Brazil

dear friends,

it's not easy for me to write letter in english. so, please, forgive me for any deadly grammar mistake. I'll be glad to explain anything that is not clear on the letter below.

i imagine that many of you have seen or heard about or read about the police in south america and, particularly, in brazil. this week, though, the world was able to see how our police treats the poor. somebody unknown taped a blitz inside a shantytown. the policemen involved were shown torturing and also killing people, without any reasonable motivation. about this sad event, there are a few things that must be said.

1) violence against the poor is not recent here. until a century ago, there were people in brazil considered to be below humanity—the slaves. in fact, very little of it has changed since then.

2) do not trust that the efforts that the government is making to punish the policemen (involved in this case) has anything to do with changing the current situation. the real objective is, in fact, to clear the countries image in order to sustain our economic links. what you probably have seen on TV can happen to me (and specially to the black + poor), when we walk at night, away from the middle-class spots in town.

3) this police (the military police) was created during the military dictatorship that ruled brazil (quite the same in latin america) from 64 to 84. its objective was to maintain the social (and political) "peace." first, destroying anything related to freedom (of speech, act, etc.). and right after (mid-70s), to keep the poor aware that they had not permission to express disagreement against the government. about this special matter, you can read (i don't know if it's translated) "ROTA—A POLICIA QUE MATA," by Caco Barcellos.

4) the policemen in brazil has a wage that is inferior to US$600 a month. but that does not mean that they are allowed to torture and kill for money. it means, though, that they are on the same level of others who choose to raise [their] "natural" wage dealing with drugs, robbing banks, or kidnapping. but it's important to note that this situation is very much adequate, otherwise it could be changed. but if the poor kills the poor, the social and political balance stays untouched.

5) on the other hand, every year, millions of dollars are sent to foreign banks by politicians (and by the politician's friends), and no one has ever gone to jail. first, because the justice is structured to protect the rich. and second, because soon after the scandals are off of the TV, the cases are closed. the reason: "insufficient [proof]." President Collor, for instance, impeached in 94, is living now in Miami. His judgment is forgotten, and he'll be soon able to run for any public position—even for president. but the ones that actually go to jail have very special privileges. while the uneducated people are put in normal cells (twenty or thirty in each cubicle), the ones that have superior education have partial freedom and have private cells—it's all in the constitution.

so, if you feel indignation against what you saw on TV, do not use it superficially. it's not an easy situation, and it will not be changed with the punishment (ninety years in prison) for the policemen involved. one year ago, several people were killed at the Caraja's Massacre, and they were only defending their right to subsist on a land that was being used for economic speculation. so far, nothing happened to the landowners that, together with the police, ordered the massacre. in 92, 111 men were killed inside a prison in São Paulo—and there was not even one policeman dead. (that makes you think about the types of weapons used by the police and by the prisoners.) after a few days, when the government felt that the subject was already cold and forgotten, the case was closed.

today, as it has always been, the few people that face the police (in fact, facing the institutional repression), have to run away or they are soon killed. it happens centuries ago, with the killing of Zumbi (an ex-slave, leader of the Palmares community). it happened last century, with the military invasion against Canudos (another community that faced the governments rule). and it is happening over and over, with the street kids, with the native brazilians, and with the landless workers.

the government that claims to have stabilized our economy hasn't done anything to develop the country's social situation. but there are still more than 18 percent unemployed people in Brazil. a teacher that works for the public schools earn around US$3 per hour—you may figure out how many hours they have to work to make their living at least decent. in order to get into a no-tuition public college (these are the best in the country), the student must have a private education that costs at least US$600 a month. but brazil's minimum wage is US$112.

if you really feel you must do anything to help, do not worry about events like the murders or massacres. it's sad, but the punishment of these policemen will not change the situation. the causes are [hidden] below what you see. what we need is citizenship (education, land, wages, etc.), and not a type of justice that is meant to be seen by the foreign public eyes.

thank you for your attention,
juliano

Inaugural Address

Fernando Henrique Cardoso

*FHC, as the media dubbed Fernando Henrique Cardoso, took the oath of office
as president of Brazil on January 1, 1995. The three preceding heads of state—
José Sarney, Fernando Collor de Mello, and Itamar Franco—had attempted
change but accomplished little. Cardoso, however, was elected with a large
popular mandate, having defeated the affable yet unpolished candidate of the
leftist Labor Party, Luís Ignácio da Silva (Lula), mostly on the strength of his
achievements as finance minister in curbing inflation. The new president set out
to assure Brazilians that his administration would respect their rights, but also
move the country forward, embracing the free market system and moving to
curtail Brazil's historical isolation from the rest of Latin America. The success
of Mercosul, the Southern Cone common market, was one sign that this policy
had a good chance of succeeding.*

Your Excellencies, Deputies, Senior Officials of the Republic,
Ladies and Gentlemen,

I have come to add my hope to the hope of all on this day that brings us
together. Before giving voice to the president, however, allow me to
speak as the citizen who made an obsession out of hope, as have so many
other Brazilians. I belong to a generation that grew up lulled by the
dream of a Brazil that would be at the same time democratic, developed,
free, and fair. The flame of this dream was lit in the distant past. It was lit
by the heroes of our independence; by the abolitionists; by the revolutionary "lieutenants" of the Old Republic.

This flame is the one I saw shining in the eyes of my father, Leônidas
Cardoso, one of the generals in the campaign called "the oil is ours," just
as it shone at the end of the empire in the eyes of my grandfather, an
abolitionist and republican.

For the students such as I who threw all their enthusiasm into these struggles, oil and industrialization were our ticket to the modern, post-war world. They guaranteed a seat for Brazil in the car of technological progress, a car that was accelerating and threatened to leave us behind in the dust. For some time, during the presidency of Juscelino Kubitschek, the future seemed to us to be very near. There was development. Brazil was becoming rapidly industrialized. Our democracy functioned, despite the fits and starts. And there were prospects of social progress. But history takes turns that confound us. The "golden years" of Juscelino Kubitschek ended on a note of heightened inflation and political tensions.

In their stead, we had the somber years that initially recouped growth, but that sacrificed freedom. These years brought progress, but only for the few. And then, not even that, merely the legacy—this time, shared by all—of an external debt that tied down the economy and an inflation rate that aggravated social ills during the decade of the eighties. And so I watched my children grow and saw my grandchildren appear, dreaming and struggling to decry the day in which development, freedom, and justice—justice, freedom, and development—would walk side by side throughout the land.

I never doubted that this day would come.

But I also never thought this day would find me in the office I enter today, chosen by a majority of my fellow citizens to lead the journey toward the Brazil of our dreams. Without arrogance, but with absolute conviction, I say to you: This country shall be a success story!

Not because of me, but because of all of us. Not just because of our dreams—our tremendous desire to see a successful Brazil—but because the time is now ripe and Brazil has all it needs to thrive.

We have recuperated what ought to be the most precious treasure of any people: our freedom. Peacefully, calmly, despite the bruises and scars that remain as a symbol to ensure that there will be no repetition of the violence, we turned the page on the authoritarianism that under many names and guises has undermined our republic since its foundation. For today's young people, who literally put on their war paint and took over the streets demanding decency from their representatives, and for the people of my generation as well, who learned the value of freedom when they lost it, democracy is an unchallengeable conquest. Nothing and no one shall make us give it up again. We have recovered our confidence in development.

It is no longer just a matter of hope. Nor is it a matter of euphoria for the two good years we just enjoyed. This year will be better. Next year will be better still. Today, there is no responsible specialist who forecasts anything but a long period of growth for Brazil. International conditions are favorable. The burden of our external debt no longer suffocates us. Here in Brazil, our economy is like a healthy plant after a long drought. The roots—the people and businesses that produce wealth—have resisted the rigors of stagnation and inflation. They have survived. They have emerged with greater strength after their travails. Our business community has proved to be capable of innovation, of retrofitting their factories and offices, of overcoming their difficulties.

Brazil's workers have proved to be capable of facing up to the hardships of arbitrary practices and recession, and the challenges of new technologies. They have reorganized their unions so as to be capable, as they are today, of demanding their rights and their fair share of the results of economic growth. The time has come to grow and blossom.

Even more important, today we know what the government must do to sustain the growth of the economy. And we shall do it. In fact, we are already doing it. When many doubted if we would be capable of putting our own house in order, we started off over the last two years to put that house in order. Without yielding a millimeter of our freedom, without breaking any agreements or harming any rights, we did away with superinflation.

We owe all of this not just to those who set a new course for the economy, but also to President Itamar Franco, who has earned the respect of Brazilians for his simplicity and honesty. At this moment in which he leaves office, surrounded by well-earned esteem, I thank Itamar Franco on behalf of the nation for the opportunities he has afforded us. By choosing me to succeed him, an absolute majority of Brazilians clearly opted for the continuation of the "Real" Plan, and for the structural reforms that are necessary to do away with the specter of inflation once and for all. As president, I shall dedicate myself to this task with all my energy, and I will count on the support of the Congress, the states, and all the community leaders of the nation. So, we have our freedom back. And we shall have development. What is missing is social justice.

This is the major challenge facing Brazil in the final days of the century. This will be the number one objective of my administration. Joaquim Nabuco, the premier advocate of abolitionism, thought of himself and his companions as having been delegated with a "mandate from the black race." Not a mandate from the slaves, since they did not have the means to demand their rights. But a mandate that the abolitionists took on even so, because they felt the horror of slavery in their hearts, and they understood that the shackles of slavery kept the entire country trapped in economic, social, and political backwardness.

We, too, feel horrified when we see our fellow citizens and—even if they aren't Brazilian—human beings by our side subjugated by hunger, disease, ignorance, violence. This must not go on! Just as was the case of abolitionism, the reform movement I represent is not against anyone. It does not seek to divide the nation. It seeks to unite the nation by rallying us round the prospect of a better future for all. But, in contrast to Nabuco, I am well aware of the fact that my mandate resulted from the free votes of my fellow citizens. From the majority, regardless of their social status. But my mandate also came, to a tremendous degree, from those that have been excluded; the humblest Brazilians who paid the bill of inflation without being able to defend themselves; those that are humiliated in hospital and social security lines; those that earn so little compared to all they give the country in factories, fields, stores, offices, hospitals, schools, on construction sites, streets and highways; those that clamor for justice because they are, in fact, aware of and willing to fight for their rights—it is, to a great degree, to all of them that I owe my election.

I will govern for us all. But if it becomes necessary to do away with the privileges of the few to do justice to the vast majority of Brazilians, let there be no doubt: I will be on the side of the majority. In all tranquillity, as is my wont, but in all firmness. Always seeking the paths of dialogue and persuasion, but without shying away from the responsibility of decision making. Knowing that most Brazilians do not expect miracles, but will demand results from the government on a daily basis. Among other reasons, because Brazilians believe in Brazil again, and are in a hurry to see Brazil improve more and more.

It is also a satisfaction for us to see that interest regarding Brazil is increasing among other countries. Our efforts to consolidate democracy, adjust the economy, and attack social problems are monitored abroad with very high expectations. Today, everyone understands that our transition to democracy was slower and occasionally more difficult than that of other countries. This was because our transition was deeper and broader. We restored democratic freedoms and began overhauling our economy at the same time. For this very reason, we constructed a more solid foundation on which to build. We have the support of society for changes. Society knows what it wants and where we should go. Speedily, at the rapid pace of communications and the liberalization of the Brazilian economy, we leave behind xenophobic attitudes that are more accurately described as the effect than the cause of our relative closure in the past.

None of the above implies that we will renounce even a fraction of our sovereignty, nor neglect the means to guarantee it. As commander in chief of our armed forces, I shall be mindful of their needs in terms of modernization to ensure that the forces will reach operational levels in line with Brazil's strategic stature and international commitments. In this regard, I shall assign new tasks to the armed forces staff, going beyond their current responsibilities. And I shall order proposals to be presented on the basis of studies to be carried out in conjunction with the navy, army, and air force, in order to tailor the gradual adaptation of our defense forces to the demands of the future.

In the post–cold war world, the importance of countries such as Brazil no longer depends solely on military and strategic factors, but on domestic political stability, the general level of well-being, and the vital signs of the economy—the capacity to grow and create jobs, the technology base, our share of international trade—and also on clear, objective, and feasible diplomatic proposals.

For this very reason, the implementation of a consistent national development program should strengthen us in a growing manner on the world stage. Times are favorable for Brazil to seek more active participation within this context. We have a constant identity and a lasting set of values that will continue to be expressed by our foreign policy. Continuity means reliability in the international sphere. Sudden changes, unmindful of the long-term view, might satisfy short-term interests, but they do not forge the profile of a responsible state. Nevertheless, we should not be afraid to innovate when our interests and values indicate this option.

During a phase of radical transformations colored by the redefinition of the rules for political and economic comity among nations, we cannot turn our backs on the course of history out of mere nostalgia for a past seen through rose-colored glasses. We must, however, be mindful of the course that history is taking in order to influence the design of the new world order. The time has therefore come to update our discourse and activities abroad, in consideration of the changes in the international system and the new domestic consensus as to our objectives.

The time has come to openly discuss what Brazil's profile should be as a sovereign nation in this world in transformation; the debate should involve the Ministry of External Affairs, the Congress, academia, labor unions, the business community, and nongovernmental organizations.

We will retire dated ideological dilemmas and outworn forms of confrontation, and face up to the new themes that impel cooperation and conflict among countries today: human rights and democracy; the environment and sustainable development; the broadened range of tasks relating to multilateralism and regionalization; dynamizing international trade, and overcoming protectionism and unilateralism. Other key themes are access to technology, efforts to ensure nonproliferation, and the struggle against the various manifestations of international crime.

We will take maximum advantage of Brazil's ubiquitous presence, both in political and economic terms. A presence that will allow us both to increase our participation in regional integration movements, beginning with Mercosul, as well as to explore the dynamism of unified Europe, NAFTA, the Asian-Pacific region. And we will also identify areas with new potential in terms of international relations, such as the post-apartheid South Africa, not to mention countries such as China, Russia, and India, which because of their continental size, face problems similar to ours in the effort to ensure economic and social development.

I believe that Brazil has a place reserved for it among the countries on this planet that will do well during the next century and I am convinced that the only major obstacles that stand in our way are the result of our domestic imbalances—the extreme inequalities among regions and social groups. We know that the development of a country in today's world is not measured by the quantity of goods that it produces. The real degree of development is measured by the quality of care a country provides to its people. To its people and to its culture. In a world in which communications are global and instantaneous, and yet, in which the target groups are becoming fragmented and specialized, cultural identity holds nations together.

We Brazilians are an extremely homogenous people in cultural terms. Our regional differences are mere variations on a basic cultural theme, the result of a fusion of Western and Portuguese with African and Amerindian traditions. Our intellectuals, our artists, and our cultural agents are the genuine expression of our people. I want to acclaim them and provide them with the conditions that will allow them to become builders of citizenship. For citizenship means not just the right of the individual, but also the pride of being part of a country that has values and a style of its own.

The priorities that I put forth to the voters, and which were approved by the majority, are those that have direct repercussions on people's quality of life: employment, health, safety, education, food production. Job creation will come with the return of growth, but not automatically. This administration will be committed to specific programs and actions in this field. And we will throw ourselves heart and soul into the great challenge—facing Brazil, and not just this or that region; facing us all, and not just those left on the sidelines—the challenge of decreasing inequalities until we have done away with them.

Providing access to hospitals and respect for those being helped, eliminating unnecessary delays, fighting waste and fraud, all these are factors that are just as indispensable to proper health care management as is the existence of sufficient funding. But health must be viewed—and so it shall be, under my administration—primarily as the prevention and not just the curing of diseases. A modern approach to health includes basic sanitation, mass vaccination campaigns, adequate food and sports for all.

The school must be the heart of the teaching process once again. Schools are not just the function of the teacher. A school is far more than that. It is a gathering place where the actions of parents, the solidarity of the social medium, the participation of students and teacher and proper administration are added together to train properly prepared citizens.

To make the great leap that will be required on the threshold of the new millennium, we can no longer coexist with massive levels of illiteracy or functional illiteracy. It is a sorry illusion, indeed, to believe that the mere consumption of gadgets will make us "modern" even if our children continue to pass through our schools without absorbing the barest minimum of knowledge needed to keep up with modernity's rapid pace.

We have had enough of a situation in which we built ridiculously monumental schools, and then filled them with badly paid and badly trained teachers, as well as unmotivated students who were not materially or psychologically ready to take full advantage of their education.

To fully exercise our mandate to do away with destitution, we must also do away with spiritual impoverishment. Let the modern media help us in our task. Together with information and entertainment, let us engage our television networks in a true national crusade to rescue citizenship through education, beginning with a tremendous effort to provide literacy and cultural education.

My mission, beginning today, is to ensure that these priorities of our people will also be our government's priorities. This will demand a broad reorganization of our government machinery. The federal administrative system has deteriorated significantly after year upon year of excesses and fiscal difficulties. Patronage, corporativism, and corruption drain away the taxpayer's money before it reaches those who should be the legitimate beneficiaries of government activities, primarily in the social arena.

The congressional investigations and the decisive steps taken by President Itamar Franco's administration began to rid us of these parasites over the last two years. It will become necessary to stir up many hornet's nests before completing our housecleaning and providing the structural reforms that are so necessary if public services are to become efficient. This does not frighten me.

I know that I will have the support of the majority of our nation. And also the support of many employees who care deeply for the civil service. The most important support, in fact, is not the kind extended to the government or to the president as an individual. The most important support is the kind we give one another, as Brazilians, and the support we all give to Brazil.

This veritable social revolution, this revolution of people's mindsets, will only occur with the cooperation of all society. The administration has a key role to play, and I will see that this role is carried out. But without congressional approval of changes in the Constitution and our legislation—some of which I pointed out in my farewell speech to the Senate—and unless public opinion is mobilized, our good intentions will be stillborn phrases in speeches.

We must stitch together new ways for society to participate in the process of change. A fundamental share of this growing awareness, these demands on the part of our citizenry and the mobilization I have described, will depend on the mass media. Our media were a fundamental part of the redemocratization processes and they have also been key to the recuperation of morality in public life. Now a new and pivotal role has been reserved for them in the effort to mobilize everyone in the building of a fairer and better society, while maintaining their critical independence and their passion for the veracity of their information.

Once Brazilians have better access to information and are in a position to be more critical of the policies that are actually implemented than of the folklore surrounding so many aspects of daily life, once they are in a position to put events into proper perspective and demand greater consistency from actions rather than judge mere intentions, then Brazilians will be better prepared to exercise their citizenship . . .

Let us ensure a decent life for our children, taking them off the streets where they have been abandoned, and above all, putting an end to the shameful massacres of children and youths. Let us vigorously guarantee equal rights to equals. To women, who form the majority of our people, and to whom the country owes both respect and opportunities for education and employment.

To the racial minorities and to some near-majority groups—primarily the blacks—who expect equality to be, more than a mere word, the portrait of a reality. To the Amerindian groups, some of them living witnesses of human archaeology and all of them witnesses of our diversity. Let us transform solidarity into the active ingredient of our citizenship in search of equality.

And our hope of seeing a free, prosperous, and fair Brazil shall beat ever more strongly in the breast of each Brazilian like a great truth. In conclusion to this speech, I wish to leave behind a heartfelt word of gratitude. To the people of my country, who with generosity, elected me to office during the very first round of voting. To the many who accompany me in our political struggles. To my family, who was capable of understanding the challenges of history.

To the Congress I served in up until today and which now swears me in, with the proclamation of the judiciary, as president of the republic. To the heads of state from countries that are our friends, and to the foreign delegations that honor us with their presence during this ceremony. To our guests. To all the citizens, men and women, of this Brazil of ours, once again I ask that you have much faith, much hope, much confidence, much love, and much work. And I call on you to change Brazil.

Thank you very much.

Fernando Henrique Cardoso:

Theory and Practice

Ted G. Goertzel

President Fernando Henrique Cardoso is, Ted G. Goertzel maintains, the most distinguished marxist scholar to lead a nation since the death of V. I. Lenin. As a young instructor, Cardoso belonged to a group that carefully dissected all three volumes of Das Kapital *and many other marxist classics. Cardoso's voluminous scholarly writings include references not only to Marx, but to many luminaries of historical materialism, including V. I. Lenin, Leon Trotsky, Rosa Luxemburg, Harry Magdoff, Paul Baran, Paul Sweezy, Nicos Poulantzas, and Louis Althusser. Academically, Cardoso is best known for his study of the dependence of Third World nations on multinational capitalism. Since his election to the presidency in 1994, however, Cardoso has been a vigorous advocate of free markets and privatization. Multilingual and personable, he travels the globe wooing investors, and has been repaid with massive infusions of corporate capital. He is also a successful macroeconomic strategist who, as finance minister, ended a stubborn hyperinflation that had defeated several previous governments.*

Cardoso's policies would be easy to understand if he had traded in his worn edition of *Das Kapital* for the collected works of Milton Friedman. And, indeed, Cardoso did publish his break with marxist economic theory as long ago as 1969, when he was in exile in France because of his opposition to the military coup d'état of 1964. But he is nevertheless proud of having mastered the marxist opus a decade before Althusser made reading Marx fashionable, and he readily acknowledges the marxist element that persists in his thinking. He unabashedly stands by everything he ever wrote and insists that, given the same circumstances, he would write it all the same way again. His critics—on both sides of the political spectrum—are troubled by his refusal to apologize for either his past or his present.

On the Left, Brazilian political scientist José Luiz Fiori labels Cardoso a puppet of the neoliberal, new colonialist, multinational business elite. Still, he doesn't believe that Cardoso has abandoned marxist theory. On the contrary, he makes the odd accusation that Cardoso is using his marxism in the service of his new masters.

On the Right, the American political scientist Robert Packenham calls Cardoso an ideologue who ignores empirical evidence. Yet Packenham observes that "no one exemplified the change in Marxist thinking in a more vivid and significant way than Cardoso." Packenham supports Cardoso politically, but he cannot forgive Cardoso his failure to repent his marxist past.

Fiori and Packenham raise a puzzling question. Isn't marxism a critique of capitalism and a harbinger of socialist revolution? If so, how can such a theory be used in defense of the new capitalist world order? What can it mean to be a marxist in a postcommunist era, when almost no one believes in a centrally administered socialist economy?

Cardoso has actually been more consistent in both his theory and practice than many people assume. In 1964, Cardoso was completing his doctorate in sociology and preparing for an academic career at the University of São Paulo when the military coup d'état forced him into exile in Santiago de Chile. He got a job with a U.N. think tank, where he was thrown into international debates about development policy. The result of these discussions was the 1972 book, coauthored with Enzo Faletto, *Dependency and Development in Latin America,* which established his international reputation. *Dependency and Development* had a leftist tone that criticized the exploitation of Latin America by imperial powers. But it also showed that Latin American nations had, at certain points in history, been able find strategies for development within the confines of the capitalist world system. It was more subtle and sophisticated than much of the literature on dependency, which portrayed Latin America as a helpless victim of Europe and North America.

Cardoso returned to Brazil when things seemed to be easing up in 1968 and won a chair in political science at the University of São Paulo, only to be forced out of academia by a military crackdown on the Left. He and a number of prominent academics were involuntarily "retired" and prohibited by law from holding university jobs anywhere in Brazil. The military leaders, however, respected their scholarly achievements and permitted them to start an applied research institute. This had the unexpected consequence of making them much more influential than they would have been as university professors. Their most significant study, a book called *São Paulo: Growth and Poverty,* documented the suffering caused by the military's economic and social policies. It was sponsored by the Catholic Church and helped to build a mass movement for democratic reform.

As a writer and internationally renowned intellectual, Cardoso was a frequent spokesperson for the Brazilian redemocratization movement. His political success owes much to the great respect that Brazilians have for intellectuals. Many businesspeople, civic leaders, and military men follow the currents of intellectual life. The leading newspapers publish lengthy scholarly essays, and Cardoso himself wrote a regular newspaper column for the *Folha de São Paulo* for many years.

Possessing both good political skills and connections, Cardoso was able to use his base of support in the redemocratization movement to win nomination as one of the major opposition party's candidates for senator from São Paulo in 1978. He came in second in the election, which in the Brazilian system, put him in line to become senator when the leader of the ticket resigned to become governor of the state. He was a respected senator, serving for a time as majority leader. He also held the posts of foreign minister and finance minister. In the latter position, he successfully ended Brazil's hyperinflation and established the conditions for a period of rapid economic growth.

How do these accomplishments relate to his marxism? Cardoso explained his view of marxism in an article published in France in 1969. At the time, he was teaching at the University of Paris campus in suburban Nanterre, a hotbed of student activism where many thought capitalism was at death's door and socialist revolution was imminent. Cardoso disagreed. Unlike many marxists who blamed political errors for the failure of Marx's predictions, Cardoso thought that Marx's economic theory had essential flaws. In his view, marxist economics simply could not account for the success of the working class in Europe, or for the division of the capitalist world into core and peripheral countries.

Why, then, didn't Cardoso simply abandon marxism? He did discard marxist economics as outdated, but he thought that Marx still had value as a sociologist and an applied philosopher of knowledge. Cardoso retained Marx's dialectical model of analysis, which combined formal economic research with sensitive political and sociological analysis. In his thinking about the philosophy of science, Cardoso has been influenced by his close friend, prominent Brazilian philosopher José Arthur Gianotti. The two of them were guiding members of the Marxist Study Group of their youth, a group now famous throughout Brazil for the distinguished scholars and leaders that it produced.

By emphasizing the dialectic as a key element in marxist thinking, Cardoso infused his marxism with a heavy dose of voluntarism. He denied that political outcomes were determined by social forces, insisting that they could be changed by strategic and tactical decisions made by leaders. He uses marxism and other theories to illuminate historical situations and to highlight alternatives, not to predict an inevitable future.

Cardoso's generation was decisively shaped by the Brazilian military coup d'état in 1964. Many leftists of the time were tragically misled by the belief that the political crisis was caused by the failure of dependent capitalism. They thought that the only options were socialist revolution or socioeconomic stagnation. In fact, there was a third choice: continued capitalist development with social reforms. What kept this from happening was a political crisis, not an economic one. The moderate reformers, who had enough votes and popular support to impose a compromise, allowed themselves to be lead astray by extremists on the Left and Right who opposed reconciliation. In his analysis of the coup d'état, Cardoso argued that "the insurrectional movement was one of the possible solutions, not the only one, as an economistic view of history would claim."

Cardoso did not need to abandon marxism for another theory because his interpretation of Marx allowed him to include all of the factors he thought important. Although he was thinking more and more like a mainstream sociologist in some ways, he continued to be emotionally tied to his marxist roots. In an interview published in 1978, Cardoso explained:

> If you want to know my personal statement of faith, I am favorable to abolishing the system of exploiters and exploited! But this is *a statement of faith,* which has perhaps a biographical or moral importance. What is important is to develop a political attitude, not a moralistic attitude. *What is important is to know which forces are moving in a given direction, to introduce the act of faith into the reality of the current situation. . . .*

Cardoso believes that in the post-Soviet world, there is no viable alternative to the capitalist mode of production. The only realistic approach in this historical conjuncture is to do whatever is necessary to make Brazil into a prosperous, modern capitalist nation. In effect, he agrees with José Luiz Fiori's argument that he is using his marxism in support of the new capitalist world order. He observes that his government "is making it possible for the most advanced sectors of capitalism to prevail. It is certainly not a regime at the service of monopoly capitalism nor of bureaucratic capitalism, but of that capitalism which is competitive under the new conditions of production. It is, in this sense, socially progressive." To advocate anything else in today's world, he maintains, would be moral posturing, good for the soul perhaps, but not helpful to Brazil.

This does not mean that Cardoso has given up on the human concerns of the Left. Like all Brazilian progressives, he is deeply worried about the suffering of the country's huge impoverished and marginalized populations, especially the landless peasants and the shantytown poor in the cities. And he is painfully aware of his government's limitations in meeting these urgent needs. He frankly concedes that his is not the "regime of the excluded, because it does not have the conditions to be. I would like to incorporate them more, but I cannot say that this will be." In Cardoso's view, since the poor are not part of the dynamic sector of the economy, they cannot be the social basis for progress. Nor can the working class be the vehicle of universal values, as Marx had anticipated. "What was Marx's grand revolutionary proposal?" Cardoso asks. "It was that there was one class, and only one, that, by its specific nature, would be the carrier of universal values. Today this is difficult to sustain, if only because this class is diminishing in quantity and changing its behavior . . . you will see that progressively the unions are no longer against the employers, they are against the government."

Cardoso wants to help the poor and dispossessed, not only for ethical reasons, but also because society cannot function smoothly with millions of people at its margins. In his phrase, the excluded are "sand in the machinery" of society, and social programs are needed to integrate them into the mainstream. However, these programs can be paid for only if the economy is vigorous, and the government cuts waste, corruption, and unnecessary bureaucracy. In terms of practical politics, he has much in common with Franklin Roosevelt or Bill Clinton.

Marxist sociology, for Cardoso, is not a set of doctrines and principles handed down from the nineteenth century; it is a body of knowledge that has to be continually revised to fit changing circumstances. This kind of sociology is very demanding, because it requires him to "read everything" and make his own judgments about each policy issue. The technical details may be left to experts, but the major decisions are dependent on his analysis of the historical conjuncture . . .

Is Brazil Hopelessly Corrupt?

Roberto DaMatta

In 1985, Brazilians emerged from the twenty-one-year military dictatorship hopeful that democratically elected civilians would address the country's grave social and economic woes. To their dismay, the fledgling democracy withered on the vine. First, the highly respected Tancredo Neves entered the hospital, fatally ill, on the eve of his presidential inauguration in 1985. His successor, José Sarney, practiced a brand of politics that featured patronage and favoritism. Then, in the 1989 presidential election, Brazilians placed their faith in the photogenic, youthful Fernando Collor de Mello. Collor never finished his term. While the country suffered spiraling inflation, Collor and his cronies bled the national treasury, thereby leading to his impeachment on charges of corruption in 1992. When other governmental scandals came to light in 1993, anthropologist Roberto DaMatta searched into Brazil's soul to explain why its leaders wantonly disregarded the law. His remarks, although critical of elite behavior, offer hope that Brazilian democracy will succeed.

Deeply revolted by the corruption of Fernando Collor de Mello, their first democratically elected president in thirty years, Brazilians cheered as Congress removed him from power last year.

But now a new scandal is shaking up Congress itself. Along with more than thirty other lawmakers, João Carlos Alves de Santos, director of the powerful National Budget Commission, is being investigated on suspicion of illegally appropriating up to $40 million. The police found $1 million in cash stuffed in his mattress.

Meanwhile, in the impoverished and corruption-ridden northeastern state of Alagoas, the governor's wife proudly parades before the peasants in gold jewelry, French suits, and Italian shoes. A true egalitarian, she says, "Poor people have just the same right to see me pretty as people in society."

Do such scandals—and they are merely a current handful—justify the conclusion that it is impossible to clean up Brazil, freeing the future from the vast corruption that permeates its past? In other words, can public and private morality be transformed as Brazil struggles on the threshold of modernization?

Brazilian corruption is the fruit of a double ethic. One kind of morality exists in the space Brazilians call *rua* (meaning street or, more broadly, the public world); another morality applies in the *casa* (house), a universe that encompasses family, followers, and friends. In the realm of the *rua,* Brazil is just like any other modern nation. It is governed by universal law and institutions that, formally speaking, apply to all its citizens. In the universe of the *casa,* however, Brazil is ruled by unwritten and unspoken norms that promulgate and protect the ethic of privilege and those who act on it. As they say, this is not the land of know-how but of know-who.

Political corruption is a connecting link between the *rua* and the *casa.* Since no moral code exists that applies simultaneously to both spheres, as in most countries that have undergone modernization (Italy is something special), when something cannot be done under the rules of the *rua,* it can be done under the ethical protection of the *casa.*

That is why Brazilian corruption is so hard to correct and prosecute. Corruption is never an individual act. It always involves groups of people bound by one fundamental rule of association: an exchange of favors. This collective corruption is founded on traditional morality, well-established friendships, and the opportunity at hand. It allows crimes to be practiced with impunity and is characterized by an intolerable arrogance.

All this has led society to build a profoundly ambiguous nation-state—a state that indulges its elite and fends off its citizens. As Brazilians say, "To our friends, everything; to our enemies, the law!" The drama has a lot to do with the childish vision of an elite convinced that it is able to manage social contradictions by manipulating the law. It is as if the state were not part of society. To understand corruption Brazilian-style, it is necessary to understand this profoundly negative relationship between a state that is considered above society and a society that wants to be insulated from the state that rules it.

This dangerous illusion is finally under challenge. Since the end of the military regime that ruled from 1964 to 1988, prodded by an aggressive and liberated news media, Brazilians have questioned publicly whether it is legitimate to use the state and politics for personal enrichment.

Now, popular demand is not so much for liberty (which was always of interest to the elite), but for equality. In this milieu, corruption is viewed as an immoral political style. How can the government ask the people to make sacrifices required by modernization if the political elite is not willing to follow the rules and if public officials profit from the emergency, deepening the crises of the state with their immoral conduct?

I interpret the recent scandals and the accompanying uproar as the final gasps of traditional politics. First, the elites have been exposed in their perversion of the political process; second, the public is no longer willing to tolerate a state more satisfied with passing laws than with enforcing them honestly.

So instead of focusing on corruption as Brazil's main problem, look at it as a sign of the change that society and government need to undergo. We also know that friendship, kinship, and personal loyalties are not pure and inviolate institutions. In a democracy, they have to submit to the law.

VI

Women's Lives

Brazilian women were traditionally assigned roles prescribed by social norms and were penalized, often harshly, when they stepped beyond the lines of permitted behavior. If women rebelled, they faced scorn or even ostracism. Even marriage was unavailable to many women. Many women were condemned to live their lives as "old maids," as Emília Moncorva Bandeira de Mello's poignant story, "Aunt Zézé's Tears," recounts here. Casting women in the role of "sainted mothers," Stuart B. Schwartz contends, left little room for feminine sexuality or independence.[1] The only women allowed to express their independence were from the upper classes, such as in the case of Tarsila do Amaral, an avant-garde intellectual and artist who found release and nurture in Paris, then returned to Brazil to defy the social mores of the day as an outspoken rebel. She was able to do this because she was both a brilliant artistic success and from the privileged classes. Patrícia Galvão, the wife of modernist icon Oswald de Andrade, got away with behavior considered even more scandalous because she was the darling of the Left, although she was caught up in the repressive atmosphere of the 1930s and forced to pay dear for her militancy.

Nonelite women generally remained silent, although some managed to be heard by gaining popular recognition as mystics and visionaries.[2] In more recent times, four professions were open to working-class women: factory work, school teaching, domestic service, and prostitution. Factories, especially in textiles, employed more women than men, yet women were overwhelmingly excluded from trade unions, even under Vargas, who went out of his way to acknowledge the role of women in society.

The informal or underground economy, in which up to half of Brazil's population participated, was also largely made up of women artisans, manufacturing hammocks, linens, hats, fishing nets, and a panoply of handmade objects sold at rural markets and to middlemen who brought them to cities to sell at high markups.

Women teachers received terrible pay, even today little more than the minimum wage, hovering around $200 monthly. Most Brazilian schools were at the elementary level, ill-equipped and impoverished; the few middle and secondary schools were invariably staffed by men. Maids down to the 1990s worked long hours—typically six and a half days a week in private homes—for virtually no wages (since they were given room and board in the tiny maid's quarters built into every house and apartment). Until the mid-1990s, they received neither benefits nor health care, unless their patrons provided them, and they were not represented by unions.

Society overlooked the plight of poor women. Thousands worked as laundresses, climbing down from their huts in favela shantytowns to pick up dirty clothing from middle-class houses (the upper class had staffs of live-in maids), take it to a river or back to the favela, hang the wash to dry, and then deliver the clothes back in bundles they carried on their heads. Lower on the economic ladder, other women worked as scavengers, picking up trash, scrap paper, and metal to be sold. Women left young children in the care of older ones or with relatives to work in the city. Often, when they returned to their homes after exhausting days, they were confronted by their men, unskilled and therefore usually idle, who when drunk, beat their women for imagined slights, out of jealousy, or simply because they were expected to be docile.

Charity for women was provided by religious bodies, but it did not reach many. Brazilians have always paid low taxes, and there is no tax incentive to donate money for philanthropy. One secular organization that did charity work among women was the fascist Integralist Party during the 1930s; members of the Integralist women's auxiliary went into poor neighborhoods and offered instruction in hygiene, child rearing, and homemaking skills. As ideologues, the Integralists also attempted to mold women according to the fascist ideal, as exemplified in "The Integral Woman" selection below. In time, government agencies took over this kind of work, but social agencies have long been underfunded and, in rural areas, their presence is all but invisible.

Women won the vote in Brazil in a backhanded manner, bestowed on them as part of Getúlio Vargas's paternalistic social largess that, in many ways, proved meaningless. First granted the vote in the late 1920s in a few of the northern states, women's suffrage was made into a campaign issue by Vargas's Liberal Alliance in 1930. A few women were chosen by indirect election, controlled by the government, to the 1933–1934 Constituent Assembly, and the 1934 Constitution granted all women the vote. But dictatorship soon canceled representative democracy, and neither women nor men actually voted in Brazil until 1946.

Women's associations emerged in the 1930s, but were tiny and had little influence. In the 1970s, however, as part of a larger mobilization of public voices seeking to end the dictatorship, small feminist groups were organized in São Paulo and Rio de Janeiro. One was the Movimento Feminino pela Anistia, a women's amnesty movement seeking the release of political prisoners and restoration of civilian government. The designation of 1975 as the International Year of the Woman by the United Nations helped encourage such movements, even while other political activities in Brazil were still banned. Feminist groups increased in the next decade as the political system "opened" and political exiles began to return.[3] Feminist scholars, especially a circle known as the Grupo Ceres, have been examining issues of sexual and social identity in Brazil. Moreover, feminist scholarship was followed by gender studies and research into alternative forms of sexual expression.

Notes

1 Stuart B. Schwartz, "Somebodies and Nobodies in the Body Politic: Mentalities and Social Structures in Colonial Brazil," *Latin American Research Review* 31, no. 1 (1966): 129.

2 Schwartz, "Somebodies," p. 131.

3 June E. Hahner, "Recent Research on Women in Brazil," *Latin American Research Review* 20, no. 3 (1985): 164.

Aunt Zézé's Tears

Emília Moncorva Bandeira de Mello

Emília Moncorva Bandeira de Mello (1852–1910) used the pen name Carmen Dolores. Her story of the sad young woman Zézé, written near the end of the nineteenth century in Rio de Janeiro, reflects the lives of many women from "good families" (as the term was used), not wealthy enough or sufficiently attractive to win suitors, but required by society to stay at home. A woman daring to leave to live alone, or to move to another city unless she lived with relatives, would be stamped immediately as a whore. Careers without a husband for such young women were out of the question. They had to become content, as the author of this not-so-fictional short story writes, with "passive obedience to routine." Bandeira de Mello assumed modest fame for her novels and collections of short stories, although she is not widely read today.

Pale and thin, for eighteen years she had lived with her youngest sister, who had married very early and now possessed five children: two young ladies of marriageable age, a third still in short dresses, and two little boys.

Maria-José, whose nickname was Zézé, had never been beautiful or winning. On her father's death, it was thought best that she should go to live with her sister Engracigna's family. Here, she led a monotonous existence, helping to bring up her nephews and nieces, who were born in that young and happy household with a regularity that brooked small intervals between the births.

A long, pointed nose disfigured her face, and her lips, extremely thin, looked like a pale crack. Her thoughtful gaze alone possessed a certain melancholy attractiveness. But even here, her eyes, protruding too far for the harmony of the lines on her face, seemed always to be red, and her brows narrow and sparse.

Of late, an intricate network of wrinkles as fine as hairs had formed at the corner of her eyes. From her nose, likewise, two furrows ran along the transparent delicacy of her skin and reached either side of her mouth. When she smiled, these wrinkles would cover her countenance with a mask of premature age, and threatened soon to disfigure her entirely. And yet, from habit, and through passive obedience to routine, Maria-José continued to dress like a young girl of eighteen, in brightly colored gowns, thin waists, and white hats that ill-became her frail and oldish face.

She would remain for a long time in painful indecision when it was a matter of picking out some piece of goods that was of too bright a red or blue—as if instinctively she understood the disharmony of these hues with her age, whose rapid oncoming they moreover placed in all the more noticeable contrast. And at such times, Engracigna and her daughters would say to her with a vehemence whose effect they little guessed, "Why Zézé! Buy something and be done with it! . . . How silly! Do you want to dress like a widow? What a notion!"

And at bottom they meant it.

None of them saw Maria-José as she really was. Living with her day by day had served to efface the actual appearance of the faded old maid. For, in the minds of the mother and daughters, who were moreover of a frivolous and indifferent sort, Zézé had grown to be the type, very vague, to be sure, but the eternal type of young girl of marriageable years who always should be well dressed and smiling.

When she would be out walking with her nieces, of sixteen and seventeen years—who wore the same clothes as she herself did, but whose graceful and lively charm became their gay colors of youth so well—Zézé's intelligence saw only too plainly the contrast between her and them; she would hold aloof from the laughing set, morose, wounded, as if oppressed by an unspeakable shame.

Ah! Who can depict the secret chagrin of an old maid who seems passed by in useless monotony her dark, loveless, despairing days, without hope even of some event of personal interest, while about her moves the busy whirl of happier creatures whose life has but one goal, who feel emotions and tenderness, and who look on her simply as an obscure accessory in the household's affairs! They all loved her, of course, but not one of them suspected that she, too, could cherish those aspirations that are common to all human beings.

Her self-denial seemed to be a most natural thing; indeed, they hardly considered her in the light of a living person; she was no longer of any consequence.

This was an attitude that satisfied the general egotism of the family, and to which they all had grown accustomed, never suspecting the grievous aspect of her sacrifice, which was hidden by a sentiment of proud dignity.

So, when they would go to the theater, and the box held only five—Engracigna, her husband, Fabio, and the three young ladies—Maria-José knew beforehand that her sister, snugly wrapped in her opera cloak, would come to her and say gently, in that purring voice of hers: "You'll stay at home with the children tonight, won't you, Zézé? Little Paulo isn't very well, and I wouldn't think of leaving him with anybody else . . . "

And she would remain behind, without betraying the revolt within her, which on each occasion of these evidences of selfishness, would make the anemic blood in her veins tremble with agitation.

Alone in the dining room, she would ply her needle mechanically, while her nephews would amuse themselves with the toys scattered on the table—colored pictures and lead soldiers. Every other moment, they would call her.

"Aunt Zézé, look at Jorge pinching me!"

"I am not! Paulo hit me first! . . . "

And the good aunt would quiet them. Then, after both had been put to sleep in their little twin beds, she would rest her elbows on the windowsill of her gloomy old maid's room and, placing her hands beneath her sharp chin, her gaze directed toward heaven, she would lose herself in contemplation of the stars that shone in the limpid sky, less lonely, surely, than she on earth. In vain did her eyes seek in the eyes of another that expression of sympathy and tenderness that alone would console her . . .

The truth is that Maria-José was suffering from the disappointment of unrequited passion. She had fallen in love with Monjardin, a poet and great friend of her brother-in-law, Fabio. Monjardin came to the house every Sunday.

Older than she, almost forty, but having preserved all the attractiveness of youth—a black moustache, a vigorous, yet graceful figure, eyes still bright, charming and wide-awake—Monjardin, without knowing it, had conquered Zézé.

This had come about in a rather curious manner. Finding the conversation of Fabio's wife and daughters too commonplace, Monjardin, when he would recite some of his poems or tell some story connected with his literary life, preferred to address Maria-José, whom he saw to be of a serious and impressive nature.

"Let's have another poem, please, Sr. Monjardin!" she would ask in a supplicating tone. "For instance, that one you call 'Regrets.' You know?"

And then he would describe in his verse the grief of a heart, disillusioned and broken by the cruelties of fate, that evoked in vain the remembrance of yesterday's lost loves, vanished in the mists of eternal despair.

He recited these bitter griefs in a strong, healthy man's voice, erect in the center of the parlor, looking mechanically, distractedly at Maria-José with his dreamy eyes; the concentrated effort of his memory brought to his face an involuntary immobility that Maria-José, most deliciously touched, drank in.

The poet had announced that he had written a poem that he would recite at Zézé's birthday dinner. The date for this was but a few days distant, and ever since the poet's announcement, the whole family had taken to teasing the old maid, christening her "the muse of inspiration," and asking her when the wedding would take place . . .

She smiled ingenuously; at such times, her face would even take on an air of unusual happiness; her features grew animated, less wrinkled, and more firm.

On the day of the celebration, Maria-José came out of her room radiant with hope. At the belt of her white dress bloomed a rose; a little blood, set pulsing by her agitated heart, brought a feeble color to her marble cheeks, from which now protruded her long nose in a manner less displeasing than usual.

"See, mama," remarked one of the nieces, "doesn't Zézé look like a young girl today?"

They dined amid merry chatter. Seated directly across from Monjardin, Maria-José, hiding her glances behind the fruit bowls that covered the table, looked at him furtively without surfeit. Her poor heart beat as if it would burst, waiting in agonized suspense for the poem in which the poet, without doubt, was to declare his intimate feelings for her. Monjardin had already pointed to his pocket as a token that he had the verses with him, and Zézé had trembled with gratification as she bashfully lowered her long face.

Champagne sparkled in the glasses, and toasts were given. Several guests of distinction spoke first, then followed the hosts and their children—frolicsome little things. Finally, Monjardin arose and unfolded a manuscript, asking permission to declaim the verses that he had composed in honor of Maria-José, the central figure of the occasion. The guests greeted his remarks with noisy and enthusiastic approbation.

"Hear! Hear!"

Engracigna and her daughters leaned over and cast malicious glances in the direction of Maria-José, but she was paying no attention to them. Her eyes were buzzing; it seemed that everything was turning round.

Monjardin, the center of all eyes, made pompous preparation; he pulled down his vest, arranged his sleeves, and in sonorous, cadenced voice, began to recite his alexandrines, scanning the lines impeccably.

His poem opened with a eulogy of the ineffable virtue, compounded of self-abnegation and chastity, that distinguished the angelic creature who, with her white tutelary wings, watched over the happiness of his dear friend's love nest. He then recalled that the date of this day commemorated the happy birth of a being of immaculate purity, Maria-José, a veritable saint who had renounced all her own aspirations so that she might consecrate herself entirely to the duties of her sister's family; gentle figure of the mother-guardian, who would soon be the beloved grandmother sharing with her sister the joys of younger households that would soon be formed, offsprings of that home that her devoted tenderness as aunt and sister at present cultivated. As he came to a close, the poet raised his cup of sparkling wine, and in exalted voice, drank to the health of Zézé amid the loud huzzahs of all present.

"Long live Aunt Zézé! Hurrah for Aunt Zézé!" cried the children, glasses in hand, while the nieces laughed loudly, blushing to the ears, for they had understood very well the poet's reference to future "younger households."

Fabio and his wife, their eyes somewhat brightened by the strong champagne, proposed in turn a toast to Zézé.

"Here's to Zézé and the eighteen happy years we've lived together! . . ."

Maria-José, as soon as she had seized the significance of Monjardin's verse, had grown deathly pale; stricken by sudden disillusionment, she felt a glacial chill overwhelm her body to the very marrow; she feared that she would faint straightaway and provide a spectacle for the guests, who were all drinking her health, their eyes focused on her. A veil of tears spread before her sight. . . . In vain, she tried to repress them, to force a smile of thanks on her face. The smile wrinkled into a dolorous grimace; she succeeded only in convulsing her contracted visage with the sobs that she sought to restrain. Overcome at last, humiliated, powerless, she broke into tears, and this unforeseen denouement put an end at once to all the pleasure of the dinner.

"Zézé! Zézé! What ails you? . . . "

Engracigna had rushed to her side in alarm; everyone rose, seeking the reason for the outburst; they surrounded the poor creature, whose head had sunk on the table, in the midst of the rose petals that were strewn in charming confusion.

"What is the trouble? . . . "

A nervous attack, perhaps? . . . Confusion produced in her by the touching poem?

Finally, they raised Maria-José's head and bathed it in cool water; whereupon the face of the poor old maid stood revealed in all the ugliness that her spasms of convulsive weeping cast over it, with her large aquiline nose, her protruding eyes, and her livid lips.

And now Monjardin drew near. Delicately raising the icy fingers of Maria-José, he lifted them to the edge of his perfumed moustache and placed on them a grateful kiss; then, turning to Engracigna's daughters, he said, with a solemn, self-complacent tone, "Aunt Zézé's tears are the most beautiful homage that could be rendered to my poor verses."

Tarsila and the 1920s

Carol Damian and Cristina Mehrtens

Tarsila do Amaral, one of the most important female painters of the twentieth century, played a critical role in Brazil's modernist movement. She was born to a life of wealth and privilege on a rural estate in Capivari, in São Paulo state, in 1886. Lydia Dias do Amaral and José Stanislaw do Amaral raised their four boys and two girls in the countryside, but they often visited the capital city and made long trips to Europe. Tarsila's family was typical of the rural aristocracy. Her father, the son of a pioneer planter, was a landowner and successful coffee grower. Tarsila's meals were served by maids on an immense table centered in a spacious colonial room lined with twelve Austrian rocking chairs arranged along opposite walls. The meals consisted mainly of simple rice and bean dishes accompanied by French wine, water, liqueurs, and Brazilian coffee. Tarsila learned to play the family Steinway piano, and was instructed by French-speaking tutors and black "nannies" (amas de leite). From these beginnings, she rose to be one of Brazil's famous painters, a unique interpreter of Brazil's non-European roots in spite of her own background in the landed elite. Few women could aspire to the kind of life she forged for herself, but she cared little about what others thought, and as a result, her life became exemplary of the independence that women, at least in the arts, could achieve.

Born in 1886, Tarsila's first schooling took place on the plantation, where a young Belgian woman taught her to write, read, and embroider. Later (1898–1904), she received a Roman Catholic elementary education from nuns in schools in São Paulo and Barcelona. After a sheltered adolescence, it came time for her to marry. As explained by her father, this event followed the traditional "three F" rule: "*falado* (arranged), *feito* (done), and *fora* (out)." Tarsila wed her mother's cousin, André Teixeira Pinto, in 1906. They honeymooned in Argentina and Chile, and soon had a daughter, Dulce. The marriage did not last, however. Tarsila left her husband and, in the mid-1920s, had the marriage annulled. Although it may seem that it has always been possible for the rich to annul a marriage, her separation from her husband was, by itself, considered shocking in her conservative social environment. In retrospect, Tarsila would explain that it happened due to "disenchantment and cultural distance," and that she coped by "writing sonnets, playing the piano, and aspiring to travel."

In 1913, when she was twenty-seven, Tarsila moved to the burgeoning city of São Paulo, where she took painting and drawing lessons. She also met the young painter Anita Malfatti, who had just returned from Europe and would have a tremendous impact on art in Brazil. Malfatti brought European avant-garde styles of abstraction to a country long dominated by rigid and conservative academic methods. Tarsila was anxious to explore the new trends in modern art. She studied sculpture with the famous Italian artist Mantovani, who had come to São Paulo to design the facade of the new Palace of Industry building. Her lessons brought her into the closed "social circuit" that was molding public spaces—stores, restaurants, cafés, theaters, and parks—and influencing new forms of public behavior.

By 1918, Tarsila was a mature woman who loved music, knew how to paint, and lived a discreet and comfortable life, but in an assertive and independent manner. She would, for instance, go out to the Jardim da Luz park to draw daily scenes. The park abutted the Luz train station, where people from all social classes paraded through on their way to work. Not only did she walk to the park, but she also painted in public, unusual for well brought up women of her day.

Tarsila passed from her "apprentice" phase in São Paulo in transition to delirious postwar Paris. In 1920, she journeyed to France to improve her painting, travel, and as her parents had done, provide her child with a European education. Dulce attended school in England, while Tarsila went to Paris to draw at the Académie Julien and paint with Émile Renard.

In 1922, one of Tarsila's paintings was accepted at the Salon Officiel des Artistes Français (Official Salon Exhibition of Art of France). Its conservative academic style of realism reflected European taste. She was not, at this time, following the avant-garde movements that were shaking the Paris art scene. Tarsila was one of three Brazilian artists admitted to the salon, and the only woman. After her painting's successful reception,

Tarsila changed its name from *Portrait* to *Passport,* claiming that it had admitted her to the world of art. More than just a name change, the event marked her acceptance by the artistic elite. On her return to Brazil later that year, Anita Malfatti introduced her to the young intellectual planners of the Modern Art Week, the event that marked Brazil's entry into the world of modern art. They formed the "Group of Five"— Tarsila, Malfatti, Menotti del Picchia, Mario de Andrade, and Oswald de Andrade—to defend the new modernist ideals while seeking to develop a "national identity." Tarsila thrived in the company of these intellectuals, and participated in the creation of a modernist language that included distinctly Brazilian and *paulista* themes, colors, and subjects. Her desire was to paint truly Brazilian art that would be of national and international significance.

Writer and poet Menotti del Picchia described Tarsila as a *paulista* painter who came from Paris and who "was one of the most beautiful, harmonious and elegant creatures he had ever seen." In September 1922, as part of Brazil's Independence Centennial held in the Palace of Industry, Tarsila presented her paintings to the public. At the same time, she began a romantic relationship with Oswald de Andrade, a poet and writer four years younger. In January 1923, they met again in Europe. Seeking new experiences, they traveled together to Portugal, Spain, and Italy. On their return to Paris, now very much a couple—Tarsiwald was the name they gave themselves—the two of them hobnobbed with Paris intellectuals. They became friends with Swiss poet Blaise Cendrars, who introduced them to Constantin Brancusi, Jean Cocteau, and Madame Apollinaire, among others. Brazilian Ambassador Sousa Dantas invited them to lunch with French and Brazilian artists. At one luncheon, Tarsila, the only woman present, was placed close to Cendrars to assist him in cutting the meat, since he had lost his right arm in the Great War. In the Europe of the day, only a woman could perform such a role.

Tarsila also took lessons at Fernand Léger's atelier, where she learned the basic tenets of cubism and painted *A Negra* (*Negro Woman*). It was a work that made a strong impression on the famous painter and would be used as an illustration for Oswald de Andrade's writings. She continued with her interest in the avant-garde of Paris and her study of cubism. Socially, Tarsila had become an enchantress. Considered one of the most beautiful women in Paris, she had long, strong, thin black hair framing a

A Negra (Negro Woman), oil on canvas from 1923 by Tarsila
do Amaral. *(Guilherme Augusto do Amaral, São Paulo)*

lovely face adorned by long earrings that touched her tanned skin. She
admired and played the music of Erik Satie, was Paul Poiret's customer,
and bought Rosine's perfume, Perugia's shoes, and Martine's furniture.
Well-known and influential people visited Tarsila's exciting studio at
9 Hégésippe Moreau Street. The language Tarsila found to express Brazil to her foreign guests did not present any difficulty. She would offer
feijoada—a black bean dish—or *canja*—a rice and chicken soup of rural
origins (*caipira*). Such a menu was a metaphor for Tarsila's influences, so
well reflected in paintings such as *A Negra* and *A Caipirinha* (*Little Country
Girl*), painted in 1923 and far more modern than her earlier academic
works.

Tarsila took *paulista* modernism to European modernism, and vice
versa, determined to create a new and unique Brazilian visual language

Black and charcoal study
for *A Negra*, drawn in
1923, by Tarsila do
Amaral. *(Guilherme
Augusto do Amaral, São
Paulo)*

Sono (Sleep), an oil on canvas by Tarsila do Amaral from 1928. *(Guilherme
Augusto do Amaral, São Paulo)*

that would be widely appreciated. From birth, Tarsila had experienced both Brazilian and European culture. Perhaps that is why, in her formulation of a new Brazilian visual language, there was a serendipitous co-existence between the search for something authentically Brazilian and her social condition. She never criticized Brazil's sociopolitical situation; rather, she explored her country and appreciated its great diversity. Tarsila's quest for a truly Brazilian art took her back to Brazil to visit places she had never seen. In 1924, she toured Rio de Janeiro and Ouro Preto, where Carnival and Holy Week rituals exposed her to a new Brazil. Tarsila found in the beautiful mining towns of Minas Gerais the colors she loved when she was a child—the verdant green landscape, deep blue skies, and whitewashed churches with their gilded steeples shining in the bright sun. She painted a series of works inspired by these travels known as her "Pau-Brasil" phase after the first painting of 1925. The series is noted for subjects that include tropical flora, the *caboclo,* black people of the area and their daily activities, and the small towns of the interior. In 1925, she illustrated Oswald's *Pau-Brasil,* and painted more than ten new works celebrating the beauty of Brazil and its diverse landscapes. Palm trees, cactus plants, exotic creatures, and the glow of a lemon-slice sun are all characteristic images of the series that would continue to be recognizable elements of her work throughout her career.

In June 1926, Tarsila had her first solo exhibition at Galerie Percier in Paris, and she and Oswald were married in October. The exhibition was a success, described by the critics with such words as "fresh," "exotic," "naïve," and "cerebral." She sold her first painting—*Adoração (Adoration)*, also entitled *Le negre du Saint-Esprit (The Black Man of Saint Esprit)*, from 1925—to someone outside the family for 5,000 francs. She also sold her first painting in Brazil, *Angels* (1925), to Julio Prestes (the president-elect in 1930 who would be deposed before taking office by Getúlio Vargas). The triumph of her Paris exhibition allowed Tarsila the possibility of financial independence, although she was secure with her family's wealth. The other significant event of the year, her remarriage, took place in São Paulo and was an important social occasion attended by such dignitaries as Brazil's new president, Washington Luís, Oswald's godfather. It brought Tarsila back to the semisecluded environment of the family plantation, which Oswald acquired from her father. The couple settled in the countryside, spending most of their time writing and painting. They traveled to Bahia to meet friends returning from a trip to

Amazonas. It was fashionable for the wealthy to travel within the country, and explore what was previously inaccessible and of little interest. In this relaxing atmosphere, Tarsila painted a new series of works, including *Manacá* (*Tree*) in 1927 and *Sono* (*Sleep*) in 1928, works that treat the Brazilian landscape from a dreamy, surreal perspective. The paintings from this period are highly simplified and imaginative interpretations of her country's natural beauty.

In 1928, Tarsila's style embraced the modernist *anthropophagy* (cannibalistic) movement, named by Andrade and their avant-garde circle to reflect their obsession with the violent origins of colonial Brazil. Tarsila's first work in the series is entitled *Abaporu* (from the Tupí-Guarani language: *Aba* = man, *Poru* = who eats). The image of a huge, solitary figure with enormous feet sitting on a bright green patch of land was painted as a birthday gift for Oswald, and became the inspiration and symbol for the *anthropophagy* movement and its quest for Brazilian independence from European cultural domination. Tarsila became more involved in the legends of the land and increasingly aware of its rapid devastation. She realized she could use her art to voice her fears for nature and for the indigenous peoples who were rapidly being displaced by civilization. These were extraordinary concerns for a woman of the 1920s, a time of little sympathy for the causes that occupy activists worldwide today.

Tarsila continued to achieve success in Brazil's elite circles with exhibitions and modernist ventures. The modernists pursued their search for a national identity with a full social circuit of activities that may appear in strange contradiction to their aspirations to recognize the country's vast diversity in their art. They invited foreign personalities, including the surrealist poets Benjamin Péret and Blaise Cendrars, to Brazil and also gave accolades to popular Brazilian personalities like the circus clown Piolim. In their own way, they sought to identify with ordinary Brazilians. They promoted some of their cultural events in such locations as São Paulo's Mappin department store and the Municipal Theater.

The world economic crisis of 1929 and Brazil's complex political issues caused fissures in the modernist ranks. Tarsila's coffee plantation was foreclosed and she lost most of her inherited fortune. With a recommendation from São Paulo's governor, she took her first job as director of restoration at the State Museum. But Tarsila's world was built on patronage, and the 1930 Revolution abruptly put an end to her connections, as well as her job. It also closed an era for a generation accustomed to material comforts and economic stability. As the modernists were forced to abandon their intellectual gatherings and quests for a Brazilian cultural language, Tarsila and Oswald's marriage also ended. The bleak colors of her single painting completed in 1930, *Composição* (*Composition*), mirrored a moment of melancholy for Tarsila and her friends. It was a year of reflection and, while her painting production endured this brief hiatus, Tarsila continued to explore new subjects as an expression of this new Brazilian reality of social change, determined to resume her career alone.

In 1931, Tarsila began to use social themes of international significance in her paintings to bring attention to the plight of struggling people everywhere. She had visited the Soviet Union to arrange an exhibition in Moscow and completed a series of paintings of faceless people enduring the hopelessness of the crowded cities. She returned to Brazil in 1932 in time for the São Paulo Constitutional Revolt. After it failed, she spent a month in jail as a political activist and communist sympathizer. She had descended from the top of her social class to the depths of social humiliation. Not discouraged, she entered the final phase of her career (1933–1972) with a renewed effort to paint the people and landscapes of Brazil, and participate in cultural activities. Now displaying a mastery of technique that combined modernist aesthetics of abstract simplification with accurate draftsmanship and bold tropical colors, she created lyrical paintings that projected a synthesis of Brazilian elements ranging from the folkloric to the mythical, and that now included more of people's daily activities.

Tarsila's modernist quest for a truly Brazilian form of expression had been an appeal for reflection, tolerance, and enjoyment of the changing social scene of the 1920s. Long recognized as "the most Brazilian of modern painters," she applied the new European aesthetic language to the themes and subjects of her own land. She worked with a sincerity of purpose and unique style to create the image of an ideal, exotic world that would be seen as quintessentially Brazilian. Between 1923 and 1972, she produced over 230 paintings, hundreds of drawings, studies, illustrations and prints, and five sculptures, and was honored with exhibitions throughout the world. Tarsila's accomplishments and experiences show that identity is not always about choice. Living through transitional and conflictive situations, her identity and choices intermingled in complex ways. Working with sincerity and dedication, Tarsila exemplified a unique elite role in generating a shared Brazilian identity that crossed class boundaries and transcended the artistic definitions of the past. Tarsila do Amaral stopped painting in 1972; she died in 1973 at the age of eighty-nine.

The Integral Woman

Província de Guanabara

In the mid-1930s, the Ação Integralista Brasileira—patterned after the fascist movements in Portugal, Spain, and Italy—set out to organize Brazilian men and women, and to foster social progress. They followed the corporatist model, emphasizing hierarchy, morality, discipline, and Roman Catholic spirituality. In the large cities, their women's auxiliaries, dubbed "Green Blouses" after the evergreen color of their uniforms, offered instruction to poor women in vocational skills and hygiene. The excerpt below appeared in the Integralist newspaper, Província de Guanabara.

In earlier times, women were classified in three categories: essential, agreeable, or spiritual. The essential woman was one who limited herself to the home, to her domestic obligations, and to the responsibilities of that position. Agreeable women flourished in society through their feminine charms, grace, and sociability. Spiritual women cultivated themselves through reading, and lived in a world of thought and intelligence. As we realize, none of these three categories for Green Blouse women is sufficient, because each is too narrow. No woman possesses only one of these traits; rather, her goal should be to blend them harmoniously. This results in what we call the "Integral Woman."

This does not mean that the Integral Woman is one of these modern feminist types who demand civil equality in a spirit of vindictiveness; the feminist who hates men and who seeks to establish matriarchal rule. In no way.

The Integral Woman is the docile daughter, the solicitous sister, the affectionate wife, the heroic mother, the loyal companion, the precursor to a new, regenerative ethical standard, the conscientious inspirer, far from those who lower themselves to the state of savagery, with their animalistic vices.

To become an Integral Woman, the female must train herself fully, to develop her intelligence, her heart, her conscience, and her character, without jeopardizing her health or being seduced by atavistic pressures. Green Blouses must become capable of lifting their lives to a state of biological and moral union. They must elevate themselves to defend the collective interests of the nation, whose base reposes in the family, on which the woman is the fundamental rock and its firmest support.

The Children Always Had Milk

Maria Puerta Ferreira

These days, it is virtually impossible to escape from the favelas infesting Brazil's major cities. They are rife with crime. Drugs and alcoholism are rampant, and the residents of the shantytowns are stigmatized as soon as they move in, so that the chance of finding a decent job in almost nil. Yet up until the late 1950s, things were different, especially in São Paulo. Families hard on their luck lived in favelas until they were able to afford permanent housing elsewhere. Maria Puerta Ferreira, from a family of Spanish immigrants, was such a person. While her husband worked, often at two jobs, she took in laundry and was also a midwife. One day, however, a baby she was delivering was born dead, and the family threatened to report her to the police. She stopped assisting at births. Until her death in 1997, she lived in a small, cinder block house in a working-class district of São Paulo. In her oral history reminiscences her memories are warm, although she does not romanticize the past.

I was Carolina Maria de Jesus's neighbor in the Canindé favela. We lived there since the early 1950s, around when Getúlio died. My children, now grown up and with families of their own, were small then, but they remember how it was. . . . I am Spanish by birth, but Brazilian in my heart. I grew up here, was married here, built a home . . .

I was a young girl when I came to Canindé. I had met my late husband, Dionísio Ferreira, in the countryside. I married him when I was fourteen. We came to São Paulo in search of work; since my father had bought a shack in Canindé, we decided to build one of our own. We lived in that little house for almost fifteen years and, thanks to God, although we were poor, we made only friends . . .

Life was hard for the favela residents. We lacked many things. There were 180 houses and, for many years, there was only one water spigot for all of us to use. When they put in a second one it helped a little. We woke

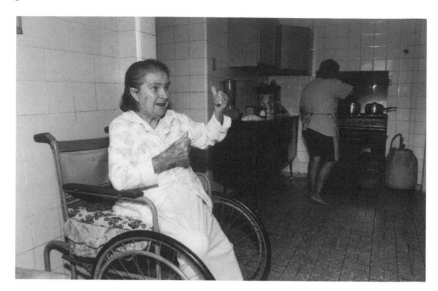

Maria Puerta Ferreira at her home in São Paulo in 1993. *(Photograph by Robert M. Levine)*

up before dawn to stand in line to get water. Whenever I got there, the line was long already. People brought their cans and waited, waited. Sometimes it took more than an hour to get to the faucet, and most of the people had jobs and couldn't be late. The ones who came late got only a few drops of water. Got that?

The main street was called Felisberto de Carvalho, and our house was on it. On each side they built shacks. Everything was simple—no bricks or anything, just some boards, tin, and whatever God provided. In January, it always rained and flooded everything. Every year it was the same thing. The favela residents couldn't buy bricks or cement, and so the roofs leaked. The only solution was to build the shacks off the ground so that the floods would do less damage. Those who had relatives in other parts of the city would leave the favela in January and return in March, when the rainy season ended. I left once, to go to my sister's, because my children were getting sick, but my old man stayed, guarding the house.

When the river went down things returned to normal. You just had to clean things up and that's it. Since we had almost no furniture, we didn't lose very much; we just had to dry things out and polish them. I used twenty-liter cans to help with the cleanup. . . . We had no shower or electric power.

Life in Canindé was filled with work, and we had little rest. Only during Carnival and the June festivals did we enjoy ourselves. In Canindé, the families who lived there were good people, honest and good neighbors. We decorated our street during the festivals; it looked beautiful! Everyone helped, cutting out decorations, cooking. . . . Everyone did something, voluntarily. No one sold anything! The little kids loved it: we had sweet potatoes, coconut patties, good things. We celebrated until dawn! The people launched paper balloons, firecrackers . . .

Once during one of these festivals, my old man was standing in front of the house. He was really happy! Our first son had been born that day, and we were celebrating. . . . But a disgrace happened: it was the custom to set off firecrackers in the street, and one of them got under his pants. Oh, it was an event! He chased after the culprit. Then the merrymaking stopped. Everyone was sad because my old man was very well liked.

We also had a procession in the favela, commemorating Christ's death and resurrection, on Good Friday. . . . We organized everything, just like at the June festivals, but with the help of the St. Vincent de Paul fathers from the church. . . . The politicians also came around to visit us. Antônio Sampaio, even [future President] Jânio Quadros came and debated how to deal with Canindé's problems. Jânio was in my house twice. Eventually, the favela was torn down. They built brick houses where the shacks had been, and they offered them to the residents. But few people could afford to buy them. . . . The politicians walked through the streets, chatted with people, and they came into my house to have coffee and eat cake. Only in mine! I made special preparations to welcome them . . .

Our family became followers of Vargas's party. He was the "father of the poor" for Brazil, until his death. . . . We were in the favela when we heard the news of his suicide [in 1954], and we felt as badly as if it had been the death of a relative. Everyone was crying, my children, the neighbors. . . . After Vargas, Adhemar de Barros and his wife Leonor showed up; she was considered "the mother of the poor." Every Christmas, she organized campaigns to distribute presents so the needy could celebrate. They were distributed from the local church, the Pacaembu stadium, the train station, and the mayor's office.

. . . It was rare for people to be hungry for more than a day or so then, unlike now. There were social workers: D. Teresinha Godinho and her staff helped us a lot! . . . People took several jobs to support their families. Twice a week they gave lessons in hygiene and health care for anyone who wanted to attend, especially women. The social work agency helped us get more water, school bus transportation for our children, and eventually financing so we could build our own houses.

. . . The people who lived in Canindé came from all over Brazil, and there were foreigners as well! There were southerners, northerners, people from the interior of the state of São Paulo. Many came from other countries. I came from Spain, and there were Italians, Portuguese, and even a Japanese woman, Mrs. Tomiku. . . . Today, someone who lives in a favela is just like a bandit . . . when you think of bandits, you think of favela people. And there is so much discrimination! It was better to have to live in a favela in the old days. After ten or twenty years, you could get out with the assistance of members of your family.

Women of the Forest

Yolanda and Robert F. Murphy

Long before Europeans arrived, Amerindian women cultivated and processed manioc, rendering even its poisonous varieties edible. In addition to providing vital sustenance, manioc helped define village social relationships. Men hunted while women ground manioc roots into farinha. *Among women, this work reinforced kinship bonds and status. During the early 1950s, ethnographers Yolanda and Robert F. Murphy lived in the Amazonian rain forest with the Mundurucú Indians, paying special attention to women. Their book,* Women of the Forest, *describes the arduous task of producing* farinha.

The sun had risen full into the morning sky, but the peak of the day's heat was still four hours away, making most of the women anxious to get their garden work done. The supply of manioc flour in the house had already been eaten, and for the last two days the women of Borai's house had been drawing on the larders of their neighbors. Borai's mother went to the open-walled shed in the middle of the village where manioc flour was made, and began to build a fire in the large earth-walled oven on which the *farinha* (meal or flour) was toasted. She directed her three daughters to fetch tubers from the stream, where they had been soaking in water for the past three days, and sent her daughter-in-law for more firewood. The daughter-in-law put an axe in her carrying basket, which she carried on her back with a bark-cloth tumpline hung across her forehead, and went through the village to ask her cousin to come help her. Borai and her sister stopped at another house to tell the women where they were going and enlisted the support of two of the occupants. The four then set out for the stream on a path which took them well below the area where they bathed and drew water, and they began to load their baskets with the softened, almost crumbling, manioc tubers. The children had been left with their grandmother, allowing the women to take another, more leisurely, bath and to discuss some of the short-comings of their sister-in-law.

The carrying baskets were heavy with the water-laden manioc, and they squatted in a genuflecting position with their backs to the baskets, passed the tumplines across their foreheads, and slowly stood up, using the full strength of their torsos and necks to lift the burdens. The sun was beating down on the path as they made their way laboriously back up the hill to the village, walking in silence to conserve their strength. Arriving at the *farinha* shed, they gratefully dropped their loads into a long hollowed-out log used as a tub and sat down in the shade to rest. Borai's baby began crying as soon as he saw her, quickly escaping from his older cousin to crawl through the dirt to his mother. She nursed him, more for comfort than food, and then let him crawl back and forth across her lap. The sister-in-law and her helper returned from the garden, where they had gathered felled, but unburned, wood and chopped it into stove lengths, and dumped the contents of their baskets next to the *farinha* oven. They too sat in the shade against one of the shed uprights and joined the conversation. Three other women drifted across the weed-choked village plaza to help and to tell of their own plans to make *farinha* in two days' time.

The work party having increased to eight, the women decided that the dull and laborious chore could be put off no longer. Borai and her mother stepped into the trough filled with soft manioc and began to walk back and forth, working their feet up and down, to break up the tubers and separate the pulp from the skins. As they worked, the water oozed out of the broken tubers, mixed with the pulp into a thick mass, and squished rather pleasurably between their toes. Another woman began picking out the skins and throwing them to one side. The sister-in-law and her cousin went off to the old garden for more firewood, and three of the other women went down to the stream to get more manioc. One woman remained seated in the shade, helping Borai's niece in keeping the children from underfoot.

Despite the tedium of the work, the conversation in the *farinha* shed never slowed. Borai's mother brought up the possibility that the trader might pay a visit to the village in the near future, a story she had heard from the wife of a young man who had been visiting on the Tapajós River. One woman added that it seemed to make little difference whether he arrived or not, as he rarely brought very much desirable merchandise. Another commented that on his last visit the trader had brought nothing but *cachaça,* the regional cane rum, and that the men had exhausted all their credit in becoming thoroughly drunk. Borai's mother reminded the critic that she, too, had drunk her fair share of the trader's rum on that occasion, and the onlookers dissolved in laughter. Given the fact that many of the women had drunk as much as the men would let them have, the subject was quickly turned to the men. One of the chief topics of conversation at the time was the visit in the village of a young man, who was in a late stage of courtship with one of the village's girls. The progress of the romance was carefully examined by the group in the *farinha* shed, and the young man's merits mercilessly evaluated. One of the women noted that the suitor had a small penis, bringing forth the sour remark that he was not much different from the other men. At least, said another, his penis showed more life than those of most of the other men. The women laughed and all looked over with amusement toward the men's house, where two or three occupants still lingered. The men, aware of the derision, became furiously intent on whatever they were doing, their eyes turned carefully away from the *farinha* shed.

In the meantime, the work was progressing at a slow and steady pace. Large wads of wet pulp were taken from the trough and placed in the open end of a *tipití*. The *tipití* was a long tube made of loosely woven palm leaves, with an open mouth at the top and closed at the bottom. The top end was suspended from a rafter, and a long pole was placed through a loop at the bottom. Two of the women sat on the end of the pole, the other end of which was secured near the ground, and the resultant lever pulled powerfully downward on the *tipití*. This caused it to elongate and constrict, squeezing out the water from the pulp and leaving the contents still moist, ready to be sieved. When only a dribble of water came from the *tipití*, the women emptied the pulp into a large sieve placed over a shallow basin and gently worked it through the mesh with their fingers. It dropped into the receptacle as a coarse, damp cereal, and the pieces that did not go through were taken by another of the women and pounded with a wooden mortar and pestle.

The day's production of *farinha* would not last the household much more than a week, and the women agreed that they should put more tubers in the water to soak. Borai and three of the other women took their carrying baskets and machetes, and headed out of the village to the gardens . . .

By the time this chore was done, the sun was almost directly overhead, and the morning breezes had died completely. The village lay beaten down by the sun, quiet and somnolent under the noonday heat. The roosters and chickens were not to be seen, and the few dogs remaining in the village were lying in the shade. One of the men in the men's house was still working on a basket, but the other two had retired to their hammocks in its shady recesses. Borai and her companions went to the *farinha* shed, where she found her baby crying lustily from hunger. She sat in the shade to nurse him, while watching her mother and another woman slowly turning and stirring the manioc flour, which was being toasted on a copper griddle above the furnace. The women each had a canoe paddle, which they used as a spatula to prevent the manioc from burning on the pan and to turn under the flour on top to expose it again to the heat. It would take well over an hour for each panful to become dry and toasted brown, and other women took up the task at intervals of about fifteen minutes to relieve the heat-parched workers.

As the work dragged on, most of its preliminary phases—such as bringing in the manioc, mashing it, running the pulp through the *tipití*, and sieving the resulting mash—were already largely completed, and many of the helpers from the other houses had drifted away to escape the heat of the oven. Borai was hungry after her morning's work and she went to the dwelling, where she put the baby in her hammock. One of her sisters had cooked some plantains in the coals of the fire and offered her some, and Borai rounded out the meal with manioc mixed with a drink made of palm fruit. She then lay down in the hammock to rest with her child and almost immediately fell into a light sleep.

My Life

Maria das Dôres Gomes Batista

*Opportunities for upward social mobility for the poor have always been lim-
ited by unwritten social rules favoring adscription (one's inherited status) over
achievement, but there have been dramatic exceptions. Black and the daughter
of slaves, Maria das Dôres worked hard and lived to see her children gain an
education, in their cases, the key to entrance to the Brazilian middle class.
Slowly building a business as a caterer, the former maid also achieved an astonishing level of economic success.*

I was born on July 25, 1908, in Campos dos Goytacazes, a town 360
kilometers from the capital, Rio de Janeiro, in the North Fluminense
part of the state. I am the daughter of slaves, who were manumitted in
1888 when Princess Isabel signed the law abolishing slavery in Brazil.

I spent my childhood on a fazenda in the district of Campos, called
Mussurepe. But in any case, the joys of running through the greenery on
the property did not last very long. The building on the fazenda where
my parents and others worked caught fire and burned. My parents died
in the blaze, I was just nine years old. My grandmother, Ina Gomes dos
Santos, took me in until I was thirteen, when I was placed in the house of
Dr. Écio Bruno de Azevedo as a servant. I had to stand on top of a
wooden box to be able to wash the dishes. For this, I was given meals and
some clothing. After a while, the masters noticed that I was bright but
unhappy, and they extended help to me. The teacher who was hired to
give lessons to the family's children was also permitted to teach me how
to write and do arithmetic. I was then entrusted with caring for the
family's laundry as well as ironing—even clothing made of lace and fine
silk that the family imported from Europe. Only me, the orphan girl,
had this level of responsibility in the house.

The years went by. In 1930, I was twenty-two and still single. I decided to go to Rio de Janeiro with a cousin. Carrying reference letters from my employers in Campos, I presented them at the house of Dr. Ariôsto Pinto, a federal congressman. His wife watched me do various tasks and carefully examined my teeth (an old habit of the elite from the days when landowners looked over slaves to buy). Because I had good teeth, they hired me as their new maid. I remained in their house for two years. In 1931, I gave birth to a daughter, Penha das Dôres Gomes. Aurino Gomes was the father; in 1933, a son was born. I have lost track of Aurino.

From the first, I learned of things linked to the political events that would transform Brazil. Lieutenant Juárez Távora, a close friend of Ariôsto Pinto, telephoned the house to say that the Revolution would break out on the night it did, exactly at 2:00 A.M. The whole family went to the Copacabana Fort to celebrate the victory of the overthrow of the Washington Luís government. Lieutenant Getúlio Vargas of Rio Grande do Sul, head of the triumphant side, was carried on the shoulders of the revolutionaries. Fireworks lit up not only the fort, but the entire beachfront.

As a maid, I saw many of the important figures of the 1930 Revolution when they visited the house in which I worked. One meeting was held in which the topic was the arrest of the deposed president, who had declared that he would remain in office until death. I also began to become aware of household problems. There was inflation: matches I needed to light the gas stove went from one *tostão* [a nickel] to three.

In 1932, pregnant with my second child, I returned to Campos and found a job ironing clothes in the residence of the most famous sugarcane mill owner in the region, Dr. Atilano Crisóstimo de Oliveira and his wife Maria Queiróz de Oliveira. These times, with young children, were arduous for me, and I was grateful to gain regular employment. I stayed with them for fifteen years, and it was while working for them, in 1933, that I met my future husband, Miguel Batista de Moraes. He had been the couple's driver for seven years. We had a child, Dulce Batista Pereira, that same year and other children after that; we married, officially, in a civil ceremony at the town hall in September 1944. Over time, when new children were born, the older ones helped to take care of them— immediately after birth, in fact.

Dr. Atilano was a wealthy *usineiro* and was descended from a rich family as well. But things were hard in 1940, and when President Getúlio Vargas visited Campos de Goytacazes to see how he could help, he stayed in the Queiróz mansion twice. During the second visit, his daughter Alzira

Maria das Dôres Gomes Batista, 1938.
(Rosane Pereira)

Miguel Batista de Moraes, 1939.
(Rosane Pereira)

came along. I was responsible for making their beds, taking care of their clothing, and supervising the other servants. At the lunches and dinners held in the house, the *usineiros* talked about their debts and about policies for the economic development of the region. I heard them ask that their debts be forgiven, that in exchange for being able to hold onto their sugar mills, they would support the government.

My own living conditions improved as well. I bore eleven children in all. Miguel, known for his soft voice and affable manner, was very esteemed by his *patrões* [employers]. He worked for them for forty years before retiring. I was able to put aside some small amounts of money and was very economical in my household. I earned twenty-five *mil-réis* [about thirty dollars] per month; Miguel only earned four *mil-réis*.

We bought our first radio in 1940. Miguel liked to listen to President Getúlio Vargas's speeches on the *Hour of Brazil*. A decade and a half later, when Vargas shot himself, Miguel heard the news on the radio, and put his head down on the table and wept copiously.

On the whole, we always were able to feed our family: beans cost 600 *réis* a kilo, rice 300 *réis*, dried meat 200 *réis*, and fresh meat 800 *réis*. In 1941, I was able to purchase a piece of land with an old shack on it. We spent twelve years constructing our own house on the plot. All of my children grew up there, and I still live in it. It wasn't considered to be a very good location, but in time, nicer houses were built there.

In 1946, having had four children already, I left the Queiróz's house and earned a living by taking in laundry. In 1948, I started to read through cookbooks. I already knew how to make sweets and began to sell them. After a while, I became known as "Dona Maria the Pastry Maker," the most popular baker around. All of the high society women fought over me to make sweets for their parties.

With this source of income, my husband and I were able to educate our children. Miguel died in 1961. I took over heading the family and continued to work very hard. Today, at eighty-nine, I only accept orders from a few people, but I still work. Because of my ironing and laundry and baking, during the 1950s and 1960s I was able to buy four more houses [to rent out]. We also managed to buy a little house on Atafona Beach, fifty minutes from Campos. When Miguel took ill, in 1955, he went there to rest. Later, the house was washed away in a storm, but with the help of some of my children, we built another one, more protected.

We purchased our first television set in 1964. Most of my children and grandchildren have studied and entered fine careers. Some went all the way to the college and postgraduate level. In 1990, I returned to the Queiróz mansion, which today is the mayor's office, and attended the graduation of a grandson who earned a degree from Campos Law School. In 1996, I attended the ceremony in which my granddaughter, Rosane Pereira, who holds a master's degree in philosophy, assumed the post of professor in arts and letters.

In fact, ten of my eleven children survive, and all of them live in Campos dos Goytacazes. They have the following occupations: federal tax agent; revenue collector; three work for the post office; three are primary schoolteachers. One is an accountant for the state petroleum company. One is a chauffeur, like his father was. Valedmar, who was a policemen, died in 1988.

When I developed health problems as I became older, I always received excellent medical treatment in the best hospitals in Campos, because my son, Roberto, who works for Petrobrás, includes me in his health coverage. The government provides two pensions for me as well: mine, based on my income as a caterer, and my late husband's.

A Healer's Story

Maria Geralda Ferreira

Maria Geralda Ferreira was born in July 4, 1906, in the Jatobá Valley, now the westernmost district of Belo Horizonte, the capital of Minas Gerais. Short and plump with age, Dona Maria, as she is known, looks out at the world from deep brown eyes. She has dedicated her life to helping others as a benzadeira, *or healer. Since her childhood, Dona Maria has participated in the Congado—the African Brazilian feast-day celebration dedicated to Our Lady of the Rosary. Although she holds no official title within the celebration, she is the central spiritual leader of the festival.*

This Congado comes from the beginning of the world. I was a child when I remember the groups of *congadeiros* passing by our door on their way to the houses of the participants there below, there on the edge of the train tracks. We would go through the backyards down there, in the middle of the trees, so we could see the Congado pass. Papai [father] didn't like it at all. He thought that the Congado was witchcraft, sorcery, only of bad things, that there was nothing good about it. Later, he asked for an explanation of the Congado, what the story of Our Lady of the Rosary was, when the blacks took her from the middle of the sea. He opened his heart to faith and love in Our Lady of the Rosary because his life turned around, and we never went hungry again.

Papai never liked schooling, not at all, and he didn't even know how to sign his name. And he didn't give a chance for us to study, to get a better life. I don't know what would have happened to me if I hadn't had those three years of schooling that my father gave me—after a lot of fighting. The old people didn't like it if girls went to school. It was a really difficult, a really sad life for both women and men. We were all raised at the end of a hoe, from Monday to Saturday. I got married when I was twenty to a young farmer. He also didn't know how to read; his father didn't let him study. But he had a formidable intelligence, he was a hard worker, and was really admired by everyone—but he was also a bum. But we survived, because no matter how bad my married life got, it was better than my life as a child, as a young woman.

Sometimes I think about the things I've been through, the work I went through raising my children. I raised fourteen children, no fifteen—twelve of mine and three others. I gave birth to them, raised them, put them in school, and all of them learned; everyone in my family knows how to read and write, not deep study, but everyone knows how to read and knows how to write. For twenty years, we were rich; we bought two *alqueires* [twenty-three acres] of land here and built a house with twelve rooms. We had fields from there below to the division of the city, that lowland was all fields. We always had five or six workers working every day. I cooked, I washed, I ironed, I had children, I sent the children to school, I carried firewood on my head so I could cook for my husband, for everyone. But I always made time to sit, and read and write. Many of my children, when they went to school, already knew how to read; I taught them every night.

These days, these girls don't know how easy they have it, no ma'am! Until I was a young woman, until I was twenty, I never got to go any-where. My folks would not let me go to parties, they never let us go out with anyone. During the years I was raising my family, sixty-three years, I never went to a party, never went, never. My girlfriends would be getting married, and their mothers would come to invite us to the wedding, and can you believe that they [our husbands] wouldn't let us? They wouldn't take us and they wouldn't let us go with anyone—it was a life of slavery that we lived.

When I was a child, a young girl, I really liked the old black women. I knew a lot of these women who had been slaves, and they loved me. There was one, very small, a beautiful little thing. She would tell me stories about the slaves that would make me cry, the cruelty that the masters showed to the poor slaves. But blacks had more courage, more power than whites. Once, there was a runaway slave who was being chased by his master, to catch and punish his slave. The black hid on the side of the road, turned himself into a termite, and the master passed and didn't see him. When the black saw the master in the distance, he got up and went on his way. That's how many blacks survived during slavery: they lived many years in the forest and no one found them, not even the blacks from other farms.

Slavery ended, but it didn't end. People work, everyone works for these companies, and people have rights, but they are all mistreated, abused! Those that want to work to earn their daily bread are mistreated, almost like slaves, only that they aren't tied to a whipping post. But everything else still exists. And there are a lot of poor souls in this world, in this Brazil, who are slaves. The poor who have no place to sleep, no place to stay—persecuted. And the police, who grab some poor guy and beat him until he falls on the ground, or drag him to a place far away, kill him, and throw him in the water. This is all from the time of slavery. And what about slavery? Did it end? Slavery didn't end! As long as the world was the world, there has been slavery. As long as the world is the world, slavery will never end.

I can recount for you the misery in which I was born, the poverty, the cold that I've already been through in my life—in my childhood. But I lifted myself out of that mess to serve Our Lady of the Rosary. Because of this—in my family, child, many have abandoned it; they don't want anything to do with the Congado—I'll die with my feet inside this Congado. Until then, come what may, I give my life to this Congado, and nothing will stop me, thank God!

Sonia, a Middle-Class Woman

Alison Raphael

Alison Raphael lived in Rio de Janeiro in 1975 and wrote up her observations for the newsletter series of the Institute of Current World Affairs. Trained in anthropology, she focused on the patterns of everyday life, especially the changing world of middle-class women. "Sonia" is a pseudonym, although her story was not unusual for women during the mid-1970s in urban Brazil.

It was a difficult week for Sonia. The job she had faithfully worked for over three years was threatened, and her housekeeper couldn't come to work. Miss Mara, the maid, had returned home on the very day she had pawned her wedding ring to pay a debt to find her husband lying dead on the floor. Now she was suffering serious pangs of remorse, as she had left her husband locked in the house with no way to call for help. This was a daily procedure, since Miss Mara's husband was a chronic alcoholic who beat his wife regularly until she devised the ingenious technique of locking him in the house.

In fact, Miss Mara worked as a housekeeper not only for financial reasons, but also as an escape from her home, her husband, her life. She would arrive promptly at 6:00 A.M. at Sonia's door, to return home some fourteen hours later. For her troubles, she received 350 *cruzeiros,* or about $9, a month (an average wage for housekeepers in Rio's Zona Norte, a predominantly working-class area). Since Sonia's apartment consists of three minuscule rooms and a small kitchen, and only two simple meals were prepared, it would seem that Miss Mara prolonged her stay long beyond the call of duty.

This week, however, the housekeeper was steeped in guilt and grief, leaving Sonia to tend to her own household chores.

When the alarm clock rang at 5:00 A.M., Sonia rose cheerfully. Despite an existence that would hardly lend itself to cheerfulness, Sonia is an exceptionally vivacious and joyful person. Far more diminutive in height than weight, Sonia boasts warm brown skin and a pleasantly plump body, which Brazilian men admire as she swings down the street. She has a smile for everyone, calls most people "Honey" or "Sweetheart," and delights in nothing more than having her two children climb all over her, showering her with abundantly returned hugs and kisses. Sonia's wit is sharp and her vocabulary rife with curse words and slang. She would give the last piece of food in her refrigerator to a friend, and probably to most anyone else who needed it.

So when she arose, awakened the children, showered, and began to prepare breakfast and lunch, she was already singing back to her two parakeets. Bread was warmed, coffee and milk mixed, and bananas sliced. Meanwhile, rice, beans, and okra with bits of beef were cooking on another burner. The latter would be warmed up by her husband at lunchtime for himself and the children. By 7:00 A.M., Sonia was ready to catch the bus that one and a half hours later, following a circuitous route enabling it to pick up all the other Sonia's in the environs, would drop them collectively in Rio's downtown area. Sonia would arrive at 8:30, just in time to punch the time clock at the large foreign-based engineering firm, from which she would be fired the following week.

SECRETARIA:

O ESSENCIAL É SER LEAL,

GENTIL E EFICIENTE.

MAS, SE FÔR

BONITA, MELHOR AINDA

The Secretary:

She must be loyal,
polite and efficient.
But if she
is beautiful as well, better yet.

—*Gente* magazine, 27 October 1975

It is common knowledge that one of Brazil's principal attractions for foreign businesses is its promise of cheap labor with no threat of strikes or union salary demands. One might assume that this phenomenon primarily affects manual agricultural and industrial laborers. Not so. Despite Sonia's eight years of secretarial experience, her position as the coordinator of two other young typists, and her knowledge (albeit limited) of English, her salary is a mere 1,400 *cruzeiros* per month—or about $36. Of this, $9 goes to pay the housekeeper and the bulk of what remains repays a debt that Sonia incurred with the firm itself.

Under the circumstances, a housekeeper might appear to be an outrageous luxury. Without her, however, Sonia would have to quit work or leave her children alone in the house until their school opens at noon. In Brazil, one woman commented to me, you can't afford *not* to have a housekeeper. Thus, the housekeeper prepares lunch and supper, cleans house, and takes the children to school—when, that is, Sonia is able to find a suitable employee. Miss Mara was the fourth in two months.

Family Life in Recife

Fanny Mitchell

It is difficult to know to what extent Recife is typical of any Brazilian town, but from brief visits to other cities in the Northeast, and conversations with many Brazilians, Recife seems to be socially more traditional and closed than others of similar size and importance. Certainly, according to both Recifenses and southerners, it is very different from towns in the South. Fanny Mitchell, a Briton, wrote her observations while living in the northern city.

Recife, with some justification, proudly claims to be the capital of the Northeast. Only two cities are possible competitors and both of these lie on the periphery of the region. Fortaleza has only the headquarters of the Bank of the Northeast of Brazil to support its claim, and Salvador gives the impression of being more preoccupied with its contact with Rio de Janeiro than its status in the Northeast. Recife conclusively established her claim when the head office of the Superintendency for Development of the Northeast, the largest and most powerful regional organ, was located there, and with it, all of the satellite organizations that naturally tend to spring up in the same place.

With a kingdom of twenty-five million inhabitants and the size of several countries of Europe put together, Recife could be expected to have a metropolitan air. While the place has physically burst at its seams, it does not have the atmosphere of a big city. The component parts—the small center, the smug sprawling suburbs, and the slums of the semi-employed poor—have not yet welded themselves together as an entity. It is a city of parts loosely joined together and still evolving painfully. Since the war, its population has multiplied at an alarming rate, with services unable to keep pace. Shops are overcrowded, traffic jams a challenge to the most ambitious traffic engineer, hospitals overflowing, and unemployment rife. Telephones are in such demand that one is lucky to buy the use of one for $300, even after a long wait.

Two factors have contributed to this explosion; the extremely high birthrate combined with a rapidly falling infant mortality, and the continued immigration of those seeking relief from their rural poverty or looking for wider horizons. Both of these phenomena are as true of the middle and upper classes as of the lower. With a retinue of maids and relatively few financial worries, parents can afford to bring up a family of eight or more in comfort. At the same time, all those with educational or professional ambitions have headed for the capital. Many children of landowners were sent to school in Recife, and then stayed, or at least maintained a house there as well as in the country.

The aristocracy used to be based exclusively on landed wealth and remarkably few families, all of which intermarried time and time again. At the turn of the nineteenth century, however, the *usineiros* (sugar factory owners), by their intermediate status, paved the way for industrialists, and today the process of integration and acceptance is virtually complete. Bankers, cotton factory owners, and others have succeeded in buying their way into society, while the wealth of those whose money lay exclusively in land has gradually diminished.

By degrees, as the closed circle is widened, the number of cross-cousin marriages is falling, but to an outsider, it still seems an extraordinarily introverted society. One factor that serves to maintain this exclusiveness is the strength of family ties, and the interest taken in their own family by both upper and middle classes. Intercousin marriages have helped to increase this still more, since relations common to both partners of a marriage are more likely to be visited than those related to only one. One girl said that she had always tried to avoid her ubiquitous male cousins, but had nevertheless succumbed in the end. Most, however, regard the liaison as natural, and harmful genetic side effects seem to be few. In one case, the offspring of a couple with only eight instead of sixteen great-grandparents between them suffered from abnormally high blood pressure, as a result of which most died in infancy. In another family, which had been marrying into itself for generations, one child was mentally retarded and another physically precocious. Most vehemently deny the dangers of such marriages and blind themselves to the possibility.

The size of families makes such a state of affairs more natural than it might be in many countries. When a family of six to eight children is the norm, uncles, cousins, and nephews immediately multiply to produce well over 100 close relatives. Furthermore, once families have arrived in Recife, they tend to stay, and as a result, they are mainly concentrated within a small radius. A few have relatives who have emigrated south, but most live in the city or the country around. There is no tendency for families to spread out as occurs often in Europe, for reasons that should become clear later.

Size alone does not satisfactorily account for the closeness of families. Far more important than this is the affection felt for fellow members of a family, a fondness, as far as I can judge, both more deeply felt and more openly expressed than between their European counterparts. This is apparent at all levels: parents devote more attention to small children and, despite the universal nanny, fondle them more; there is no teenage rebellion against authority, and even as adults, uncles, aunts, cousins, or brothers and sisters generally see far more of each other than all but the very closest friends.

The family is regarded as a closed and sacrosanct unit. It is considered very bad form to criticize members of one's own family in a destructive way, nor would any friend or acquaintance do so. Family affairs are a private matter and not a proper topic of conversation: while a polite interest is expected, a normal curiosity is considered inquisitive. With time and energy expended mainly on relations, friends tend to be restricted to colleagues, former colleagues, and more distant cousins who are treated as friends rather than relatives. In these circumstances, it is not surprising that even among Brazilians, Recife society has a reputation for being closed and, consequently, difficult to enter. An initial warmth, no doubt largely curiosity, with open invitations is common, but as the novelty wears off, one realizes that Recifenses' real interest lies in their own kith and kin.

Most women lead vacuous lives: armed with a full complement of maids to cope with all the household chores and even to do most of the shopping, their main concern is their children, to whom they devote much attention and affection, and secondly their husbands. Apart from these two interests, they have little to occupy their thoughts. Many envy the relative freedom of the American or European woman, and complain that their husbands will not let them lead more varied and demanding lives. As it is, the daily routine is more or less as follows: The morning is spent at home supervising the maids and playing with children too young to go to school. After lunch, a visit to the dressmaker or hairdresser, a guitar or language lesson, or a visit to some close relative break the monotony. The evening, in all probability, is spent watching television.

To fill idle moments and satisfy creative desire, a curious local art form, which could be described as a sign of desperate underemployment, flourishes among this sector of society. A passion for decorating useless objects to adorn the house or give as presents, and covering any shape or size of container with plastic frills, at times amounts almost to a mania. One such addict became really upset that she would not have time to finish painting enough shells gold and sticking ribbons onto them before Christmas. This particularly futile occupation, when so much desperately needs to be done for others, has rightly made some of the more socially aware angry.

Although almost all are Catholics, and most would maintain they were good Catholics, religion does not loom large. Sunday mass is not an institution, and many regard an annual confession as sufficient, but all go through the formalities of baptism, church weddings, and mass at the major festivals. Little interest is shown in charities or church activities, and while on the one hand most women are superficially aware of all the poverty around and never cease to bring it to one's notice, they are on the other hand, not concerned enough to do anything about it. One who carries on any form of voluntary work is highly regarded by others, but they show little inclination to join in.

With their very limited lives, conversation is also naturally restricted to one or two recurring topics: children, maids, clothes, and the inevitable gossip. Considerable care is taken with appearance, but fashion lags months behind Rio de Janeiro, and a strong preference is shown for bright colors with little subtlety. Also, on the most sophisticated beach, a bikini is thought sufficiently daring to receive widespread comment and to be forbidden by many of the more conservative parents.

Yet, however much women complain about their lot, the environment seems to have been remarkably successful in bringing up children. Most are happier, less complicated, and more mature than their European counterparts. Both parents lavish them with affection: a childless couple is universally pitied, and it is thought a distinct abnormality for a couple not to want children immediately. The pleasures of parenthood are increased by the fact that the chores and less attractive jobs are left to the nanny, usually a young girl from the interior, and only in the very richest houses does one find the traditional strict nanny in a stiff-collared, starched uniform. With all this care, small children always look clean and scrubbed, and from an early age, are highly conformist in behavior. When they are difficult, they show signs of being spoiled rather than neglected.

As children grow older, they spend a certain amount of time with friends of their own age, but at no stage is there a clear wish to break away from home and the authority of their parents. Since schools of all types operate on a shift basis, with classes either in the morning or the afternoon, they have a great deal of free time. Boys go off to the beach or cinema with their friends, and as they get older, to bars. A rather nebulous group known as the Jovem Guarda (young guard) is the Brazilian equivalent of the "with it" generation, but as far as Recife is concerned, it masquerades itself as no more than an addiction to popular music and long hair. A boy with long hair is known as a playboy, and indeed, it is one of the signs to the poor of a young *rico*. Popular music, not jazz—which curiously is considered old-fashioned—of national, American, and European origin fills much of the emptiness of the local youth. As soon as they are seventeen, boys divert part of their energy to cars, and the wealthier are given cars of their own. Motor bikes have not arrived. Yet, however much their interests lie outside the home, boys continue to live there and to remain on very close terms with their parents until they get married.

Girls also stay at home until they find a husband, but they are far more carefully supervised, and the accepted code of behavior for an unmarried girl is similar to that in England some forty years ago or more. This tradition is gradually weakening; a few of the more enlightened parents let their daughters go out without a chaperone, and a closer examination reveals that what is actually done and what is said to be done are not the same thing. Until she is officially engaged, a girl may not go out alone with a boy, but must either go with a group (which may break up in the course of the evening) or a third person as chaperone (often chosen to turn a blind eye). Extremely high value is laid on virginity; if she loses it, a girl virtually forfeits her chance of marriage. Therefore, everything is done to protect her from this misfortune. The system is vicious, since men know how carefully most girls are guarded, and so are far more likely to try and take advantage of one left unprotected.

Girls naturally complain about these restrictions, but ineffectually and more as a matter of form than through any deep-felt frustration. While grumbling, one nevertheless admitted that it would not be worth breaking away from her parents, since such behavior would create a scandal and she would only succeed in making herself a social outcast. Certainly, the outcry that another created by living for a time with an artist seemed to me totally disproportionate to the offense: her parents finally succeeded in removing her and sending her to Rio de Janeiro "to recover."

Xuxa and the Televisual Imaginary

Amelia Simpson

Popular culture in Brazil in the 1980s and 1990s is indelibly marked by the media stardom of Maria da Graça Meneghel. Better known as Xuxa (pronounced SHOO-sha in Portuguese), the tall, blond, blue-eyed Brazilian has become an unparalleled cultural icon. Born in 1963 to a middle-class family, Xuxa began modeling in her teen years. Her well-publicized romance with soccer champion Pelé provided exposure that led to invitations to act in films and on television. Xuxa hosted her first children's television program in 1983, and in 1986, hit the jackpot with the Xou (pronounced "Show") da Xuxa, a five-hours-a-day, six-days-a-week show broadcast on Brazil's TV Globo, the world's fourth largest commercial network. Mass audiences of all ages watched the program and surrendered to a euphoric experience of group indulgence. In the late 1980s and early 1990s, at the height of her stardom, Xuxa was Brazil's national fantasy. She gave her audiences a make-believe Brazil ruled by a blond "Rainha dos Baixinhos" (Queen of Kids), the idol of teenagers, the stuff of men's dreams and of women's envy and aspirations.

The *Xou da Xuxa* and the star's subsequent programs (such as *Xuxa Hits,* which began airing in January 1995) attract because they dissolve unseemly differences of race, gender, and class in a televisual pandemonium of generic happiness and idol worship. Xuxa's image assembles in one tidy package a set of unwieldy, mutually contradictory ideas. She celebrates an ideal of femininity that is both erotic and domestic. She relentlessly markets a consumer-driven model of modernity in a country where the basic needs of many citizens are not met. And she presents a white ideal of beauty in a nation with the second-largest population of African descent on earth. Xuxa's image thus reconciles, without resolving, the deep fissures of race, gender, and capital that divide Brazil. The manipulation of these key ingredients of the charismatic star's image has rendered Xuxa what her Internet homepage in 1997 proudly calls an "authentic national institution." Like samba and soccer, Xuxa is a form of celebration of Brazilianness. She helps to create and maintain the consensus through which Brazilians negotiate a complex and divided identity.

Xuxa's ability to build consensus began to slip in late 1991 when two young men allegedly tried to kidnap her and one of the Paquitas, the all-blond group of teenaged girls who serve as aides to the star on her shows, in Rio de Janeiro. Since then, the star's image has become less stable in a Brazil where citizens are less able to sustain the old myths of a fundamentally genteel society. Still, although attention has shifted to other figures and episodes, Xuxa remains inscribed in Brazilian culture as an icon of unusual authority. A 1996 poll published in *Veja* magazine, for example, ranked her tenth on a list of the country's twenty most powerful people.

The most striking development in the star's narrative in the late 1990s is the appropriation on her newer television programs, *Xuxa Park* and *Xuxa Hits,* of stylistic markers that allude to the Brazilian funk phenomenon. Since its emergence in the 1970s, Brazilian funk culture has passed through several stages, including the mid-1970s period when funk dances served as forums to assert black identity and pride. In the 1990s, the huge dances presided over by disc jockeys with giant sound systems address a variety of interests. Funk is associated with youth, poverty, and nonwhite Brazil, as well as rap and hip-hop culture from the United States. In the mid-1990s, funk also attracted middle-class, whiter kids, and is increasingly viewed as a profitable sector of the Brazilian entertainment industry.

As a result of the appropriation of elements of Brazilian funk culture, Xuxa's programs have taken on a more racially integrated look and style in the late 1990s. The incorporation of the nonwhite hip-hop group You Can Dance and of a mulatta called Bom Bom in the regular cast of *Xuxa Hits* means television audiences in Brazil have a better chance to see people on the screen who look like most of them. Moreover, the Paquitas Nova Geração [New Generation Paquitas], while still all white, are no longer blond replicas of the star, as the original group was. Other features as well suggest a significant impulse on the part of Xuxa's image managers to accommodate diversity. One example was the choice of a twelve-year-old black youth to star as an angel opposite Xuxa in her 1993

Christmas television special. Another sign of willingness to use Xuxa's huge following to construct a more racially inclusive project of national consensus was the July 1996 celebration of Xuxa's anniversary of ten years with the Globo network. The highlight of the television special was a video of the star performing in the symbolic center of Brazil's African heritage, Salvador, Bahia, with members of the Afrocentric percussion ensemble Olodum. These and other televisual experiences clearly denote openings for people of color alongside Xuxa in spaces that had been closed or relatively inaccessible.

At the same time, the raced view of difference that the *Xou da Xuxa* affirmed in the 1980s and early 1990s was still very evident in the second half of the 1990s. Although the funk identity of *Xuxa Hits* established a link with a cultural phenomenon that has represented a challenge to Brazilian racial conventions, it is hard to say how meaningful the connection has been. The appropriation of funk in Xuxa's consensus-building narrative of national identity clearly constitutes a genuine opening of televisual space for programmatically underrepresented subordinate groups. Yet the new funk look and sound of Xuxa's shows enhance her ratings without altering the structure or questioning the ideological premises of her projected version of Brazilian identity. As for the Paquitas, Michele Pires Martins became the first black finalist in March 1995. In the end, however, she was not selected to join the elite group, which remained all white.

The racial configuration presented by the image of Xuxa with You Can Dance, or with her black Christmas angel, echoes the many portraits, mostly from 1980 to 1986, of Xuxa and Pelé. Their six-year, very public romance was crucial to her symbolic embodiment of Brazil's myth of racial democracy. By visually marrying white and black in the persons of two media superstars, Xuxa's image vanquishes difference while remarking it. She is able to affirm Brazil's myth of racial harmony while removing the threat that black and white as equals implies by placing the image in special circumstances—the celebrity soccer champion and his beauty, or in later versions, the Christmas angel and his "Queen," or You Can Dance with their *funkeira*.

It is hard to ignore the complexity and contradictions expressed in an image such as that of members of Olodum in Salvador backing up Xuxa in celebration of an anniversary of her collaboration with a television network that plays a definitive role in defending Brazil's status quo. Only two months later, Xuxa announced her intention to feature on an up-coming television special the controversial performer Tiririca, whose hit tune "Veja os Cabelos Dela" ("Check out Her Hair") had been de-nounced by Olodum and other black organizations. They called for a store recall of Tiririca's CD because of racist lyrics that, in part, describe a black woman as a "stinking animal" (*"bicha fedorenta"*). The success with which the Xuxa icon absorbs and controls counterimages and contesta-tory voices points to the difficulty of producing a politics of representa-tion in Brazil that can maintain the clarity and integrity necessary to mobilize for meaningful, structural change. The roles of those who lend their color to create a more integrated television screen tend to confirm rather than challenge Brazil's racial hierarchy of white privilege. The hypereroticized mulattas who appear on *Xuxa Hits* point to the stra-tegic use of gendered representations, as well, to displace racial issues and leave undisturbed an underlying structure of racial inequality and injustice.

The authority that the Xuxa icon commands in Brazil can be partly measured in hard currency. In 1991, Xuxa became the first Latin Ameri-can to appear on the *Forbes* list of the world's best-paid entertainers. Around the same time, another reflection on the distance the star had put between herself and ordinary Brazilian mortals surfaced in the form of a rumor that a Xuxa doll, one of many products the star markets, had wept blood. Features of the Xuxa phenomenon had long hinted at the idea that the media star might be endowed with divine or special powers. The star shared the stage of her *Xou da Xuxa,* for example, with an oversized sculpture of herself paired with a replica of the Christ the Redeemer statue, Rio.de Janeiro's famous landmark. Xuxa gave inter-views in which she discussed miracles that had occurred on the *Xou*—a mute began to sing, a paralyzed child to clap. The lyrics to the opening tune of the star's 1994 updated version of the *Xou da Xuxa* liken her to the Virgin Mary, declaring in one verse that she "gave birth without getting pregnant" (*"deu a vida sem engravidar"*).

It is little surprise that Xuxa's image makers should attempt to inscribe their media star in a context outside the motives of the marketplace. Xuxa's fortune implicates her in the fate that the less-fortunate majority of Brazilians experienced during the 1980s and 1990s. Her immensely lu-crative career was built on affirming a status quo that, by the mid-1990s, earned Brazil top ranking among countries with the greatest disparities between rich and poor. The strategic use of spectacle and religious and pseudoreligious imagery to market the star draws attention to the symbols of power and away from the details of its exercise. Xuxa's television and other performances work symbolically to close social gaps even as these grow perceptibly wider.

Dreams of Uneducated Women

José Carlos Sebe Bom Meihy

José Carlos Sebe Bom Meihy interviewed thirty-one women for his research on the dreams of lower-class women. It is interesting to note that he attempted to ask men about their dreams but they balked. The women recounted dreams that were apparently inspired by Bible stories, mythology, and in northern Brazil, folklore. In only two cases did women account nightmares. Even when questioned about "bad dreams," many replied that they preferred to forget them, that they only remembered "good dreams." Their lives were harsh enough. Three of the dreams are excerpted here.

Maria Rosário Silva Jesus (dona Rosa) is a washerwoman who lives with an unemployed stoneworker and her two children, one fourteen months old and the other three and a half years of age. She was interviewed by myself and two colleagues, donas Filó and Zilá. Her long and cooperative conversation dwelled on her long, hard life, often without income and, consequently, on the edge of starvation; her testimony was further complicated by the role of her "husband" (they were not legally married), who drank excessively and whose temperament brought additional instability to the relationship. The dream she recounted was about a quarrel with the man that she had to run away from with her two children, one hanging onto her neck, the other being pulled along by the hand:

"I was with my old man outside. . . . It was Sunday. . . . He had drunk quite a bit and I was waiting around. . . . My daughter Izildinha was around my neck—she's still a baby—and Emerson, my son, was holding my hand. He had a pacifier in his mouth. We went to buy some macaroni and go to his sister Socorro's house to find out how her family was doing. . . . He stopped to talk with another man . . . [and] we had to wait a long time for him—like women have to when their men drink. . . . I saw that the 'thing' was going to get hot because they always fought. There were five of them against him . . . he stood alone. . . . I think it was about some soccer game or a woman, who knows . . . I wasn't close by. . . . Then the beating started . . . all of them against my man. . . . He really hadn't drunk so much . . . he was able to run away . . . he grabbed us and began to run. We couldn't do this easily: he was drunk and I had the two children. . . . We fell behind . . . but still we ran. . . . He began to shout for us to run faster . . . then I passed him; I got ahead of him, and the clown yelled to run faster. . . . Things got bad because he began to catch up with us. . . . I was terrified for my children. . . . Then he began to say this: run, run, and don't look back . . . or you will turn into a stone. You will turn into a STONE. Imagine that, I, a stone! And the children, too."

Dinalva Santos, in an interview held in a shantytown "chapel," spoke of another kind of biblical dream. She recounted that she came from a rural place in the interior of the State of Maranhão, where she with her mother took care of pigs and their large family. Her brother asked her to come to São Paulo and take care of his shack in the favela. She dreamed: "I was very tired and I slept. . . . It was hot as hell. . . . In the dream we were all together; my brothers from Maranhão were here, too . . . but they didn't know each other any more. There were all types: Bahians, people from Pernambuco, from Salvador, from the North. The neighbors were all types: Japanese, Arabs, Bahians, Italians, from all over the world. Everyone spoke different languages, a damnable mixture, like devils. You couldn't understand anything. . . . Everyone shouted and gestured with their hands. It was total confusion. I remained quiet. . . . The worst were those who lived in my house. No one understood one another. I thought: Ah, Dinalva, why did you come to this place? When the noise got worse and I couldn't stand it, I woke up."

Maria Kaufman, sixty-four years old, grew up in a German-speaking household in Campinas das Missões, Rio Grande do Sul, where in 1938 all foreign language schools were closed by the government. Indeed, during the war, it was forbidden to speak anything but Portuguese in public. She could not attend school because she did not speak Portuguese, so along with other German children, Maria stayed home, in isolation. She recounted one of her dreams: "I was in a beautiful place . . . it was at a lake. There was beautiful music and some lovely women, dancing. Then they mounted horses, and the horses also danced. The girls suddenly turned into soldiers and always were victorious. After the war, they returned to the same place to ride. . . . The dream was in color."

VII

Race and Ethnic Relations

Searching for an image to describe Brazilian music and culture, the modernist Brazilian poet Olavo Bilac writes that they represent the "loving flower of three sad races" (*flor amorosa de três raças tristes*). Bilac draws on two persistent themes in the way that Brazilians see themselves: as a product of multiracial national origins, and as inherently sad or nostalgic, longing for their ancient homelands, whether Portugal, Africa, or the forests of Brazil before the Europeans came.[1] The enormous legacy of slavery weighs heavily on racial attitudes, although Brazilians have often bought into the myth, popularized by Gilberto Freyre, that the institution of slavery was more humane in Brazil. In *The Masters and the Slaves*, Freyre argues that Brazil achieved "one of the most harmonious unions of culture with nature and of one culture with another that the lands of this hemisphere have ever known."[2] Others contend, further, that unlike the United States, where race was defined legally as a matter of ancestry and genetics, in Brazil a more complex (and more tolerant) system of classification evolved, never embraced by law although definitely operative in informal relations.

News of how blacks fared in the United States horrified Brazilians when they read travel accounts, or listened to relatives who had visited Virginia or Mississippi. Although nonwhite Brazilians invariably clustered at the bottom of the social and economic ladder, Brazilians were adamant that this was the result of lack of skills, and in a society where family name was often more important than material status, they could claim that there was little or no prejudice in Brazilian life solely on the basis of skin color. Writers of mixed-race background, moreover—

including Joaquim Maria Machado de Assis, the abolitionist poet Antônio de Castro Alves, the black symbolist poet João da Cruz e Sousa, and Lima Barreto—were accepted as central figures in Brazilian literature. The modernists, led by Mario de Andrade, were less willing to champion racial fusion, preferring, instead, racial juxtaposition. Andrade, as David Haberly observes, was sensitive to the term *mulatto,* and he employed it in a pejorative sense, "implying phoniness and dissimulation." His prose masterpiece, *Macunaíma,* explores the modernists' shock at the reality of Brazil's racial heritage, presenting Macunaíma, the central protagonist, as a trickster and "hero without character." He is a black-skinned Indian who becomes white, blond, and blue-eyed when he steps in a pool of holy water. He then muddies the pool, so that others who bathe in it become darker. Moving from infantile sexuality to adult potency, he is portrayed as a sadomasochist, a destructive rather than creative force.[3]

It is ironic that the official view of the Brazilian government, even during the period of the repressive military dictatorship, was that Brazil was a "racial democracy" and that if discrimination existed in Brazil, it was a function of class not race. In the 1960s, racial discrimination and segregation were outlawed, although Brazil remains one of the most residentially segregated countries in the world. Brazilian academics, frequently marxist in their orientation, studied race thoroughly as an element of dependency. They emphasize the adaptation of racism to the structural characteristics of industrial capitalism.[4] More recently, however, Brazilians not only have become more aware of the realities of discrimination against nonwhites but have also been exposed to television programs and articles in journals such as *Veja* and *Istoé,* with stories about nonwhites who have achieved success in business, public service, and the professions. Whether these latest achievements signal profound changes in Brazilian race relations or merely gloss over long-standing patterns of racial inequality, as occurred during the 1960s, remains an open question.

Notes

1 David T. Haberly, *Three Sad Races: Racial Identity and National Consciousness in Brazilian Literature* (Cambridge: Cambridge University Press, 1983), p. 1.

2 Gilberto Freyre, *The Masters and the Slaves* (New York: Alfred A. Knopf, 1946), p. xii.

3 Haberly, *Three Sad Races,* pp. 139–55.

4 See Pierre-Michel Fontaine, introduction to *Race, Class, and Power in Brazil* (Los Angeles: Center for Afro-American Studies, University of California at Los Angeles, 1985), p. 2. Scholars who have researched race relations in Brazil from this perspective include Florestan Fernandes, Otávio Ianni, and Fernando Henrique Cardoso.

A Letter from Brazil, 1918

José Clarana

The following letter published in a 1918 edition of The Crisis, *the official magazine of the National Association for the Advancement of Colored People, contains a Brazilian's critique of race relations in the United States. References to Texas, and particularly to the city of Waco, figure prominently in the letter. Waco was the site of a grisly lynching in 1916, known as the "Waco Horror." Coincidentally, Gilberto Freyre, the great memorializer of Brazilian race relations, began studying at Waco's Baylor University in 1918. Furthermore, Freyre's older brother had previously attended the same school. Was José Clarana a pen name for the young Freyre or his brother? Regardless of the answer, Freyre certainly came face-to-face with Jim Crow in Waco. One can only guess how that confrontation influenced his later, seminal works on Brazilian race relations.*

In acceding to your request that I send you "one or two letters about the color problems in Brazil," I keep within the limitations of my capacity, and comply with your admonition that I "make them as short as possible," by writing one letter with the simple statement that there is no color problem in Brazil.

By way of explanation, however, I must add that this does not mean that a black skin is an open sesame to any and every drawing room, and a shibboleth of easy access to the heart of any maiden and the purse of her father. It means, for one thing, that a man is not necessarily black because his skin is not so white as somebody else's skin. In the terms of the "social equality" that the telegrams say that German spies have been trying to obtain for the not-quite-white-enough in Alabama, it means that the color of the pelts in a drawing room is the exclusive business of the people who wear them, and that if the son of some gentleman violates the servant girl, there is no law to prevent him from marrying her because she does not come up to the popular specifications as to complexion. In a word, in Brazil the mere possession of a white skin does not entitle a man to superior civil rights and opportunities, nor does an increased pigmentation condemn its owner to the status of a pariah.

Occasionally, an attempt is made in Brazil to establish a standard of whiteness to which all aspirants to a life of the greatest usefulness must conform. Generally, if not always, these attempts to divide the Brazilian people are made by foreign residents. For instance, the son of a colored teacher was not long ago refused admittance to a college conducted by Belgian priests. I do not know how this affair ended, but the action of the rector of the school was severely criticized by the newspapers. A striking contrast to the attitude of the Belgian friar is the fact that, recently, one of the largest and wealthiest churches in Rio was crowded with people attending a mass of intercession for the early triumph of the ideals of the allies, including, of course, those valiant defenders of the rights of oppressed peoples who used to cut off the hands of the natives on the rubber plantations in the Congo. Most of the worshipers at that mass were altogether white and many of them were distinguished foreigners. The celebrant was a colored man, who when he is not saying mass or singing in the choir of a church, conducts a school whose students are nearly all white.

Americans, of course, are not slow in attempting to establish caste discrimination, especially when they first come here. A friend of mine told me, shortly after he arrived here, that the Negroes ought to be separated from the whites in public places. I do not know whether he got that notion so much from having resided in Alabama as from reading *The Outlook,* which is ashamed to tell the American public that in trying to show how superior they are to the "niggers," white people have disgraced their civilization by committing acts of savagery unexcelled by the lowest tribes in the heart of Africa. It does not mind libeling the colored people of the States by characterizing as "envy" the natural desire of a decent man to sit in a clean railway carriage, or to enter a restaurant without fear of buying a steak fried with spit or sharing the fate of the colored Georgian who, in neutral Chicago, was killed for the crime of unwittingly seating himself at the side of a Texan at a public lunch counter.

I got the Chicago story from an eyewitness, the son of a Confederate officer, who told it, with the greatest sangfroid, at lunch in a Brazilian boardinghouse. I mention it here in the hope that some of the editors, politicians, and countinghouse anthropologists who make the color question in the United States, and who are really responsible for crimes against civilization and against the good name of the United States, like the Waco Horror, may have another concrete example of the effect of the "social equality" humbug in a land where nearly everyone has some learning, but too many of the people have only enough to enable them to read a newspaper.

Perhaps one reason for the absence of a color question in the countries of South America, where there is any great variation in the color of the inhabitants, is the fact that there are not so many people who can read as in the United States, but proportionately, more persons who do more than just read, because they have more time, let us say. One of the thinking readers of Brazil and unquestionably one of the greatest intellects of all America, Rui Barbosa, in speaking of slavery and its consequences in this country, says: "For three generations we were free, prosperous and rich at the cost of the oppression of our fellow-men. We are today undergoing the great expiation which never fails, which does not pardon historic outrages and capital crimes against humanity."

The fact that slavery was a crime against humanity and not merely an economic mistake is, I think, something that no important public man in the United States would admit without reserve. In Brazil, it is the essential immorality of the institution, the inherent injustice to its victims, that is most emphasized. The date of the abolition of slavery, May 13, is duly commemorated as a national holiday, and there is no effort to reintroduce it in any form. Whatever penalties the nation may now be paying for the original error of importing and maintaining African slaves, there is no desire to postpone the day of atonement and increase the sacrifice by aggravating the old offense.

A friend of mine, a very likable fellow in himself, assures me that "the only way to handle an American 'nigger' is to knock him on the head and talk to him about it afterward."

African blood is, perhaps, as plentiful in the States of Bahia and Rio de Janeiro as in Georgia or Texas, but in a country where great statesmen think and feel that the humblest blacks are their *fellow men,* it would not be possible for white men to drag a man through the streets, bleeding from head to foot from the nails and knives thrust into him, burn him, still living, and wear his dead teeth as charms to "keep the 'nigger' in his place."

Brazilians are very religious, but they are not quite that superstitious. Among them, everyone finds his place naturally. If one can afford to travel in a first-class public conveyance, no one will attempt to make him go second class and pay first-class fare. If a man wants a cup of coffee or a glass of milk or cane juice, which are the most popular beverages among the Brazilians—who, by the way, are not prohibited from drinking whiskey—if they want to, no café will refuse to serve him if he is clean and decent. They even serve Americans and Europeans who get drunk, so long as these do not offend other people. When the new minister of foreign affairs, whose policy is to be one of approximation to the United States, embraces the lawyer who makes a public address of Godspeed and presents the minister with a gold pen with which to sign his first official act, nobody has any objection to make because the minister is white and the orator brown. The newspapers do not even mention the color of the people concerned. They never do, except sometimes, in reporting civil statistics, accidents, and crimes. In such cases, the person is not called black if the skin is not black. Whether white or mixed, the color is mentioned only once, parenthetically, for identification, and not used to substitute proper nouns and pronouns, in a manifest effort to associate complexion with crime, as in the two-inch paragraph I once cut from the *New York Times,* which contained nine references to the color of a man accused of a commonplace crime. The man, of course, was a Negro, more or less.

Nobody wastes any time in the Republic of the Southern Cross in trying to determine the moral and intellectual potentialities of a people by skin color or facial configuration. In this country, a man's accomplishments are the measure of his ability. Even before the complete abolition of slavery, the greatest statesman of the Empire was a mulatto. A black of the deepest dye was a commanding figure in journalism. Today, there are men of Negro blood in the national and state legislatures, representing citizens of any and all hues. One of the most important diplomatic representatives of Brazil would be called a Negro in law and a "nigger" by custom in the United States. In short, in every walk of life, from the highest and most useful callings to the humble and unproductive one of begging and the less honorable but less prevalent one of stealing, Brazilians are engaged, without let or hindrance, purely because of their own or their grandmothers' color.

But withal, white civilization is still supreme, and is constantly increasing its power and influence, for it is supported by the national conscience of a people passionately devoted to the practice of liberty and justice within their own borders and among their *fellow men*. Such a civilization must always endure, for it is only when [German chancellor] Bethman Hollweg declares, "We'll knock Belgians on the head, and then talk to them about it afterward," that Waco becomes Verdun and white civilization commits suicide.

The South American countries have had their Wacos and Verduns, and for this reason, they are not anxious to pay more than they can help of the penalties for wrongs done unto them rather than by them. For 400 years, Europeans, Africans, and American aborigines have toiled together, according to their gifts, to make this continent what it is today. Out of this long experience has been evolved the attitude toward men and citizens of the various countries, which is thus expressed by Don Francisco Garcia Calderón, former minister of Bolivia to the United States, in an essay titled "Pan-Americanism, Past and Future": "The biological notion of race, that internal fatality as inexorable as destiny of old, which is revealed by the cranial line and the color of the skin, is declining in prestige. Sociologists have given up discovering pure blood in confused nations, they do not recognize the hereditary pre-eminence, which used to be attributed to particular ethnic groups; they contest the summary opposition between Indo-Germanic and Semitic which explained, in the mind of ambitious historians, the development of the drama of peoples, their progress and decadence, the construction of empires and philosophies, the mission of Orient and Occident. But we do not abandon the idea of race as the synthesis of the diverse elements of a definite civilization. Religion, art, language, lengthy inhabitation of the same territory, tradition, moral affinities which fix, through the centuries, lasting cultures and unmistakable psychological characteristics."

This idea of race as being synonymous with nation holds true in Brazil. Perhaps, in the Great Republic of the North, the time is not far distant when an American will be no less than an American, no matter what the shape of his head or the color of his skin. And then, when you have no more Wacos, you need fear no Verduns. At least, you will have the satisfaction of knowing that none of the blood and treasure that you would generously spend for the redemption of Belgium is being paid in needless sacrifice for the slavery that you maintain at home.

Growing Up Black in Minas Gerais

Carolina Maria de Jesus

*In twentieth-century Brazilian history, virtually no descriptions exist of the lives of poor people. Carolina Maria de Jesus (nicknamed Bitita) was an illegitimate black child, the granddaughter of slaves, who grew up in the 1920s in Sacramento, a small city in Minas Gerais where traditional Roman Catholic values and a rigid class system bestowed on her the status of a social pariah. Her memoirs, written in the 1970s after she briefly achieved fame for publishing her diary of slum life (*Child of the Dark*), only to fall back into poverty, offer remarkable detail about lower-class life and social relationships. Edited versions of her reminiscences were published in France shortly before her death, in Brazil a decade later, and in English as* Bitita's Diary, *but the following excerpts, discovered in manuscript form in 1998, reveal a greater degree of torment and offer more thick description than the sanitized, published editions of her autobiography.*

I found some of the old books. . . . When I arrived in Sacramento, my relatives received me with hostility. By now, I was more intelligent and studied their rancorous expressions. I thought: "They didn't miss me." My mother told me that if I came back, I would be sorry. "Didn't I tell you to stay there? I'm not saying this out of a lack of care for you, but it is for your own good. It is very hard for me to watch them ostracize you." Humiliated . . . I showed them my dresses; my mother thought them pretty. The cloth is from São Paulo. My employer bought it. "Ha . . . you had an employer? Stop being a liar. You want us to believe you, but I doubt it." I showed her the necklaces. She took the yellow one and left the green one for me. I bought a parasol and noticed that my cousins were envious of my clothing. When they bought clothing, I never was jealous. What I didn't respect was useless vanities. They worked just to buy clothes. They could have, instead, worked to buy a piece of land and construct a small house, the most important thing we can have.

I spent the days reading Camões's *Lusiadas,* with the help of my dictionary. I wanted to learn new things, since I understood that educated people are able to cope with the subtle aspects of life.

Since I had been treated with several medicines, my legs were beginning to scar. I began to make plans. I'm going to be well. I had to know the city of São Paulo, that the people called the land of milk and honey. In São Paulo, there is a district named Paradise. And the city of São Paulo is a paradise for poor people. It had more railroad tracks than any other state.

Through books, I learned of Brazil's wars. The War of the Farrapos. The Paraguayan War. I condemned this brutal and inhuman form that men find to solve their problems. I sat in the sun to read. Passersby looked at the dictionary and commented on how thick it was. "It must be the book of São Cipriano." This is the only book that these ignorant people have ever heard about. They said that I was studying to be a witch, to frustrate their lives. Witches pray, they said, and not rain but hail falls. When my mother found out what was said, she told me: "It's better for you to stop reading these books. They're saying that its the São Cipriano book. That you are a witch." I laughed heartily. People who read become enlightened and prudent, and know how to confront life. I want to heal so I can leave and not come back. I was content because my wounds were drying out. I wanted to surprise my mother. I was following the advice of the nun in Jardinopolis, that if I return home, I would get better.

In my house, I was calm. I didn't feel like a rebel, nor did I feel the old internal anguish. When I didn't read, I embroidered something or another. My brother hung around. What pain I felt for these poor youths. They couldn't hang out in the town because the police would get after them.

Poor men looked at the police the way cats look at dogs. But this is foolish because the policemen were also poor, understanding the difficulties people have to survive. . . . One day I was reading when some youths passed by, stopped, and asked to see my dictionary. I gave the book for them to see; they looked and said, "Ah, it's the São Cipriano book. Look how heavy it is." I was pained, because literature benefits men as much as women. I wanted to be healthy so I could work. When the youths left, they went to tattle to the police sergeant, telling him that I called him a ragpicker. That he goes after poor people. The sergeant was my cousin Leonor's godfather and ordered his soldiers to pick me up. I was in the house and I didn't like to go out anymore because of the way I attracted trouble.

I realized that rich people who are born in small cities can be born naked, but poor people have to be born dressed in patience to be able to put up with all the ignorance surrounding them.

I had a fright when I saw the policemen stopping in front of the house and saying that they wanted to arrest me. I didn't ask why I was being taken in. I just obeyed.

My mother interfered, saying that I hadn't done anything wrong. "Quiet. You're arrested also." My mother wept, telling me that I shouldn't have come back to this place. . . . Why don't you stay with the *paulistas* [people from São Paulo]? When we arrived at the jail, everyone knew that I was being arrested. They put us into a cell, and I remembered the nun's advice to go home because I could rest and heal there. We stayed in jail two days, with nothing to eat. On the third day, the sergeant made us wail and beat our hands together at the front of the jail. People came by just to see us. On the fourth day, we wailed until midday. My hands hurt. My wounds became inflamed again for lack of ointment. At 1:00 P.M., the sergeant called us to interrogate me.

"Do you still say that I am a ragpicker?"

I understood. It was Li [Leonor] who told him.

"I told Li that the malady I have has turned me into a human derelict, inferior to the others. I don't like it when they mock my illness. It's not my fault I am infected. When I heal, I want to go to work."

"Are you still reading the São Cipriano book? You're going to practice witchcraft on whom?

"I don't believe in witchery and I don't have the São Cipriano book."

"I have it." And he gave me the book to look at.

I love books, and took it gratefully and with care, as if I were holding a newborn infant. But I was nervous to read it.

"They say that you go out at night and wander the city." My mother said: "She doesn't go out at night."

"Shut your mouth, you vagabond." We returned to the cell. The sergeant sent a black soldier to beat us. He beat us with a hard rubber hose. My mother tried to protect me. She held her arm in front of me, receiving the blows. Her arm broke and she fainted. I tried to help her, but the soldier kept beating me. Five days in jail without anything to eat. My aunt visited us and brought a meat stew with farinha. My legs swelled. I thought that these people must be descendants of Nero, who loved cruelty. My mother's arm hurt. She cried. A soldier named Isaltino cursed at me. "This vagabond lives in the street. Proper girls don't do that." I said that I was going to São Paulo. I asked my aunt to speak with Mr. Aureslino de Campos, the bank manager, to get me out; I would pay him back later. He said that he couldn't do this. I had to pay the jailer twenty *mil-réis*. My legs started to reek.

My cousin Paulo came up with the twenty *mil-réis* [half a month's wages] and got me out. I'll have to consider him as my only relative. My wounds became inflamed. My mother couldn't wash clothing. We wandered through the countryside begging, my mother with her broken arm and I with infected legs. We got rice, beans, lard, soap, cheese, leftovers. My mother said that I had to leave. OK. I agreed. I thought of the generosity of the *paulistas*. Here, parents forbade their daughters from talking to me, as if I'd contaminate them . . .

Worries kept me from sleeping. Will I be happy in this city? What fear I had of big cities. And I had no money. I went up "Nostalgia Avenue." I arrived at the Santa Casa charity hospital and asked for an appointment. They applied a salve and said that I should return in three days. This frightened me: where would I stay? Then I remembered that Aunt Ana lived in the city, and I decided to find her. I asked around and I found her place. She lived in Vila Tibério. When I arrived, it was 6:00 P.M. They were having dinner. I stopped at the door and said hello:

"Bless you, Aunt Ana."

She didn't respond. But even without an invitation, I came in and sat down. My feet were swollen inside my shoes. It was Saturday. Aunt Ana told me: "You surely have eaten." "No, ma'am," I replied. She gave me a furious look. She put down a small serving of beans and rice, and said: "I'm not interested in having mouths visit me. Visits of arms, yes. How did you find my house?" "A woman told me." My aunt became furious, cursing: "Ah! A disgraceful, infamous woman. . . . She can go to hell." I ate but I remained hungry. My cousins were getting dressed. They were going to a dance in a rented ballroom.

They decided that I should go, because they didn't know me and couldn't leave me alone. "We don't know if she is a thief." Mulattoes make me most nauseous of anyone. They dissipate the blacks; it's tough putting up with their boastings and lies. Aunt Ana's house was filled with decorative things. How many cushions on the floor! I went to the dance. Marcelina went from one side to the other. She was engaged to a boy, Octávio. A serious guy.

The people present were special. Well dressed. The men wore fine suits. I wondered if they were rich. At midnight, they raffled off a roast chicken. What a temptation I felt to get close to that chicken and run away with it. I was seated near Aunt Ana. Watching them dance and thinking that they are from the other side of the world. Good health. For me, it was just a stage that I could watch, but not take part in. Now I was calmer, realizing that being petulant wouldn't help anything in the state I was in, something that couldn't go on. Sick people have to be quarantined. But it is hard to accept this. I had the impression that I was in a prison with no chance of winning my freedom. Next to my aunt sat a woman more than fifty years old. Who was she? My aunt looked me over minutely and said: "She's a beggar who comes from time to time to my house to ask for alms."

"Poor thing! How young and already incapacitated in being able to deal with life. How you are charitable!" And Aunt Ana basked in the woman's praise.

I was sleepy but I couldn't lay down. To mark the end of the dance, they had a quadrille. But there weren't enough women. So they asked my aunt, the other woman, and me.

What a torment it was to lift my legs. They were swollen and as heavy as if they were made of lead. I wanted to say: "Fellow, I can't dance. I'm sick." But then he might say to me: "The place for sick people isn't a ballroom, it's a hospital."

I accepted the invitation. He smiled at me. I smiled also. I hadn't danced in quite a while. It wasn't my favorite pastime. I was badly dressed, a fairy-tale character. I implored God to make the quadrille finish. I didn't know how to follow the music, and in such pain I couldn't follow the steps. The other dancers smiled; I felt like groaning. What a relief when the quadrille ended. The people said goodbye to one another and we went home. When we arrived, my aunt gave me a rug on which to lay down on the cement floor. When I breathed, I smelled the dust. I couldn't sleep because I was too cold. I got up and sat in a chair. I wasn't sleepy because I was hungry. My cousin José Marcelino entered the kitchen, heated coffee, drank it, and left without saying anything to me. He was a train engineer on the line to Sertãozinho.

When day came, I went out to warm in the sun. They didn't give me coffee. They complained about the entrance fee to the dance, 12,000 *cruzeiros*. I was only allowed to stay in the yard. At midday they ate, and my aunt gave me two spoons of rice and two of beans, complaining that I was being a burden to her. "Why don't you beg? Go to the city. I'm sick of you being here in my house. I left Sacramento so I wouldn't have to be mixed up with your family. . . ."

I decided to leave. I went to Barbara's house. When she saw me, she slammed the door. I thought: if some day I get healed, and prosper, I won't have anything more to do with my relatives. I think that if they saw me drowning in the sea they would not save me. If I weren't sick, I wouldn't know the negative side of my relatives. I returned to Aunt Ana's house and sat in the yard. I slept. When I awoke they had eaten dinner. I was struck by how Aunt Ana didn't ask about her relatives, if they were well. She separated herself from her family because the others were blacks. I thought of the sacrifice mulattoes make to give the appearance of being rich. I was dirty after three days without a bath in Ribeirão Prêto, in insupportable heat. But they didn't let me take a bath. Three days in my aunt's house and I ate just two times. But God was protecting me. I didn't feel hungry. What horrified me was to have to sleep on the dirty floor, covered with dust. I understood that they were treating me nastily so I would leave their house. At 4:00 A.M., I awoke and sat down on a chair. At 5, my cousin José Marcelino awoke to go to work. He looked at me with disgust and asked me: "When are you going to leave?" I cursed him mentally: "dog," "disgusting," "rotten scoundrel." I thought: "Where are these girls, the ones Aunt Ana raised, the daughters of Aunt Sebastiana, Vicente, Joaquim, Adálio, and the son of José Marcelino with Maria Generosa?" I didn't speak even ten words to these brazen people. This is how I consider mulattoes.

When my aunt got up, she told me: "Go out and beg. You were born to be a beggar. If you don't get money, you don't need to come back here." I took my bundle and left. I felt hungry. I decided to ask for a piece of bread. I looked at the houses, thinking about which one I should ask.

I rang the bell of a house. When the woman opened the door, I asked: "Could you give me a piece of bread?"

"Ah, go to work, you vagabond. My poor husband works all day in a horrible job to earn money for me to give bread he buys after such sacrifice to you? Work you people don't want."

Exotic Peoples

Indian Protection Agency

When released by a government agency at the turn of the century, this photo was titled, *"Indian, S. Paulo. Aged 14."* (Nevin O. Winter, *Brazil and Her People of Today* [Boston: Page Company, 1910])

Agencies of the state sought to demonstrate the benefits of their civilizing influence. The first photograph, made available to foreign news services during the beginning of the twentieth century, was labeled, "Indian, S. Paulo. Aged 14." The girl is wearing an urban dress, although it is tattered. The patronizing attitude of the photographer and the agency editor is obvious in every aspect of the composition and captioning. The second photograph, captioned "Kaingang Indians. Dressed for the first time," shows four barefoot girls, one of them wearing tribal markings, in angel-like Western robes.

The official caption on this photo read, *"Kaingang Indians. Dressed for the first time."* (Nevin O. Winter, *Brazil and Her People of Today* [Boston: Page Company, 1910])

Brazil:

Study in Black, Brown, and Beige

Leslie B. Rout Jr.

The late Leslie B. Rout Jr. centered his academic career by specializing in Latin American diplomatic history, but as an African American and a jazz musician who liked to travel and visit places other than libraries and archives, Rout published a few articles in the mid-1960s on his personal experiences in Brazil. His first person narrative sheds revealing light on the myths and attitudes about race in Brazilian society.

If you're like me, you've probably read Gilberto Freyre or Frank Tannenbaum, or watched a couple of CBS reports. . . . Perhaps you've talked to a Brazilian or two. If you've done any of these things, you know already that "no racial problems exist in Brazil." Maybe the Brazilian you talked to was more discreet. He would then have informed you that there is less racial discrimination in Brazil than any place else in the world.

As the story is usually told, unlike the Anglo-Saxons who set up shop at Jamestown or Plymouth Rock, the Portuguese gentlemen who migrated to the New World had significantly fewer qualms about "nighttime integration." The result was that in addition to the obvious black slaves and white masters, there appeared an increasing myriad of colored persons who were part of both, but not really of either. Accordingly (and this is in keeping with the legend), the Brazilians adopted the converse of the formula adopted by the Anglo-Saxons. Where the English settled, any measure of Negro blood made you a Negro. In Brazil, any discernible quantity of white blood made you at least a *pardo* (mulatto). Ultimately, it was probably very much a question of what one could get those higher up in the pecking order to believe.

In today's United States of America, where racial troubles can no longer be swept under the carpet, the Brazilian legend exercises a peculiar influence. For Afro-Americans, such as this writer, Brazil beckons as a kind of tropical Shangri-la. As a friend once put it, "Man, after I make my pile here, then I'm splitting for coffeeland where I can enjoy it." Others wonder how a nation that maintained slavery until May 1888, where illiterates possibly outnumber literates, and where political democracy can hardly be said to have taken giant strides, could do what the "gringo Goliath" could not: satisfy the hopes and aspirations of its nonwhite citizens.

This story really begins the second time I saw Walt Disney's *Saludo Amigo*. There was José Carioca and lots of samba, and seemingly a country where the living was easy rather than hectic. Then there was *Black Orpheus*, lots of samba and a plenitude of Carnival. More important, Orpheus, although a lowly *bondes* (streetcar) driver, seemed to possess a peculiar kind of personal security. In the land of the Anglo-Saxon, without identification signs as big as life, Senator James Brooke of Massachusetts and/or Congressman William Dawson of Illinois are like George Washington Jones of Birmingham, Alabama: "Niggers" to be kept in their place. Afro-Americans in the land of Uncle Sam are acutely aware of their dependence on "Whitey," lock, stock, and credit card. Orpheus was black like me, and so poor he could hardly have afforded a free lunch. Yet, his view of himself as a functioning member of the Brazilian body politic gave him a kind of quiet support black Yankees cannot achieve, Cadillac or no Cadillac, education or no education. Orpheus felt he belonged; Afro-Americans do not believe they do.

In June 1961, the Paul Winter Sextet, of which I was a member, won the Intercollegiate Jazz Festival held at Georgetown University. As fortune would have it, somebody in Washington, D.C., noticed that the six members of the group were split even-up—three blacks and three whites. Could you have dreamed of a better combination to send on a government-sponsored tour of Latin American colleges and universities? A seven-month tour was dropped into our laps. Secretly, I resolved that if Brazil resembled the land of Orpheus, Carioca, Tannenbaum, and Freyre, it must eventually open its arms to a new immigrant—me.

Arriving in Porto Alegre (May 1962), the first thing I tended to notice was that *brancos* in Brazil found nothing strange about fraternizing with Negroes. One saw *pretos* and *pardos* frequently, but as my Portuguese was limited to such terms as *macanudo* (and the usual unprintable terminology you always seem to learn first), it was nearly impossible to communicate with them. Exceedingly noticeable on the campuses of the universities and in the theaters was the absence of Negroes at sextet concerts. Whites I questioned assured me that although the concerts were free, most Afro-Brazilians were of the lower economic classes, and rarely attended affairs where middle- and upper-class *Senhores* predominated. Previous experiences in South America had convinced me that some kind of class system would be found everywhere. The explanations given were logical, but in my opinion, insufficient. Somehow or another, I had to meet a few *pretos* and get their side of the story.

Jazz musicians meet their counterparts wherever they seem to go in the world, and with the music as a medium, friendships are forged. Through Cepú, a black tenor saxophone player I met in a Rio nightclub, I finally met some *pretos* who spoke English. Speaking directly to the gentlemen (both of whom were musicians), I remarked that none of the black members of the sextet had encountered any incidences of discrimination in Brazil. One of the Brazilians smiled and said, "Things are not as they seem; they are more subtle here. . . . " This was to be inkling number one, you might say.

In this regard, probably the most interesting character I would meet was a young Negro from Omaha, Nebraska, named Bill Waters. Waters had decided to take one year off, go to Brazil, and see whether he wanted to move there permanently. When I met him, his stay in Rio had exceeded ten months. He stated that while he liked Brazil, it had not been the racial nirvana he'd hoped to find. Indeed, he was amazed at the ease with which the black members of the sextet moved among Rio's social elite. He later confided in me that he felt certain that the prestige of the Department of State opened doors otherwise hermetically sealed. At the time, I was enjoying myself to such a degree that Waters's reservations seemed sour grapes. The whole issue reemerged about three months later when Bill stopped in Chicago on his way to Omaha. Having just returned to the United States, I threw a small party and invited Waters. Afterwards he remarked, "You know, Les, I saw more integration here tonight than I saw in twelve months in Brazil." What he really meant was miscegenation, and secretly I had to admit that while everywhere in Brazil one sees *pardos,* I had seen precious little intermingling on a social level. Admittedly, it was the *pretos* you saw pushing the brooms, but the witness of my own adventures as a musical diplomat in Sambaland were a kind of insulation against the other reality. Bill was a great guy, but . . .

Two and one half years would pass before I could again travel to Brazil. This time, there would be no fanfare or ballyhoo. Under the guise of traveling graduate student doing dissertational research, one Les Rout would continue to investigate whether or not Brazil was where I wanted to belong. Fortunately, my Portuguese had come along and I had maintained contact with about half a dozen Brazilians I'd met the first time around. The years 1962–1965 had convinced me that racial discrimination in the land of the free and home of the brave would end in 2965 at the earliest. Hopefully, the Brazilians had more satisfactory answers. Boarding the jet, I could already hear João Gilberto singing *"Samba da Minha Terra . . ."*

There is the oft-told tale about the astronauts who landed on Mars and were approached by one of its thirty-eyed, forty-legged, three-foot-high inhabitants. Despite their obvious disparity, the astronauts and the Martians got along fine. However, the latter cautioned the space travelers about one thing: "We don't want you messin' around with our females, you dig?"

There were times in Brazil when it occurred to me that I must have resembled an astronaut. For example, there was the time in late July 1965, when I attended a theater in Porto Alegre, in company with a fair young Brazilian girl of German parentage, whom I shall call Karen. There were, I believe, two shows that night. There was one on stage, and there was Karen and I. Probably everywhere except maybe New York and Paris, when black boys appear in polite society with attractive blondes, eyebrows go up a few inches and there is some gnashing of teeth. In Alabama, both of us would have been lynched. In Porto Alegre, they pointed their fingers, wagged their tongues, and murdered us with their eyes. Never was I so happy to have the houselights dim and the play begin! At intermission, it started all over again, however. The man sitting directly in front of me turned around so many times that I can still see in my mind where the moles were on his face. As for Karen, within five minutes she had been frightened out of her wits. After we joined a large group in a nightclub, she still could not relax. She agreed to dance with me only reluctantly, and then only after she had taken time to gauge the impact this event would have on the other customers. Violence? Naked force? There is nothing quite like social pressure to bully reluctant parties into line.

Later that night, while reflecting on what had been a most unpleasant experience, I imagined myself calling Karen on the phone and hearing the maid answer—"She is not here. She just went out to visit all her remaining friends in Porto Alegre. She should be back in five minutes."

One might argue that despite its population of 800,000, Porto Alegre is hardly a center of cosmopolitanism. This is correct, but matters did not seem to be remarkably different in that haven of the hip, Rio de Janeiro. Still sharply in focus is the November evening on which I performed as special guest artist at the Boate K-Samba, for the Club de Jazz e Bossa Nova do Rio. Friends introduced me to a sparkling *branca* who taught Latin in a local private school. As is often the case when boy meets girl, boy asks girl if he might see her on another occasion. The young lady enthusiastically agreed to have dinner with me the following evening. Just before leaving the club with friends, this Afro-American again confirmed the date of the engagement with the Brazilian *branca*. Here is an approximation of the conversation that followed the next day:

He: "When may I come for you?"

She: "I am sorry, it is impossible."

He: "Well, how about lunch tomorrow?"

She: "That also is impossible."

He: "What about dinner tomorrow evening?"

She: "That is out of the question. I am sorry."

He: "Well, is it possible for me to visit you at all?"

She: "Unfortunately, there are problems . . . that also is impossible."

Checking with friends later, I discovered that the young lady was not married, had not come to the club with another man. I had not forced her to accept my invitation or attempted to embarrass her. Assuming that I did not appear to be the previously described astronaut, did not have leprosy or trench mouth, the readers must pardon me if I chalked this experience up as another pigmentation misadventure.

Reflections

Although these events took place about four years ago [in 1964], it was literally impossible for me to write about them until now. Quite foolishly, I had assumed that there was a land of Oz, that there really was a "somewhere over the rainbow." My journey to Brazil had put me eyeball to eyeball with grim reality. Black boy, you can run, but you cannot hide!

Some may conclude from what I have written that neither *pretos* or [*sic*] most *pardos* can aspire to greatness in Brazil. This is hardly the case. Among the more celebrated *pretos* and / or *pardos* (and here, I include everyone whom I would conceive as being considered a Negro if they were in this country) are Pelé (Edson Arantes), the soccer star; such personal friends as Jair Rodrigues and Lenni Andrade, vocalists; Raul de Santos ("Raulzinho"), musician; and Antentor Carlos Vaz, artist. It is not my intention to denounce all whites as being deluded or racist. People are people all over the world. Gradually, the hate and disillusionment subsided. Eventually, it became possible to make some kind of reasonably objective comparisons:

First. In the United States of America, the installation of the Jim Crow system forced mulattoes and blacks together. Mulattoes did not prefer things that way, but they were unable to force any significant change in the situation. Thus, while "light" Negroes and darker ones remained at odds for many years, the inability of parlaying lightness into privilege brought about a black unity that would not have been possible in 1900. If you question this supposition, take a good look at [the light-skinned Harlem Congressman] Adam Clayton Powell. Considering that God supposedly draws good from every evil act, one might say that "Whitey" did us a favor.

In Brazil, the official ideology is "Brazilianization," or more accurately, amalgamation of the races. The general impetus, however, is toward "whitening" the nation. The *pardos,* therefore, distinguish themselves from the *pretos,* for they see themselves as farther along the lightening process than their "brothers." A *preto* might consider himself as marrying "up," if he could forge an alliance with a *pardo,* but a lighter-skinned female would be considered as marrying "down." Indeed, animosity between *pardos* and *pretos* seemed very strong in Brazil. One might well ask if some kind of race war occurred in Brazil, which way would the *pardos* go? It has also passed through my mind that possibly the cleverest way to keep nonwhites divided would be to perpetrate a system whereby *pardos* yearn to become lighter, and *pretos* yearn to become *pardos.*

Second. From an economic standpoint, the Afro-American appears much more prosperous in general than *pretos* or *pardos* in Brazil. This is a simple reflection of the fact that the United States of America is a richer nation than the United States of Brazil. In neither nation can it be argued that nonwhites had an equitable share of whatever there was to get. However, migration to the northern urban areas and three major wars since 1917–1918 have put Afro-Americans in a position where some of the funds that came their way could be invested or used to buy property.

Most amazing to this observer was the almost total absence of Afro-Brazilians in the business world. In the industrial south of Brazil, where miscegenation is far from a virtue, one hardly expected to see *preto* bank executives. But even in the northern areas, *preto* or dark *pardo* bank or office clerks were as rare as [Charles] de Gaulle supporters in the State Department. Apparently, the *brancos* owned everything. *Pretos* and *pardos* might sing, dance, and play soccer, but the mysteries of commerce were somehow beyond their grasp.

Immigrant Ethnicity in Brazil

Jeffrey Lesser

Scholarly and popular sources on Brazilian society often focus on the African roots of much of the population, ignoring the millions of immigrants who settled over the nineteenth and twentieth centuries. The largest numbers came from Europe (namely, Italy, Portugal, and Spain) and were considered desirable by elites who hoped to "whiten" Brazil, and thereby mirror both the industry and status of central Europe and the United States. Yet hundreds of thousands of non-European immigrants also settled in Brazil, challenging the monolithic hegemony of the ostensible Brazilian "race" that elites hoped to create. Most numerous were Arabs and Japanese, who sought to establish compound ethnicities for themselves as Japanese Brazilians (called nikkei) *or Arab Brazilians (called Syrian Lebanese), even though the dominant discourse suggested only two possible social groups, "Brazilians" or "foreigners." Thus, the common terms for a third- or fourth-generation Brazilian of Japanese descent is "Japanese," not "Japanese Brazilian" or "nikkei."*

Arab and Japanese immigrants entered Brazil in greatest number between the last decades of the nineteenth century and the middle ones of the twentieth, composing about 11 percent of the total immigrant pool (300,000 of 2,731,360). Some 107,000 Arabs, mainly Greek (Melkite) and Marronite Catholic or Orthodox, entered, but the overwhelming majority (almost 91 percent) arrived from Syria and Lebanon in the thirty years starting in 1904. At least 189,000 Japanese immigrants settled in Brazil between 1908 and 1941, with another 50,000 arriving after 1950. Most Arab immigrants came independently to Brazil, and many began their working lives as peddlers, eventually settling in large and small cities, where they opened shops (often selling textiles and related goods) and later factories. Japanese immigrants, however, came as part of a large-scale labor migration that was formally arranged between the Japanese

Imperial Government and individual Brazilian states. These migrants were almost uniformly agricultural workers and, by the early 1920s, often settled on colonies where the Japanese government was the de facto owner.

In spite of the differences in both occupation and official home-country interest, Arab and Japanese immigrants and their descendants had something in common: both groups sought to integrate into the "Brazilian nation" by claiming a more "original" or "authentic" Bra-zilianness than members of the European-descended elite. One way they did this was through the construction of myths that justified their own places in Brazilian society. Two of the most common were the following.

Myth One: Beginning in the nineteenth century, a number of well-respected French crackpot theorists suggested that King Solomon sailed the Amazon River, and that the Quechua and Portuguese languages were offshoots of ancient Hebrew. Such theories were repeated fre-quently by the most prominent Arab Brazilian intellectual of the 1930s, Salomão Jorge, a prizewinning poet, author, and radio commentator. Jorge modified the myth to suggest that King Solomon was the "ances-tor of the Syrians," and thus, Brazil's indigenous tribes descended from Solomon and, by extension, Jesus.[1]

Myth Two: In the late 1920s, Hachiro Fukuhara, owner of the Com-panhia Nipponica e Plantações do Brasil and one of Japan's most power-ful businesspeople, visited the area around Belém do Pará with the inten-tion of setting up a colony. In a series of interviews given to the Japanese and Brazilian press, he claimed that Brazil was "founded by Asiatics" since "the natives who live along the River Amazon look exactly like the Japanese. There is also a close resemblance between them in manners and customs . . . [and] a certain Chinese secretary in the German Em-bassy at Rio [has] made a careful study [of language] and concluded that these Indians descended from Mongols." Fukuhara even claimed he knew of a Buddhist ceremony performed in the Himalayas where a woman holds a tree as she is bearing a child and her husband walks around her, exclaiming happily, "I saw the same thing in the Amazon."[2]

Arab and Japanese immigrants and their descendants were able to promote these myths effectively because Brazil's elites lacked ideological clarity about the place of immigrants judged neither white nor black. While "whites" were generally seen as desirable and "blacks" as undesir-able, those immigrants who fit neither category caused confusion and debate. Policy makers and intellectuals were thus deeply divided about whether nonwhite / nonblack immigrants should be allowed to settle in Brazil. Those in favor believed immigrants provided a perfect bridge between European and African labor, and that these foreigners would help to transform Brazil from "black" to "white." For others, the social cost of allowing nonwhites to settle was so high that even substantial economic gains were not worth the risk of "infecting the blood" of an already "too dark" Brazil.

These different attitudes did not prevent elites from placing Arabs and Asians in a single, and controversial, "racial" group whose "value" became a constant source of debate among those seeking to transform Brazilian society. This linkage stemmed from, and created, a multiplicity of images about Arabs and Asians among the elite. Many sought to place the origins of the Amazonian indigenes in Asia Minor making Iberia's conquest by the Moors, and the thrill of European reconquest and the excesses of the Inquisition, a kind of ethnic consolidation. Arabs and Asians thus had a special place, as both friend and enemy, as exotically different yet somehow familiar. A perfect example of this conflation between self and other can be seen in Plínio Salgado's (the nativist leader of the fascistic Ação Integralista Brasileira) diary of a 1930 trip to the Middle East: " . . . I hear, coming from one of the boats . . . (in) the guttural accent of the Asiatics, the roguish [Carnival] music of Brazil, at the far limits of the Mediterranean, with its indescribable flavor. We are in Beirut."[3]

The notion that Arabs and Asians might somehow form a part of Brazil's social soul was quickly picked up by immigrant elites. In 1922, a commission composed of members of São Paulo's Syrian Lebanese community placed a bronze monument in the Parque Dom Pedro II to honor the centennial of Brazilian independence. The ceremony celebrated, according to the widely read newspaper *O Estado de São Paulo,* "the traditional friendship that unites the hardworking Syrian community to the Brazilian people," and included a parade by over 2,000 soldiers and speeches by the mayor. In his speech to the assembled crowd, Nagib Jafet, president of the commission, emphasized the biological connection between Brazilians and Arabs, evoking images of family and nature, and referring to the Syrian Lebanese community's "Syrian Brazilian soul." A poem by Elias Farhat engraved at the base of the monument also implied that Arab immigrants were original Brazilians. It transformed the Middle East into a region of mobile cultural and religious strength, suggesting that Arab ethnicity was not related to place but to person and could coexist easily within other national cultures. Another Farhat poem asserted that while Lebanese immigrants were indebted to Brazil for allowing them to settle, the Lebanese presence in Brazil had increased its prestige as a "Christian nation" since Arabs, regardless of the religion they practiced, were at the heart of Christianity.

> If we cut all the cedars in Lebanon
> —and the cedars are the base of our inspiration;
> and with them we built a temple
> whose towers crossed the clouds;
> if we snatched from Baalbeck and Palmira
> the vestiges of our glorious past;
> if we plucked Saladin's Tomb from Damascus
> and the Sepulcher of the Savior from Jerusalem;
> if we brought all of these treasures
> to this great independent nation
> and its glorious children
> we would still feel that
> we had not paid our debt
> to Brazil and the Brazilians.[4]

Japanese immigrants and their descendants viewed their ethnic space in Brazil much as did the Syrian Lebanese. In 1935, a group of students from São Paulo's São Francisco Law School founded the Nippo-Brazilian Student League to sponsor cultural, educational, and sporting events. The name itself, with its explicit hyphen, emphasized that ethnicity and nationality were two separate yet compatible items, a position explained with regularity and care in the League's Portuguese-language monthly, *Gakusei* (Student). One article written by José Yamashiro (who would later become a well-known journalist) told the story of a conversation between an older immigrant and a young Japanese Brazilian student. The hypothetical exchange revolved around how hyphenated ethnicity might work to the advantage of Brazilian society. The younger wanted to know what the concept of *Yamato damashü* meant, and the elder interpreted it as a "Japanese soul" that led to an undying loyalty to the emperor. The younger man responded with shock, wondering why even he, born in Brazil, had to be loyal to the emperor. The elder's response, however, emphasized the value of a hyphenated Japanese Brazilian identity: "[You] should defend the Brazilian flag with the same ardor, with the same dedication, as the Japanese soldiers defend their sovereign. What you should not do is interpret '*Yamato damashü*' as only linked to the Mikado. . . . If you promise to defend the integrity of the Brazilian fatherland, its institutions and order . . . this is the essence of '*Yamato damashü*.' " Put differently, something in the corporal nature of Japanese descent made *nikkei* the most loyal Brazilians possible.

Brazilian society cannot only be understood in terms of blacks and whites. Thousands of nonwhite / nonblack immigrants settled in the country, and many, including large segments of the Arab- and Japanese-descended communities, established themselves in the upper echelons of Brazil's social, economic, and political spheres. Using deeply rooted Brazilian myths about race and culture, members of these groups created a world for their hyphenated ethnicities by reconstructing elite discourse on "whitening" and "miscegenation." In many ways, the hegemony of the elite was broken as the descendants of Arab and Japanese immigrants fought to create a place for themselves as Brazilians.

Notes

1   Viriato Correia, "O Rei Salomão no Rio Amazonas," in *Album da Colonia Sírio Libanesa no Brasil,* edited by Salomão Jorge (São Paulo: Sociedade Impressora Brasileira, 1948), pp. 471–79.

2   Hachiro Fukuhara, "Brazil Founded by Asiastics?" in *Japan Times and Mail,* 26 June 1927; Hachiro Fukahara, "Nipponese Gets 2,500,000 Acres as a Basis for a Vast Colony," *Japan Times and Mail,* 11 May 1930.

3   Plínio Salgado, "Oriente (Impressões de Viagens) 1930," in *Obras Completas,* vol. 18 (São Paulo: Editôra das Americas, 1954–1956), p. 307.

4   Elias Farhat, in *Dinheiro na Estrada: Uma saga de imigrantes,* edited by Emil Farhat (São Paulo: T. A. Queiroz, 1986), p. 3. Translated into Portuguese by Afonso Nagib Sabbag.

The Myth of Racial Democracy

Abdias do Nascimento

The first voice protesting Brazilian racism against nonwhites was Abdias do Nascimento's. A black man born in the small city of Franca in São Paulo state to a mother who made candies to sell and a father who repaired shoes, he worked from the age of six as a delivery boy. He managed to study accounting and later economics, and fought in both the 1930 and 1932 military uprisings. By then, he had become a militant and worked for the betterment of conditions for blacks. After the 1964 military coup, he went into exile, joining the faculty of the State University of New York at Buffalo as well as the University of Ifé in Nigeria. He published more than twenty books on racial issues and, in 1994, founded the Negro Experimental Theater in Rio de Janeiro; he is also a painter and poet. In February 1997, Nascimento was elected to the Senate on the ticket of the small Democratic Labor Party. Blunt and outspoken, he was ignored by most Brazilian intellectuals, although those on the Left paid lip service to his criticisms of society. The following statement on race was made by Nascimento in a thematic issue of the left-wing journal Cadernos Brasileiros *on the eightieth anniversary of the 1888 "Golden Law" abolishing slavery. Nascimento was well aware of the U.S. civil rights movement, and frequently quoted James Baldwin and Martin Luther King as well as Jean-Paul Sartre.*

Now that eighty years have passed since the abolition of slavery in Brazil, it is opportune to look objectively at the results of the law of May 13, 1888. Are the descendants of African slaves really free? Where do Brazilian blacks really stand in relation to citizens of other racial origins, at all levels of national life?

More than ten years ago, a reporter from a prominent Rio de Janeiro magazine asked various persons of color to respond to these questions. But the interviews were never published, although the questions obviously remain valid and hold the same significance, because since then nothing has changed in the way blacks live in this country.

The abolitionist campaign stopped abruptly in 1888. . . . Abolition was a facade: juridical, theoretical, abstract. The ex-slaves were driven to the brink of starvation; they found only disease, unemployment, complete misery. Not only the elites, but all of Brazilian society closed the avenues through which blacks might have survived; they shut off the possibility of a decent, dignified life for the ex-slaves. They created a fabric of slogans about equality and racial democracy that has served to assuage the bad national conscience. Abroad, it presents our country as a model of racial coexistence; internally, the myth is used to keep blacks tricked and docile.

There was a phase during which the condition of blacks awakened the interest of scholars, especially in the Northeast. But although sincere, the intellectuals dealt with black culture as ethnographic material for their literary and academic exercises . . . [when, instead], the situation of blacks cried out for urgent practical action to improve radically their horrible existence . . .

It is a characteristic of our racial democracy myth that it accurately defines a "pathology of normality. . . . " There is no exaggeration here. We remember that Brazilians of dark pigmentation number nearly thirty million. Certain apostles of "whitening" would like to see the extinction of the Negro as an easy way to resolve the problem. . . . The white portion, or the less-Negro population, would continue to monopolize political power, economic power, access to schools, and to well-being, thanks to the legacy of the wretched "Golden Law," which Antonio Callado has correctly dubbed, "The Law of White Magic." Under the law of white magic, the black is as free as any other Brazilian. In practice—without any white or black magic—the Negro is simply this: a racial pariah consigned to the status of a subaltern.

Why should the Negro be the only one to pay for the onus of our "racial paradise"? I stand corrected. The Indian, as well, has been treated in the same way. According to a study by the federal government itself, practices to liquidate indigenous peoples have been employed in the [current] decade of the 1960s. Another mask yanked off the face of our vaunted Brazilian humanism, tempered with compassion and Christian spirit . . .

It is imperative for human dignity and a civic duty for Brazilians to struggle—blacks and whites—to transform the concept of racial democracy into reality. The Negro should organize to take up the promise deeded to him by history. This should be done without messianism, without hatred or resentment, but firmly and steadfastly in pursuit of the just place to which we are entitled. The Negro should create pressure groups, instruments for direct action. In the process, we will encounter our qualified leaders. Only through dynamic organization will the Negro obtain equality of opportunity and the status of a better life . . . not only for Brazilian blacks, but for all the Brazilian people.

Naturally, anything directed against the status quo runs risks. But Negroes run risks from the instant of their birth. Do not fear the label of "black racist," because the product of intimidation is docility. It is enough for us to know that our cause has integrity, and follows our conscience as democrats and humanists. Our historical experience shows us that antiracist racism is the only path capable of extinguishing the differences between races.

The National Day against Racism

Revista MNU

Formal protests against racism in Brazilian life have been rare, although groups organized in Salvador (Bahia) and São Paulo during the 1970s. They staged public demonstrations on May 13, the anniversary of the abolition of slavery in 1888, which they called a "national day against racism." Few whites responded to these protests, however, rejecting claims of prejudice by citing Brazil's lack of Jim Crow laws and its nominal achievement of racial democracy. The Movimento Negro Unificado (Unified Movement of Blacks or MNU) published a newspaper, Revista MNU, in which this article appeared in 1981.

Participating in São Paulo's antiracism campaign, more than 2,000 blacks protested on May 13 [Emancipation Day] in the Largo de Paissandú as well on the steps of the Municipal Theater, in remembrance of [what we have designated] the National Day against Racism. Other protests were held in Belo Horizonte, Salvador, Rio de Janeiro, and Brasília. Many of the speakers criticized the national government and the unemployment problem. "The worst victims of unemployment are us," said one of the members of the national executive committee of the MNU. An open letter distributed to the public asked everyone to look around them, in homes and among friends, to ascertain the gravity of the problems caused by unemployment in Brazil today. "Who does not have one unemployed friend today?" the leaflet asked. Members of the national executive committee also denounced the rising wave of police violence against the black population. "We are being abused psychologically as a part of a police plan to attack our mental condition as the first step in completely dominating us," said Milton Barbosa. Mrs. Geralda Severino, a domestic and the founding member of the association in her category, was roundly applauded when she said that domestics are treated as if they were slaves by Brazilian society. "I have been a maid all of my life and treated inhumanly. I worked so that you, the younger generation, can be better prepared to fight for our people. You have to do this, because I do not know if I will have enough time to fight until victory is achieved," she said, referring to her more than fifty years of life. She also encourages black women to fight: "we are women and we also have to claim our place in the sun. We have to fight alongside our comrades . . . and we have to organize, even if we are [only] domestic servants."

The Church

Tries to Combat Prejudice

Bernardete Toneto

Since the 1930s, Brazilians have boasted of their racial democracy. In recent years, however, an increasing number of Afro-Brazilians have denounced racial democracy as a myth. They point to discrimination in employment and education, the high poverty rates among Afro-Brazilians, and the many racial insults hurled at them daily. The Roman Catholic Church, historically a conservative institution in Brazil, has not escaped accusations of racial bias. The following article from the magazine Sem Fronteiras *discusses racism in the church. Its very publication in this church-sponsored journal indicates that Brazilians are ready to enter a new dialogue concerning race.*

"The Negro still is discriminated against by Brazilian society and the Catholic Church." The assertion is by Bishop José Maria Pires of the archdiocese of Paraíba. One of the principal Negro voices of the Catholic Church, "Dom Zumbi"—as he likes to be called and is most endearingly dubbed—calculates that, of the 400 Catholic bishops in Brazil, only 5 are Negroes. In the case of priests, the mathematics presents a balance even less exalting: of the approximately 14,000 clerics, some 200 are Negroes. "Organization and consciousness of our value and culture are still missing."

Dom Zumbi, at seventy-six years, thirty as bishop of a region where Negroes and Indians predominate, says that he never suffered open discrimination. But he remembered a pastoral visit made years ago to a small city in Paraíba. He was received with ceremony by the lady of a house who, during his departure, shot: "Look, to be sincere, I am seeing the color of his skin. But, as the gentleman is a bishop, for me he stopped being Negro."

He remembers that there was an era in which the Negroes remained in the church doorway, as if they were inferiors. Today, in his opinion, the Catholic Church is awakening to the Negro culture. "It is perceiving that the Word of God succeeds by means of being from the people." For him, after the awakening, the phase now is [one] of organization. A sign of this is the growth of seminary participation by religious men and women of the Agents of Pastoral Negroes. "There still is a long path to traverse, but we are showing a new way for the Church, based on the end of prejudices and on the recognition of our identity."

Father Antônio Aparecido da Silva, nicknamed "Toninho," agrees. Ex-director of the Our Lady of Assumption School of Theology and professor of theology at PUC [Catholic Pontifical University] of São Paulo, Toninho perceives advances in the Afro-pastoral: the Negro population is today the theme of pastoral reports and studies, and the priority in the majority of diocesan pastoral plans in the large cities. In the field of theology, studies and reflections are emerging that did not sprout from an academic form, but from communal experiences brought to the faculty chairs. "The point of departure for Afro-theology is the God of the poor. A Negro God, who is revealed in the very history of the Negro population, marginalized, that has him as the only source of safety."

Toninho was one of those who suffered discrimination when trying to enter the seminary. He prefers not to cite names, but he relates that he passed through a diocese and a congregation that did not accept him. He ended up entering the congregation of Dom Orione. "It is undeniable that prejudice exists. The CNBB [National Conference of Brazilian Bishops] itself recognizes that, until the Second Vatican Council, the diocesan seminaries and congregations that admitted male and female Negroes were rare." The theologian defends a liturgy that revives the principal elements of Negro culture, that in his opinion, are "efficient for representing the foundation for the project of the Kingdom of God, for expressing the utopia of the Christian faith." They are the clothes, the colors, the foods, the song, and the dance [of the Afro-Brazilians]. Bishop José Maria Pires thinks in the same manner. "The celebration cannot be with arms crossed, listening to lectures and hearing sermons. The people have to participate, dance, sing. They have to be excited when celebrating God's praises, not only with the mind but with the entire body. These are details that make up part of the Negro culture."

What Color Are You?

Brazilian Institute of Geography and Statistics

This list was drawn up in 1976 by the government agency responsible for taking the census—the Brazilian Institute of Geography and Statistics (IBGE)—to collect the terms used by people to describe their skin color. Polltakers simply asked people to identify their skin color; the results yielded the 134 different terms listed below. The study was commissioned in response to complaints that the five categories used by the agency—white, black, brown (parda), Indian, or Asian—were insufficient. Several of the expressions on the list describe physical attributes beyond skin color—crioula, for example, and agalegada. Brazilians have always considered such racial characteristics as hair texture, the shape of lips and noses, facial and body shape, as well as pigmentation of skin and hair. In North America, as we have noted, people are "white" or "black," although African Americans within their own community historically have used dozens of terms for shades of skin color and phenotype, like "high yellow." In the 1990 census, based on the IBGE's five terms for skin color, the Brazilian population divided up as follows: 55.3 percent white, 39.3 percent brown, 4.9 percent black, and 0.5 percent Asian; no statistics for Indians were provided. It is interesting that some people described themselves with terms that, when used by others, have pejorative connotations.

1. *Acastanhada* (cashewlike tint; caramel colored)
2. *Agalegada* (an often derogatory term for a Galician; features considered gross and misshapen)
3. *Alva* (pure white)
4. *Alva-escura* (dark or off-white)
5. *Alverenta* (or *aliviero,* "shadow in the water")
6. *Alvarinta* (tinted or bleached white)
7. *Alva-rosada* (or *jambote,* roseate, white with pink highlights)
8. *Alvinha* (bleached; whitewashed)

9. *Amarela* (yellow)
10. *Amarelada* (yellowish)
11. *Amarela-quemada* (burnt yellow or ochre)
12. *Amarelosa* (yellowed)
13. *Amorenada* (tannish)
14. *Avermelhada* (reddish, with blood vessels showing through skin)
15. *Azul* (bluish)
16. *Azul-marinho* (deep bluish)
17. *Baiano* (Bahian or ebony)
18. *Bem-branca* (very white)
19. *Bem-clara* (parchmentlike; translucent)
20. *Bem-morena* (very dusky)
21. *Branca* (white)
22. *Branca-avermelhada* (peach white)
23. *Branca-melada* (honey toned)
24. *Branca-morena* (darkish white)
25. *Branca-pálida* (pallid)
26. *Branca-queimada* (sunburned white)
27. *Branca-sardenta* (white with brown spots)
28. *Branca-suja* (dirty white)
29. *Branquiça* (a white variation)
30. *Branquinha* (whitish)
31. *Bronze* (bronze)
32. *Bronzeada* (bronzed tan)
33. *Bugrezinha-escura* (Indian characteristics)
34. *Burro-quando-foge* ("burro running away," implying racial mixture of unknown origin; the opposite of *cor-firma*)
35. *Cabocla* (mixture of white, Negro, and Indian)
36. *Cabo-verde* (black; Cape Verdean)
37. *Café* (coffee)
38. *Café-com-leite* (coffee with milk)
39. *Canela* (cinnamon)
40. *Canelada* (tawny)
41. *Cardão* (thistle colored)
42. *Castanha* (cashew)
43. *Castanha-clara* (clear, cashewlike)
44. *Castanha-escura* (dark, cashewlike)
45. *Chocolate* (chocolate brown)

46. *Clara* (light)
47. *Clarinha* (very light)
48. *Cobre* (copper hued)
49. *Corada* (ruddy)
50. *Cor-de-café* (tint of coffee)
51. *Cor-de-canela* (tint of cinnamon)
52. *Cor-de-cuia* (tea colored; prostitute)
53. *Cor-de-leite* (milky)
54. *Cor-de-oro* (golden)
55. *Cor-de-rosa* (pink)
56. *Cor-firma* ("no doubt about it")
57. *Crioula* (little servant or slave; African)
58. *Encerada* (waxy)
59. *Enxofrada* (pallid yellow; jaundiced)
60. *Esbranquecimento* (mostly white)
61. *Escura* (dark)
62. *Escurinha* (semidark)
63. *Fogoio* (florid; flushed)
64. *Galega* (see *agalegada* above)
65. *Galegada* (Ibid.)
66. *Jambo* (like a fruit the deep-red color of a blood orange)
67. *Laranja* (orange)
68. *Lilás* (lily)
69. *Loira* (blond hair and white skin)
70. *Loira-clara* (pale blond)
71. *Loura* (blond)
72. *Lourinha* (flaxen)
73. *Malaia* (from Malabar)
74. *Marinheira* (dark greyish)
75. *Marrom* (brown)
76. *Meio-amerela* (mid-yellow)
77. *Meio-branca* (mid-white)
78. *Meio-morena* (mid-tan)
79. *Meio-preta* (mid-Negro)
80. *Melada* (honey colored)
81. *Mestiça* (mixture of white and Indian)
82. *Miscigenação* (mixed—literally "miscegenated")
83. *Mista* (mixed)

84. *Morena* (tan)
85. *Morena-bem-chegada* (very tan)
86. *Morena-bronzeada* (bronzed tan)
87. *Morena-canelada* (cinnamonlike brunette)
88. *Morena-castanha* (cashewlike tan)
89. *Morena clara* (light tan)
90. *Morena-cor-de-canela* (cinnamon-hued brunette)
91. *Morena-jambo* (dark red)
92. *Morenada* (mocha)
93. *Morena-escura* (dark tan)
94. *Morena-fechada* (very dark, almost mulatta)
95. *Morenão* (very dusky tan)
96. *Morena-parda* (brown-hued tan)
97. *Morena-roxa* (purplish tan)
98. *Morena-ruiva* (reddish tan)
99. *Morena-trigueira* (wheat colored)
100. *Moreninha* (toffeelike)
101. *Mulatta* (mixture of white and Negro)
102. *Mulatinha* (lighter-skinned white-Negro)
103. *Negra* (Negro)
104. *Negrota* (Negro with a corpulent body)
105. *Pálida* (pale)
106. *Paraíba* (like the color of *marupa* wood)
107. *Parda* (dark brown)
108. *Parda-clara* (lighter-skinned person of mixed race)
109. *Polaca* (Polish features; prostitute)
110. *Pouco-clara* (not very clear)
111. *Pouco-morena* (dusky)
112. *Preta* (black)
113. *Pretinha* (black of a lighter hue)
114. *Puxa-para-branca* (more like a white than a mulatta)
115. *Quase-negra* (almost Negro)
116. *Queimada* (burnt)
117. *Queimada-de-praia* (suntanned)
118. *Queimada-de-sol* (sunburned)
119. *Regular* (regular; nondescript)
120. *Retinta* ("layered" dark skin)
121. *Rosa* (roseate)

122. *Rosada* (high pink)
123. *Rosa-queimada* (burnished rose)
124. *Roxa* (purplish)
125. *Ruiva* (strawberry blond)
126. *Russo* (Russian, see also *polaca*)
127. *Sapecada* (burnished red)
128. *Sarará* (mulatta with reddish kinky hair, aquiline nose)
129. *Saraúba* (or *saraiba:* like a white meringue)
130. *Tostada* (toasted)
131. *Trigueira* (wheat colored)
132. *Turva* (opaque)
133. *Verde* (greenish)
134. *Vermelha* (reddish)

Mixed Blood

Jefferson M. Fish

Dr. Jefferson M. Fish, a Caucasian clinical psychologist, and his African American wife, Dolores Newton, an anthropologist, have a daughter, Krekamey, who has just passed her medical board examinations. His essay on the differences in the way North Americans and Brazilians look at skin color and race is based on his daughter's experiences in Brazil, as well as on the way she looks at herself.

Last year, my daughter, who had been living in Rio de Janeiro, and her Brazilian boyfriend paid a visit to my cross-cultural psychology class at St. John's University. They had agreed to be interviewed about Brazilian culture. At one point in the interview I asked her, "Are you black?" She said, "Yes." I then asked him the question, and he said, "No."

"How can that be?" I asked. "He's darker than she is."

The short answer to the question, What is race? is: There is no such thing. Race is a myth. And our racial classification scheme is loaded with pure fantasy.

Consider the avocado—is it a fruit or a vegetable? Americans insist it is a vegetable. We eat it in salads with oil and vinegar. Brazilians, on the other hand, would say it is a fruit. They eat it for dessert with lemon juice and sugar.

How can we explain this difference in classification?

The avocado is an edible plant, and the American and Brazilian folk taxonomies, while containing cognate terms, classify some edible plants differently. The avocado does not change. It is the same biological entity; but its folk classification changes, depending on who's doing the classifying.

Perhaps the clearest way to understand that the American folk taxonomy of race is merely one of many—arbitrary and unscientific, like all the others—is to contrast it with a very different one, that of Brazil. The

Krekamey R. Fish.
(Dolores Newton)

Portuguese word that in the Brazilian folk taxonomy corresponds to the American *race* is *tipo*. *Tipo,* a cognate of the English word *type,* is a descriptive term that serves as a kind of shorthand for a series of physical features. Because people's physical features vary separately from one another, there are an awful lot of *tipos* in Brazil.

Since *tipos* are descriptive terms, they vary regionally in Brazil—in part, reflecting regional differences in the development of colloquial Portuguese, but also because the physical variation they describe is different in different regions. The Brazilian situation is so complex, I will limit my delineation of *tipos* to some of the main ones used in the city of Salvador, Bahia, to describe people whose physical appearance is understood to be made up of African and European features. (I will use the female terms throughout; in nearly all cases, the male term simply changes the last letter from "a" to "o.")

Proceeding along a dimension from the "whitest" to the "blackest" *tipos,* a *loura* is whiter than white, with straight blond hair, blue or green eyes, light skin color, narrow nose, and thin lips. Brazilians who come to the United States think that a *loura* means a "blond," and are surprised to find that the American term refers to hair color only. A *branca* has light skin color, eyes of any color, hair of any color or form except tight curly, a nose that is not broad, and lips that are not thick. *Branca* translates as "white," though Brazilians of this *tipo* who come to the United States—especially those from elite families—are often dismayed to find that they are not considered white here, and even worse, are viewed as Hispanic despite the fact that they speak Portuguese.

A *morena* has brown or black hair that is wavy or curly but not tight curly, tan skin, a nose that is not narrow, and lips that are not thin. Brazilians who come to the United States think that a *morena* is a "brunette," and are surprised to find that brunettes are considered white but *morenas* are not. Americans have difficulty classifying *morenas,* many of whom are of Latin American origin: Are they black or Hispanic? (One might also observe that *morenas* have trouble with Americans, for not just accepting their appearance as a given, but asking instead, "Where do you come from?" "What language did you speak at home?" "What was your maiden name?" or even, more crudely, "What are you?")

A mulatta looks like a *morena,* except with tight curly hair, and a slightly darker range of hair colors and skin colors. A *preta* looks like a mulatta, except with dark brown skin, broad nose, and thick lips. To Americans, mulattas and *pretas* are both black, and if forced to distinguish between them, would refer to them as light-skinned blacks and dark-skinned blacks, respectively.

If Brazilians were forced to divide the range of *tipos,* from *loura* to *preta,* into "kinds of whites" and "kinds of blacks" (a distinction they do not ordinarily make), they would draw the line between *morenas* and mulattas, whereas Americans, if offered only visual information, would draw the line between *brancas* and *morenas.*

The proliferation of *tipos,* and the difference in the white-black dividing line, do not, however, exhaust the differences between Brazilian and American folk taxonomies. There are *tipos* in the Afro-European domain that are considered to be neither black nor white—an idea that is difficult for Americans visiting Brazil to comprehend. A person with tight curly blond (or red) hair, light skin, blue (or green) eyes, broad nose, and thick lips, is a *sarará.* The opposite features—straight black hair, dark skin, brown eyes, narrow nose, and thin lips—are those of a *cabo verde. Sarará* and *cabo verde* are both *tipos* that are considered by Brazilians in Salvador, Bahia, to be neither black nor white.

When I interviewed my American daughter and her Brazilian boyfriend, she said she was black because her mother is black (even though

I am white). That is, from her American perspective, she has "black blood"—though she is a *morena* in Brazil. Her boyfriend said that he was not black because, viewing himself in terms of Brazilian *tipos*, he is a mulatto (not a *preto*).

There are many differences between the Brazilian and American folk taxonomies of race. The American system tells you about how people's parents are classified, but not what they look like. The Brazilian system tells you what they look like, but not about their parents. When two parents of intermediate appearance have many children in the United States, the children are all of one race; in Brazil, they are of many *tipos*.

Americans believe that race is an immutable biological given, but people (like my daughter and her boyfriend) can change their race by getting on a plane and going from the United States to Brazil—just as, if they take an avocado with them, it changes from a vegetable into a fruit. In both cases, what changes is not the physical appearance of the person or avocado, but the way they are classified.

VIII

Realities

Everyday life obscures from view the exertions of millions of Brazilians to earn enough to make ends meet. The coping strategies that the poor use are creative and diverse, but they do not always work. They include tactics to create and stretch income; political tactics (organizing, voting as a bloc, negotiating with politicians); economic ones (the irregularity of work patterns, for example); and cultural ones (the adoption of beliefs, symbols, and attitudes that govern behavior). Language can be a tool to sustain morale and fight back.

But the poorest Brazilians do not have the luxury of devising long-range strategies because they have to scratch to provide enough food to assuage hunger. Homeless people and shantytown residents in Brazilian cities eat the foods left on the ground in *macumba* offerings. When people are hungry, or when acting aggressively or according to socially unacceptable norms promises to yield more benefits than allowable behavior, more desperate behavior often ensues, even among people considered docile. Over the centuries, around the world, those in dire need have turned to begging. Brazil is no exception. For generations, beggars have thronged the streets of Brazilian cities, many deformed, displaying diseased limbs or vile rashes, scooting legless down the sidewalk on crude wheeled boards, or holding infants screaming from hunger. Many sat in the same place—at the foot of bridges or in front of important buildings—for years. Blind beggars had children in tow to guide them.

During the 1960s, Rio de Janeiro's governor, Carlos Lacerda, was believed to have ordered the police to clear the streets of beggars, gathering them up in trucks and dumping them in sacks into the river; similar stories were believed in Recife and many other cities in the Northeast. The affect of these "street cleanings" lasted only a few weeks, however, as swarms of new beggars from the interior took the place of the ones displaced. Affluent Brazilians learned to avoid beggars, just as Americans avoid homeless people in the streets. "They never get to keep what one gives them," one explanation went; others swore that mendicants earned too much from begging, or that they spent what they got on alcohol, which may have been true in some cases.

Street life also is home to public festivities, and especially the exuberant annual pre-Lenten festival of Carnival, that permit the temporary suspension of status and the flight of passions in percussive rhythm, movement, and revelry. These activities, however, often deteriorate into *brigas* (violent brawls), whereby drunken men beat women, robbers prey on bystanders, and street brawlers fight and stab one another with knives. Most Carnival participants channel whatever aggression they may have through mimicry, in their costumes, and in musical forms of stylized belligerence. Carnival tolerates aggression by labeling it play, and by ignoring the year's harvest of Carnival injuries and murders in clubs, bars, and on the street. Mimicry requires agreement from both parties, and when this agreement breaks down, violence may result. Carnival affords opportunities to *desabafar,* to get things off one's chest, to expel the year's accumulated frustration and anger. When it ends in bloodshed, it is a sign that the system has broken down.[1]

Brazilians have adopted marvelous ways of coping with the reality of their lives. Millions play the lottery and the ubiquitous numbers games daily, placing bets in bars, shops, and on street corners in every Brazilian town and city. Clayton S. Cooper's excerpt below offers details from 1917; in many ways little has changed, although in recent decades, the chiefs of numbers operations have gone public, sometimes flexing their political power, or becoming prominent in samba schools and soccer team management. Today's numbers games are interwoven with crime and drugs; earlier times seemed—at least outwardly—more innocent. Other realities of Brazilian life include abortion, which is illegal—but used to terminate one in five pregnancies; religious diversity (evangelical Protestantism and Afro-Brazilian spiritism vie with Roman Catholicism for the attentions of the faithful far more than one might imagine); and a spirited, tolerant joy of life that in its own way serves as a powerful coping mechanism in a world that does not treat individuals equitably.

Note

1 See Daniel Touro Linger, *Dangerous Encounters: Meanings of Violence in a Brazilian City* (Stanford, Calif.: Stanford University Press, 1992); and Robert M. Levine, *Brazilian Legacies* (Armonk, N.Y.: M. E. Sharpe, 1997).

The Animal Game

Clayton S. Cooper

The Jogo do Bicho (Animal Game) is a most curious Brazilian institution. On almost any Brazilian street corner, one might see a bicheiro (bookie) routinely taking bets and making payoffs. While tax and vice laws make this form of gambling doubly illegal, in effect, the game's popularity and the wealth amassed by Bicho's kingpins have ruled out serious enforcement of the laws. A visitor, Clayton S. Cooper, described in 1917 Brazilians' fascination with gambling.

Certain it is that Brazil goes other Latin American republics one better in her daily lottery (Argentina seems satisfied with a weekly lottery), occasional state lotteries, private lotteries, and the special joy of the whole populace, the daily Jogo do Bicho. To say that the native club life and much of the amusement hall life of the larger cities centers about the gaming table, with its "57" or more varieties of games of chance, would not be far from the truth. The capital city, Rio de Janeiro, is the national center of this form of amusement, as it is the guide and gauge of so many other things Brazilian. The main streets in the federal city are provided with lottery vendors' counters, and on the main thoroughfares, he who would invest his *mil-réis* on a turn of the wheel, or the winning numbers, will find tickets at his hand in cigar stores, small book stalls, and in the outstretched hands of newsboys, beggars, and even small children. Sometimes the seller may have but a single piece of crumpled, bluish paper that he proffers you for a small sum—but there is always the chance that it may carry the triumphant arrangement of figures when the afternoon announcement is made.

It is at least gambling in the open. There is no hypocrisy about it, no subterfuges, no sneaking away behind barred doors. It is too universal with high and low to be associated with any suspicion of disgrace. It is a remark commonly heard in Rio that "everybody buys a lottery ticket, if not daily, at least occasionally," and even the foreigners do not seem to be immune, but fall more or less generally into the national habit, especially at the times of the special and Christmas lottery drawings. When the day of "muckraking" and reform movements strikes Brazil, if it ever does, when pestiferous committees of "investigation" follow as they have here in the United States, their members being paid salaries to unearth evils rather than try to build up the good, the lotteries and the gambling habits will probably be the last and toughest proposition they will tackle. One prominent Brazilian told me that if the police tried to close up gambling, there would be a popular revolution.

Here again, one sees striking contrasts with conditions in the North. The national lottery is a government affair, and as much of a Brazilian institution as the national library or the Brazilian Chamber of Commerce. A federal concession is given to the Companhia Loterias Nacionaes do Brazil for drawing lotteries throughout the Republic. This company takes pride in the fact that it conducts its business with strict regard to honesty and the elimination of fraud; (whatever this proud boast may mean to the losing participants, who find that there are many chances to one against them in the matter of ever beating the "machine," may be conjectured).

Yet in a country where it is maintained by many that lotteries are a necessity for the people, it is an advantage to have them conducted decently, in order, and under the inspection of the government. The customers rarely find fault with the lottery companies, no matter how hard the results may go against them, which would seem to argue that the enterprise is conducted in a mechanically correct fashion.

Charities benefit largely by the lottery. Asylums, schools, and charitable houses of various kinds all over the country are beneficiaries, since apart from the prizes distributed daily, the company is obliged by law to contribute yearly somewhat more than $500,000 to charities that the government selects, plus 5 percent of the prizes exceeding in amount 200 *mil-réis*. There is a strict government inspection and supervision, and the lottery company is evidently in a most prosperous condition, its shares standing high in the market. The directors are chosen from among the prominent men in the nation, the names of ex-ministers of government and members of the leading commercial associations of the land being found on the company's board of governors. It is thus apparent that Brazil does not "tolerate" the lottery; she originates, governs, and promotes it, and in a fashion complementary at least to the Brazilian's business ability in organization.

The Brazilian or foreigner who draws the first prize in the government lottery receives a comfortable sum, ranging from 16 *contos* ($4,000) to 500 *contos* ($125,000). The wheel of chance turns often toward the clerk, the small shopkeeper, or sometimes to the head of a very poor family in the rural sections, where the tickets are sold almost as generally as in the cities. There are also compensations for many who fail of the first prize, since each daily list contains many prizes, and the drawer gets back the value of his ticket, if he draws only the last digit of the chief winning number.

On any afternoon in the federal capital of Rio de Janeiro, one who is on the watch will witness a Sister of Mercy trailing a number of young orphan children along the Avenida Rio Branco toward the lottery company's offices, where the drawings are made at about three o'clock. At the time of the drawings, a small Brazilian maiden is posted at each of the six or seven or ten wheels, as the size of the day's lottery requires, and each small miss twists her wheel in unison with the others at the given command. When the wheels stop, the spectators look with that peculiar intentness known to the devotee of the whirligig of fortune, to see the total figure made by the combined twists of the wheels. This is the first prize number. Now, a blasé gentleman with a bored and apathetic expression calls out impassively, *"Cem contos de reis"* or *"Ducentos mil-réis,"* as chance may have it. It is at this highly interesting and thrilling moment of the Brazilian day that thousands of little red signals begin to bob up all at once in the distracted eyes of the telephone girls in the exchanges, and from the rich coffee fazenda in the rural sections to the suburban residence of the capital's Copacabana district, they are asking the same thing—the winning number—after hearing this, things go on as usual, and the next day the same thrill is repeated.

But popular as is the national lottery, the little animal known as the *bicho*—in Portuguese, this word means insect, animal, or thing—and which represents the form of gambling that is the particular joy of the common people as well as those higher up, holds the front of the stage in fortune's show. The Jogo do Bicho is "illegal," but despite this fact, it is just now the universal favorite among Brazilian games of chance, and the authorities make only spasmodic and false-alarm attempts to check its merry career. This form of gambling, which is based on the numbers that come out in the national lottery, affects more directly the pockets of the working people and Brazil's poor, for which reason it is undoubtedly a pleasure with a sting to it. I asked the superintendent of the municipal lodging house in Rio de Janeiro what brought the majority of the 1,000 men there nightly, and he answered, "the Bicho." In the United States, the reply under similar circumstances would probably be "drink," but liquor is not the national vice in Brazil. The weakness of the lower-class man in this republic runs in the direction of the gaming table, or the too-excessive attention to the game of love and women. The emotional, romantic temperament is not confined to the poets and statesmen; it runs a continuous thread through the entire national fabric of life. The same traits seek for expression in the fishman who brings you the daily fish and in the rich planter; it would be difficult to find a waiter, a ditch-digger, a stevedore on the great docks, or a policeman who lifts his hat obsequiously at your question, who does not take his more or less regular fling at these small magic *bichos,* the midget animals that swim in silver seas before the eyes of those who live laborious days in the great tropical republic.

How Brazil Works

Robert M. Levine

*Brazilians spend untold time entangled in the bureaucratic labyrinth. Some
cases of hopeless dealings stretch out for years. Starting in the early years of the
twentieth century, for those who could afford it or who possessed political influence, however, an antidote emerged in the person of the* despachante, *a professional facilitator able to cut through the red tape. Sometimes, bribery was involved, or small favors, but usually* despachantes *simply got things done (for a
fee) faster and without hassle because they knew the right people on the inside.
Some veteran* despachantes *seemed to have magical powers. Passports for
which mere mortals have to wait in line for hours, then return for a second or
third or fourth time to wait at the federal police headquarters, are issued in
minutes. Documents not available at all by legal means materialize the same
way. The first part of this section shows how* despachantes *form part of the
world of the* jeito, *the Brazilian way of getting things done.*

*Another practice is the intimidating ritual. In urban Latin America, where
the gap between the very rich and very poor is great indeed, and where in many
cases, rich and poor work or even live in close physical proximity, the affluent
intimidate to get their way, as portrayed in the second part below. The mulatto
novelist Affonso Henriques de Lima Barreto satirized the use and abuse of titles
in his World War I–era novel,* Recordações de Escrivão Isaías Caminha; *his
novel about the imaginary republic of the United States of Bruzundanga, a
pseudo-Brazil, mocks the entrance examinations required by prestigious Brazilian professional schools: "Passing the preliminaries, the future leaders of the
republic, the United States of Bruzundanga, take courses of study and end up
more ignorant and presumptuous than they were when they entered. They are
the sort who loudly boast, 'I have a degree. You are talking to a man with a
degree!'"*

I. The *Jeito*

M., a maid working in an affluent condominium complex in São Paulo, at twenty-four married a seventeen-year-old young man and had a child. When her mother-in-law told her that she couldn't care for the baby all the time, M. sent for an eleven-year-old girl from the interior, telling people that she was "adopting" her. The girl, who presumably attended school a few hours each day, otherwise worked without papers (or wages) for M. as her servant.

What M. did is as much a part of the informal economy as it is a legal ruse, since she did not have to obtain permission from any civil authorities to bring the girl to her home. In cases where regulations have to be confronted, Brazilians pride themselves on being especially creative in their array and variety of gambits suitable for bending rules. Most of these ploys work best, of course, for those with connections, even as low level as a friend of a relative who works in a certain office or department. The system also bends for those who can throw their weight around. Thus, facing down a policeman trying to write a ticket on an illegally parked car is easy for someone wearing a Rolex and educated in an elite private school, because the weaker party to the action knows full well that society expects him to back away.

One element in the political culture that is available to almost everyone possessing a modicum of poise and self-respect is the *jeito*. The *jeito* (diminutive, *jeitinho*) is the "way" to grease the wheels of government or the bureaucracy to obtain a favor, or to bypass rules or regulations. *Jeitos* fall halfway between legitimate favors and out-and-out corruption, but at least in popular understanding, they lean in the direction of the extra-legal. Favors, in addition, imply a measure of reciprocity, a courtesy to be returned. One never pays for a favor, however, but a *jeito*, which is often granted by someone who is not a personal acquaintance, must be accompanied by a tip or even a larger payoff.

Peter Kellemen's 1963 tongue-in-cheek *Brazil for Beginners* offers an example of how the system worked even within the bureaucracy. A recent graduate of a European medical school was applying for a visa to emigrate to Brazil at the Brazilian Consulate in Paris. When he appeared, the Brazilian consul changed the applicant's profession from physician to agronomist. When the candidate protested, saying that he did not want to sign a false statement, the consul told him: "In that way I can issue you a visa immediately. You know how these things are? Professional quotas, confidential instructions from the department of immigration. Utter nonsense! . . . In any event, this way will make it perfectly legal." The consul explained that he was helping the applicant by employing the *jeito*. After the physician took up residence in Brazil, he understood: he had immigrated to a country, law professor Keith S. Rosenn notes, "where laws and regulations are enacted upon the assumption that a substantial percentage will be disobeyed," and where, quoting Kelleman, "civil servants, be they small or powerful, create their own law. Although this law does not happen to correspond with the original law, it meets with general approbation, provided that it is dictated by common sense."

Several kinds of behavior are associated with the *jeito*. Officials fail to perform a legal duty (for example, contracts to the highest briber); persons employ subterfuges to circumvent a legal obligation that is proper (underinvoicing import shipments, receiving part of the purchase price abroad in foreign currency to evade currency control and taxes on part of the profits); speedy completion of paperwork only in exchange for a bribe or because the official knows the applicant; skirting an unreasonable or economically prejudicial legal obligation (for instance, laws requiring compensating bank balances or deposits at low interest); failure to enforce rules or laws because the official thinks that the law is unjust or unrealistic (the example of the visa applicant). The first three cases are corrupt, but the last two fall into a grey area where public purposes are arguably served by evading legal obligations. Some applications of the *jeito,* of course, involve mixed kinds of motives, combining payoffs or favoritism with a sense that the outcome will be reasonable and even legitimate.

Jeitos affect everyone. Once I was traveling to the interior of Rio Grande do Norte, a desolate backlands region with few signs of life. The van in which I was riding broke down outside a tiny, dusty town. The passengers and driver walked to the village to attempt to find parts to fix the motor; while we were sitting in a café, waiting, a man came in and identified himself as the police chief. He wore no uniform and showed no badge, but everyone in the café showed him deference and we assumed that he was some kind of official. He then asked to see our documents. The Brazilians had their federal identity cards; I had my passport.

The official demanded that each of the Brazilians pay the equivalent of $6 for being given "refuge" in his town, and he "fined" the driver of the van a slightly lower amount for having obstructed the roadway. Then he turned to me. He asked me what a foreigner was doing in his town. I told him. He then asked to see my passport, taking it and thumbing through the pages one by one. "Why had I gone to Mexico?" he asked me, seeing a visa stamp issued in Mérida. "Venezuela?" "France?" Was I working for the "U.S. Intelligence Service?" I assured him that I was carrying out historical research. "What do you have with you?" he asked. I showed him my camera and lenses, and my notebook. He then grabbed my camera bag and passport, and stalked out the door.

More than two hours later, well after midnight, he returned. The van had been fixed by then and was sitting with its motor running because the driver was impatient to leave. I had visions of being stuck in this town or even being put in jail. Then the man returned. With a broad grin, he handed me my camera case and passport. On one of the blank visa pages, he had painstakingly issued a "visa" for me to enter his town. It was handwritten, with various misspellings, and it had a cutout printed paragraph from what probably was the state *Diário Oficial* pasted in—a regulation covering one rule or another that did not seem even closely pertinent to this case. He then demanded $140 for the "processing fee." At this point, my Brazilian host interceded, pulling him aside in conversation. He then hustled me and the others out to the van, and we drove off. He told me later that he had given the man about $2 and told him that he "should be honored to have a university professor passing through his jurisdiction."

II. Intimidating Rituals

When a *porteiro* (doorman), dressed in a frayed uniform and carrying his starchy lunch in a tin box as early as 5:00 or 6:00 A.M. after walking down hundreds of steps from his favela house (or arriving from a two-hour bus ride over bumpy roads from the periphery of the city), is asked by an impatient, immaculately dressed professional man or woman to carry something, or to run back for something forgotten, or hastily to clean their car of the dust accumulated overnight, sparks may fly, but the door-man is expected to react humbly, without complaint. Many such employees, fearing the loss of their jobs, respond by adopting an air of near-total silence, often interpreted by employers as docility. Sometimes, this is internalized and becomes part of that person's personality, exhibited even outside of the employment framework. In other cases, the door-man (or the domestic servant, or the dishwasher, or the crossing guard) goes home and becomes another person, sometimes a tyrant, a hard drinker, or a wife or child abuser. These behavior traits are not seen by the employer class, because the private lives of the poor are well hidden, rendered all but invisible except for moments when that aggressive be-havior crosses back over the boundary, such as in instances when a *mar-ginal* (marginalized man or woman) breaks the law, and is arrested for drunkenness or stealing.

This situation is exacerbated by the attitudes of some persons of higher status. Roberto DaMatta has captured the elite's expectation of defer-ence and special treatment in identifying the ritual importance of the phrase, *"Você sabe com quem está falando?"* ("Do you know who you're talking to?"), the embodiment of the ritual that plays out when someone powerful is challenged by someone of lower status, such as in the case of a policeman confronting someone who has parked illegally, blocking traffic. Even physical size can be a factor in this kind of exchange: traffic cops are usually small and thin (in comparison to the burly members of the military police, or the police *delegados* who deal with crime), in con-trast to the wealthy, who can be fit and athletic. Even if the offensive big shot is short and paunchy, his use of intimidating language makes per-fectly clear what DaMatta terms the "radical and authoritarian separa-tion between two social positions that are objectively or conceptually differentiated in terms of the rules of classification of Brazilian culture." This behavior reflects the true nature of social distance, and belies the myth endorsed by Gilberto Freyre and others of the Brazilian as cordial and tolerant of others. It takes other forms. For example, the common practice by affluent teenagers of cutting ahead in line, or cheating in school, because they are privileged.

Whether intentional or not, people in high positions intimidate. Being a *filho de papai* (the father's son, implying nepotism) counts for a great deal in Brazilian life. Verbal and behavioral reminders of status, in fact, have in many cases grown in use in recent decades, as traditional marks of social position—for men, for example, the cream-colored linen suits worn by true whites of seignorial class, or fountain pens and walking sticks—went out of fashion. As a researcher in Brazil, I found this out the hard way. Waiting in line at a bakery counter in Ipanema on a Sunday morning during the military dictatorship, I was rudely pushed back by a man wearing shorts who bolted ahead of me. I muttered something about *"falta de educação"* and beckoned to the clerk to do something about what was, by any account, a blatant violation of propriety. The clerk looked away, as did everyone else in line. Walking away after the purchase was finally made, another person who had been standing in line with me whispered that I'd better be damned careful. The man who had cut into line was a colonel in the military police, he told me, who usually sent a servant to buy things for him while he waited in his car.

I also remember Asís, the doorman of a residential apartment house on Recife's Boa Viagem. An emaciated *caboclo* born in the *zona da mata* a half hour to the east of the city, with sunken, swollen eyes, he lived with his family in a hut that could not have been more than fifty square feet in size, behind the elevator. When residents of the building approached, Asís would lower his gaze to the pavement, avoiding eye contact in the same manner as slaves and other blacks on the streets of colonial and nineteenth-century Brazil. There was a chute near the elevator on every floor into which maids threw refuse, and Asís, several times a day, would tip back the dumpster on the ground floor, taking out anything in the garbage that was edible or could be scavenged. Sometimes, Asís permitted ragged children from the neighborhood to enter the dumpster room with him. One day, I saw him being confronted by the head of the building's *condomínio,* the residents' association, and ordered to stop "abusing" his position by taking the garbage. *"Mais amor e menos confiança,"* I heard the man say: "Show respect and less impertinence." Asís groveled and promised to obey. Within a month or so, one of Asís's small children died. Rats now infested the grounds of the building. Then Asís and his family disappeared; another doorman took his place. It turned out that when Asís asked the *condomínio* president for an advance from his salary to pay for the burial of his child, he was fired on the spot.

Iansã Is Not Saint Barbara

Ilé Axé Opô Afonjá

Scholars routinely debate whether Brazilian Candomblé is a syncretic religion. Simply stated, one side considers it a true marriage of African and European religions, while the other claims that slaves only used Catholicism to disguise their African beliefs. Consulting the faith's actual practitioners would certainly enrich the discussion. The following selection from the Internet not only tackles syncretism, but also addresses the public's recent fascination with Candomblé.

The word *Candomblé* is synonymous with African religion. It was always used in this sense, and still is today. This explains lots of things. Let's see. The Negro was uprooted from his land and sold as merchandise, enslaved. Here he arrived as slave, object; from his land he departed as a free man. During the journey, the slave traffic, he lost his personality, identification, but his culture, his history, his landscape, his experiences, they came with him. These seeds, this knowledge, found a soil, an earth that resembled Africa, although strangely inhabited. Fear imposed itself, but the faith, the belief—what they knew—had an urge to express itself. There emerged the cults (*Onilé*—later confused with the cult of *Caboclo,* one of the first versions of syncretism), there emerged the anger and the necessity of being free. The spells (*ebós*), the *quilombos,* appeared.

The 300-year history of Negro enslavement in Brazil shows, before all else, the resistance, the organization of the Negroes. The African culture lived, for them, through their belief, through their religion. What one believes, desires, is stronger than what one experiences whenever there is a limited situation. The religion, its organization in *terreiros* (terrace or cleared land near a house, also a *Candomblé* temple) and *roças* (small farms), was—as it was extensively written—the resistance of the Negroes. They resisted because there was organization. Organization within one's self. Every Negro used to have, or knew that his grandfather had, a light, a guide, a protective *Orixá* [a *Candomblé* spirit].

The culture survived, the *axé* (sacred spirit) grew, and it appeared in society under the form of the *Candomblé* houses (religion of the Yoruba Negroes). It was a "Negro thing," and as such, something furtive, ignorant, despised, and quickly translated as a bad thing, the devil's doing; good and bad, right and wrong, white and black. Those were the oppressing antagonisms, without any alternative possibility. The Negro, to be accepted, decided to behave as if he were a white. He used to say: "Sir, we are dancing and playing to *Senhor do Bomfim,* your saint, my Sir! It is not to *Oxalá,* or rather, *Oxalá* is the father, he is the same as *Senhor do Bomfim.*" Syncretism was installed. It was a way of resistance that generated a great burden, severe disfigurement, and scars. The dynamic, the social process is implacable. Immobility does not maintain itself. The sons of the Africans now said they did not have confidence in Brazilian-born Negroes (the *sigidi,* for example, an enchantment for invisibility, and a basic teaching, was not taught). Many things were lost, the African land was reduced to small portions, but *Candomblé* had effectiveness; the patron used to look for the old Negro woman to do a spell, to give him a bath of leaves, to give him an amulet. It began the proliferation of *terreiros*. Alienation, massification, tourism, folklore.

But the great initiates, like the ones who created the African land in Brazil, still exist. Odé Kayode–Mãe Stella de Oxossi in 1983 said: "*Iansã* is not Saint Barbara." She showed that *Candomblé* is not a sect; it is a religion independent from Catholicism. The earth trembled; some people began to complain: "We always went to the mass, always the last blessing, after the initiation, was in the church, we do the mass with the corpse present when someone dies, this can't change." It was the alienated tradition versus the coherent revolution, it was the breaking of the last chain. The dam was broken, and the water fertilized the almost sterile fields of survival. The Negro is free. He came from Africa, he has a history, a religion equal to any other, and what's more, it is not polytheist but monotheist: *Olorum,* the creator of the cosmos, is above all the *Orixás*. Raimundo Nina Rodrigues told us that once he asked a *Babalorixá* [a male *Candomblé* priest] why he didn't receive *Olorum,* and he heard the following answer: "Doctor, if I were to receive him, I would explode."

Now a new limit, a new configuration installs itself. At this end of the century, with the deterioration of the traditional religious institutions, with the appearance of new religions, with the alternative esoteric doctrines, *Candomblé,* now taken as a religion, is also seen as an efficient agency: it solves problems, cures diseases, calms the head. The whites want to be Negroes, we no longer hear of "the Negro with a white soul." Now the privilege is to be white with a Negro soul, to have ancestry, "to have an intrigue, a history with the saint." The *Iyalorixás* [female *Candomblé* priests] and *Babalorixás* question themselves as never before. The traps, the "bounty hunters," are installed. They are the congresses, the television—the media—the books, the "web" in a sense. We transform all this into tongs to separate wheat from chaff, that is the reason we are here. Saying what we are, we give conditions to perceive what is posed and to understand the supposed, the opposed, and the apposed. Differentiation is knowledge; *Candomblé* is a religion, it is not a sect.

The *Iyalorixás* organize the head. The process of organizing the *ori* is *awo* (secret). *Candomblé* is a religion that works with the secret, the silent side of the being, what belongs to *Olorum. Candomblé* organizes what is fragmented, opening channels of expression to the human being.

Upward Mobility Is Possible

Alcides Nazário Guerreiro Britto

*Although Brazil's rigid class society and the paucity of free public education
made it very difficult for ordinary people to better their station in life, some did.
This is the story of a young man from a poor family in the far north who set out
to make his fortune and managed to better his situation significantly through a
career in the armed forces. He was not from the poorest class—his father and
mother both held jobs, the mother as a teacher—but neither was his a life of
privilege. His story illustrates how Brazil's modernization opened undreamed-
of opportunities for some.*

Alcides Nazário Guerreiro Britto was the sixth of seven children born to
a poor family in Belém, in the state of Pará. He was a runt when he was a
baby, small and thin. In this regard, he was just like most of the other
children born into poverty in that place. His father could not afford a
hospital, so he was born at home. Nor were there either taxis or am-
bulances, because on July 24, 1924, there had been a military insurrection
in the Belém barracks, and Alcides was born four days later.

When he was six, his parents sent him to primary school because they
could not pay for private school tuition. It was a good school, but without frills, and it provided no social connections. His family lived in a tiny
house alongside the railroad tracks. Cinders from the wood-burning
engines frequently wafted into the house and onto the street where
barefooted children played. The smoke affected their lungs. His father
was a doorman; his mother an elementary teacher. Alcides always remained short in stature. When he reached his full height, he only stood
1.60 meters high.

Belém, from the end of the nineteenth century, had been one of the
most prosperous cities in Brazil as a result of the rubber boom. But when
it ended, after World War I, the regional economy became depressed.

Alcides Nazário Guerreiro Britto
as a young officer in the 1940s.
*(Rosane Pereira and Alcides Nazário
Guerreiro Britto)*

The people of Belém were never forced to live in misery, however, because the river teemed with fish and the tropical forests surrounding the
city yielded fruit.

Alcides's family, because his parents had jobs, were part of the urban
lower-middle class. Many youths with rudimentary education opted to
migrate south, since there were more jobs there. Alcides decided to leave
with the others. His mother had died in 1934, some of his older brothers
had already migrated, and his oldest sister, Luiza, could stay at home and
take care of the younger ones. Meanwhile, the depression made life even
more precarious. Government agencies no longer paid in cash, but issued "tickets" (scrip). His mother was paid this way until her death of a
heart condition. Life was harsh. Families in Belém who could not feed
their children often had judges from the juvenile court system send their
young girls to state orphanages, which then loaned them out to families
as maids in exchange for room and board. Unfortunately, the young men
of these families often initiated themselves sexually with these maids,
and when the girls became pregnant, they were kicked out and sent to
brothels.

In 1943, after a thirty-day trip by canoe, on boxcars, and on the back of a mule, Alcides arrived in Recife. He had finished primary school in Belém. Although the city had an active commercial life, he could neither find a job nor a place in a secondary school. Abandoning Recife, he migrated to Rio de Janeiro, the federal capital, where he knew some colleagues who had gone there from Belém. He went by ship, on a commercial steamer that had been commandeered during wartime by the navy to transport troops. It was empty, so he was given a ride without having to pay his passage. He found a job as an office boy.

A year later, Alcides sat for the entrance examination at Rio de Janeiro's military academy. He passed the test, was admitted as a student, and received a stipend to pay for uniforms and books. He graduated three years later as a subofficer (*aspirante*). The upward trajectory of his career had started.

In 1947, he was assigned to Natal, on Brazil's northeastern bulge. The city had been transformed during the war by the presence of thousands of soldiers, sailors, and airmen from the United States who had been stationed there. In Natal, Alcides met his future wife, Maria, who would become the mother of his only child, Angelo, named after his paternal grandfather. He then was transferred to Belém, the city of his birth. He tried to reunite with his family, but his father had died, and most of his family members and friends had left. Economic conditions in Belém were still precarious, but the army paid Alcides's salary and provided housing.

He rose through the ranks. When he made captain, he was transferred to the south of the country, to Santa Maria. There, he encountered another Brazil, a world totally different from what he had known, a region dominated by immigrants from Italy, Germany, Poland, and the Ukraine. It was now the early 1950s, and Alcides decided to study engineering. He took and passed the entrance examination for the Military Engineering Institute (IME). He graduated in 1958. After an initial assignment as a military engineer that he dispatched successfully, he was sent for eighteen months to Belgium, where he did graduate work in engineering. When he returned, he was named to the IME's faculty. By this time, he had reached the rank of lieutenant colonel. He spoke French; he owned his own home; he owned a *sítio*, a rural property where his family could relax; he possessed an automobile.

He was promoted to full colonel and named commander of the army proving grounds at Marambaia in the state of Rio de Janeiro. His marriage failed, however, and he divorced his wife. In 1970, he joined the faculty of the new Gama Filho University. Angelo, his son, graduated with a degree in business administration. Of Alcides's four grandchildren, the oldest took a degree in civil engineering. Angelo owns a house, an imported car, has health insurance, and his younger children attend private school. Alcides retired from the army in 1982. In 1997, he was seventy-four years of age. He is remarried, and because he retired with the rank of army general, he receives a pension of U.S.$78,000 a year. He lives in a penthouse in one of Rio's most elegant neighborhoods, owns several foreign cars, and spends two months every year traveling in Europe.

Crab and Yoghurt

Tobias Hecht

*Tobias Hecht is a writer, literary translator, and anthropologist. He is the author of a book of nonfiction based on ethnographic fieldwork with homeless children in Brazil (*At Home in the Street: Street Children of Northeast Brazil*). Like his ethnography, this short story is set in the city of Recife. "Crab and Yoghurt," based loosely on a tale told to the author by a homeless girl, concerns the encounter between a young, gun-toting but still thumb-sucking prostitute and her crippled client. Victim and perpetrator, hatred and mother-adoration merge in this glimpse of Recife's underworld, as the young girl watches her legless client climb the stairs and skate to his room in a boarding house.*

Conceição wondered how the man would ascend the steep, narrow staircase. He wasn't old, not nearly so old as João Defunto, whom she met from time to time at the Chantecler nor half so frail as Seu Dário, the watchman at the post office. She could even discern the muscles that bristled tentatively around his shoulders and forearms. He did not totter from side to side because one leg was made forever childlike from polio. Nor did he lurch haltingly like the old ladies in the favelas who drag a bloated foot at the end of a leg, thin and tired but spared as yet from elephantiasis. The man simply stopped in the middle. He had no feet. He had no legs.

The street urchins called him Caranguejo, for he moved like his namesake, the crab. Through the veil of inhaled glue, it seemed to the children that when the man slid along the sidewalks, one hand thrust frenetically before the other, he had not one pair of hands but several. He would weave along the sidewalks among Recife's languid strollers, surprising those he passed that the top half of a man could not only move of its own accord but was possessed of an urge to move faster than they. Some of the children even thought the man suspended his body in the air an inch above the ground with the reluctant strength of his arms. But Conceição knew otherwise.

She discovered his secret when once he had passed quite close to her. Conceição was sitting along the wharves. She realized that Caranguejo did not bob in the way one would imagine fitting for a man who *walked* with his hands and carried his torso. His body remained at a steady elevation above the earth, never descending fully to slap the hot pavement. As he approached, Conceição heard the pained cry of rusty metal.

Caranguejo's hands propelled him, but the wheels nailed to the board below his torso were the key to his movement. It was difficult to know where the man ended and the contraption began. He would tuck his shirttails under the board, uniting the ends of the fabric with a pin, in this way leaving no part of the wood or the wheels beneath exposed.

Caranguejo surveyed the stairs, planning his ascent. His calculating gaze reminded her of the look she had seen many times in the eyes of Seu Zé, her sometimes stepfather. Before he would thrash out against Conceição or her mother, Dona Marinefa, or a figment of his drunken imagination, he stopped to consider his tactics. His eyelids would widen, his brow furrowed. His body would tense like a frightened rodent. He required several moments to decide whether to clasp an empty bottle, to unfurl his belt, to lift a chair by its back. She remembered how once he had grabbed a lightbulb dangling from the ceiling on a thin wire. He wrapped his hand around the bulb and socket, and yanked. Before the cord snapped from the ceiling, the bulb popped in his hand. His weapon fell to the floor, limp and demure. Angry that his plan had been foiled, he did not notice the shards of fine glass embedded in his palm, the red drops pattering to the floor. He forgot that he had planned to hit Conceição and grabbed instead the plastic relic of Preto Velho from Dona Marinefa's pantheon. He threw Preto Velho on the floor, pounding his sinewy heel into the saint.

"You ugly nigger! You never looked my way. Marinefa's a whore, so why do you listen to her? And she gave birth to more whores and knaves than I can count." He lifted the saint, thrust its plastic head in his mouth, and clamped his teeth. He pulled on the body, but it would not separate from the head. He bit harder and saliva bubbled from the corners of his mouth.

Caranguejo raised his left hand and grasped the rail. He held his right hand behind him, then thrust it violently counterclockwise. At the same time, he heaved his torso upward and hopped onto the first step. He repeated the movements many times, pausing at each step, never loosening his left hand lest he sail backwards. Conceição stood at the top of the stairs, arms akimbo, as the crab ascended. He looked only as far ahead as the next step, never at Conceição. The rusted wheels gave him an uncertain perch.

Conceição began imagining what she would do with the money she would get off the crab. She wanted to fill her mother's refrigerator with new things that came in plastic containers, like Dannon yoghurt. She wanted to surprise her mother with all sorts of food. She wanted a few of those pills that only Come-Rato knew how to get. She wanted sweetbread and Coca-Cola, a tank top and sunglasses, shoes and a colorful knapsack. She wanted all the things once unleashed on her by a pity-stricken foreigner.

The crab took a long time to climb the stairs. When he was about halfway up, Conceição remembered Bochecha—for no apparent reason. He lost his willy to a bottle of glue. There he was, his bare toes clasping the back bumper of a bus, one hand thrust through an open window, the other wrapped around the hot tailpipe. Conceição imagined the wind blowing through the boy's hair as the driver reached ever-faster speeds. Bochecha stretched his neck around the corner of the bus to take in more of the view. The bus lurched from side to side. A group of children at one stop taunted him—"glue sniffer." He spit into the wind, even knowing his cob would never reach them. As the bus accelerated, leaving the stop, Bochecha took another look back at the kids. He felt his right hand burning on the tailpipe and released it. He aimed to grab a piece of trim on the corner of the coach, but before he had a chance to get a solid grip, the bus swung around a sharp curve. The vehicle sank to the right onto its tired shocks. Bochecha lost his hold on the windowsill where his left hand rested and spun wildly into the air, then onto the pavement. The first part of his body to make landfall was his head. It slammed into the curb. Then his torso settled into the pavement to the gentle crackle of glass and ribs. The bottle that once bore honey, but that Bochecha had filled with carpenter's glue and placed inside his shorts, had shattered. When he awoke in the corridors of the Restauração, he no longer had a penis. He pissed through a hole they made in his belly. Conceição had seen it.

Afterwards the kids would tell him, "Bochecha, you should give in to death, you can't go on living like that. How are you going to screw a girl?" He said, "No problem, with my finger or my tongue."

When Caranguejo reached the penultimate step, Conceição retreated. She let her arms fall along her flat hips. She noticed the beads of perspiration that had gathered across his forehead and she felt tall for the first time as she looked down at the bearded crab. Usually she had to careen her neck upwards to look at Johns. Sometimes she would stand on a box or a bed so they could rub their lips across her face, breathe into her ears.

When she was alone, sometimes Conceição sucked her thumb, the left one. She had recently wrapped the same thumb around the handle of a Mauser. Matuto had lent her the pistol. It was so much heavier than she had ever imagined. But even though it was difficult for her to lift it into the air, she liked the feeling of grasping it in her hand, the crisscross pattern of the grip imprinting itself on her palm as she held it ever tighter. Now she raised her thumb and hooked it through an empty belt loop. Caranguejo skated into room seven. Conceição followed.

The grimy window in room seven faced east and caught no wind. It looked out on a police station, boîtes, and a church, whose only visitors were toothless, stubble-faced men who pestered Father Rogério for a sip of wine, a taste of wafer. The father usually obliged, even when their breath stank of *cachaça*. He knew of no other way to attract parishioners, and the archbishop had already threatened to close the church and transfer Father Rogério to the backlands, where he hated the dust and feared the parching sun and empty sky.

Caranguejo bent his neck backward and scaled Conceição's body with his eyes. She smirked, and he didn't know why. It was not the smile of giddy shame he would have welcomed. It was the look he saw a hundred times a day. How could half a man move? How could half a man fuck? She wondered if the crab was like Bochecha, if he peed through his belly and screwed with his tongue.

"I don't do this for nothing," Conceição said.

"I know. You told me already, 200,000."

"Yeah, and next month it'll go up. It goes up every month. Everything goes up every month."

He said nothing. He reached inside his shirt pocket and pulled out four ruffled bills of 50,000. He stretched out his arm to lay them on the bed. Conceição saw that the spot from which he had removed the bills still bulged. Caranguejo rolled closer to her. His hands propelled him gently.

The wheels squeaked. Another sound intermingled with the crying of the wheels. Caranguejo stopped and turned his head reluctantly. He saw Matuto stepping toward him, Mauser in hand.

"It's in his shirt," Conceição said.

The crab's eyes opened wide, his brow furrowed. Just like Seu Zé. Only she knew he could not pick up a chair, unfurl a belt he'd never worn. The smirk deepened on Conceição's lips. The crab didn't move. He was still, like a mechanical doll whose batteries had suddenly run out. Matuto handed the Mauser to Conceição. She looked at it. It seemed so big inside her hand. She pointed it at Caranguejo. Matuto ripped off the crab's shirt. Caranguejo, no longer attached to his board, tumbled to the side, writhing to steady himself against the bed. He was naked without his shirt. From his back sprouted black, knotted hairs. The crab clawed at Matuto's legs. Matuto kicked him, once in the ribs. The second time in the jaw. A third time, in the ribs again. The crab fell supine, and Matuto stepped on his neck. He meant to merely stomp on him for a moment, but he realized that if he kept his foot there and raised his body so that all his weight rested on the crab's neck, the half man would soon stop writhing. Conceição wondered if the crab's neck was as strong as Preto Velho's. His arms thrashed, his eyes opened even wider. Then his entire body arched, just like with the other Johns. Suddenly it all stopped, and he fell as limp as the cord Seu Zé had yanked from the ceiling. Matuto picked up the rest of the money that had fallen across the floor.

Conceição went to see what was in the refrigerator. It was a tiny refrigerator, no taller than the crab himself. Conceição swung open the door. He had beer—in those little, tiny bottles. Conceição removed two of them and let them tumble on the floor. In the back, she saw a plastic container of yoghurt. She picked it up. "Danone," she said, unable to read the blue letters. It was famous. She held it in one hand and wondered what her mother would think when she received the gift.

Voices from the Pavement

Cláudia Milito and Hélio R. S. Silva

Voices from the Pavement *is an ethnography of street children, street educators, and the terrified middle classes of Rio de Janeiro. The following vignettes concern a young boy who works in the street, an elderly man who seeks revenge for an attack on his wife, and the authors' argument that "avoidance" has come to characterize Brazilian society's approach to street children.*

Eduardo lives with his parents in neighborhood of Austin (pronounced "A-ooh-stheen) in the Baixada Fluminense, in the state of Rio de Janeiro. He attends third grade at a state school, the afternoon shift, from 1:00 to 6:00. Like his father, forty-eight, and one of his brothers, he sells peanuts. Altogether, he has nine siblings, all from the same thirty-two-year-old mother.

His body carries the marks of a beating his father inflicted on him with a stick. The incident has left him with a big swollen spot on the head. In a calm, objective voice, Eduardo explains the reasons for his recent beating. Making his way to his place of work, a bar called Petisco da Feira, he'd caught the number 415 bus (Usina-Leblón) at dawn. But he was sleepy and dozed off, only to waken in Leblón—without his valuable supply of peanuts. His father wouldn't forgive him.

Likewise, his father is said not to forgive him when Eduardo sells few peanuts. In his defense, he asks, "What am I supposed to do, point a gun at the clients so they'll buy?"

But that's not how the father sees it. The boy must have been playing rather than selling in earnest. The lack of sales could only result from his bumming around, from being irresponsible. With little emotion, Eduardo swears he'll run away from home if his father beats him again. He speaks of an aunt in Niterói (adjacent to Rio) and of his godmother who lives in Caxias (a vast, gritty suburb of Rio). If he ran away to his aunt's house, he says, his father would never see him again. But he doesn't seem very resolute. His graceful smile and little white teeth light up his face, which seems too young for his alleged age of twelve.

His family is from Governador Valadares, a city he does not remember because he was so little when they left there. His father recalls that he was beaten a lot as a child, which is why, Eduardo insinuates, he also inflicts beatings. The boy suggests the possibility that there might be something like a generational pattern of domestic torture, a Brazilian tradition that makes us recall the belt episode in Graciliano Ramos's *Childhood*.

He explains that peanuts come from the land. Hélio wants to know what land they come from, and Eduardo says that they were bought in Austin. He recites the names of the stations that come after Austin en route to Japeri: Queimados, Comendador Soares. . . . He swears that in Austin, whoever beats up a woman is as good as dead. Then he tells a long, utterly unintelligible story that involves a woman, a threat, a revolver, a man walking around his house, and his father "filming" the whole thing.

His oldest sister is seventeen and his youngest brother just four months: "He's a little tyke who doesn't even know how to walk."

He says that when he is unable to sell his entire stock, he doesn't go back home. He hangs out and catches a snooze on the buses.

He tells of spending Christmas and Christmas Eve with his grandfather, as well as New Year's and New Year's Eve, and Carnival. He asks, "Is there such a thing as Carnival Eve?" He describes with wonder the table full of cold drinks, alcohol, sweets, and food.

Hélio asks the boy if he skips school when he does not go home because he has not sold enough peanuts. He says he skips from time to time, but the teacher doesn't get worked up about it.

He yawns continuously as he talks, the sleepiness weighing heavily on his tired eyelids. It's close to midnight, and he has scarcely sold anything. He fashions his sole piece of paper money into a little airplane, flies it, and philosophizes: "Copacabana isn't a good place for selling things; it's good for robbing gringos."

The willingness to exterminate precedes the realization of the traumatic act. The gentleman, retired, about sixty-five years of age, is in the bar on Carlos de Vasconcelos Street, where Hélio regularly gets a snack while doing fieldwork. The man talks about the kind of gun he uses. He's on the lookout for three boys who held up his wife in front of the army barracks, at the little square where the avenues Barão de Mesquita and Maracanã intersect. His wife resisted, and the resulting accident not only cost her a broken leg and other complications—she suffers from diabetes and hypertension—but also made him relinquish any moral resistance. The animal-out-to-kill, who lacks a conscience or remorse, is quite composed. What the children made off with was his cherished dream of a peaceful senior life in a traditional neighborhood, at the side of his companion. Now, it seems, anything goes. In nothing like hushed tones, he feels at ease telling the researcher, whom he doesn't know, of his intention—his obsession—to find and punish the three. The weapon is in his bag. The scene is reminiscent of American Westerns: the lone gunman set on settling a score.

The residents of Rio want civilization at any price.

Avoidance is better understood if we don't think of it as a quality exclusive to beasts, typecast criminals, or potbellied soldiers with a thirst for blood and destruction. "Killing those little dirty things" might be suggested by the upright doctor who offers free, humanitarian care, a man flanked by his children and grandchildren. Just as easily, it might be suggested by the university anthropologist who, after a brief period in the field with the kids, is pontificating, searching for a way to translate into sanitary, intellectual argot the mentality that he, as a resident of Rio, shares with the vigilante exterminators, soldiers, members of organized crime syndicates, and frivolous housewives: "They don't want citizenship; they want to take over the city."

Pixote's Fate

Robert M. Levine

Hector Babenco's 1981 film Pixote *depicted the violent world of abandoned and outlaw children in Brazil, and the failure of the system to offer any remedies. It was the third most commercially successful Brazilian film up to that time ever made. The other two*—Dona Flor and Her Two Husbands *and* Bye Bye Brazil—*were lighthearted and fanciful, in contrast to the brutality of* Pixote *(pronounced "pee-shoat," loosely translatable as "Pee-Wee"). Babenco, an Argentine making movies in Brazil, first intended to produce a documentary about Brazil's urban juvenile detention centers, the stark state institutions housing orphans and street children, but officials abruptly and without explanation canceled his permission. He and Jorge Duran then bought the rights to a novel about the same subject, journalist José Louzeiro's* Infancia dos mortos, *although in the end they wrote an original script about street youths, using only a small part of Louzeiro's narrative.* Pixote *was the result. Following in the tradition of Luis Buñuel and Vittorio de Sica, writer-director Babenco used seven real street urchins in his casting. Fernando Ramos da Silva, the eleven-year-old boy who played the title role, grew up in abject poverty in the gritty industrial district Diadema; unlike* Pixote, *however, he still had a family. When the film opened, Rio de Janeiro's chief youth court judge sought Babenco's indictment under the National Security Law "for inciting corruption of minors, advocating drug usage, and undermining social institutions."*

The most tragic byproduct of the film was the fate of its lead actor, Fernando Ramos da Silva. After his fame from the film had subsided, Fernando had drifted into petty crime and was arrested twice for minor offenses. He complained that the police were out to get him, that they could not distinguish him from the role he played in the movie. At the age of nineteen, in August 1987, the boy who had been selected out of 1,300 applicants to play the title role of the thieving street kid in the film was shot to death by the police.

Fernando was born on November 29, 1967, the sixth of ten children, into a family whose poverty deepened when his father, João Alves, died when Fernando was eight. His parents were peasants from the northern state of Pará who had migrated to the coffee fields of Paraná before moving on to the city of São Paulo, where they hoped to find more reliable work. His mother, Josefa Carvalho da Silva, received a pension of less than $10 a month; to survive, she and all of her children sold lottery tickets in the city streets. They were light-skinned and, therefore, did not face racial discrimination, but their status as rural migrants marked them as outcasts. Fernando attended grade school, but did not learn to read or write very well; at seven, he won a small part in a play put on by a theater group. He had no record of delinquency as a child.

The movie's national and international success came when Fernando Ramos da Silva was twelve, a year after the movie was made. *Pixote* was seen by an estimated two and a half million people in twenty countries, mostly in art cinemas. After his acting success, Ramos was signed to a one-year contract by TV Globo to play a small part in a prime time soap opera and was cast in the role of an errand boy in Bruno Barreto's film of Jorge Amado's novel, *Gabriela, Clove, and Cinnamon*. Globo dropped him for being lazy and because he couldn't read his lines, although his clumsy mannerisms and street vocabulary likely made people afraid of him. He was hired briefly to advertise UNICEF Christmas cards on Brazilian television. Moved by Fernando's story, the mayor of Duque de Caixias, a depressed-income city on the outskirts of Rio de Janeiro, gave him a house there and a scholarship to an acting school, but his mother and other family members moved back to Diadema some months later. He dropped out of the acting school after two days. "I don't think he truly wanted to be an actor, a job that requires a lot of dedication and patience," the actress Fernanda Montenegro was quoted as saying. In 1984, he was arrested on robbery charges in his old neighborhood. After his second arrest, in 1985, he told a reporter that he wanted the public to forget his image as Pixote. "I want a chance to live as a man, without being persecuted," he said. "They created a Pixote, but they did not know how to prepare him for life." He pleaded with José Louzeiro to write a sequel to his romance-reportage in which Pixote would be redeemed. The request was not considered viable, however. "I pulled him out of this absurd dream, to wake him up for other projects, but he didn't seem to believe," Louzeiro said in response.

His brothers and sisters said that Fernando felt persecuted by being typecast as Pixote and wanted to play romantic roles. In 1985, now nineteen with two tattoos on his arms and a sparse beard, he married a sixteen-year-old girl from a family of migrants from the interior of Minas Gerais, Cida Venâncio da Silva. Fernando settled down to an ordered life after the birth of their daughter, Jacqueline. His wife later said that Fernando always had two personalities: the aggressive and self-sufficient character of Pixote, and a more emotional, romantic, and sensitive face, which she called the "real Fernando." His last job was in the Northeast, where he had been acting in a play, *Atalpia My Love,* in the part of a hired assassin.

When he returned to his family, he was playing cards in a neighborhood tenement when he learned that the military police were conducting raids in the area, looking for criminals. Fearing that he would be harmed, he fled unarmed to another house. The police found out about his flight, and although they had no formal charge against him nor any warrant, pursued him and dragged him out from under a bed where he was hiding. He pleaded with his captors not to harm him—he was overheard by several residents of the tenement as saying that he was the father of a small daughter that he had to raise—but was shot to death. The official police report claimed that on August 25, Fernando and a young boy were caught trying to holdup a pedestrian on a street near Diadema, and that in the ensuing chase, he opened fire on his pursuers with a .32 caliber revolver. His family vigorously denied this, and produced witnesses to swear that he was not involved in the street mugging. Virtually no one believed the official story.

His mother and wife cried to reporters that the shooting had been a police execution. The body had seven bullet holes in it; two in the right arm, five more in the chest. A forensic examination revealed that on the basis of the powder marks on his white cotton shirt, the youth had been shot with the gun nearly touching him while he was lying on the ground, but the official police report blandly said that he had died while resisting arrest. Police spokespersons, attempting damage control, rationalized the youth's violent end by emphasizing that he was a known bandit and that he used his fame as Pixote to demand clemency when he was caught. "Every time he was detained," Mario Miguel Bittar, the police officer who first arrested him claimed, "[he] promised to straighten out, and he cried a lot. . . ." What Bittar did not mention was that each time that Fernando was arrested, the boy had been tortured with electric shocks, and that the police had treated him all the more roughly than other youths in their custody because of his fame. Fernando's death produced an outcry across Brazil, but it quickly subsided. A thin paperback book authored by Cida, Fernando's widow (skillfully edited, presumably by a professional), appeared, blaming the military police for murdering him. The three policemen who had killed him were dismissed from the force. One dropped out of sight, but the other two started a lucrative private security firm in Diadema, accusing the left-wing media of trumping up the charges against them.

On one hand, then, the outcry against what had happened suggested that people did care, that the success of the film *Pixote* and the publicly expressed sympathy at what had happened to the film's baby-faced title actor was a positive sign. But the fact was that nothing changed. Several of Fernando's own brothers died violent deaths without public outcry: they were, of course, unimportant *marginals* without the aura of film stardom. Six months before Fernando's murder, his older brother Paulo, twenty, was lynched by a crowd of more than fifty persons who left the body so badly mutilated that it took days to identify it. The motive for the lynching is not known, although Paulo was infamous for his womanizing. Three years later, another brother, Waldemar, was shot to death. Two of the surviving three brothers fled Diadema in fear of being killed as well. Of the seven child actors in *Pixote,* only the boy who played the androgynous Lilica, Jorge Julião, briefly succeeded in an acting career. The others fell back into poverty.

By deciding not to use professional child actors, the street children's performances, although minimal, were expressive and graphic, above all spontaneous. At the same time, they were complemented by the mature performances of the film's professional actors, notably Marília Pera, customarily cast as a comedienne, who played Sueli, a bitter, aging whore. Director Babenco revealed later that his street children–actors taught him so much about street life that he invited them to change the script as they worked through it. He estimated that, in the end, perhaps 40 percent of the original script was rewritten. Every day, Babenco held a workshop on that day's shooting, and everyone improvised. An assistant, a prison therapist, talked with the children every day to help them relax and to discuss the things they had to do in front of the cameras. At one point, Babenco piled the kids into his car and took them to a moviola studio to show them how editing worked so that they would not gripe so much about having to retake scenes over and over. The shooting took sixteen weeks, and the film cost twice as much as budgeted. Overall, Babenco never relinquished control. His imprint remains indelible throughout the film. Some of the story's violence is quick and brutal; other scenes are choreographed like a soccer play; when the kids rob a pedestrian, the camera pulls back, giving us a view of the whole area, so that we "get the social picture."

In *Pixote*'s opening scene, Babenco introduces the eleven-year-old Fernando with his real mother in front of their shack. Babenco looks strikingly like a grown-up version of Fernando, but one gets the idea quickly that the boy from the slums will never make it to the director's age. The director tells the audience that "Brazil has 120 million people of which approximately 50 percent are under twenty-one years of age. About twenty-eight million children have a lower standard of living than that stipulated in the UNs Children's Rights Declaration. Almost three million are homeless and have no real family." But it is important to know that the people who live in a slum work. Babenco points out that he is standing in "a working-class neighborhood in São Paulo, the great industrial center of Latin America, responsible for 60 to 70 percent of the gross national product of Brazil. . . . Typically, both parents work and the children stay home. Usually, the elder sister baby-sits, or a neighbor who is paid. Fernando, the star of the film, lives with his mother and nine brothers and sisters in this house. The whole film is acted by children who have this common background." The camera then shifts to Fernando, who becomes Pixote, a fictional wide-eyed and apprehensive new inmate hauled away in a police sweep of street kids (*trombadinhos*) brought in following the death of a prominent judge, who died after being pushed in front of a moving car during a mugging. Pixote is "a little camera taking it all in." He is quick: he learns that you keep your mouth shut, you do whatever stronger people tell you to, and you watch out for yourself.

In the hellish, Dickens-like juvenile center, Pixote witnesses a homosexual gang rape and other sordid scenes, climaxing in the killing of one of his comrades. He and several other suspects are singled out and taken to a city jail, where two are murdered. On their return to the juvenile center, they are confined to sleeping naked under a stairway. The prison and the detention center are nearly exclusive male worlds; the women who appear briefly bring caring and help, but these interludes are very short. During one lyrical scene, a kind teacher helps Pixote learn to write, but the movie shrugs off sentimentality. Throughout the film, the police are depicted as arrogant, corrupt, violent, and accountable to no one—a wholly accurate portrayal, despite the official line defending police as enforcers of law and order. Babenco conveys this mood astutely by shooting mostly at night in confined spaces, casting a feeling of unrelieved, ominous gloom. The detention center—one of its pavilions named for the eminent writer Euclides da Cunha—is unerringly exact in the way it is depicted.

Pixote intersperses shocking images relieved occasionally by fleeting moments of tenderness dashed by the intrusion of sordid reality. When brief scenes of tragicomic adventures occur, they are followed by events that take the children deeper into the world of alienation and pathos. The first part of the film, set in the institution and in the adult prison to which some of the children are taken, is brutal and violent. The story line demonstrates in short order how the children are doomed. They school themselves in the ways of the street, play at robberies, teach one another how to react under police interrogation, sniff glue, smoke marijuana, play soccer, and form a kind of family unit.

An ineffective investigation by a police official whose superiors are leaning on him to find a scapegoat leads to the savage beating death of Fumaça, one of the youths accused in the crime that had led to the roundup. After Fumaça's body is found in a city dump, a television newscast blames his death on Diego, one of the older adolescents in the detention center. When the rest of boys learn that Diego has been beaten to death by the authorities, they riot, wreck their dormitory, and escape. The breakout is accompanied by an abrupt change in mood. Visually, after the harrowing and dark opening part, the film becomes suffused in pale, dawnlike hues; at night, the pastel-colored light gives way to garish, raw neon—red, pink, and orange. The scene changes to the street, although its freedom becomes as confining as the detention center. Pixote joins with three others for solidarity and protection.

Each of the film's child characters are stereotypes. There is Lilica, the seventeen-year-old transvestite, ringleader "queen"; Chico, an abandoned street kid; seventeen-year-old Dito, a black kid the police are waiting for when he turns eighteen, sensitive and searching, and Lilica's lover; and Pixote, babylike and vulnerable. They snatch purses and pick pockets, philosophize about life, and eventually travel to a grayish Rio de Janeiro, where they become involved in selling cocaine. They are soon enticed into a drug deal, but are ripped off. By the end of film, Pixote has killed three people, run drugs, and pimped, but he remains a child. He murders one of his victims by sticking a knife into her. He wants her money, not to kill anyone. The argument between the woman and the child is just like a kindergarten fight, Babenco recalls. "Give me my pocketbook." "I don't want to give it to you." "Please give it to me." "Whap."

While Pixote and his friends escape, they remain confined to a prison of degradation. Eventually, the boys buy the "rights" to the alcoholic whore Sueli, using her as a decoy to rob her clients. One of the schemes goes sour, and Pixote shoots both Dito and an American businessman who has come to Sueli's flat. Sueli, who earlier had aborted her fetus with a knitting needle, briefly comforts Pixote by taking him to her breast, but then, after thinking about escaping with him to the country to pose as mother and son, she expels him. The film ends with the boy walking impassively down a railroad track, kicking cans, with a gun in his pocket, heading for trouble. His friends have been killed, he has been rejected by his mother figure, and he is dazed by what he has seen, likely destined for a violent end himself.

A Letter to President Cardoso

Caius Brandão

The Brazilian government acknowledges that 200,000 to 700,000 children live or pass their days on the streets. The true number may run into the millions. Impoverished, without schooling and frequently fleeing abusive households, children entering street life immediately become prey for police death squads. To protect street children, the government recently adopted the United Nations Convention on the Rights of the Child and passed the Child and Adolescent Act. Much remains to be done. The following 1995 letter from the International Child Resource Institute's Brazil Project to President Fernando Henrique Cardoso beseeches further action in defense of these children.

Dear President Cardoso,

We write to you today both to congratulate you as you initiate your presidency, and to wish you success in your efforts to lead Brazil to a better future for all its citizens. But what bring us together in addressing you is our deep concern for those citizens of Brazil that comprise its future generations: its children and adolescents.

Over the last decade a serious movement on behalf of the rights of children has grown in Brazil, and its achievements have been impressive. Yet, in spite of these gains, destitute children and adolescents continue to be murdered with impunity. We urge you to use the full power of your office to end the extrajudicial killings of children and adolescents in Brazil and to bring to justice members of death squads and others responsible for these crimes.

We share the indignation felt by many Brazilians over the impunity enjoyed by murderers of poor adolescents and children. Professional killers continue to profit from these crimes, and, if anything, killings of children and adolescents have escalated. We cite the following statistics:

—According to the National Movement of Street Children (MNMMR) and the Brazilian Institute for Social and Economic Analyses (IBASE), 1,937 children and adolescents were killed during the period of 1984 to 1989.

—According to the Attorney General (Procurador General da República), 5,644 children between the ages of five and seventeen were victims of violent deaths in the period between 1988 and 1991.

—According to Rio de Janeiro state government's own statistics, in 1992, 424 children under the age of 18 were victims of homicide in Rio de Janeiro. In the first six months of 1993, 298 children were killed in that state.

The Center for the Mobilization of Marginalized Populations (CEAP) states that the majority of the victims are impoverished male adolescents of African descent. In addition to being at risk of homicides, these young Brazilians are frequently humiliated, tortured, and mutilated at the hands of their assailants.

The History of the Huni Kui People

Siã Kaxinawá

Few indigenous people remain in Brazil, and fewer still have achieved the degree of stability and protection necessary for them to preserve their culture and identity in a shrinking world. Siã Kaxinawá, of the Huni Kui (Kaxinawá) tribe, was educated on his people's lands in remote Acre, near the border with Bolivia, as he describes in his essay on his people's contemporary history.

The story of our Kaxinawá people's association with whites goes back more than one hundred years. It started with the raids, when the rubber barons seized our lands by force, cordoning off the land and putting the rubber prospectors there. This was the time of the rubber fever. Many different groups appropriated our forests to produce latex.

These first whites saw the Indian as a threat to their aims. They remedied this by killing. They shot to death many of our relatives; they surrounded our villages and murdered children, women, and old people.

Many Kaxinawá managed to flee deep within the rain forest or to escape through the river system. Our people became dispersed to all corners. The only ones who got away went up many different rivers: the Taruacacá, Envia, Purus, Curanja, Muru, Humaitá, Jordão, Tejo, Breu, and the Juruá. Even so, they eventually became slaves of the rubber prospectors who took control of all of our lands.

After the period of conquest ended, we worked for the rubber producers, clearing the rain forest to provide roads for them to ship the rubber away. We carried heavy bundles of rubber on our backs or by traveling by river. We cut down trees and we planted crops on the rubber prospectors' lands. We learned to tap for rubber.

We were given no rights and lived barely at a subsistence level. Many of the Indians were branded on their bodies with the initials Felizardo Cerqueira (FC), the name of one of the rubber companies. This was to show that we were the company's property.

Dispersion of the Indians, a drawing by José Mateus
Itsairu Kaxinawá. *(Commissão Pro-Acre)*

We lived like this for many years in the condition of slaves, from the beginning of this century to 1975, when Txai Terri Vale de Aquino began to study the problem of our lands, our state of health, education, and to identify the locations to which our people had been dispersed along the many rivers and tributaries of the Purus and Juruá rivers. Through the work of this great friend, we learned that there are protective laws in this country and that we have the right to receive assistance for our communities. On the basis of this study, FUNAI (the Indian Protective Service) began to chart our lands. But much of this was only on paper.

Our lands remained in the hands of those who had taken them long ago. They still bought and sold our land with us on it. Because of this, we

At the Center of the World, a drawing by José Mateus Itsairu Kaxinawá.
(Commissão Pro-Acre)

began to tire of FUNAI's promises that our land would be returned to us
from the rubber prospectors occupying it. We resolved to fight for our
rights.

To do this, we established our economic cooperative that allows us to
buy and sell collectively. We stopped paying tolls to use the rubber ship-

ment roads and we refused to give any of the rubber we produced to the occupiers. In 1978, we made an arrangement with the Federal University of Acre to buy what we produced in exchange for tools, cloth, and other needed material. We obtained a 10-horsepower Brigg[s] motor to transport our goods. In this way we began to reorganize our lives.

Later, with the help of others, we obtained some small resources for us to move forward with our cooperative. Little by little, we made progress negotiating with the landowners and managers with the goal of guaranteeing protection for us from all types of invaders. Thanks to the work of our cooperative, we have been able to bring to the Jordão River reserve many of our relatives who had been driven out by the rubber prospectors. When the cooperative began in 1978, there were 350 of us Kaxinawá. Now we are more than 1,000 Indians living on our land.

One problem that we had to confront at the outset of our cooperative's existence was that no one knew how to read or write, which was needed to set up an accounting system, to write down sales to our customers and the goods they took. We asked for help from the Pro-Indian Commission of Acre, which made it possible for many of our relatives to study in Rio Branco to, in turn, become teachers among us. Today we have six Indian teachers on our land, and for the last nine years they have been offering classes and training for all members of our community.

We have learned to read and write, not only in Portuguese but in our own language. We also know a little mathematics, so we will no longer be tricked and taken advantage of in our commercial transactions in neighboring towns and cities. Besides encouraging the creation of schools with teachers from our own people, the cooperative has taken steps to train six health agents, taught by physicians and nurses from the Health Service.

In these ways we are continuing our struggle, organizing our people, taking control of the production and commercialization of our rubber, and dealing with the needs of education and medical assistance in our community. In this way we are guaranteeing [our ownership of] our land, our survival, and our liberty.

Urban Indians

Juliano Spyer

São Paulo is the greatest industrial center in South America and one of the three largest cities on the globe, along with Tokyo and Mexico City. Its budget, the third largest in Brazil, is superseded only by the federal budget and that of the state of São Paulo. Nearly fourteen million people call greater São Paulo home. Many are migrants or the children of migrants, who trekked to the industrial South from the hinterland and points north to escape the misery of the North and Northeast. Within this melting pot of cultures and ethnicities, one group in particular stands out for having made headlines in the press. This is the Pankararu, a group of Indians who already make up a small "tribe" of almost 1,000 people, located within the city limits of São Paulo. Why did they leave their home village in northeastern Pernambuco on a journey of more than 1,200 miles to the distant shantytowns of São Paulo?

The Pankararu are the remnants of the Tapuia tribe, formerly inhabitants of the semiarid backlands of the Northeast. They have received little attention to this day from ethnographic or linguistic scholars. The little that is known about their precolonial history is that they likely lived on the coast, but were expelled from the region by the expansion of the Tupí peoples. They then encountered resistance from the Gês, who stopped them from moving further west. Trapped, they established themselves in the middle-lower São Francisco River Valley, in the border area of the present-day states of Bahia and Pernambuco.

The Pankararu dialect has, even today, elements of the Gê and Tupí languages. This raises the possibility that their ability to negotiate with other indigenous cultures helped them in the period after first contact was made with the Portuguese in the seventeenth century when missionaries arrived. Mission priests founded the hamlet of Brejo dos Padres, deep in the interior of Pernambuco, which eventually became home to the Pankararu.

Pankararu Indians outside their São Paulo favela. (*Photograph by Juliano Spyer*)

During the nineteenth century, Emperor Dom Pedro II ceded rights to 35,000 acres to the Pankararu. Decades later, in 1941, the reservation was mapped by the federal Indian Protection Service (SPI); by then it had shrunk to 20,000 acres. The presence of non-Indian landowners on the Brejo dos Padres reservation, however, had lasted for centuries. The rapid depletion of the soil from sugar-intensive cultivation encouraged small farmers to flee the coast, and some came to the Pankararu lands near to the São Francisco River Valley. The arrival of whites brought disaster for the Indians. According to contemporary accounts, Indians who refused to speak Portuguese had their tongues extracted.

The shrinkage of their protected lands as neighboring farms and ranches expanded led to massive outmigration after 1950. Many now trekked south to the industrial cities of the Center-South. In São Paulo, the first Pankararu families settled in favelas near Morumbi, the wealthiest neighborhood in the city, and the site of the Cícero Pompeu de Toledo Stadium under construction. Later, the Pankararu migrants moved into small shacks in the nearby Real Parque neighborhood.

There were some advances in São Paulo. The building boom of the 1950s brought secure employment opportunities for the tribe: in factories and the construction industry for the men, and as domestics for the women. But unlike the vast majority of migrants from the Northeast, who sought the cities as places to reside permanently, the Pankararu migrants tended to stay in São Paulo only for brief periods, usually six months, after which time they returned home. They saved money, when they could, to buy seeds and tools for their plots of land in Pernambuco. This practice made it difficult to send children to school in São Paulo and robbed the community of a stable base.

Nowadays, the Pankararu work cycle involves hundreds of families, and is encouraged by FUNAI (the National Indian Foundation). Some tribe members receive air tickets by claiming the need to go to São Paulo for health reasons. The continued pattern of migration south has emboldened 400 or so non-Indian squatter families to settle on or near Pankararu lands in Pernambuco. Migrant workers' siblings are left to maintain the land and prevent more seizures, although in general it is a losing battle.

In spite of this, the Pankararu circular migratory pattern between São Paulo and Pernambuco has lasted into the 1990s. That the Pankararu hold firm deeds to their reservation has helped them fare better than Indian groups without deeds. They are eligible, for example, for assistance with planting during the growing season.

The confrontation between Indians and landowners on the Brejo dos Padres reservation in Pernambuco actually has become something of a contradiction for human rights organizations. The parties involved in this case do not play the traditional role of the "oppressor" and the "oppressed," as there are no clear and defined entities; instead, they are trapped in a complex social web that emanates from familial, cultural, and labor bonds.

When they migrate to São Paulo in search of employment, the Pankararu help meet the demand for unskilled labor and, therefore, assume the risk of facing the violence within the poverty belt, as often is the fate of those who are illiterate, low-wage workers. They also must deal with the disadvantages of receiving government assistance, which outside the villages, carries the mistaken assumption that Indians receive help because they are incapable of working. In other words, a person with an Indian birth certificate often finds himself frozen out of the work market.

By 1990, the more than 1,000 Pankararu Indians living at least part of the year in the Real Parque favela in São Paulo was drawing considerable media attention. Media interest in the Pankararu of São Paulo is not only based on the fact that they live in the city. Most news items published about them serves to remind the public of their presence in the shanty-town, exposed to problems of violence from gangs of thieves as well as the police, and living in conditions of almost absolute misery. Photos frequently chosen by newspapers show families outside their shacks, constructed from leftovers of urban trash. The media also like to run full view images of the shantytown; the mass of wooden houses, separated by twisting dirt trails, contrasts markedly with a romanticized idea of life in the village. In one report, a camera crew from the CNT / Gazeta net-work, wanting to interject a bit of color into their broadcasts, asked the Pankararu to put on a dance just outside the shantytown, where the camera could get the best picture of sewage floating in broad daylight, along with the sleek architecture of the nearby aluminum-constructed office towers.

Even though the Pankararu received treatment from the media that was more sensationalistic than humanitarian, and which lost its impact after a while, the Pankararu gained visibility nonetheless, and their de-nouncements against the official agencies responsible for the migratory process and the conditions of city life started to have an effect. The facilitated access given to human rights organizations within the city of São Paulo, and the constant clashes between the tribe and the govern-ment, ultimately helped to establish institutions to negotiate with the "white" culture on the Pankararu's behalf.

Two distinct and recent problems remain to be solved. One has to do with the food distributed by the state government on Indian reservations in São Paulo. The Pankararu are excluded from this arrangement be-cause the government fears protests from other favela dwellers who do not receive such aid.

More serious is the growing apathy among a part of the Pankararu born in São Paulo to tribal traditions. As children, they spend a good percentage of their weekdays in public schools, where they are often teased by their classmates and even teachers about being Indian. These youths have become accustomed to city life, attending movies, dances, and soccer games with friends from inside and outside their community. Village life back in Pernambuco is devoid of such luxuries. If the land claims were settled and the Pankaruru returned to their ancestral home, the younger generation would face traumatic readaptation. Yet on the whole, the modernization process that the Pankararu had to undergo to adjust to city life demonstrates their ability to build bridges with the predominant culture without losing their own identity. One of the tribal association's next projects, in line with this thinking, seeks to revive the original language so that in the future, bilingual schools can be opened both on the reservation and in São Paulo.

The Pankararu phenomenon becomes even more important from a social context in light of the fact that other indigenous groups are following suit. There is the case of the Fulni-ô, numbering almost 100 residents in another shantytown on the periphery of São Paulo. Members of the Guarani Mbya and Guarani Nhandeva, ancestral tribes to the south, have also relocated to urban settings. Within the city limits of São Paulo, three Guarani Mbya favela communities are surrounded by non-Indian neighbors. This is all relatively new and blurs the lines between assistance to Indians and other needy groups.

Mayor Orders Billboard

Shacks Destroyed

Juliana Raposo

The article translated here appeared in Correio da Cidadania, *a newspaper started in 1996 to promote civic awareness and responsibility. It tells the story of a decision by the mayor's office in São Paulo to burn out squatters who had constructed makeshift shacks behind advertising billboards, called "outdoors" in Brazilian slang. The squatters were ordered out two days before the running of the city's marathon, whose route was to pass by the billboards in question. Juliana Raposo, a young woman of student age, came on the scene by chance. She witnessed it, interviewed the people involved, took several photos, and delivered the story to her newspaper. The article is detailed and spares no sarcasm in its description of events. The reporter conveys indignation not only at the fact that families were made homeless, but also that they had lost even though they had played by the rules: the squatters had held jobs, had been victimized by robbers, and had been turned down for aid by bureaucrats who preferred to split up families by sending children to bleak state-run institutions rather than find ways to help them stay together. There was no other media coverage.*

On one of the main thoroughfares in the city of São Paulo—Avenida Sumaré, up to last Wednesday—there were two shacks lodged behind large billboards. Behind the advertising, five families lived in misery.

Last Thursday, for the second time, the São Paulo mayor's office ordered the shacks removed. "Operation Clean-Up" started at 3:00 P.M. and was completed by 5:40 P.M.

The operation was supervised by the city police department. Gilmar Almeida de Lima, an employee of the Lapa district's Child Welfare Agency, and a social worker, Dóris Curcino, along with Isabel Gazel from another agency, also participated in the operation.

A shack built behind a billboard in Avenida Sumaré.
(*Photograph by Juliana Raposo*)

A municipal employee burns the remnants. (*Photograph by
Juliana Raposo*)

Twelve men were sent to carry out the orders. Two trucks were needed
to remove the belongings of the new members of the city's homeless.

"People lived here in subhuman conditions," agent Gilmar Almeida
de Lima said, pleased with the operation. A policeman added that the
neighborhood had complained of what they had seen in their headlights.

According to Rogério Alves dos Santos, eighteen, one of the residents
of the demolished hovels, members of the military police arrived earlier,

Gilmar Almeida de Lima, Lapa district employee, and Dóris Curcino, social worker. (*Photograph by Juliana Raposo*)

Hermes Justino da Silva, in his police uniform, with his family. (*Photograph by Juliana Raposo*)

around 2 P.M., and set fire to his family's shack without waiting for them to retrieve their possessions and leave. "The military policemen are the same ones who usually hang out at that coffee and snack shop over there. They set fire to everything: to the wood and to old clothing," Rogério recounted.

Three families lived in Rogério's shack, including a child only a year old. The homeless youth shouted: "This is the end! They threw out the

Elisete Vicente da Silva and her daughter.
(*Photograph by Juliana Raposo*)

baby's food!" At this moment, Rogério became aggressive, smashing dozens of dishes on the ground. The shards hit some of the cars passing by on the street.

According to policeman Oliveira, the metal gas canister had been returned to the homeless family. He denied that food had been left on the stove. "They were cooking rice and they threw it on the ground," he said.

One shack on the same street was not destroyed in the operation. It sits on a private plot of land on the corner of Avenida Sumaré. Edson Barnabé Queiroz, the squatter who lives in the shack, explained that the owner of the property is Germano Buchardi. Queiroz is in charge of taking care of the property. "If they come here, they will see that my boss asked me to look after his property," he said.

The social workers spoke with the families, urging them to send the children to a city agency. "We tried to talk with them about the legal status of the children," Isabel Gazel said. According to her, the children would be taken to the Lapa Temporary Children's Shelter and could stay there for up to three months. "They even have Jacuzzis there for the children to take hydromassage," she commented. When the three months are up, the children would be sent to a permanent shelter.

According to Gazel, the shelter's role is "to restructure the lives of its children." She claimed to be taken with the Silva family in particular. "It's a true family. I admire the efforts of the mother to stay with her children at whatever the cost."

Elisete [the mother] refused. She said that she wanted to send her children to Rio, to relatives. "The lady over there said that she would pay for the bus fare, but she didn't say anything else. I have to do something right now or they will take my children away." Elisete said that the shelter would allow her to stay only one night. She earns tips by watching cars in front of the Brunella snack shop.

One of the social workers offered to make a list of the possessions of the families so that they could claim them later. For Hermes da Silva, Elisete's husband, the worst thing was when they took away two audio speakers, two bottled gas canisters, two sofas, and a stove—none of which were returned to them. "Today they want to have a list, but first they took away everything I had." At this moment, three of the men assigned to demolish the ruins tossed a stove to the ground approximately three meters beneath the ledge where the shacks had been perched. Not onto the truck, but to the ground.

Hermes Justino da Silva and Elisete Vicente da Silva had been residents of the destroyed shacks for the last year and a half, living there with their four children. Two of them were born to the couple—fifteen and sixteen—and two of them were "adopted" (they rescued them from the street)—ten and fourteen. Elisete and Hermes had been arrested on October 24, in front of the shack, and terrorized for two hours in a police van belonging to the special operations squad. During this time, both of them, but principally Elisete, were insulted, called vagabonds, and threatened with beatings. Because they had no identity papers, they were taken to the police station at Perdizes, but were subsequently freed for lack of any charge against them.

The Silva family is from Rio, but has lived in São Paulo for eleven years. They came first to Osasco, where Hermes worked as a municipal policeman for six years, between 1986 and 1992. Elisete was a cook at a day care center run by the Osasco city government. They lived in a shack in the Baronese favela, built on land given by the mayor, Celso Giglio. On payday, however, Hermes was mugged in the favela. He and his wife were beaten by the thieves. He spent a week recuperating in the Hospital das Clínicas. When he was released, fearing further reprisals, he went to Rio and hid there for eleven days.

On his return, with his four children, he found another family living in his shack. They had assumed that the Silvas had died. Complaining to the mayor's office did no good; [after all,] their documents had been confiscated. They then were ordered out of their shack, which with the others was destroyed. . . . The police came two days before the city marathon that passes by Avenida Sumaré and ordered the family out. "I had nowhere to go," Elisete said. A day later, the policemen arrived with the two trucks with city drivers. "They started knocking everything down while my children were still sleeping." She pleaded with them to wait, but they refused. "They took everything, even my radio and my television set," she said. "They wanted to take my children to the institution but I refused. . . . They left my family with nothing, huddled under a blanket during the heavy rain."

Cultural Imperialism

at Its Most Fashionable

Roger M. Allen

"If I were Brazilian," Roger M. Allen writes, "this new cultural imperialism would bother me. For that matter, I'm American and it bothers me. American schlock is shoving aside Brazilian things of real value. If there were huge demonstrations against the American cultural invasion I'd find myself more than a little sympathetic." Allen, who spent several years in Brasília as the spouse of a member of the diplomatic corps, offers interesting observations about commercialism and attitudes that are not calculated to win friends, but that merit consideration as the global economy bears down on Brazil and feeds its long-held love of what is foreign.

Imagine, if you will, going to the largest and fanciest shopping mall in the most fashionable suburb of Washington, D.C.—the nation's capital. Imagine that you notice that one shop has a German name. Then imagine that the next store over also has a German name—and that several German words appear in the signs hanging in the window. After strolling about for a bit, it suddenly dawns on you that something like a quarter or a half of the stores in the mall have German-language signs or German names. As you go into the shops, you notice many items have at least some German on the label and many of the highest-priced items are festooned with signs saying "IMPORTED." Sure enough, the products in question—CDs, computers, clothes, kitchen gadgets, food items, just about anything—are imported, but otherwise are of perfectly ordinary quality. You start to get the impression that being imported is, in and of itself, a good thing, which in turn carries with it the implicit assumption that anything of domestic manufacture is no good.

You turn your attention back to the stores, and recognize several actual German companies and restaurants that have opened branches. Many local stores have obviously based themselves on German models and have taken German names. Almost all the movies at the multiplex cinema are German. The bookstore has a special section of German-language books and another of German-language magazines. German music—even bad German music—is all the rage in the music stores, and the mall's public address system is playing some schmaltzy Muzak-version of an old German pop tune. It's Christmas time, and the mall is adorned with holiday decorations—with a more or less accurate representation of the standard German Christmas symbols and images as the central motif.

And then you notice the strangest thing of all about what's going on. No one is bothered by it. No one thinks it strange. As best as you can tell, no one feels any paranoia toward the Germans or is up in arms about German cultural imperialism. . . .

Welcome to Brasília, capital of Brazil. Go through the first section of this article and change "Washington, D.C." to "Brasília," change the word "German" to "American" or "English-language," as appropriate, and you'd have an utterly nonexaggerated description of a visit to our local shopping mall. (For that matter, the mall itself is clearly patterned on an American model, and the name of the place is Park Shopping. In fact, *shopping,* the gerund form of the English verb "to shop," has become a noun in Brazilian Portuguese, meaning "shopping mall." The phrase "I am going to the mall" would be translated as something like *"Eu vou ir a shopping."*) Odds are that at least six of the eight movie screens will be showing American films. You can eat at McDonalds, treat yourself to a Dunkin Donut, bowl a few frames at the Brunswick bowling alley, pick up a copy of the latest Danielle Steele novel or any of several American or British magazines (which usually are about a month out of date), watch the kiddies sit on Santa's lap, buy yourself a Compaq computer, or even wander down to the General Nutrition Center to get yourself some brewer's yeast. My hunch is that some brands are so well established that the locals don't even know they aren't local. Fanta, Coca-Cola, and Sprite are totally localized, to coin a term. (But if you want a Sprite, ask for a SPREET-CHE. Unless, of course, you want a Sete-Uppe to wash down your potato chips.)

Everywhere you look at Park Shopping, you'll see people wearing their Disneyland regalia, their T-shirts emblazoned with the image of Bugs Bunny, or the New York Giants logo, or this Las Vegas hotel, or that Los Angeles night spot. Baseball-style caps with team names on them are very popular. Basketball is played a fair amount down here, and basketball teams are the most popular choice on hats and shirts, with football teams a close second, and baseball far behind. Certain teams and cities are the most popular. The Chicago Bulls and the New York Giants are very hot, understandably enough. Those are big towns, and very visible teams. Less explainable is the popularity of anything bearing the name of the Charlotte Hornets or the Georgetown Hoyas. And I'm not quite sure why University of Kansas Jayhawks caps were on sale in Forteleza, a city in the north of the country.

The choice of one logo over another might be mysterious, but the motive for wearing the caps and shirts is not. They are fashion statements and status symbols. If you wear a Giants T-shirt down here, it proves (or at least suggests) you've been to New York, and that you're hip, stylish, and rich.

It isn't just the shopping malls, either. Anything advertised in English becomes fashionable, and anything American is very chic. English-language schools are all over the place. (My favorite advertises itself as an *academia de idiomática,* or literally, academy of idiomatic expressions. The sign shows a cartoon figure with a globe of the world for its over-sized head. The figure is wearing an Uncle Sam hat, and has its hands splayed out of either side of its head, thumbs in its ears, while it sticks its tongue out through a goofy grin. I can't help wondering how strong their grasp of American idiom really is.) American news gets a fair degree of prominence in the papers and on television. In *Veja,* a news-magazine comparable to *Time* or *Newsweek,* there is a weekly two-page spread of celebrity gossip called *"Gente,"* very much like the "People" page in *Time.* It is rare, indeed, for *"Gente"* to fail to mention at least one American film star or celebrity of one sort or another.

Many grocery stores have special import sections, where you can buy (allegedly) fancy delicacies from around the world. The English jams and jellies and the French canned mushrooms are there as well, but much of the shelf space is given over to such gourmet items as Heinz ketchup and Shop-Rite salad dressing, and other totally generic American store-brand or no-name products are also quite visible. (It makes me wonder just how fancy those Brit jellies really are.) Gatorade is very big. For no reason I can figure out, Pringles, the American potato chip substitute, are wildly popular and very hip. I noticed recently that a common Brazilian brand of condom, Blotex (I swear I'm not making that name up), had vanished from the racks over the checkout stand at a local grocery store, to be replaced by Trojan-brand condoms. The packets, in Portuguese, boasted that the Trojans were not only *Importado,* but also approved by the *FDA.* I'm not quite sure if this shoving aside of a domestic condom brand is the apex, or the nadir, of cultural imperialism, but at least it makes Saturday night just that much more international.

No discussion of American cultural imperialism in Brazil would be complete without a mention of Uncle Walt. More than 50 percent of Brazilian visa applicants list a desire to visit Disneyland or Disney World as a reason for wishing to visit the United States. It has become a terrifyingly expensive tradition for well-to-do, fifteen-year-old girls to get trips to Disney World in lieu of the old-fashioned coming-out party. Any aircraft traveling from the United States to Brazil is likely to be carrying at least one such young lady (though they usually travel in groups). She'll be the one lugging back a Mickey Mouse or Donald Duck stuffed animal, which is, generally speaking, somewhat larger than herself.

Brazilian shoppers in Florida have been compared to clouds of locusts by frazzled but happy shopkeepers. As with locusts, there is nothing at all left once the Brazilians have swarmed through one's store. On my various trips from the United States to Brazil, I have noticed an interesting phenomenon at baggage claim: on average, for every one suitcase that trundles down the baggage conveyor, there is one box containing an electronic gizmo or consumer gadget of one sort or another. I've seen computers, computer printers, televisions, VCRs, fax machines, baby strollers, even an artificial Christmas tree in Brazilian luggage. Given the price differences between Brazil and the United States, a clever shopper can actually finance his or her trip by bringing the goodies home and reselling them for enough of a profit to cover the cost of airfare, hotels, and so on. (All very illegal, of course, but that never stopped anyone.) There are, rumor has it, people who run whole cottage industries on this basis; for example, there is supposed to be a woman here in Brasília who runs either a dress shop or clothing store out of her house, with her entire stock coming in via suitcase express.

This sort of shopping has gotten so out of hand that some airlines that serve Brazil-U.S. routes have let it be known they will no longer accept cardboard boxes as regular baggage during peak travel periods, for the very good reason that all those VCRs and televisions are crowding out the regular suitcases. I will omit any description of the various adventures with carry-on luggage that I have witnessed, leaving them to the imagination of the reader. One bit of urban folklore has it that the Brazilian soccer team, in the United States for the 1994 World Cup, chartered a plane just to carry back the results of their shopping spree. The customs official who actually dared suggest that the team's luggage be searched was practically thrown in irons.

For many years, it was official government policy to limit foreign imports in order to encourage domestic production. Not very surprisingly, eliminating competition also eliminated the impetus to improve quality, with the result that many Brazilian products are second-rate—a fact that became distressingly apparent when trade barriers were relaxed. For everything from condoms to canned goods to cars, Brazilians are discovering that the imported version really is better. Doubtless, competition will improve the Brazilian versions, but for now, it is taken as a given that the foreign version is better—and there is a strong element of truth to this idea.

All of this cannot help but make English fashionable. And when a language is used more or less as a fashion accessory, coherence is all but sacrificed on the altar of attempted sophistication. The first morning my wife and I arrived in Brazil, jet-lagged and staggering around the airport, we noticed a lunch counter advertising "smell chicken." We decided not to try it. And I doubt the smartly dressed young lady we saw the other night really understood all the layers of meaning there were in a South American person wearing a shirt that promoted the Banana Republic clothing store. I certainly hope another young woman I saw didn't understand—or at least didn't mean—the satire of the Nike motto on her shirt. In letters eight inches high, the shirt read "JUST DO ME." If Ford of Brazil decides to market their big, brawny, four-wheel-drive in an English-language country, they'll have a lot of trouble unless they change its name to something besides "Deserter." And I don't believe many American visitors are eager to try the Brasília airport restaurant, named (in English) the Albatross. The name of the airport bar (also in English) is Good Head. As they used to say on *Mystery Science Theater* when the setup was just too obvious, insert joke here. I could offer plenty of other examples, such as the Tip Dog Restaurante and the Foot Free shoe store (for amputees?), but you get the idea. To be honest, I make so many appalling mistakes in Portuguese that I'm reminded of the old saying about people who live in glass houses.

But even if it is not always used perfectly, English is very big here, and there are lots of factors that will all but guarantee it will get bigger. Anything related to computers and electronics will almost certainly provide yet another avenue of invasion for the English language and American culture. American brands—Compaq, IBM, Hewlett-Packard—dominate the market. As in the United States, Japanese brands, especially of printers, also do well—but most of the Japanese (and other third country) brands that arrive in Brazil are the American version, with English instructions. The same applies to legitimately imported televisions, stereos, and so on. One newspaper offered an English-Portuguese dictionary as a premium for subscribing, and the ads for it portrayed a frazzled consumer trying to make heads or tails of her stereo's instruction manual. Only her free dictionary could save the day. Having usable instructions is so rare that it is a selling point: some gizmos advertise themselves as including instructions in Portuguese. While a fair number of computer programs have been translated into Portuguese, many have not. And, of course, English is the lingua franca of the Internet. Brazil's main "backbone" links to the Internet almost all pass through the United States. An E-mail message going from one neighborhood in Rio to another would quite likely travel back and forth across the equator in order to travel a dozen miles.

Cultural imperialism could be said to start at home. Switch on the television and the odds are very good that you'll see something American—and also pretty good that it will be American trash. The Brazilians produce a lot of their own programming, and a lot of it is pretty slick—but you can find plenty of badly dubbed old American movies, along with badly dubbed half hour infomercials for cleaning products and gizmos to help you stop smoking. If you have cable, you've got CNN, HBO, TNT, and MTV in Portuguese and Spanish, the Warner Brothers and Sony stations (featuring shows produced by those studios), and of all things, Country Music Television. (Most of the music on MTV, and virtually all of the music on CMT, is American, or at least in English, with a smattering of Latin music thrown in. But there are these strange crossovers. Just last night I was treated to the sight of a Brazilian picking on his banjo.) . . .

Go back home, flip on the radio, and chances are good that what you'll hear will not be samba or bossa nova, but Lionel Ritchie. (I just switched on the radio at random and got what sounds very much like the Pretenders doing the old Air Supply song "I'm Not in Love." What the hell is *that* doing on the air?) For some reason, the cheesiest 1970s' English-language schlock is all over the airwaves. Maybe just because it's cheap. Show up at a party, and odds are the dance music will be—get this—disco from the Paleolithic era. Gloria Gaynor announcing "I Will Survive" is very big. (Now the radio is pumping out some generic cover of "Stop in the Name of Love." I may have to take an ax to it.) Just a note from later on in the process of writing this article: the same radio station just played at least six English-language songs in a row, most of them god-awful. Having had enough of listening in the interests of reporting, I have now shut the radio off with a distinct sense of relief.

The Brazilians, of all people, don't need to do this. If there is one country on earth that doesn't need to import popular music from the damned Yanquis, it is this one. Nor, in a larger sense, do they need any of the other cultural bric-a-brac they get from us. I feel more than a little uncomfortable with it all, and I am astonished that more of the Brazilians don't—as they certainly felt in the past. "Yankee Go Home" used to be the flavor of the day, not so many years ago—and with some justice. Uncle Sam can be a bit overbearing at times. Why there has been no backlash to the present cultural invasion is a mystery to me. Maybe the answer is that the backlash is yet to come.

The Gay and Lesbian Movement

in Brazil

James N. Green

Gay and lesbian movements developed in three Latin American countries in the early 1970s—Mexico, Puerto Rico, and Argentina. During this period, the Brazilian military dictatorship (1964–1985) entered its worst phase of political repression. By 1975, however, faced with a domestic economic crisis and mounting opposition to their rule, the generals initiated a gradual and uneven process leading toward political liberalization and the eventual return to civilian rule. As student, intellectual, and most significantly, working-class mobilizations against the dictatorship's policies expanded, new movements emerged to challenge the political status quo. These movements included feminists who questioned both widespread societal sexism and its manifestations in the left-wing opposition; adherents of the black consciousness movement who blasted the generally accepted concept that Brazil was a racial democracy; and advocates for gay and lesbian rights. The Brazilian gay and lesbian movement evolved from the interaction of the international movement and the changing political situation in Brazil, which provided catalysts for the organization of gay men and lesbians to fight for their political, social, and democratic rights. This essay follows the movement as it developed during the first years in São Paulo, Brazil's political, economic, and cultural center.

Attempts were made in 1975 and 1976 to organize homosexuals in Brazil, but the political climate proved unfavorable. For example, the First Congress of Brazilian Homosexuals was called by an unknown and probably fictitious União do Homossexual Brasileiro (Union of Brazilian Homosexuals), to be held in the gardens of the Museum of Modern Art in Rio de Janeiro on July 4, 1976. As reporters gathered to cover the event, which had been announced in a leaflet circulated three days earlier, twenty police cars, including eight arrest vans with seventy men from the General Department of Special Investigation, surrounded the museum. As a result, no congress took place. In the same year, João S. Trevisan, a writer from São Paulo who had lived in the United States in the early 1970s and was in contact with the San Francisco gay liberation movement, attempted to form a discussion group on homosexuality among gay university students. The initiative failed, largely because participants questioned the validity of discussing their own sexuality and argued that a more important priority was to overthrow the dictatorship.

In late 1977, João Antônio Mascarenhas, a lawyer from Rio de Janeiro who had connections with gay activists in Europe and the United States, hosted a visit by Winston Leyland of the San Francisco–based Gay Sunshine Press. Leyland had been traveling throughout Latin America collecting material for an anthology on gay Latin American literature. A whirlwind of interviews in the opposition and mainstream press, as well as meetings with gay intellectuals in Rio de Janeiro and São Paulo, inspired the formation of a collective to publish a monthly newspaper for homosexuals as a vehicle for discussions on sexuality, racial discrimination, the arts, ecology, and machismo. The first issue came out in April 1978 under the title *Lampião da Esquina,* which has a double meaning— "lamppost on the corner," in reference to gay street life, and Lampião, a Robin Hood–type bandit figure who roamed the Brazilian Northeast in the early twentieth century.

A month after *Lampião* first appeared, a modest association in São Paulo that evolved into Brazil's first gay liberation group was established. Initially called Núcleo de Ação pelos Direitos dos Homossexuais (Action Nucleus for Homosexuals' Rights), its activities included consciousness-raising and discussion sessions. In spite of its limited membership and semiclandestine profile, the group achieved some public exposure in an open letter denouncing homophobic representations in the mainstream tabloid press. In December 1978, because of an internal debate about how to broaden its appeal, the group changed its name to SOMOS: Grupo de Afirmação Homossexual (We Are: Group of Homosexual Affirmation). In addition to the "coming-out" implication of the name, the group's new designation paid political homage to the Argentine Homosexual Liberation Front (HLF) of 1971–1976 and its magazine *Somos.* (A former member of the Argentine organization living in São Paulo at the time had brought news of the group, which was seen by several members of the Brazilian organization as a political model and inspiration.)

On February 8, 1979, university students invited SOMOS to participate in what proved to be a historic debate on minorities held in the social science department of the University of São Paulo. More than 300 people jammed into the auditorium to hear representatives from SOMOS and the editorial board of *Lampião* talk about homophobia in Brazilian society. The discussion soon shifted to a heated critique of the antigay positions held by many currents of the Brazilian Left. In response, student representatives from pro-Soviet, pro-Albanian, and pro-Cuban organizations argued that instead of addressing issues such as sexism and homophobia, people should unite in a general struggle against the dictatorship. Following the event, SOMOS became more widely known, and many new people joined the group, including a significant number of women.

Concurrently with SOMOS's new public profile and growth, the Brazilian government moved against *Lampião*. Since August 1978, the paper had been the subject of a police inquiry in Rio de Janeiro and São Paulo on a charge of offending "public morality." A leaked government document revealed that the military intended to shut down the publication. In early 1979, the military accused *Lampião* editors of committing offenses against "morality and propriety," which could have resulted in imprisonment for up to a year. Intellectuals, cultural and artistic figures, the journalists' union, and the Brazilian Press Association denounced the government's measures. SOMOS members, in one of their first acts of political activism, formed a committee in defense of *Lampião* that circulated a protest petition. Eventually, the dictatorship ended the financial audit and dropped the charges against the editors of the gay press.

In October 1979, SOMOS reorganized in response to its participants' desire to be more activist oriented. During this period, the group's composition expanded from a membership base among lower-middle-class white-collar workers and students to include more Afro-Brazilians, older people, and lesbians. As more women joined the organization, they tended to meet separately to discuss sexism within the group, the emergent women's movement, and feminism. Ultimately, most opted for a semiautonomous status as Ação Lésbica-Feminista (Lesbian Feminist Action). SOMOS's second public political effort involved support for the incipient black consciousness movement, known as the Movimento Negro

Unificado (United Black Movement or MNU). SOMOS members joined the MNU-sponsored march against racial discrimination on November 20, 1979, carrying a huge banner publicly identifying the organization.

As new groups came together in Brazil's largest cities inspired by reports about SOMOS in the pages of *Lampião,* its editors called a meeting in Rio de Janeiro of representatives from different groups to discuss the possibility of organizing a national gathering. Delegates to the meeting unanimously decided to hold such a conference in São Paulo in April 1980.

In the weeks prior to the conference, a massive strike wave shook the industrial suburbs of São Paulo, and directly challenged the economic and political policies of the military regime. Workers received widespread public support, and at the opening ceremonies of the gay and lesbian movement's first national gathering, the body unanimously endorsed the goals of the strike. The over 100 activists from eight groups attending the meeting claimed a membership base of approximately 300 nationwide. As in most gatherings of this kind, the first two days' activities concentrated on workshops and networking. One controversy, however, split the conference. During a plenary session, a participant introduced a motion that the gathering join a massive May Day march being organized to support the working-class strike. After fierce debate, the body voted fifty-four to fifty-three against the motion. Opponents argued that the working class was homophobic, and that the gay and lesbian movement had no business getting involved in other people's struggles. Members of São Paulo's SOMOS, still the strongest group in the country, also split, with a majority voting in favor of participating in the demonstration.

The third day of the national meeting, a rally in a local theater, was attended by over 800 people. It was the largest public gathering in favor of gay and lesbian rights to take place in Brazil up to that time. Immediately thereafter, the majority of SOMOS members decided to join the May Day protest. A contingent of fifty lesbians and gay men marched under the banners "Stop the [Governmental] Intervention in the Unions: Homosexual Commission for May 1st" and "Stop Discrimination against Homosexual Workers." A leaflet distributed by the ad hoc Commission of Homosexuals in Favor of May 1st, which had organized the contingent, expressed solidarity with the strikers, linked their struggle with that of the oppressed (blacks, women, and homosexuals), pointed to examples of discrimination that lesbians and gay men suffered as workers, and called on the unity of the working class to end such discrimination.

The May Day celebration was held in a climate of repression. To cut down on participation, military police blocked all the major roads from São Paulo to the suburban industrial center where the march took place. Army helicopters flew overhead to disrupt the demonstration. Nevertheless, over 100,000 workers and supporters marched to a rally site in a soccer stadium, where another 50,000 awaited their arrival. When the gay and lesbian contingent entered the stadium, the crowd received them warmly. The group within SOMOS that opposed joining the demonstration organized a picnic at the city zoo instead. Several weeks later they split from SOMOS, arguing that the group had been taken over by left-wing elements. Coverage about the event in the pages of *Lampião* reinforced the antileftist critique of SOMOS's actions. About the same time, a majority of SOMOS's lesbians also withdrew from the organization to work autonomously, although they maintained friendly ties with the group.

Soon after the departure of the more conservative male members and most of the lesbians, SOMOS faced a new challenge. In May 1980, the São Paulo police initiated a campaign to "clean up" the downtown area by arresting the gays, lesbians, transvestites, and prostitutes who frequented the city's nightlife district. SOMOS members called an emergency meeting, which included representatives of the spin-off groups, to plan a response. On June 13, 1980, 500 people gathered on the steps of the Municipal Theater, a traditional free speech area, to protest the more than 1,500 arrests that had taken place the previous month. Activists called for the removal of the police chief and urged the rally to march through the streets of São Paulo. Slowly, the crowd moved through the downtown area, its numbers growing to almost 1,000. This was by far the largest political act of the movement to date, and it was considered one of the reasons that police raids and roundups ceased soon after. Following this successful event, SOMOS members raised funds to rent a headquarters in downtown São Paulo, the first public gay and lesbian center in South America.

In December 1980, representatives of sixteen groups from around the country met in Rio de Janeiro to plan a second national meeting. It became clear, however, that the movement was still small. Groups were not growing. There was widespread confusion about the movement's overall direction. In fact, the planned second national meeting failed to materialize. Seven months later, the editorial board of *Lampião* decided to close down the monthly. The turnout at the June 13, 1981, demonstration in front of the Municipal Theater to commemorate the 1980 march of 1,000 against police repression amounted to only several hundred protesters.

The waning of the movement coincided with the severe economic recession of 1981–1982 and the resulting downturn in the labor movement. During the same period, there was a general retrenchment of middle-class-based social movements in the face of limited political successes. SOMOS members and most of the other groups that had attended the first national gathering in 1980 folded by late 1983. Many lesbian activists moved into the growing feminist movement, where they won a political space to raise issues about homophobia. Only a few other groups managed to survive the downturn, mostly notably Grupo Gay da Bahia, led by the energetic anthropologist Luiz Mott.

After the return to civilian rule in 1985, a slow resurgence in movement activities took place, in part to enact provisions against legal discrimination and respond to the burgeoning AIDS epidemic. By 1991, more than a dozen new groups had formed. In January 1995, fifteen years after the first national conference held in São Paulo, representatives of thirty-one organizations founded the Brazilian Association of Gays, Lesbians, and Transvestites. Currently, there are over sixty groups throughout the country, and the pride marches in Rio de Janeiro and São Paulo attract over 1,000 participants, making them among the largest in Latin America.

Had Brazil not been under the domination of a military dictatorship in the late 1960s and early 1970s, the Brazilian gay and lesbian movement could have developed somewhat earlier than it did. The political opening in Argentina from 1971 to 1975 provided the opportunity for a movement in that country, and a comparable movement could have coalesced in Brazil had the political conditions been favorable. Just as the gay and lesbian activism of the early 1970s in the United States and Western Europe was impelled by the student, civil rights, feminist, and antiwar movements, so the belated Brazilian movement was encouraged by the mobilization of students and labor that destroyed the myth of the military's invincibility.

The international movement had a direct impact on the Brazilian movement through the visits of activists from the United States and the experiences of Brazilians living abroad. The movement as a whole looked to Western Europe and the United States for ideas and inspiration. Moreover, former activists from the Argentine HLF provided encouragement in its first stages. The key to the movement's growth, however, was the fact that it was rooted in the political and social realities of Brazil.

From the early days of SOMOS, the vanguard organization during the movement's first phase, a sector of the membership understood the relationship between the political openings won by students and labor, and the comparable political and social space that they needed to develop within Brazilian society. Whereas in 1975–1976 attempts to form support groups had failed as participants doubted their own need to organize and questioned the possibility of success, in 1977–1978, there was a marked change in the consciousness not only of gay men and lesbians, but of other oppressed groups as well, most notably the working class, women, and Afro-Brazilians. Thus, the first public contact of the leading gay organization was SOMOS's Committee in Defense of *Lampião,* which sought support from the alternative leftist press, prominent artists, and intellectuals opposed to the regime.

Because the dominant ideology within the movement espoused a natural affinity between gay men and lesbians and organized groups of women and blacks, it was logical that feminists and the Unified Black Movement were its first organizational allies, or at least the first groups that it sought as allies. Although the movement's more conservative wing carried out a systematic campaign against the Brazilian Left between 1979 and 1981, there was no comparable criticism of the MNU, which accepted the solidarity of SOMOS at public demonstrations, but made no real overtures in return for united action. A critique of the MNU might have shaken the ideological model defended by the conservative wing, which pitted women, blacks, and gays against the Left. The vision presented by the movement's left wing of strategic alliances with sectors of labor and the Left was countered by the contention that the Left was homophobic, and that it only wanted to manipulate gay and lesbian groups for its own political agenda. Antileft activists also argued that the movement was too weak to work with labor, which according to their analysis, was also homophobic and hostile to any alliance. The proposal to participate in the 1980 May Day march and the subsequent march of 1,000 against police repression, initiated and led by SOMOS and its left wing, reinforced the militant forces within the movement. It also provided the impetus for the historic step of opening a public headquarters, a goal that had been discussed since 1977.

In the long run, the affinity of SOMOS's left wing with other social movements proved to be well founded. In 1980, militant labor leaders and left-wing opponents of the dictatorship founded the Workers' Party. Over the last decade, congressional representatives of the Workers' Party have been in the forefront of supporting a constitutional amendment prohibiting discrimination based on sexual orientation and legislation establishing same-sex civil status not unlike domestic partnership, as well as denouncing violence against gays, lesbians, and transvestites.

Although there is currently a new wave of lesbian and gay activism in Brazil, homophobia and oppression have not disappeared. Authoritarian regimes in Latin America have historically turned to traditional family values and rigid Christian morality to justify their rule. Homosexuals are an easy target for these regimes. The history, experiences, and lessons of the first Brazilian movement—its tactics and strategies, its perspectives and alliances—are important both for those interested in the sociology, politics, and history of that time, and those interested in supporting the new wave of gay and lesbian activism that is sweeping Latin America.

Liberation Theology's Rise and Fall

Robin Nagle

Late on the morning of October 19, 1990, five trucks of military police arrived at the praça *on the Morro da Conceição (Hill of the Immaculate Conception), a low-income neighborhood in the northeastern coastal city of Recife. Their charge was to take back the local church and parish house from "rebel" Catholics, who had held the buildings for several months in defiance of Recife's bishop, Dom José Cardoso, who had suspended their priest for insubordination a few months earlier. They believed that they were in negotiation with Dom José to get the ousted priest reinstated, or at least to have a say in his replacement. The bishop had other ideas; it was at his request that a local judge ordered the surprise police raid that day. Anthropologist Robin Nagle's analysis of the relationship between a poor northeastern community and the institutional Roman Catholic Church illuminates why reform-minded ideals often fail when confronted by day-to-day reality.*

When the police surrounded the Morro church, they were soon confronted by hundreds of angry, shouting residents. Jostled and taunted, the police held their line, but their nightsticks were drawn and their gun holsters unsnapped. Television news teams, on the scene within minutes, added to the chaos. After it was all over, no one knew how it had not become a riot. The Virgin Mary—Our Lady of the Immaculate Conception—seemed the only calm presence on the *praça* that morning. She stood a dozen yards away, a tall statue with an eternally benevolent expression.

The arrival of the police put the Morro at the center of one of the most dramatic expressions of religious tension that Latin America had seen in years. When events leading up to that day were pieced together later, however, the confrontation was not entirely surprising. Some community residents, local witnesses, and even international observers called it an invasion, a brutish and unnecessary use of force, but others said it was inevitable, and even a relief. This difference of interpretation was not limited to the Morro, but arose from a division within Roman Catholicism that encompassed ideas about faith, history, politics, and basic understandings of how the world works.

Liberation versus Conservation

The Morro had been at the center of a disagreement between the parish priest and the bishop for many months. That conflict, in turn, reflected a rift between those Catholics, clergy and laity alike, who wanted to guard the church's traditions and those who advocated a newer, more politically engaged Catholicism. The debate took shape around the controversies inspired by liberation theology, a religious and social movement felt in many parts of the Latin American Roman Catholic Church from the late 1960s until the early 1990s. Brazil provided especially fertile ground for the movement; Recife in particular was one of its hotbeds.

Liberation theology read the Bible as a blueprint for social change, and encouraged Catholics to make political awareness and action a part of their religious practice. It was not enough to pray for salvation, say the rosary, or listen to sermons, explained liberation clergy; to be in harmony with God's will, one's faith must serve as a guide toward changing larger patterns of social oppression and political injustice. This work should blend local initiatives—say, helping someone rebuild a home washed away by rains or starting an adult literacy program—with analyses of regional and even global systems of inequity. Marxist language of class analysis was used creatively. When it was at its height, some analysts claim, Brazilian liberation theology attracted between one and two million adherents, organized in as many as 100,000 *comunidades de base,* or base communities (CEBs), groups of neighbors who read the Bible together, and reflected on its implications for their work and critical analyses.

In Recife, no parish was more famous for liberationist activism than the Morro da Conceição. Reginaldo Veloso, the priest whom the bishop suspended, had a charisma and soft-spoken style that attracted hundreds who had been disillusioned by traditional Catholicism. To those Brazilians drawn to it, the goals of liberation theology seemed essential when the nation confronted a dictatorship in 1964 and then fashioned a return to democracy throughout the 1980s as the military eased out of power.

The problem was that liberation-style Catholicism became the Morro's only expression of the church. While it delighted many parishioners, it alienated many more. There were plenty of Morro residents who had been content with the church's traditional expressions of faith. These practices had resonated with what they had learned as children, and with stories they knew from earlier generations of what the church was supposed to be and do. The quiet of the church sanctuary, for many such Morro dwellers, was one of the few places they could go for refuge from an often troubling world, and the age-old rituals were sources of solace and comfort. Liberationism seemed to erase the fundamental distinction between what belonged outside the church and what belonged inside.

With Reginaldo's tenure, the very substance of the Mass was changed. Secular problems were made part of sacred time. Even the community's huge annual festivity honoring Our Lady of the Immaculate Conception was reconfigured. It was no longer a celebration of her holiness and willingness to intercede on behalf of petitioners. Liberation theology–minded *festa* organizers, said more religiously conservative Morro residents, turned it into a series of political rallies, with people praying for causes like Afro-Brazilian empowerment and the rights of landless sugar-cane cutters.

At first, these disaffected Morro dwellers weren't a problem for liberationist Catholics. In fact, if they were noticed at all, they were not given much attention. Most either left the parish to worship at a church down the hill or stopped attending Mass completely. For years, they were quiet. But they were always numerous, and when Dom José became bishop, they discovered an ally.

Dynamics of Religious Conflict

A religious tradition must blend orthodoxy with malleability to survive. If it aspires to longevity, it must help its followers understand not only the world around them, but also the history that shaped that world across time. Liberation theology presented an interpretation of history that rearranged conventional depictions by putting "the poor" at the center of both secular and sacred powers. Secular powers had consistently wronged the poor, they said, as Jesus's own life story made clear. Liberationists noted that Jesus was a carpenter and fisherman, thus a worker as humble as any other. That he was also the Son of God, they continued, who chose to take human form in such a simple role demonstrated that all the poor, and all workers like him, were a chosen people. Governments that allowed great disparities of wealth and need, and relations between nations that created imbalances of resources and wants were sources of poverty for millions of people all over the world, liberationists argued; if the poor are indeed God's chosen people, then it is the duty of all Christians to work toward eradicating the structures that create and perpetuate poverty.

As Brazil's dictatorship grew more brutal and silenced growing numbers of people in the late 1960s, the Roman Catholic Church slowly became an umbrella under which a disparate collection of activists and protesters found some protection. As the country's original transnational institution, the church had immunity from the government's most repressive measures (though individual clergy were singled out for torture, expulsion, and even murder).

At the heart of its message, liberation theology contended that the poor had been exploited long enough; it was time for them to become creators of their own history. In parishes that embraced liberationist teachings, this shift of emphasis was reflected in the Mass, in prayers of petition and thanks, in saints' feast celebrations, and in community political dynamics. On the Morro da Conceição, parishioners involved in the liberationist church became the founders of the residents' council, mother's club, sewing cooperative, day care center, and the school for retarded children. It was they who first won running water—and later, bus service, garbage pickup, and street paving—for the entire neighborhood. The liberation-trained laity welcomed the emphasis on their abilities, and flexed newly discovered political muscle with quickly learned sophistication and effectiveness.

Perhaps this would have caused uniform celebration among the Morro's Catholics if it had not signaled a complete replacement of older religious practices. It is true that when the residents' council succeeded in wresting public services from a reluctant city government, the entire hill benefited, and no one wished for a return to the days when household water came by bucket from a few public spigots. But the politicization of the hill had started wthin the church, and the church's expression of its tradition reflected the change. Instead of embracing the new emphasis on materiality, community problems, and activism, traditionalists believed that their church was sullied by such secular concerns. They found that they no longer had a place to go that was only about devotion. And the liberationist interpretation of history meant an entirely uncomfortable assumption of responsibility for problems that had always before seemed rooted in distant, untouchable sources. It was, for traditionalists, the transformation of a sure and necessary refuge into a hotbed of agitation no longer recognizable as a spiritual center.

The traditionalists on the hill were not alone in their dismay. Church leaders in Recife, in other parts of Brazil, and even in Rome, watched the liberation theology movement with growing alarm. It represented a trend away from church orthodoxy toward a materiality that many felt was inappropriate. When Dom José was made bishop of the Olinda / Recife diocese in 1985, he was given a mandate to bring that region's church back into alignment with the church proper, and he went after his charge with a vengeance. Within the first five years of his arrival in Recife, Dom José dismantled most of the structures dedicated to liberationist themes, which had been more than twenty years in the making. Catholics and others all over the region were stunned—and helpless. They protested that the liberationist style of church Dom José seemed to hate was, in fact, a "people's" church, and they accused him of ignoring the needs of his flock.

There were two problems with these assertions. First, the Roman Catholic Church is not and never has been about democracy or listening to the will of "the people." It is a hierarchical organization with clear and rigidly enforced chains of command, responsibility, and obedience. Second, the bishop was serving the will of the people—but not the people loyal to a liberation church. Dom José's expression and understanding of Catholicism supported a much older set of religious practices, and his return to those traditions eased the worry of many in the diocese. The liberation trend, many felt, had moved the church in an entirely wrong direction. While protesters chanted in the streets that Dom José should be removed, many others quietly applauded his efforts.

The same trend has been repeated throughout Latin America. As bishops across Central and South America have retired or left the church, Pope John Paul II, in office since 1978, has replaced them with clergy who support the church's orthodoxy without recourse to social criticism or marxist economic analyses. The moment that was liberation theology's represented a brief era in which the church's prophets tried to turn the institution toward a new future. They were met by the church's guardians of tradition, who refused to allow such a transition.

This does not mean that liberation theology was a failure. On the contrary, hundreds of people schooled in its ideologies have become successful advocates for a variety of socially just causes. But religious expressions of liberationist Catholicism in Latin America have grown rare. While the impulses that found expression through the movement have not been quelled, the Roman Catholic Church will not host them again for some time to come.

IX

Saudades

Saudades are nostalgic longings for things that are distant, that have ebbed from experience. Brazil's first European visitors saw it as an Eden, an immensely rich land that provoked desire, fascination, and curiosity. In time, the Edenic past receded.[1] In 1931, as the economic depression's hold deepened, the critic Paulo Prado reported endemic melancholy— "in a radiant land there lives a sad people. This melancholy is the inheritance of its discoverers, who revealed it to the world and peopled it."[2] In later decades, wags taunted: "Brazil is the Country of the Future—and always will be."

This is wrong, because Brazilians do not permit their exuberance for life to be extinguished by setbacks. Brazilian *saudades* are rarely as sad as the soulful Portuguese *fados* sung in Lisbon cafés. Brazil recovers. Its democratic character survived the military dictatorship. Brazilian culture respects the past. The nineteenth-century musical *choro* has been revived several times. Steps are being taken to preserve the architectural patrimony. Children of all ages love Monteiro Lobato's rustic characters Jeca Tatú, Narizinho, and the Visconde de Sabugosa. All esteem Brazil's great soccer teams of past World Cups—even if the 1998 squad came up three goals short in the final match in the Stade de France before 2 billion television spectators worldwide. Even as a vise tightened over the hearts of would-be celebrants as the French team pulled ahead and a wave of introspection and finger-pointing descended minutes after the final whistle, some fans broke into irrepressible sambas. "We played well," said a woman comforting her distraught daughter. "We're a country that came up from poverty to reach victory. We're a country of soccer, illuminated by God, with a destiny. We can't win all the time. We have to give a chance to other countries, who are also God's children."[3]

Notes

1   Richard G. Parker, *Bodies, Pleasures and Passions: Sexual Culture in Contemporary Brazil* (Boston: Beacon Press, 1991), p. 13.
2   Paulo Prado, *Retrato do Brasil,* 3d ed. (Rio de Janeiro: F. Briguet and Cia., 1931), p. 11.
3   Fátima Santos, quoted by Diana Jean Shemo, *New York Times,* July 13, 1998, C15.

Bananas Is My Business

Helena Solberg

This excerpt is from the script of Helena Solberg's 1994 documentary about the life of Carmen Miranda. Born in Portugal but raised in middle-class circumstances in Rio de Janeiro, Miranda worked in a milliner's shop before gaining fame as a samba singer. In 1943, when she was brought to the United States by Broadway impresario Lee Shubert, she became the highest paid entertainer in show business. Miranda paid a high price for this: typecast as a flamboyant, ditsy Latin bombshell wearing baskets of fruit on her head, she was booed off the stage by elite Brazilians for selling out to Hollywood when she visited Brazil on tour. Returning to Hollywood, her career spiraled downward. She suffered from depression, and in 1955, collapsed on camera while taping a television show and died at the age of forty-six.

Shots of Rio de Janeiro

Announcer: Hello, hello Brazil! Once again, the city of wonder and the city of skyscrapers are brought together by the modern miracle of radio and the supreme power of love. Together, they now bring to all you in Brazil the affectionate sentiments of your own Carmen Miranda.
Carmen Miranda: My dear, beloved listeners in Brazil. The applause I hear every night on Broadway feels like the echo of your applause, pleased to know that your music is so successful in the United States. Once again, I assure you that I will always do whatever is necessary to repay your great kindness and love. Goodbye, Brazil! Until we meet again!

Like all good Brazilians, we didn't believe in her success—despite the reports that she was an amazing hit. But no one accepted that, because in those days, in Rio de Janeiro, in Brazil, samba was considered "Negro music," music from the slums.

Scenes of Carmen Arriving in Rio

Carmen was a great success in New York, and a year and a half later she
came back to Brazil. A big reception was prepared. The government
office of communications and propaganda held an official reception! Her
arrival was a smash! The next day, the newspapers gave her hell. They
said this was too good for a samba singer, that they should only have this
kind of reception for the arrival of a great scientist or classical musician,
somebody from the upper crust of society. But Carmen was just one of
the people, not one of the elite! Just like the samba! That's the way it was.

Shot of Rio by Night, then Interior of Casino da Urca

Inner Voice: This is another night at the same casino where Shubert first
spotted Carmen. It's her first appearance since returning from New
York. A night full of excitement for the selected guests invited by the
president's wife. It's not the popular audience that Carmen is used to.

   She salutes the audience in English: "Good night, people!" The silence
that follows feels like ice.

   She sings "South American Way"—not known, of course, as a Brazilian song. The silence persists.

   After a couple more songs, it's clear that she cannot continue.
Newspaper: "Carmen Miranda is sick. Has to cancel her show at the
Casino." They did her a great injustice. It was something she could never
forget even if she lived 100 years. And she never did forget it. She cried
bitterly, "I who love Brazil so much."

   It was cold, like ice—it was something no one expected!

   The next day, the newspapers attacked her again! They said she was no
longer "Carmen Miranda," that we had lost our "Carmen Miranda,"
that she had become Americanized.

Inner Voice: She will never understand what really happened: the conflict-
ing criticism, the harsh judgment, maybe the jealousy. She had made up
her mind, she will sing one last time in Brazil to the audience that always
loved her.

*Carmen performing at Casino da Urca, sings "Disseram Que Voltei Amer-
icanisada."* And she sang,

They say I came back Americanized / full of money, rich as hell: / And now I can't stand to hear a tambourine / And the "cuica" just makes me yell. . . . For so long as there's a Brazil, my heart is with my homeland still!

Inner Voice: After reassuring us of how Brazilian she was, she is surprised by a telegram: a new contract with Twentieth-Century Fox. She crosses the ocean, this time fourteen years will pass before she comes home again.

Shots of ocean. Synval Silva / Carmen Miranda duet: "Adeus Batucada."

"Farewell, samba . . .
Farewell, my people's drum and tambourine . . ."

The Invention of Tradition

on Brazilian Radio

Bryan McCann

Nationalism set the tone for the entire Vargas era. Campaigns to develop Brazilian-owned steel and petroleum industries were economic forms of nationalism. Politically, a stronger central government came to prevail over what formerly had been a loose confederation of states. Brazil's significant involvement in World War II further contributed to national unity and pride. In many ways, however, these manifestations of nationalism altered traditions that, in many eyes, constituted the essence of Brazilianness. Culture, perhaps, best reflected that contradiction.

On the night of March 19, 1947, Henrique Foreis Domingues, better known as Almirante, the admiral, took to the airwaves of Radio Tupí and Radio Tamoio of Rio de Janeiro to announce a new program. Almirante, "the ranking officer of radio," had earned his nickname as a teenager in the Naval Reserves. He had long since abandoned the navy, dedicating his life instead to radio: first as a singer; more important, as a producer, writer, director, researcher, and announcer. (It was not unusual to wear many hats in those feverish radio days, but even so, Almirante stood out for the diversity and scale of his endeavors.) In fifteen years on the air, the vast majority of that time in Rio, Almirante had become the most respected producer in Brazilian radio, and a new Almirante program was always an eagerly awaited cultural event. That night's program would go on to particular success, remaining on the air in weekly broadcasts for nearly seven years, surviving several changes in stations and short periods off the air. Even afterwards, in the mid-1950s, the program engendered music festivals, tours, television broadcasts, and records. In short, the program became a cultural phenomenon, attracting popular interest that went far beyond merely tuning in a local station for a half hour's worth of musical delight.

Such success was unexpected, given that the program seemed to buck every cultural trend of the moment. Those were days of international cultural cross-pollination: Bing Crosby and Frank Sinatra were climbing the Brazilian charts. Cuban bandleader Xavier Cugat had recently completed an extended tour of Brazil. Even in terms of domestic production, Rio seemed to be losing its stranglehold on the nation's musical attention: a new rhythm from the Brazilian Northeast called the *baião* was encroaching ever farther into the territory of Rio's samba. The new and the foreign were in, the old and the local were out. And Almirante's *O Pessoal da Velha Guarda,* or *The Personnel of the Old Guard,* as the name begins to suggest, was a program designed to feature the old masters of Brazilian popular music and reaffirm their role as the true guardians of the nation's cultural soul.

For Almirante, there was never any question that that soul was *carioca.* Almirante himself was a *carioca,* a native of Rio, and he believed implicitly in Rio as the musical capital of Brazil (and the world). The musicians he chose for his program were almost all locals. Moreover, the music they performed was overwhelmingly *carioca,* featuring the rhythms of samba, *xote, lundu,* and above all, *chorinho. O Pessoal da Velha Guarda* stirred a *chorinho* revival (a Brazilian adaptation of European polkas, waltzes, and other forms set to an Afro-Brazilian syncopation, originating in the 1860s and newly popular in the 1930s), making it more popular nationally than it had ever been before. Musically, the program marked the birth of a new phase of *chorinho,* expanding the possibilities of the genre. But such innovations and novelties were hidden by the program's constant emphasis on tradition and the preservation of the nation's cultural riches. Thus, the program's unlikely success illuminates not only that cultural moment in Brazil, but the place of cultural nationalism and the invention of tradition within Brazilian popular music.

If the degree of the program's success was surprising, it was not entirely a matter of chance. In addition to the impeccable Almirante, the program featured the talents of a host of excellent musicians. Foremost among them was Pixinguinha (Alfredo da Rocha Vianna), a composer, arranger, and musician of surpassing brilliance. Born in 1897, Pixinguinha had played professionally for over thirty years, had written hundreds of compositions in various styles, and through his work as an arranger for the Victor record label in Rio in the 1930s, had done more than any other single artist to develop the hallmarks and standards that came to define the Brazilian popular music of the era. In the 1940s, however, Pixinguinha's star had fallen a bit. He was known primarily as a flautist, but had lost confidence in his mastery of the instrument, and had limited himself completely to his second instrument, the tenor sax. The switch left audiences puzzled. Demand for his talents as an arranger had also fallen off. For Pixinguinha, *O Pessoal da Velha Guarda* was an opportunity for work and exposure.

Pixinguinha shared musical leadership of the program with Benedito Lacerda, another flautist, composer, and arranger. Only a few years younger, Lacerda was distinctly Pixinguinha's disciple, largely following in the elder's footsteps in all of his musical endeavors. Before *O Pessoal da Velha Guarda,* Lacerda had been most influential as a radio bandleader, developing the *conjunto regional,* a flexible small group capable of accompanying almost any radio act. For Lacerda, the new program offered a chance to seize the spotlight from the master, playing as the featured soloist on flute with Pixinguinha in a supporting role on sax.

The format of the program was simple and straightforward, Almirante introduced the orchestra and let it play, which it did marvelously well. In between the musical selections, he gave information about the composers and rhythms, recounted anecdotes, and as the program developed a regular audience, read sections of letters from listeners. He gave the twin themes of nationalism and preservation constant emphasis, introducing the program as "uma audição brasileiríssima" (an extremely Brazilian broadcast), "perhaps the most Brazilian on radio," and praising "the noble work of this restoration of our authentic popular music." The logic behind such assertions was frankly circular: the program was authentic because it was Brazilian, Brazilian because it was authentic, and noble because it was Brazilian and authentic. The only way to give such logic any meaning was to stress the inviolability of traditional standards. Almirante complained of "those singers who dilute the melody of our songs," insisting that "the singer should not, for any reason, change the melody written by the composer." And he affirmed that *O Pessoal da Velha Guarda,* of course, would never do such a thing. On another evening, Almirante declared, "performers of popular music: the greatest benefit you can give to Brazilian popular music is to sing samba as samba, *marcha* as *marcha*, waltz as waltz . . . none of this imitating the Bing Crosbys and Frank Sinatras. The effects they use for the fox-trot might be good for the fox-trot, *but not for our music.* On this point, the *Pessoal da Velha Guarda* plays our music with the greatest rigor."

Such nationalism was not limited to music. Speaking of Vinhos Único, the vintner who sponsored the program for one stretch, Almirante proclaimed: "Brazilians now have confidence in the things that other Brazilians produce. They are confident that our industry has completely surpassed that of foreign industries." But if other things (wine, poetry, the plazas of downtown Rio) occasionally earned that adjective of highest praise, *brasileiríssimo,* popular music was, for Almirante, the truest expression of national character. And *chorinho,* in particular, communicated something essentially Brazilian. The program's emphasis on *chorinho* was not at all axiomatic: samba, after all, was a more popular genre, one already deeply linked to nationalist sentiment following the wave of *samba-ufanisto,* or boastful samba, of the Estado Novo, and one associated internationally with Brazilian identity through the fame of Carmen Miranda. (Almirante himself, moreover, had favored samba as a performer.)

Chorinho, or *choro,* in contrast, remained primarily a local genre of Rio de Janeiro. Rhythmically, it was closely related to samba, and shared common roots. It had begun to coalesce as a genre at least two decades earlier than samba, with the compositions and arrangements of Anacleto de Medeiros for the City Fire Department's Band just before the turn of the century. But in dramatic contrast to samba, it was principally instrumental rather than vocal, perhaps one of the reasons it had not attained the popularity of its younger sibling. *Chorinho* was certainly known throughout the country, and had been since Pixinguinha led his group on an extended tour in the early 1920s, and even earlier, through the dissemination of sheet music and records. But it had never inspired a national trend, much less become a national symbol, in the way that samba had. Before *O Pessoal da Velha Guarda, chorinho* had attained its broadest fame through vocalist Orlando Silva's 1939 recording of "Carinhoso," a Pixinguinha composition with lyrics by Braguinha. That success had not sparked a broader trend: by the mid-1940s, *chorinho* had noticeably declined in popularity. But it was precisely this diminished appeal, in tandem with *chorinho*'s historical continuity of style (in comparison with samba, it had changed little over the previous twenty years), that made it the perfect candidate for Almirante's curatorial preservation. *Chorinho* remained authentic, apparently unchanged, undiluted by national and international commercial success, and it was in danger of fading away.

If the need for preservation provided the reason for the program's existence, it was the assertion of *chorinho* as an expression of a Brazilian essence that gave that project its importance. Almirante summed up his vision of *chorinho* as the carrier of national identity in a 1948 broadcast. Speaking with a passion that contrasted with his usual professorial mode, he confessed a belief in the power of popular music to pacify the world. "In that case," he added, "each of us should make sure that a good number of our songs cross the world's borders, bringing to other peoples the certainty of our existence and a way to recognize our creatures." He concluded by recommending that Brazilians, when traveling abroad, identify themselves by whistling the most famous *chorinho* composition, "Carinhoso."

O Pessoal da Velha Guarda is a clear example of the phenomenon that English historian Eric Hobsbawm describes as "the invention of tradition"—the use of the rhetoric of defense of ostensibly old and cherished customs (in reality, not necessarily either) to serve current purposes. For Hobsbawm, the word "invention" does not mean that the protected cultural expression (in this case, *chorinho*) did not exist previously, but rather that through the emphasis on preservation and tradition, the cultural expression gains an importance and a meaning that it did not possess in the past. The golden age that the inventors of tradition profess to defend is, to a certain degree, imaginary. With *O Pessoal da Velha Guarda*, Almirante imagined a glorious past for *chorinho*, one in which the genre was not only locally but nationally cherished. He affirmed that his program would preserve that past and insisted that this project was vital to the cultural interests of the nation.

Almirante's program was explicitly a reaction to the cultural upheavals of the day. He feared that American mass culture, an increasingly powerful presence in Brazil following the cultural exchange campaigns of the Good Neighbor Policy during World War II, would wipe out domestic culture. He feared that swept away by the fox-trot, Brazilians would forget Pixinguinha and "the most legitimate Brazilian musicians." The danger from without came from Bing Crosby. The danger from within came from Brazilian singers like Dick Farney, who incorporated and imitated American styles. Almirante's fears were not entirely misplaced: those were indeed years of great change in the cultural market. On the radio, for example, soap operas increasingly dominated program schedules and advertising revenue. Musical programming had also begun to change markedly. In addition to the fad of the *baião,* the late 1940s saw the rise of the famous *Cantoras do Radio,* pop divas such as Emilinha Borba, Marlene, and Angela Maria, whose overwhelming success depended on a complex package of charisma, promotion, musical ability, and endless personal interaction with their fan clubs. They performed primarily on weekend afternoon variety shows, a genre that quickly became the most popular type of musical show on the radio. In great contrast to Almirante's programs and the sophisticated orchestral elaboration characteristic of programs of the early 1940s, these programs sacrificed musical refinement in favor of a noisy ambiance of festivity and delirium. Musically, they nourished the ascendance of the slow, melodramatic Mexican bolero and its Brazilian counterpart, the *samba-canção.*

These cultural changes coincided with technological transformation. *O Pessoal da Velha Guarda* reached its greatest popularity in the early 1950s, precisely the years of the infancy of television in Brazil, and equally important to the music industry, that of long-playing records. Economically and politically, the most divisive issue of the day concerned the development of Brazilian oil deposits. Nationalists, encouraged by President Getúlio Vargas, rallied to the cry "o petróleo é nosso"—the oil is ours. Those they labeled *entreguistas,* or sellouts, supported bits of Standard Oil and Shell to expand operations within Brazil. Almirante's program responded to this climate of cultural and technological change, and reflected—and indeed participated in—political debates regarding the protection of national resources versus the pursuit of international capital and its potential for modernization. Almirante's brand of cultural nationalism, however, had a complex and often paradoxical relationship with the economic nationalism of the defenders of Brazilian oil. *O Pessoal da Velha Guarda,* for example, made its debut on the Rio stations owned by Assis Chateaubriand, a fervent supporter of multinational investors and the most vocal *entreguista* in the country.

Such small ironies did not hinder the program's success. *O Pessoal da Velha Guarda* met the trends of fox-trot and variety shows head-on, and fared well. The program never led the radio polls, but it maintained a significant share of the audience, both in its regular broadcasts on the Rio stations and in special programs in São Paulo. In fact, the entire phenomenon of *Velha Guarda* became even more popular in São Paulo. It was there that Almirante organized the Festivals of the *Pessoal da Velha Guarda,* in 1954 and 1955. (The first formed part of São Paulo's quadricentennial celebration—one more effort to place *chorinho* at the center of the nation's historical imagination.) These festivals brought tens of thousands of fans into public plazas to applaud Pixinguinha and company. The shows came to Rio afterwards, but they did not gather the same energy that they had achieved in São Paulo: the invention of *chorinho* as a national symbol was embraced most passionately far from the birthplace of the rhythm. A Rio critic noted this, writing, "this has created a paradox: these days whoever wants to hear Brazilian music in Brazil has to go to São Paulo." (A gripe that reveals just how completely Rio had previously dominated the national music industry.)

And the news media, far from consigning *Velha Guarda* to history, gave it a place of prestige. The São Paulo festivals were broadcast with great fanfare on local television, and in the mid-1950s, *O Pessoal da Velha Guarda* musicians recorded three long-playing records. These triumphs were only part of the success story. Between 1946 and 1951, Pixinguinha and Lacerda released thirty-six records (singles with B-sides), with sales bolstered by extensive promotion on the radio show. The response was not limited to Rio and São Paulo: the program registered in the ratings in several cities around the country, a feat unusual in a period when local programming generally surpassed the powerful broadcasts of Rio and São Paulo outside those areas. Almirante underlined this success by reading enthusiastic fan mail from listeners throughout the country. With material success came prestige: in 1949, Pixinguinha was finally transferred from a long-held position as an inspector of public sanitation to the more appropriate post of director of the municipal band. (The transfer was largely an issue of title, as Pixinguinha had been directing the band for years and had never shown much concern for public sanitation.) And in 1951, prodded by Almirante's encomiums, the mayor of Rio finally bestowed the title of professor of music on the great Pixinguinha.

O Pessoal da Velha Guarda, then, was a successful invention of tradition. (At least at the moment: in subsequent years, *chorinho* once again faded in popularity, made a comeback in the 1970s, faded again, and is now in the midst of yet another revival.) One paradox of that success was that the emphasis on tradition and preservation precluded recognition of the program's innovations. *O Pessoal da Velha Guarda,* for instance, featured several young musicians, such as flautist Altamiro Carrilho and mando-linist Jacob do Bandolim. Both of these men went on to brilliant careers, pushing *chorinho* in new directions. On the program, however, their emerging talents went largely unrecognized. Almirante referred to them as *"os novos da Velha Guarda"*—the young ones of the Old Guard—a phrase that in its awkwardness, suggests the difficulty of acknowledging novelty within a "traditional" performance. Likewise, the program de-buted compositions that later became classics of the genre, such as Jacob's "Treme Treme," but did so utterly without fanfare.

Most important, *O Pessoal da Velha Guarda* initiated a new phase of *chorinho,* not merely in terms of national recognition but in terms of musical expression. In his duets with Lacerda, Pixinguinha developed a striking and ingenious language of musical counterpoint that opened up a wealth of harmonic possibilities within the genre. Counterpoint had always formed a part of *chorinho,* and in his arrangements, Pixinguinha had been experimenting with parallel but distinct melodic lines for years. But it was only when he began to play a supporting role to Lacerda's flute solos that he pushed that technique to new heights, writing and improvising simultaneous melodies that contrasted boldly with each other and yet fit together with the precision of Chinese boxes. In the words of musician and scholar Brasílio Itibirê, the contrapuntal inven-tion of Pixinguinha and Lacerda "is one of the most complex elements, and one of the greatest aesthetic consequences that exist in Brazilian popular music." It was a musical innovation as significant as the contem-poraneous birth of bebop in the jazz clubs of New York City, but with the striking difference that Charlie Parker and Dizzy Gillespie acted like the brash geniuses of a daring new style, and became famous in that image. With *O Pessoal da Velha Guarda,* on the other hand, innovation always wore the mask of tradition.

Almirante was by no means solely responsible for the invention of *Velha Guarda*. The musicians participated as well, dressing in a style evocative of the 1920s: in straw boaters, bow ties, and white linen suits. (Can anyone imagine Charlie Parker in a straw boater and bow tie?) The concept of the *Velha Guarda,* furthermore, was not a new one. Pixin-guinha had formed a small band known as the Grupo da Guarda Velha as early as 1931, as part of his work as an arranger and bandleader at Victor. At the time, Pixinguinha was thirty-four. His fellow bandmates Donga and João da Baiana had already reached the terribly advanced ages of forty-two and forty-four, respectively. They were, of course, far from old, and were making some of the hippest music recorded that decade, exploring the shared terrain of samba and *chorinho*. But even then, they did so under the rubric of tradition, buttressed by its implications of authenticity.

If the concept of the *Velha Guarda* within Brazilian popular music had been around for some time, however, it was *O Pessoal da Velha Guarda* that gave that concept its first national exposure and extended promotion, precisely at a moment when the preservation of national treasures had a larger resonance. Since then, the concept has formed a constant theme of Brazilian popular music. The idea took root even more firmly in regard to samba than to *chorinho*: every samba school has its *Velha Guarda,* considered the embodiment of soul, tradition, authenticity. Within *chorinho,* the idea is explicit in the very names of the groups: Época de Ouro (Golden Age) and Rio Antigo (Old Rio) are two of the most successful current acts. As is by now evident, however, this *velhaguardismo* often finds expression in innovative language. Composer Moacyr Luz's recent "Anjo da Velha Guarda" (Angel of the Old Guard), for example, is an unusually poetic, almost hagiographic invocation of the spirit of Brazilian popular music. Not entirely coincidentally, Luz pays homage to the icons of the straw boater and white linen suit.

To dismiss the various manifestations of the concept of the *Velha Guarda* as mere nostalgia would be too simple. Brazil has maintained a domestic music industry more successfully than any other country in Latin America. International pop music is, of course, a constant presence in Brazil, but it has never threatened to take over the market share or the airtime of domestic production. That production is famously rich and varied: surprisingly, much of it is still given over to samba. The Mexican bolero and Argentine tango, to draw two roughly contemporaneous analogies, have largely been consigned to specialty markets and nostalgia bins. Jazz, in its many varieties, accounts for only a small share of the American music industry. Samba, on the other hand, is as rich and diverse as it has ever been, and still dominates the airtime of many of the country's most popular radio stations. There are many reasons for the genre's continued vitality: one is the constant presence of the concept of the *Velha Guarda,* the idea that the authentic, traditional, time-honored Brazilian popular music communicates something essential about national identity, and therefore, must be preserved and disseminated. This may be a fiction, or an exaggeration, but it is certainly a beguiling one.

Bahia Music Story

Bill Hinchberger

Between sessions, house musicians at a Salvador jingle factory threw together a spicy version of Simon and Garfunkel's "Mrs. Robinson" and packed the single off to local DJs. The jocks went for it. So did listeners. That 1983 cover and the now-defunct band Acordes Verdes (Green Chords) presaged a distinct regional style identified with this city of 2.1 million, the capital of Bahia state in the Brazilian northeast. The recipe was simple but unique: add jazzlike solos to Afro-Brazilian percussion and lay over a basic melody. "What's noteworthy about this music is not the harmony and lyrics but the melody and rhythm," says Wesley Rangel, who owned the jingle factory and runs WR Discos, a thriving music production firm that has a label but mostly brokers Salvador acts to the majors.

Percussionists Olodum (who backed Paul Simon on his *Rhythm of the Saints* album), singer Margareth Menezes (a David Byrne cohort), and percussionist-composer Carlinhos Brown (founding Acordes Verdes member, and holder of a rare joint record deal with EMI Brazil and Virgin France) contribute to the estimated three million in annual CD sales by this new wave of Salvador artists. Daniela Mercury's 1993 release "O Canto da Cidade" sold 1.2 million copies, ranking Salvador's most popular singer up there with perennial Brazilian crooner Roberto Carlos.

Bahia always supplied a generous share of conscripts to the Brazilian popular music army: João Gilberto, Caetano Veloso, Gilberto Gil, Gal Costa, and Tam Zé all hail from the state. But only in the 1980s did Salvador develop and popularize a distinguishable sound.

Sometimes labeled *axé* music (from an Afro-Brazilian term meaning "sacred spirit be with you"), that sound owes its soul to Salvador's version of Brazil's popular pre–Lenten Carnival festival. Unlike the spectator-oriented parade in Rio de Janeiro, Salvador's Carnival features musical groups that circulate through downtown. Common folks can tag along; the line between formal participant and spectator is blurred.

Stirred by the U.S. civil rights movement, a group of black activists founded Ilê Aiyê in 1974 partly as an outlet for their militancy during Carnival. "We were going to call it Black Power," says President Antônio Carlos Vovô, "but the police advised us not to." With Brazil in the middle of a 1964–1985 military dictatorship, the leaders relented.

Rather than play samba in the Rio de Janeiro tradition, like most everybody else in Salvador back then, Ilê Aiyê mixed in heavy rhythms that commonly accompany ceremonies of the Afro-Brazilian Candomblé religion. The concoction is called Ijexá. In 1982, composer Edil Pacheco and singer Clara Nunes popularized the form with their tune by that name.

Collectively dubbed *blocos afros* (African blocs), other groups followed—each with its own twist. Founded in 1979, Olodum pioneered something called samba-reggae. "It was samba with reggae's [social and political] discourse," says Olodum President João Jorge Santos Rodrigues. "You needed more time to fit in your message, and therefore a longer measure. The rhythm approached that of reggae." It was a samba-reggae composition, "Elegibô," that Margareth Menezes took to the top of the Billboard World Music charts in 1988.

About that time, Carlinhos Brown was backing a Cuban jazz band at a local club. And periodic private jam sessions involving Salvador's top percussionists were thriving downtown. Soon, as musician-musicologist Fred Dantas recalls it, percussionists were playing jazzlike solos on Afro-Brazilian instruments. "Before the large tambours just kept the beat," says Dantas. Brown won an invitation to back Sergio Mendes on the Grammy-winning hit "What Is It?" He then founded the percussion troupe Timbalada.

Back then, white folks tended to like their Carnivals set to frenetic *frevo,* a style imported from further north in Recife, mixed with rock elements. Bands played on giant stage-topped sound trucks known as a *trios elétricos,* invented by the father of a musician, Armandinho, who perfected another of his father's inventions: the Bahian guitar, a dissonant electric bandolin-ukelele developed before anybody in Bahia had heard of Les Paul and his electric guitar. "Our [recently reunited] band Cor do Som [Color of Music] was a hit in the 1980s," says Armandinho. "It took the *trio elétrico* and gave it national standing."

The *trio elétrico* business is lucrative. There are an estimated 200 of them in Salvador: together they earn an estimated twenty million dollars a month for staging replays of Salvador's Carnival across Brazil during the course of the year. This year, the Mexican resort Cancún imported Salvador's off-season Carnival. Hurting for material in the 1980s, trio groups like Banda Mel borrowed the characteristic beat from the *blocos afros* and raided their library of compositions, earning commercial success. A 1988 album by a band called Reflexus sold a million copies. Daniela Mercury's first hit was a cover from a *bloco afro*.

Seeing others popularize their songs and garner dividends, the *blocos afros*—most of them, anyway—committed what some decried as sacrilege: they added guitars and keyboards to their heretofore singularly percussionist entourages. Soon, *trio* bands and *blocos afros* were marching toward crossover middle ground, notes sociologist Milton Moura. "Olodum's beat is akin to war drums, but they made a deal with the opposing army," he laughs.

As for the jingle factory, it was producing most all of these folks, and WR Discos became Salvador's version of Sun Records, the Memphis company that launched Elvis Presley and other rockabilly stars in the 1950s. Rangel claims to have midwifed 400 new artists and recorded over 5,000 songs in his studio since 1985. By his count, WR Discos is responsible for introducing Brazil and the world to seventy new rhythms, most thanks to the musical mixing and matching that seems Bahian second nature. "There's lots of versatility here," notes singer Menezes.

Rangel hopes to keep the raw material flowing. This year, he is hiring academics to scour rural Bahia for undiscovered sounds and talent. As Rangel works to mine new sources of raw material, others fear that decadence is setting in. Ironically, it was the progressive militants in Olodum who opened the door to this creeping creative demise. The hit song in the lead up to Carnival in 1994 was Olodum's "Requebra" ("Shake Your Booty," roughly translated). The simple, upbeat "Requebra" came replete with a stylized, risqué dance. Quick butt moves and sexy grinds replaced the methodical, rhythmic dance steps reminiscent of Africa. "Olodum achieved commercial success, but it broke the link," notes musician-musicologist Dantas. "Before, the dances were all sacred, emanating from the Afro-Brazilian deities, or they represented motions from manual labor."

" 'Requebra' brought change," notes Olodum's João Jorge. "It opened things up for these *pagode* groups that began to appear." *Pagode* was once championed in Rio de Janeiro by groups like Fundo de Quintal, who led a march back to more melodic samba, distancing themselves from the rabid beat that now characterizes Rio's Carnival theme songs. In Salvador, *pagode* was speeded up, stripped down to the most basic chords, and transformed into sex music. One hit song is an unabashed ode to the striptease. Others come with names like "Dança do Bumbum" ("Butt Dance") and "Dança da Garrafa" ("Bottle Dance"). As their titles imply, the songs come with ritualistic dances. The Bottle Dance involves the female partner grinding her hips while she lowers her crotch in the direction of a beer bottle. The biggest phenomenon, É o Tchan, sold two million copies of its album *Na Cabeça e na Cintura* (*On the Head and the Waste*) in just over two months after its 1996 release. The group's star is not a musician, but a wide-hipped, bleach blond backup dancer named Carla Perez.

Fred Dantas is no prude, but the musician decries the lack of creativity in Salvador's *pagode*. "There were great advances made by the *blocos afros*," he notes. "The musical gain with *pagode* is zero. There are only four chords. There's no way to work with it." *Pagode* is pretty vacant content-wise, too, contends Dantas. Gone are stated or implied relationships to the black civil rights movement, and the subtle sensuality emanating from Afro-Brazilian culture but common to most Bahian men and women.

Hope can emerge from unusual places, though. Once again, Bahia may infuse itself with elements borrowed from the international musical cauldron. Carlinhos Brown has made incursions into heavy metal, teaming up with Brazil's Sepultura on the popular rock band's last CD before they broke up. A new Salvador band called Catapulta integrates Bahian percussion and a radical rock aesthetic in their first CD. Lyrics from the band's first single deal with *capoeira*, the Afro-Brazilian martial art, and the arrangement makes room for the *berimbau* (a twangy, single-stringed instrument) and tambourine, instruments customarily played during *capoeira* exhibitions. "The beat of Bahian percussion is as heavy as rock and roll," says Catapulta's vocalist Moisés. Just as punk shattered rock and roll's stagnation in the 1970s, aggressive young Bahian musicians may help derail *pagode*.

O Axé de Zumbí

Paulo Lima and Bernadete Toneto

As samba, axé *music,* blocos afros, *and* pagode *find acceptance in the mainstream culture industry, marginalized youth create new, sometimes radical, musical styles. In part, this reflects economics. Once their music achieves mass appeal, the marginalized must compete with performers who have better formal education, business connections, and access to expensive musical instruments. Their attraction to alternative cultural expression, however, also represents a voluntary move. In effect, the marginalized assert their identity and carve out their own social space by means of a distinctive communicative form. The following article about rappers in São Paulo's periphery illustrates the special value that impoverished youth place on alternative music.*

On the wave of recognition of Negro culture, the young in the peripheries of the large cities swing. With much *axé* and movement, they join together in organized groups, singing and dancing to the sound of rap. One of them is Zinho, leader of the Negro Power Gang, one of the largest of the western São Paulo periphery. At eighteen years of age, Zinho is unemployed, as are the majority of the friends who form his "gangue." To chase away the disenchantment, they pass the nights composing songs in strong and syncopated rhythm, speaking of racism, police violence, and Negro leaders who emotionally touch the gang, among them Zumbi.

Zinho was expelled from the João Amós Municipal Primary School, in Jardim Vista Alegre, because of acts of vandalism. He broke desks, destroyed bathroom faucets, and generally stirred up commotion. He fled from classes to paint nearby walls, in protest against a ritualistic and moralizing school. "I did not have anything to do in the school. What they teach there does not mean anything in my life." He assumed violent attitudes and intimidated the community, which associates poor and Negro kids with drug traffic and violence.

One day, he met Professor Maria Stela Graciani, coordinator of the Center for Community Work of the Catholic Pontifical University of São Paulo. He was found with youth from other neighborhoods and rival groups. In September 1994, he happened to participate in an unprecedented event: one Saturday, twelve groups organized from the periphery and painted the walls of the school that earlier they had destroyed. Instead of cuss words, they designed symbols of the Negro youth culture. With spray paint, they asked for equality, opportunities. On the stage erected next to the community center, Zinho felt stardom while singing "raps" that spoke of poverty, violence, and the Negro *axé*.

The young rappers movement is also strong in Santa Madalena Park, in the eastern zone of São Paulo. The kids arrive wearing baggy shorts, dark T-shirts, black sneakers, and the inseparable hat. Every Wednesday and Saturday, at the headquarters of the Center for Defense of Children's and Adolescents' Rights (Cedeca), more than fifty youths hold a meeting marked by the Afro-American musical movement that arrived in Brazil in the beginning of the 1980s. There, they reflect, discuss, and sing about their problems.

An abbreviation for "rhythm and poetry" (*ritmo e poesia*), rap sprang up among Negro Jamaicans, but became famous in the poor neighborhoods of New York, in the United States. Toninho, one of the Negro youths of Santa Madalena, denies that his gang might only be following a musical style. "With our music, we demand what we do not have; it gives [comfort] to whoever feels pain. Even if we are arrested, we will continue with our tone of denunciation, of criticism."

Enthusiastically, Toninho sings how the "Rap in Festival," an event dreamed up by the group of children in August, was important for the community. To celebrate Zumbi, the youths of Cedeca organized a festival. In the first week of registration, more than fifty groups jostled for an open spot. "We made a serious study about the life of Zumbi and the Quilombo of Palmares, we saw films, we read history. After the festival, there were many people who came here to seek information about the Negro people's struggle, something that never happened before." In the swinging of rap, the youths are organized. In Santa Madalena Park, the Cedeca Posse (a union of rap groups), which has a full schedule, was born. It frequently receives invitations to perform in schools, at parish parties, and at charitable bazaars. Two other groups, Swing Rap and Código Penal (Penal Code), have already recorded disks. And a proposal is on the table: there might be a meeting of musical groups where Negro and white slum dwellers, women and men, would unite in the community struggle.

At Carnival

Pedro Ribeiro

A man at Carnival, circa 1990.
(Photograph by Pedro Ribeiro)

A woman at Carnival, circa 1990.
(Photograph by Pedro Ribeiro)

Two Poets

Sing the New World

Jessica Callaway

Attempts to explain poet and composer Caetano Veloso to non-Brazilians typically refer to him as a Brazilian John Lennon or Bob Dylan. The comparisons come easily. Like Lennon and Dylan, Veloso came from the same impassioned generation, exploded onto the cultural scene in the late 1960s—pioneering a raucous and enormously influential new music, and an equally shocking counterculture style—and has become a hallowed figure in popular music. Jessica Callaway, however, argues that if comparisons must be made, in spirit and sensibility, Veloso is more aptly described as a close comrade of Walt Whitman. Veloso embodies Whitman's rebelliousness and constant restlessness to provoke. At the same time, like Whitman, Veloso takes it as his mission to define the country in which he lives, or "to prove this puzzle the New World," as Whitman phrased it.[1] The similarities between the two poets hint at connections between the worlds of which they sing; both Whitman's United States and Veloso's Brazil are revealed to be fragmented societies, almost overwhelmed with contradiction. Tropicália, the movement that Veloso led in the late 1960s, treats many of the same themes as Whitman's Song of Myself. *Both are statements of the awakened potential of a nation, while simultaneously, proclamations of the creativity inherent in the individual, embodied in the speaker-poet.*

In 1967, a twenty-five-year-old Veloso presented the song "Alegria, Alegria" ("Happiness, Happiness") to a stunned group of judges at a song festival. The judges, as well as the audience, were expecting to hear another folksy, relatively heavy-handed anthem condemning rural feudalism, the type of song presented by the majority of participants. Instead, Veloso offered a complex, fragmented, rock and roll march tune in which a seemingly apathetic speaker drifts casually between veiled protests against the military dictatorship, superficial thoughts about his personal life, fascination with the mass media, and surrealistic dreams about "the heart of Brazil."

Veloso's "Alegria, Alegria," a disjointed series of flickering images and fleeting ideas, lacked the straightforwardness of usual protest songs. With a chorus that asked merely, "Why not? Why not?," it was difficult to fit into any category and clashed with the usual bill of fare offered to the song festival crowds. Worse, at least to a leftist audience that saw rock and roll and electric guitars as in league with North American imperialist ambitions, Veloso's song featured a rock band. Tastes were offended, critics were befuddled, conservatives were outraged—all the trappings of the creation of a new style, which became Tropicalismo after one of Veloso's songs.

In the midst of a harsh military dictatorship, the tropicalists gleefully surveyed all aspects of both Brazilian and international culture, snagging whatever suited a moment's interest. Carmen Miranda was snatched up as a tongue-in-cheek icon along with Roberto Carlos, a rock singer often cited as "the Elvis of Brazil," and João Gilberto, pioneer of the bossa nova. Tropicalists often took to adopting brash, colorful, and carnivalesque stage personas, and performing playful, dadaistic stunts: during an episode of their brief television show *Divino Maravilhoso* (*Divine Marvelous*), Veloso pointed a gun toward the audience while singing Christmas carols. Within a short time of its conception, this "antimovement" was put to rest by its creators; Veloso held a televised burial of Tropicalismo, complete with a fake casket and banner, reading, "Here Lies Tropicália."

Where might Whitman fit in comfortably with all this? There is no question that Whitman shares with Veloso an iconoclastic image as the individual rebelling against society. In the opening lines of "Alegria, Alegria," Veloso suggests a multifaceted rebellion: "Walking against the wind, without handkerchief or document."[2] "Without handkerchief" here refers to a rebellion against bourgeois social convention, just as stepping out without one's documents implies an intentional disobedience of the rules of the dictatorship. Whitman strikes a similar tone of societal rebellion in *Song of Myself*: "I wear my hat as I please indoors and out."[3] Whitman's refusal to remove his hat has the same effect as Veloso's absence of a handkerchief; both constitute a deliberate bucking of convention, a staunch thumbing-one's-nose at the governing social dictates.

The call for an uprising against societal conventions parallels the desire for the liberation of a unique, national artistic expression. "Unscrew the locks from the doors! / Unscrew the doors themselves from their jambs!" the speaker proclaims in *Song of Myself*.⁴ Whitman calls for a revolt against the old, urging readers to look to themselves for material to revitalize culture: "Stop this day and night with me and you shall possess the origin of all poems. . . . You shall no longer take things at second or third hand, nor look / through the eyes of the dead, nor feed on the specters in books."⁵ In the context of the relatively young United States, Whitman's stance struck a particularly strong chord: his glorification of personal rebellion, and the epic power and creativity of the individual, provided an inspiring cultural model for a nation struggling to define itself in relation to Europe. The "eyes of the dead" and the "specters in books," then, represented the outdated cultural models of the Old World.

Veloso's rebellion had many of the same aims as Whitman's. Tropicália began as a reaction to the narrow conventions and stagnation of Brazilian popular music. Yet the significance of the movement expanded to inspire a new concept of Brazilian national and cultural identity. During a famous outburst at another music festival in 1968, Veloso took on a prophetlike tone, railing against the conservatism of Brazilian music, proclaiming his own reforms, and encouraging listeners to follow suit.

The incident occurred when the song festival audience, on seeing the rock band that Veloso had brought with him to perform a song entitled "É Proibido Proibir" ("Prohibiting is Prohibited"), began shouting him off the stage. In this already explosive atmosphere, Veloso yelled back: "So you're the young people who say you want to take power! You don't even have the courage to applaud a type of music, this year, that you didn't have the courage to support last year. . . . You're out of it! You just don't get it! . . . Here's the problem: you all want to police Brazilian music! . . . Gilberto Gil and I are here to put an end to the imbecility that reigns in Brazil! To end it once and for all. . . . If you're the same in politics as you are in aesthetics, we're finished. GOD IS ON THE LOOSE! . . . And I say YES! And I say NO to NO! I say PROHIBITING PROHIBITED! . . . ENOUGH!"⁶

Astute observers of pop culture (Whitman mentions "the hurrahs for popular favorites," for instance, while Veloso's songs are crammed with lyrics from songs and names of singers and movie stars), both Whitman and Veloso are expert at creating a captivating public image. Whitman included a photo of himself, slouching in an open-necked shirt and looking provocatively into the camera, on the frontispiece of *Leaves of Grass.* The photo became almost as famous as the book, so shocking was Whitman's rumpled, "common man" image.

Equally startling in Brazil more than 100 years later were Veloso's performances before the public, both onstage and off. Even thirty years after Tropicália, Veloso continues to be an icon for Brazilian youth and is credited with introducing to Brazil a unique version of the international counterculture; Veloso was unquestionably the most famous hippie in Brazil. It is interesting, although perhaps not surprising, that both the United States and Brazil—two vast countries that are each responsible for building some of the largest media empires in the world and churning out pop culture products at a seemingly hourly rate—would embrace as national heroes poets who are adept at marketing themselves as national icons.

The persona that appears in the poetry of both Whitman and Veloso, however, is paradoxical and constantly shifting. For all of their vehemence in regard to overturning societal norms, both poets step back from taking a traditional romantic, heroic role as national leaders. For instance, rebellion for both poets often as not entails a defiant sort of inactivity: in Veloso's case, an antirebellion, befitting an antimovement. In Tropicália, the speaker declares: "I organize the movement, / I lead the carnival," but in "Alegria, Alegria," the speaker merely wanders through the city past a newsstand. Ironically, rather than being a catalyst for political action, passing the newsstand only lulls him into a drowsy revelry: "*The Sun* on the newsstand fills me with happiness and laziness. Who reads all this news?" There is a certain sense of distancing, as if the speaker has retreated into his own space with no immediate or direct connection to the temporal, political, and social world. Instead of being inspired or angered, on seeing the leftist student newspaper *The Sun,* the speaker is stubbornly ambivalent. The feelings that the leftist student movement provokes are "happiness" and "laziness," two traits diametrically opposed to the spirit of the leftist movement and that carry with them a legacy of foreign stereotypes in regard to Brazilian national identity. What the speaker claims as his own right, and what Tropicália claims as a key to unleashing a true Brazilian culture, is contradiction, in whatever form it might take.

Contradiction is, likewise, famously embraced by Whitman: "Do I contradict myself? / Very well then I contradict myself, / (I am large, I contain multitudes.)."[7] As with Veloso, these contradictions include the introduction of the poetic revolutionary who sometimes feels nothing but laziness, or in Whitman's case, the poet-loafer of *Song of Myself*: "I loaf and invite my soul, / I lean and loaf at my ease observing a spear of summer grass." Whitman's loafing, in the context of a country still entrenched in the Puritan work ethic, constitutes social rebellion. The speaker is stepping away from the mainstream, taking a moment to do something as utterly impracticable as contemplate a humble spear of grass. Like Veloso's speaker in "Alegria, Alegria," the loafer here has staged a passive rebellion: he has simply taken to living on his own time, indulging whatever thoughts and feelings might settle on him. It is the statement of the refusal to adhere to and tirelessly promote a set agenda or ideology, which looks instead to the endlessly evolving creativity of the individual.

The only set ideology of the Tropicália movement was to be constantly aware and suspicious of the hardening of an ideology. Celebrating contradiction was one way to revolt against the strict, opposing agendas of the different factions of Brazilian society. Bristling under the rightist dictatorship and the unyielding ideologies of the leftist intelligentsia, the drifting speaker of "Alegria, Alegria" retreats to a utopic world of his own imagining, "without books or rifles, without hunger, without telephones in the heart of Brazil." The quixotic impossibility of this vision is evidenced by the fact that it is surrounded by a kaleidoscopic reality, constantly ridiculing the idea of such a pure, unadulterated core at the heart of Brazil.

Both poets portray a world so full of stimuli, so overflowing with diversity, that while they attempt to celebrate it, they can only perceive it in fragments. Whitman's loafer and Veloso's drifter open themselves up to all possibilities so entirely that they are both unwilling and unable to settle on any one avenue in particular. In "Alegria, Alegria," Veloso sings: "The sun scatters into crimes, spaceships, guerrillas, into pretty (Claudia) Cardinales. I keep going into the faces of presidents, into epic kisses of love, into teeth, legs, flags, bombs and Brigitte Bardot." It is a dazzling, restless tangle of international pop culture, politics, sappy sentimentalism, and the rush of people on the street. The speaker's reality is chaotic, without order or meaning; the only order is the complete lack of coherence and endless stream of contradictions.

Whitman tends to catalog in much the same way as Veloso:

> The bride unrumples her white dress, the minute-hand of the clock moves slowly,
> The opium-eater reclines with rigid head and just open'd lips,
> The prostitute draggles her shawl, her bonnet bobs on her tipsy and pimpled neck, . . .

In these few verses, Whitman touches on the essence of the Tropicalist sensibility. The bride is mixed in with the opium eater and the prostitute sandwiched near the president. It is a colorful satire of American life, life in a city, and the endless contradictions of the modern world. Yet, like Tropicália, the satirical element never overshadows the strong sense of celebration. Whitman's *Song of Myself*, Veloso's "Alegria, Alegria," and the tone of the Tropicalist movement all found a sense of optimism in an eternally contradictory world. Not an optimism that a goal would eventually be reached, but a complacent acceptance that the world would continue to hold fascination through all of its infinite possibilities. "I keep going," Veloso sings, "Why not? Why not?"

Notes

1 Walt Whitman, *To Foreign Lands,* in *Leaves of Grass* (New York: W. W. Norton and Company, 1973), p. 3.
2 Caetano Veloso, "Alegria, Alegria," on *Caetano Veloso,* Phillips 838 557–2, 1990.
3 Walt Whitman, *Song of Myself,* in *Leaves of Grass* (New York: W. W. Norton and Company, 1973), p. 47.
4 Ibid., p. 52.
5 Ibid., pp. iii, 30.
6 Caetano Veloso, *A Arte de Caetano Veloso,* Polygram 838 238–2, 1988.
7 Whitman, *Song of Myself,* p. 88.

Two Essays on Sports

Janet Lever and José Carlos Sebe Bom Meihy

I. National Madness

JANET LEVER

In the mid-1980s, sociologist Janet Lever published a notable study of Brazilian soccer, Soccer Madness. *This essay brings her analysis up to date, examining the great changes that have occurred inside Brazil not only in terms of soccer— Brazil's first love—but also in regard to other sports in which Brazilians have emerged as world-class performers. Oddly, perhaps, few broad analyses of the role of sports in Brazilian life have appeared. While there are ghost-written autobiographies of players, there is a great need for research on sports. We know little about professional sports in the poorer states, where even successful athletes earn barely more than the minimum wage. We know little about athletes' lives, the impact of success (and failure) on their families, and the character of the interaction between athletes (who are almost all from poor and nonwhite backgrounds), their fans, and the affluent, elite society into which star players are thrust by virtue of their financial rewards. It would be telling to learn about the downward trajectories of athletic careers, to learn what happens to athletes whose skills end abruptly because of injury or decline over time.*

When people think about world-class soccer, they usually think about Brazil. It is the only country that has qualified for all fifteen World Cups and won four times. Brazil is the birthplace of many of the sport's most celebrated players, including the legendary Pelé, considered the most gifted player in soccer's history. The players' nimble attacking game combined with the loud, colorful, samba-dancing fans who travel by the tens of thousands to support the national team have made Brazil almost everybody's favorite second team, after their own . . .

Brazil won in 1994, but it was hardly the "dream team" that won the tri-championship in 1970. After tying the lesser-regarded Swedish team one-one in the first round, they barely beat them one-zero in the quarter-finals and left the field while being booed by their own fans. The win in the final match against Italy was far from decisive, settled by a penalty kick showdown after 120 minutes of lackluster, scoreless play.

Yet after twenty-four years without a World Cup trophy, runaway four-figure inflation (over 3,000 percent in 1993), and political scandal, the Brazilians were ready to celebrate any victory they could get. Close to 100 percent of the population tuned into the last games via television or radio. The country literally stopped for the final matches—Congress adjourned, schools closed, and businesses shut down. After the victory, people poured into the streets, creating a noisy carnival of dancing and fireworks. There were no riots. Casualties included those in car accidents caused by inebriated drivers and people with high blood pressure who got sick from excitement.

When the players returned home two days later, there was no national holiday declared, as there had been in 1970. But Brazilian President Itamar Franco received the team in Brasília, no doubt with hopes of boosting his party's popularity ratings before the general elections. He was borrowing a tarnished image, however, for the players themselves were soon caught up in a national scandal when they tried to bring in eighteen tons of excess baggage (a second jumbo jet was needed to carry the cargo) without paying the estimated one million dollars in duties. President Franco supported the players' privilege while the nation's tax chief resigned in protest, and according to a newspaper poll, 79 percent of Brazilians thought their heroes should pay up like anyone else. In addition to the unauthorized excise tax bonus, each player was rewarded by the federal government with $150,000 for the victory. Star players were paid large lump sums for appearances in support of political candidates, and seventeen-year-old Ronaldo filmed an advertisement for the Brazilian army, encouraging young people to enlist.

World Cup victories notwithstanding, domestic Brazilian soccer has suffered a long slump. In the 1970s, the clubs were on the verge of financial disaster due to skyrocketing player salaries. Things have gotten worse, not better. Brazilians' real wages have fallen, and general admission to stadia climbed from $1.75 to $7.00. Attending local games, once a way of life, had become a luxury for many. Broadcast rights are small, so only important away games are televised (and occasionally a sold-out home game). Cable television is just beginning, and to date, systems have only contracted for major championship games to show their small elite group of subscribing viewers.

Clubs are dependent on advertising revenue from corporate sponsors who pay large monthly fees to have logos emblazoned on team uniforms, leading some to say that the players have turned into running billboards. Not only are the players sporting product logos, but in a controversial ploy, Brahma, one of Brazil's leading beer manufacturers, turned fans into billboards, too. The company purchased large blocks of field-level tickets, offering free entry to those who would hold up cards or a giant banner displaying the product symbol during a major game. For a bargain price, Brahma's visual message got forty-three minutes of unpaid advertising, while a competitive brewery received only a few minutes of airtime for its expensive paid advertisements. Unfortunately, the clubs do not benefit from unpaid advertising.

Star athletes who can command one million dollars on the global market cannot be paid their worth in Brazil. Many do not control their own contracts, but have managers or personal bosses who get the bulk of transfer fees when their players are sold to another team. Whether free agents or pawns, the players have made an exodus, leaving Brazilian teams without their homegrown talent. Eleven of the twenty-two-member 1994 national team play in Europe (including eight of the starting eleven); by contrast, all of the 1970 team remained with Brazilian teams. This is a vicious cycle: the more players leave, the worse the quality of regular league competition becomes, and consequently, fewer fans are willing to pay to see their teams.

A new law is just taking effect that may radically change the financial conditions of the soccer clubs. Until now, the clubs have been nonprofit organizations. The new law, designed to encourage amateur sports, says that any club that sponsors at least three Olympic sports (including soccer) can show a profit from certain fund-raising activities. As a result, soccer clubs have opened their own bingo salons and get to keep a small percent of the profits to support Olympic sports. Although full-service gambling casinos are forbidden in Brazil, bingo salons are allowed. Many clubs have hopped on Brazil's bingo-fever bandwagon.

There are other changes on the Brazilian soccer scene that are similar to changes in parts of Europe. Brazil's greatest soccer crisis stems from

the rise of violence between rival teenage fan groups, which the press
has likened to gang warfare. At least six people have been killed in fights
and shootouts after games. Members of fan clubs with up to 40,000
members have brought knives, bottles, and even homemade bombs to
games. Disturbances on the streets, as well as on trains and buses, have
become routine. Fans in Rio and São Paulo are staying away from stadia
in record numbers; average attendance has dropped to fewer than 10,000
fans in stadia built for 150,000. The great Pelé—the cabinet's "extraordinary" minister of sports—has pleaded with the people of his country not
to ruin the sport: "Soccer must be a party to the fans and not a tragedy."

By contrast, stadia in smaller cities like Belo Horizonte and Curitiba
have improved the party atmosphere such that they are now more welcoming of girls and women than in the past. Brazil has even accepted
women as referees and line judges for men's professional competitions,
including the national championship games. Women, however, are still
not supported as players. Early attempts to cover women's soccer on
television failed. They have virtually no support from Brazil's big soccer
clubs.

Over the years, some soccer fans have switched allegiance to other
sports, such as professional volleyball and basketball, two sports in which
Brazilians excel. Both the men and women's teams took some important
international titles: the gold medal from the 1992 Olympics and the 1993
championship of the World Volleyball League; in 1994, Brazilians won
the women's world basketball championship.

Further, the real heroes during soccer's lean years were Brazil's Formula One racers. First, Emerson Fittipaldi was named World Driving
Champion in 1972 and 1974, [and in 1989] became the first non-American
winner of the Indianapolis 500 since 1966. Then, Nelson Piquet took that
honor in 1981, 1983, and 1987, followed by Ayrton Senna in 1988, 1990, and
1991. Senna, the three-time champ, died tragically in a racing accident
just a month before the 1994 World Cup began. When these three out-
standing Brazilian drivers captured eight Formula One titles, racing became more important than soccer for many of their compatriots. Even
poor Brazilians could watch their race car drivers reflect glory on the
troubled nation on free television. Brazilians say that when Senna died,
the country experienced an unprecedented national mourning. In Brasília, the World Cup winners hoisted a yellow crash helmet to the welcoming crowds and dedicated their victory to Ayrton Senna, Brazil's true
national idol.

. . . Tradition established that the first country to win three World Cups would get to keep the Jules Rimet Trophy in perpetuity. The 1970 final match between Brazil and Italy was hotly contested because both sides were two-time champs. Brazil won and put the cherished historic cup on display at the Brazilian Football Federation in Rio de Janeiro. In 1983, the Jules Rimet Trophy was stolen and never recovered. There were no ransom requests, and some authorities believe that since it was made of solid gold, it was possibly melted down. Whether it became a prized, albeit hidden, possession of a crazed fan or was destroyed by a selfish criminal remains a mystery. The Brazilian branch of Eastman Kodak, in a master public relations stroke, beat competitors to the idea of paying for an exact reproduction of the trophy and donating it to the Brazilian people. It is available for public viewing in Rio.

II. A National Festival

J. C. SEBE BOM MEIHY

Perhaps because it so deeply pervades their lives, Brazilians devote less time to analyzing futebol *in the abstract. Beyond a few hagiographic biographies ghost-written by professional writers and feature films of the same ilk, there are few books, novels, or documentaries on the sport itself. José Carlos Sebe Bom Meihy, however, a historian at the University of São Paulo and a skillful analyst of popular culture, offers a broad view of soccer as a part of Brazilian tradition.*

Without a doubt, *futebol* is an expression of the "spirit of the Brazilian people." In the popular mind, soccer stands side by side with popular music and religious devotion as a defining element of national character. Just as it is said that "Brazil is the largest Roman Catholic country in the world," or "samba is in the Brazilians' blood," we hear as well that Brazil is "the country of *futebol.*"

When one talks about Brazilian soccer, one usually is referring to the professional level. For most soccer fans, the idea of soccer as a metaphor for Brazilian society holds little interest—for example, examining the various worlds of soccer below the national level, such as the leagues in the small towns of the countryside. Professional soccer, to be sure, dominates. Soccer as big business touches an enormous public and is bolstered by a sizable publicity apparatus. The repetition of certain slogans is fundamental to this process of diffusion. The arguments about the

Quando eu Durmo, from a Dorival Caymmi poster.
(Robert M. Levine Collection)

História Pro Sinhozinho, from a Dorival Caymmi poster.
(Robert M. Levine Collection)

superiority of Brazilian soccer have the effect of a kind of carrying card of Brazilian nationality.

Brazilian soccer functions somewhat like a national festivity. National life devotes a certain time for music, other time for religiosity, and a season for soccer. Celebration fits into a programmable calendar.

From the perspective of soccer as a business, the year 1950 was the watershed. This was when Marancanã, the then-200,000-seat stadium in Rio de Janeiro, was built—in time for the disastrous upset loss to Uruguay in the World Cup finals, the first soccer game to be televised in Brazil. Politically, from its roots as an elite sport played in private clubs to its mass standing today, soccer has performed a major role. It is played out for the "great public," but it is run by *cartolas*—club administrators with great power beyond the soccer stadia. For *cartolas* and politicians both, the immense numbers of soccer fans represent a passive audience. Soccer, as well, serves as fodder for ideological fantasies, useful to some groups. Oddly, it has been ignored by academics, who have failed to see how it deserved analysis, although, for example, it is a marvelous vehicle to study the persistence of social values and the changing character of the Brazilian people. Soccer is a sport that encompasses various contradictory elements. It unifies and separates; it promotes and destroys; it makes people ecstatic and also sad.

Soccer has been used to explain what some call the weaknesses in the character of the *povo*—the mass of the population. On the other hand, to survive as a national institution, soccer has adopted the language of officialized culture: "unity," "the Brazilian *povo*," "our thing," "the national sport," "*raça*"—the concept that Brazilian soccer prowess is inherited genetically. We are told that soccer is an organ that unifies Brazil. The *Gazeta Esportiva Illustrada* [a leading soccer magazine] boasts that it is read "from Oiapoque to Chui, from the far North to the far South of this great country."

Then there is the question of race. Gilberto Freyre, gathering together various stereotypes from Brazilian tradition, posited the theme of the whitening of the Brazilian population. Abroad during the decade of the 1920s, Freyre returned from his travels with ideas about the way Brazilian society worked. As time passed, his theories evolved until, in 1945, he wrote in *New World in the Tropics* that "the Brazilians play soccer as if it were a dance. This is probably the result," he added, "of the influence of those Brazilians who have African blood or are predominately African in their culture, for such Brazilians tend to reduce everything to dance, work and play alike, and this tendency, apparently becoming more and more general in Brazil, is not solely the characteristic of an ethnic or regional group."[1] Critics of Freyre, in contrast, argue that if Dionysian influences from the Afro-Brazilian heritage have influenced the ways in which Brazilians play soccer, so have the "Apollonian" ways inherited from the English, who brought soccer to Brazil. This convergence, then, gives Brazilian soccer its uniquely national character.

Note

1 Gilberto Freyre, *New World in the Tropics* (New York: Vintage Books, 1963), pp. 111–12.

Suggestions for Further Reading

The amount of good writing on Brazil is large and spans many languages. The suggestions here are just that: suggestions for where to start. When an important book written by a Brazilian exists in translation, we list it here, although readers who know Portuguese should consider reading the original. Libraries with significant Brasiliana collections are increasingly able to be accessed on the Internet, which is a good place for supplementary searching. Some of the sources listed below fit into more than one category.

I. Origins, Conquest, and Colonial Rule

Bethell, Leslie, ed. *Colonial Brazil*. Cambridge: Cambridge University Press, 1987.

Boxer, Charles R. *The Golden Age of Brazil*. Berkeley: University of California Press, 1969.

Burns, E. Bradford. *A History of Brazil*, 3d ed. New York: Columbia University Press, 1993.

Capistrano de Abreu, João. *Chapters in Brazil's Colonial History, 1500–1800*. Translated by Arthur Brakel. New York: Oxford University Press, 1998.

Dean, Warren. *With Broadax and Firebrand: The Destruction of the Brazilian Atlantic Forest*. Berkeley: University of California Press, 1995.

Maxwell, Kenneth P. *Conflicts and Conspiracies: Brazil and Portugal, 1750–1808*. Cambridge: Cambridge University Press, 1973.

Russell-Wood, A. J. R. *The Santa Casa da Misericordia of Bahia, 1550–1755*. Berkeley: University of California Press, 1968.

Schwartz, Stuart B. *Sugar Plantations in the Formation of Brazilian Society*. New York: Cambridge University Press, 1985.

II. Imperial and Republican Brazil

Barman, Roderick J. *Brazil: The Forging of a Nation, 1798–1852*. Stanford, Calif.: Stanford University Press, 1988.

Borges, Dain. *The Family in Bahia, Brazil, 1870–1945*. Stanford, Calif.: Stanford University Press, 1992.

Graham, Richard. *Britain and the Onset of Modernization in Brazil, 1850–1914*. New York: Cambridge University Press, 1968.

Leal, Vitor Nunes. *Coronelismo*. New York: Cambridge University Press, 1977.

Levine, Robert M. *Vale of Tears: Revisiting the Canudos Massacre in Northeastern Brazil, 1893–1897*. Berkeley: University of California Press, 1992.

Lewin, Linda. *Politics and Parentela in Paraíba: A Case Study of Family-Based Oligarchy in Brazil*. Princeton, N.J.: Princeton University Press, 1987.

Needell, Jeffrey D. *A Tropical Belle Epoque*. Cambridge: Cambridge University Press, 1987.

Stein, Stanley J. *Vassouras, A Brazilian Coffee County, 1850–1900: The Roles of Planter and Slave in a Plantation Society*. Princeton: Princeton University Press, 1985.

Topik, Steven. *The Political Economy of the Brazilian State, 1889–1930*. Austin: University of Texas Press, 1987.

III. Slavery and Its Aftermath

Conrad, Robert E., ed. *Children of God's Fire: A Documentary History of Black Slavery in Brazil*. Princeton, N.J.: Princeton University Press, 1983.

Freyre, Gilberto. *The Masters and the Slaves*. New York: Alfred A. Knopf, 1946.

Karasch, Mary C. *Slave Life in Rio de Janeiro, 1808–1850*. Princeton, N.J.: Princeton University Press, 1987.

Klein, Herbert S. *African Slavery in Latin America and the Caribbean*. New York: Oxford University Press, 1986.

Nabuco, Carolina. *The Life of Joaquim Nabuco*. Translated by Ronald Hilton. Stanford, Calif.: Stanford University Press, 1950.

Nabuco, Joaquim. *Abolitionism: The Brazilian Antislavery Struggle*. Translated by Robert Conrad. Urbana: University of Illinois Press, 1977.

Reis, João José. *Slave Rebellion in Brazil: The Muslim Uprising of 1835 in Bahia*. Translated by Arthur Brakel. Baltimore: Johns Hopkins University Press, 1993.

Toplin, Robert Brent. *The Abolition of Slavery in Brazil*. New York: Atheneum, 1972.

IV. The Vargas Era

Dulles, John W. F. *Vargas of Brazil: A Political Biography*. Austin: University of Texas Press, 1967.

Frank, Waldo David. *South American Journey*. London: Victor Gollancz, 1943.

Hilton, Stanley E. *Brazil and the Great Powers, 1930–1939*. Austin: University of Texas Press, 1977.

Lesser, Jeffrey. *Welcoming the Undesirables*. Berkeley: University of California Press, 1995.

Levine, Robert M. *Father of the Poor?* New York: Cambridge University Press, 1998.

Lévi-Strauss, Claude. *Tristes Tropiques*. Translated by J. and D. Weightman. New York: Atheneum, 1974.

Loewenstein, Karl. *Brazil under Vargas*. New York: Macmillan, 1942.

McCann, Frank D. *The Brazilian-American Alliance*. Princeton, N.J.: Princeton University Press, 1973.

Wolfe, Joel W., ed. "Getúlio Vargas and His Legacy," special issue of the *Luso-Brazilian Review* 31, no. 2 (winter 1994).

Zweig, Stefan. *Brazil: Land of the Future*. New York: Viking Press, 1941.

V. Seeking Democracy and Equity

Amnesty International. *Brazil: Authorized Violence in Rural Areas*. London: Amnesty International, 1988.

Erickson, Kenneth Paul. *The Brazilian Corporative State and Working-Class Politics*. Berkeley: University of California Press, 1977.

Fernandes, Florestan. *Reflections on the Brazilian Counter Revolution*. Armonk, N.Y.: M. E. Sharpe, 1981.

Flynn, Peter. *Brazil: A Political Analysis*. London: Ernest Benn, 1978.

Huggins, Martha K. *Political Policing*. Durham, N.C.: Duke University Press, 1998.

Jaguaribe, Hélio. *Economic and Political Development: A Theoretical Approach and a Brazilian Case Study*. Cambridge, Mass.: Harvard University Press, 1968.

Parker, Phyllis R. *Brazil and the Quiet Intervention*. Austin: University of Texas Press, 1979.

Purcell, Susan Kaufman, and Riordan Roett, eds. *Brazil under Cardoso*. New York: Americas Society, 1997.

Schneider, Ronald M. *Brazil: Culture and Politics in a New Industrial Powerhouse*. Boulder, Colo.: Praeger, 1996.

Skidmore, Thomas E. *Politics in Brazil, 1930–1964*. New York: Oxford University Press, 1967.

Stepan, Alfred, ed. *Democratizing Brazil: Problems of Transition and Consolidation*. New York: Oxford University Press, 1989.

Weyland, Kurt. *Democracy without Equity: Failures of Reform in Brazil*. Pittsburgh, Pa.: University of Pittsburgh Press, 1996.

VI. Women's Lives

Besse, Susan K. *Restructuring Patriarchy: The Modernization of Gender Inequality in Brazil, 1914–1940.* Chapel Hill: University of North Carolina Press, 1996.

Caulfield, Sueann, ed. "Changing Images of the Brazilian Woman," special issue of the *Luso-Brazilian Review* 30, no. 1 (summer 1993).

Hahner, June E. *Emancipating the Female Sex: The Struggle for Women's Rights in Brazil.* Durham, N.C.: Duke University Press, 1990.

Jesus, Carolina Maria de. *Bitita's Diary.* Armonk, N.Y.: M. E. Sharpe, 1997.

——. *Child of the Dark.* New York: E. P. Dutton, 1962.

——. *I'm Going to Have a Little House.* Lincoln: University of Nebraska Press, 1997.

Landes, Ruth. *The City of Women.* New York: Macmillan, 1947.

Levine, Robert M., and José Carlos Sebe Bom Meihy. *The Life and Death of Carolina Maria de Jesus.* Albuquerque: University of New Mexico Press, 1995.

Patai, Daphne. *Brazilian Women Speak.* New Brunswick, N.J.: Rutgers University Press, 1988.

Scheper-Hughes, Nancy. *Death without Weeping: The Violence of Everyday Life in Brazil.* Berkeley: University of California Press, 1992.

VII. Race and Ethnic Relations

Andrews, George Reid. *Blacks and Whites in São Paulo, 1888–1988.* Madison: University of Wisconsin Press, 1991.

Butler, Kim R. *Freedoms Given, Freedoms Won: Afro-Brazilians in Post-Abolition São Paulo and Salvador.* New Brunswick, N.J.: Rutgers University Press, 1998.

Degler, Charles N. *Neither Black nor White.* Madison: University of Wisconsin Press, 1986.

Freyre, Gilberto. *New World in the Tropics.* New York: Vintage Books, 1963.

Haberly, David T. *Three Sad Races: Racial Identity and National Consciousness in Brazilian Literature.* Cambridge: Cambridge University Press, 1983.

Hanchard, Michael George. *Orpheus and Power.* Princeton, N.J.: Princeton University Press, 1994.

Marx, Anthony W. *Making Race and Nation: A Comparison of the United States, South Africa, and Brazil.* New York: Cambridge University Press, 1998.

Skidmore, Thomas E. *Black into White.* New York: Oxford University Press, 1974.

Wagley, Charles, ed. *Race and Class in Rural Brazil.* Paris: UNESCO, 1952.

VIII. Realities

Baer, Werner. *The Brazilian Economy: Growth and Development,* 4th ed. Westport, Conn.: Praeger, 1995.

Bruneau, Thomas. *The Political Transformation of the Brazilian Catholic Church.* London: Cambridge University Press, 1974.

Conniff, Michael L., and Frank D. McCann Jr., eds. *Modern Brazil: Elites and Masses in Historical Perspective.* Lincoln: University of Nebraska Press, 1989.

Evans, Peter E. *Dependent Development.* Princeton, N.J.: Princeton University Press, 1979.

Gay, Robert. *Popular Organization and Democracy in Rio de Janeiro.* Philadelphia, Pa.: Temple University Press, 1994.

Havighurst, Robert J., and J. Roberto Moreira. *Society and Education in Brazil.* Pittsburgh, Pa.: University of Pittsburgh Press, 1965.

Linger, Daniel Toro. *Dangerous Encounters: Meanings of Violence in a Brazilian City.* Stanford, Calif.: Stanford University Press, 1992.

Mainwaring, Scott. *The Catholic Church and Politics in Brazil, 1916–1985.* Stanford, Calif.: Stanford University Press, 1986.

Vot Mettenheim, Kurt. *The Brazilian Voter.* Pittsburgh, Pa.: University of Pittsburgh Press, 1995.

Wagley, Charles. *Introduction to Brazil,* rev. ed. New York: Columbia University Press, 1971.

Wood, Charles W., and J. A. Magno de Carvalho. *The Demography of Inequality in Brazil.* Cambridge: Cambridge University Press, 1988.

IX. Saudades

Appleby, David P. *The Music of Brazil.* Austin: University of Texas Press, 1983.

Guillhermoprieto, Alma. *Samba.* New York: Random House, 1990.

Hess, David J., and Roberto DaMatta, eds. *The Brazilian Puzzle.* New York: Columbia University Press, 1995.

Johnson, Randal. *The Film Industry in Brazil: Culture and the State.* Pittsburgh, Pa.: University of Pittsburgh Press, 1987.

Lever, Janet. *Soccer Madness,* 2d ed. Chicago: Waveland Press, 1995.

Levine, Robert M. *The Brazilian Photographs of Genevieve Naylor.* Durham, N.C.: Duke University Press, 1998.

Novaes, Sylvia Caiuby. *The Play of Mirrors: The Representation of Self Mirrored in the Other.* Austin: University of Texas Press, 1997.

Acknowledgment of Copyrights

the Great River São Francisco, from Sabará to the Sea, Vol. 1, by Richard F. Burton (New York: Greenwood Press, 1969).

"Scenes from the Slave Trade," part 1, from *African Repository and Colonial Journal* (September 1841); part 2, from *Remarks on the Slavery and Slave Trade of the Brazils* by Thomas Nelson (London, 1846); part 3, from *O Captiveiro* by João Dunshee de Abrantes (Rio de Janeiro, 1941), cited in *World of Sorrow: The African Slave Trade to Brazil,* Robert E. Conrad (Baton Rouge: Louisiana State University Press, 1986).

"Cruelty to Slaves" from *Life in Brazil; or, a Journal of a Visit to the Land of the Cocoa and the Palm* by Thomas Ewbank (New York: Harper and Brothers, 1856).

"Slavery and Society" from *O Abolicionismo* by Joaquim Nabuco (London: Abraham Kingdon, 1883).

"Laws Regulating Beggars in Minas Gerais, 1900" from *Leis Mineiras, 1900* (State of Minas Gerais).

"The Social Question" from the Platform of the Liberal Alliance, Presidência da República Collection, National Archives, Rio de Janeiro.

"Manifesto, May 1930" from "Manifesto em Maio de 1930" by Luís Carlos Prestes, DOPS [Police] Archives, Rio de Janeiro.

"Where They Talk about Rosa Luxemburg" from *Industrial Park* by Patrícia Galvão, edited and translated by Elizabeth and K. David Jackson. Copyright © 1993 by the University of Nebraska Press. Reprinted by permission of the University of Nebraska Press.

"Seized Correspondence from Communists, 1935–1945" from Departamento Federal de Segurança Pública, Serviço de Informações, Pasta 20, "Correspondências Comunista" [*sic*], Arquivo do DOPS, State of Rio de Janeiro.

"The Paulista Synagogue" by Gustavo Barroso (Rio de Janeiro: Editorial ABC, 1937).

"Why the Estado Novo?" by Francisco José de Oliveira Vianna from *Antônio Figueira de Almeida, A Constituição de Dez de Dezembro Explicada ao Povo* (Rio de Janeiro: DIP, 1940).

"New Year's Address, 1938" by Getúlio Vargas from *Boletim do Ministério do Trabalho, Indústria and Comércio* 41 (January 1938).

"A New Survey of Brazilian Life" by the Brazilian Institute of Geography and Statistics (Rio de Janeiro: IBGE, 1939).

"General George C. Marshall's Mission to Brazil" from *Together Annals of an Army Wife* by Katherine Tupper Marshall (New York: Tupper and Love, 1946).

"Comments on the Estado Novo" from "Correspondence and Writings—Brazil, 1941" by Bailey W. Diffie. Reprinted by permission of the Archives and Special Collections, Otto G. Richter Library, University of Miami, Coral Gables.

"Educational Reform after Twenty Years" by Anísio S. Teixeira from the Brazilian

National Archives, Rio de Janeiro, AP 48, Caixa 18, Pasta 40. Courtesy of Jens Hentschke.

"Ordinary People," part 1, Apolonio de Carvalho, interview by José Carlos Sebe Bom Meihy, Rio de Janeiro, 4 March 1994.

"Ordinary People," part 2, Geraldo Valdelírios Novais, interview by Fábio Bezerra de Brito.

"Ordinary People," part 3, from "A Carreira Profissindal de um Pedreiro de Subúrbio" by Frederico Heller from *Sociologia* 4, no. 1 (1942).

"Ordinary People," part 4, Maurílio Thomás Ferreira, interview by Marieta Ferreira Moraes. Rio de Janeiro.

"Ordinary People," part 5, Joana de Masi Zero, interview by Edson de Oliveira Balotta, São Paulo, 6 September 1996.

"Vargas's Suicide Letter, 1954" by Getúlio Vargas, Brazilian National Archives, Rio de Janeiro. Translated by Robert M. Levine.

"Rehearsal for the Coup" from *How Brazil Stopped Communism: The Story of the Brazilian Revolution of March–April,* by Araken Tavora, translated by Lydio de Souza (Rio de Janeiro: Sociedade Gráfica Vida Doméstica, 1964).

"The Military Regime" reprinted by permission of Antonio Pedro Tota, São Paulo.

"Excerpts from the 1967 Brazilian Constitution" courtesy of the Embassy of Brazil, Washington, D.C., 1968.

"Pelé Speaks," Edson Avantes Nascimento da Silva, interviews by *Playboy Brasil* (São Paulo) 5, no. 1 (August 1980) and *Playboy Brasil* 18, no. 1 (August 1993). Copyright © 1980 and © 1993 by *Playboy Brasil*. Reprinted by permission of the publisher.

"The Maximum Norm of the Exercise of Liberty" from "Construindo o Brasil," a pamphlet circulated by the Group for Moral and Civic Education, Rio de Janeiro, 1973.

"Families of Fishermen Confront the Sharks" from "A união faz o peixe" by Paulo Lima from *Sem Fronteiras* 239 (April 1996): 19. Reprinted by permission of Paulo Lima.

"The Reality of the Brazilian Countryside" from "A Realidade do Campo Brasileiro," ⟨http://www.sanet.com.br/~semterra/mst1.htm⟩; "Manifesto dos Sem-Terras ao povo brasileiro," ⟨http://www.sanet.com.br/~semterra/manif.htm⟩. Reprinted by permission of Zenaide of the Movimento Sem-Terra.

"The 'Greatest Administrative Scandal' " from *"Civilized" but Discontent: The Xavante Indians and Government Policy in Brazil, 1937–1988* by Seth Garfield (Ph.D. diss., Yale University, 1996), chapter 7.

"Life on an Occupied Ship" from "Boletim da Intersindical," *InterPortuS intersindical portuária de santos* (April 97), ⟨http://www.portodesantos.com/sindicatos/

navio1.html⟩; ⟨http://www.portodesantos.com/sindicatos/navio2.html⟩. Reprinted by permission of Mauri Alexandrino, Intersindical Portuaria de Santos.

"Inaugural Address" by Fernando Henrique Cardoso translated and published by the Brazilian Foreign Ministry over the Internet.

"Is Brazil Hopelessly Corrupt?" by Roberto DaMatta from the *New York Times*, 13 December 1993. Copyright © 1993 by the *New York Times*. Reprinted by permission of the *New York Times*.

"Aunt Zézé's Tears" from *Brazilian Tales* by Carmen Dolores. Translated by Isaac Goldberg (Boston: Four Seas Company, 1921).

"The Integral Woman" from Ação Integralista Brasileira *Provincia de Guanabara* (Rio de Janeiro) 1, no. 2 (10 April 1937).

"The Children Always Had Milk," Maria Puerta Ferreira, interview by the University of São Paulo oral history project, 1992.

"Women of the Forest" from *Women of the Forest,* 2d ed., by Yolanda and Robert M. Murphy. Copyright © 1985 by Columbia University Press. Reprinted by permission of Columbia University Press.

"My Life," Maria das Dôres Gomes Batista, based on an interview by Maria Lisbôa and Rosane Pereira, Campos dos goytacazes, 17 March 1996.

"A Healer's Story," Maria Geralda Ferreira, from interview by Elizabeth W. Kiddy, Jatobá Valley, Belo Horizonte, Minas Gerais, August 1996.

"Sonia, a Middle-Class Woman" from *Observations on Women in Brazil* by Alison Raphael. Copyright © 1975 by the Institute of Current World Affairs. Reprinted by permission of the Institute of Current World Affairs.

"Family Life in Recife," by Fanny Mitchell. Copyright © 1967 by the Institute of Current World Affairs. Reprinted by permission of the Institute of Current World Affairs and Fanny Mitchell.

"A Letter from Brazil, 1918" by José Clarana from *The Crisis* (April 1918).

"Growing up Black in Minas Gerais," by Carolina Maria de Jesus, edited by Robert M. Levine from handwritten autobiographical notes. Courtesy of Vera Eunice de Jesus Lima.

"Brazil: Study in Black, Brown, and Beige" by Leslie B. Rout Jr. from *Negro Digest* 19 (February 1970): 21–23, 65–73. Reprinted by permission of Kathleen Rout.

"The Myth of Racial Democracy" by Abdias do Nascimento from *Cadernos Brasileiros* 10, no. 47 (May–June 1968): 3–7.

"The National Day against Racism" from "Os Negros Queriam Continuar Protestando" by the Movimento Negro Unificado, from *Revista MNU* (São Paulo) 81, no. 4 (August 1981).

"The Church Tries to Combat Prejudice" from "Igreja tenta reverter preconceito" by Bernardete Toneto from *Sem Fronteiras* 234 (November 1995): 18,

Index

Robert M. Levine is professor of history at the University of Miami. He has published extensively on Brazil and is former chair of the Columbia University Seminar on Brazil. Levine is also coeditor of the *Luso-Brazilian Review*. John J. Crocitti is completing his Ph.D. in history at the University of Miami, writing on the social and demographic history of Barra do Piraí, South America's largest railroad junction.